NONLINEAR DYNAMICS
AND EVOLUTIONARY ECONOMICS

NONLINEAR DYNAMICS AND EVOLUTIONARY ECONOMICS

Edited by

Richard H. Day
and Ping Chen

New York   Oxford
OXFORD UNIVERSITY PRESS
1993

Oxford University Press

Oxford   New York   Toronto
Delhi   Bombay   Calcutta   Madras   Karachi
Kuala Lumpur   Singapore   Hong Kong   Tokyo
Nairobi   Dar es Salaam   Cape Town
Melbourne   Auckland   Madrid

and associated companies in
Berlin   Ibadan

Library of Congress Cataloging-in-Publication Data
Nonlinear dynamics and evolutionary economics : proceedings of the
international symposium, University of Texas at Austin, Austin,
Texas, April 16-19, 1989 / edited by Richard H. Day and Ping Chen.
p.   cm.
Includes bibliographical references and index.
ISBN 0-19-507859-4
 1.   Economics–Congresses.   2.   Economics, Mathematical–Congresses.
 3.   Statics and dynamics (Social sciences)–Congresses.
 4.   Evolution equations, Nonlinear–Congresses.   5.   Chaotic behavior in systems–
Congresses.   I.   Day, Richard Hollis, 1933–   .   II.   Chen, Ping.
HB71.N66   1993
330–dc20   92-22603

9 8 7 6 5 4 3 2 1

Printed in the United States of America
on acid-free paper

Dedicated to Ilya Prigogine

who has pioneered the use of nonlinear dynamics in explaining complex physical and chemical processes, who recognized very early the relevance of nonlinear methods for understanding the wider world of biological and human processes, and whose leadership, example, and personal support have encouraged others to develop social science in this promising direction.

Preface

The physical, biological, and social sciences are currently going through a rapid development that reflects the growing influence of nonlinear mathematics and evolutionary thinking. The theory of dissipative, self-organizing systems has shown how physical processes create complex structures through their internal dynamics and how those structures may change and evolve when subjected to external forces. Computers have made it possible to illustrate the astonishing array of potential behaviors that can occur when nonlinear interactions are present. Advances in mathematical analysis are providing an ever more precise and general understanding of these phenomena. Perhaps more surprising is that social scientists have learned how similar phenomena emerge in economic processes and are showing how complex and sometimes erratic developments can be explained in theoretical terms that exploit common mathematical tools. The purpose of this symposium was to consider these developments in the context of economic science.

It is too early at this stage to contemplate a universal dynamic theory. It is too soon, also, to begin the process of refining and standardizing. Rather, it is a time to explore promising lines of inquiry, to try out new methods, to compare alternative approaches, to see how ideas in various disciplines are related, and how they can be used to enrich one another. Correspondingly, the conference was organized with this perspective in mind.

The present volume contains a small sample of the papers presented that illustrate the varying work and methodological perspectives on economics by researchers in various disciplines. A number of papers report new technical findings. Others provide summaries and reflections of previous work.

The papers are organized into six sections. The first introduces in broad terms the major themes of the conference: nonlinearity, dynamical systems, and evolution in economic processes. The second section is devoted to nonlinear analysis of macroeconomic growth and fluctuations. The third section describes analyses of economic adaptation, learning, and self-organization. The fourth section concerns a specific market: that of equities using nonlinear analysis, controlled experiments, and statistical inference. The fifth section touches on estimation and inference when nonlinearity plays an essential role in data generation. The sixth section contains a special, honorary lecture by Richard Goodwin that chronicles his personal involvement in the field. The papers are followed in the seventh section by an edited transcript of the Round Table Discussion.

Although the papers are only loosely related, they all illustrate some of the central issues, fundamental concepts, and tools of analysis that will be involved in the future development of dynamic economics and related fields.

The conference itself was one of an ongoing series of interdisciplinary conferences sponsored by the Prigogine Center for Statistical Mechanics at the University of Texas, Austin. The organizing committee consisted of Ilya Prigogine and Richard H. Day (Co-Chairs), Ping Chen (Conference Coordinator), Peter Allen, Robert Herman, Michele Sanglier, William Schieve, Raymond Smilor, and Luc Soete. Additional input was provided by Brian Arthur, William Barnett, Gerald Silverberg, and Walt Rostow. Some 50 scholars drawn from physics, biology, economics, engineering and related fields attended in Austin, Texas. The Conference was held April 11–14, 1989 at the IC^2 Institute.

In addition to the resources of the Prigogine Center, financial support was provided by the IC^2 Institute of the University of Texas, directed by Dr. George Kozmetski, the Solvay International Institute in Bruxelles, directed by Professor Prigogine, the MERIT Institute, directed by Luc Soete, the International Research Center of Ecotechnology at the Cranfield Institute in England, directed by Peter Allen, and the Economics Modelling Research Group of the University of Southern California, directed by Richard H. Day.

The logistic support of the IC^2 Institute was crucial and special thanks are due Amy Pearson and Pam Loflin whose timeless efforts made the conference a pleasant as well as rewarding occasion. The manuscript was given its final shape by Barbara Gordon, to whom we are glad to give our thanks on behalf of both authors and readers.

When the conference convened, almost immediately, as the opening addresses were being delivered, a special spirit of intellectual adventure and comraderie emerged. We all felt something important was occurring, that we were participating in an exciting effort, in widely diverse ways to be sure, but with a sense of common purpose: to help develop methods of dynamic, nonlinear, adaptive, evolutionary analysis, and to explore how these might advance understanding of economic experience. And also, perhaps, there was the hope that the world might some day become a better place because of these efforts in a still under-researched scientific direction.

Los Angeles   R.H.D.
June 1992   P.C.

Contents

Contributors, xv

I NONLINEAR, EVOLUTIONARY DYNAMICS: ALTERNATIVE PERSPECTIVES, 1

1. Bounded Rationality: From Dynamical Systems to Socio-economic Models, 3
   Ilya Prigogine
   Note, 13
   Bibliography, 13

2. Nonlinear Dynamics and Economics: A Historian's Perspective, 14
   W. W. Rostow
   A Quick Historical Survey of Nonlinearity in Economics, 15
   Some Tentative Conclusions, 16

3. Nonlinear Dynamics and Evolutionary Economics, 18
   Richard H. Day
   Some History of Thought, 19
      Equilibrium and Evolution, 19
      Nonlinearity and Complex Behavior, 22
   Complex Dynamics, 24
      Dynamical Systems, 25
      Essentially Nonlinear Systems, 25
      Chaos in the Sense of Li and Yorke, 25
      Ergodic Behavior, 26
      Deceptive Order, 27
      Statistical Equilibrium, 27
      Multiple Phase Systems, 27
      Frequency in Phase, 28
      Escape and Evolution, 28
   Economic Theory, 28
      Optimal Economic Growth, 29
      An Adaptive, Neoclassical Growth Model, 30
      Simple and Complex Dynamics, 32
      Endogenous Structural Change, 34
      Alternative Developmental Scenarios, 36
   Some General Reflections on Economic Adaptation and Evolution, 37
      Toward a General Modeling Approach, 37
      Viability and Evolving Populations of Agents, 38

Institutional Innovation and Policy Analysis, 39
Notes, 39
Bibliography, 40

II NONLINEAR MACRO DYNAMICS, 43

4. A Marx–Keynes–Schumpeter Model of Economic Growth and Fluctuation, 45
   Richard M. Goodwin
   Background, 45
   The Model, 47
   Numerical Example, 49
   Endogenous Innovation, 51
   Compensatory Fiscal Policy, 52
   Wages, Leisure, and Growth: The Policy Options, 56
   Notes, 57

5. Mode Locking and Nonlinear Entrainment of Macroeconomic Cycles, 58
   Erik Mosekilde, Erick Reimer Larsen, John D. Sterman,
   and Jesper Skovhus Thomsen
   Illustrations, 60
   The Model, 64
   Mode Locking, 68
   Amplitude Dependence of Entrainment: Structure of the Arnol'd Tongues, 75
   Lyapunov Exponents and Lock-In Time, 77
   Conclusion, 80
   Notes, 81
   Bibliography, 81

6. From Micro Behavior to Macro Dynamics: The Case of Vehicular Traffic, 84
   Robert Herman
   Notes, 88
   Bibliography, 88

III ADAPTATION, LEARNING, AND SELF-ORGANIZATION, 89

7. Emergence and Dissemination of Innovations: Some Principles
   of Evolutionary Economics, 91
   Ulrich Witt
   The Basic Concepts, 91
   Emergence of Innovations — Prerevelation Analysis, 93
   The Question of When Innovations Are Likely to Occur, 94
   Dissemination of Innovations — Aspect of Postrevelation Analysis, 96
   Notes, 98
   Bibliography, 98

8. Evolution: Persistent Ignorance from Continual Learning, 101
   Peter M. Allen
   Spatial Evolution of Urban Systems, 102

Evolution in Natural Resource Systems, 103
Evolutionary Drive, 104
Conclusions, 111
Bibliography, 112

9. Adaptive Firms and Random Innovations in a Model of Cyclical Output
   Growth, 113

   John Conlisk

   A Benchmark Static Model, 115
   The Dynamic Model, 116
      The Timing of a Period, 116
      Behavior of an Innovator Firm, 116
      Behavior of an Imitator Firm, 119
      Labor Market Clearance, 120
      Entry and Exit, 121
   Model Behavior, 124
      Stationarity, 124
      Economic Properties of the Growth Path, 126
   Appendix. Profit Rate Effect of an Additional Firm, 130
   Note, 130
   Bibliography, 130

10. Rationality, Imitation, and Tradition, 131

    Robert Boyd and Peter J. Richerson

    The Basic Model, 133
    The Evolutionary Stable Amount of Tradition, 137
    Heterogeneous Environments, 138
    Biased Imitation, 141
    Natural Selection, 142
    Cultural Mechanisms Leading to the ESS Amount of Imitation, 144
    Discussion, 146
    Note, 148
    Bibliography, 149

11. Self-Organization as a Process in Evolution of Economic Systems, 150

    Jacques Lesourne

    The Birth of a Labour Union, 151
       The Market, 152
       The Individual Decision-Making Process, 153
       The Company Decision-Making Process, 153
       The Adaptation of the Demands of the Actors and of the Union, 154
       Long Run Dynamic Behavior, 156
    The Creation of Professional Skills by the Labor Market, 157
       The Market, 158
       The Dynamics of the Model with Invariant Competence, 158
       The Dynamics with Modification of Individual Competence, 160
       The Characteristics of Stable States, 161

The Significance of the Results, 161
The Irreversible Structure of Space, 162
   The Concepts of Optimality, 163
   The Concepts of Stability, 164
   The Problem of Convergence, 165
Notes, 166
Bibliography, 166

IV STOCK MARKET DYNAMICS, 167

12. Chaotically Switching Bear and Bull Markets: The Derivation of Stock Price
    Distributions from Behavioral Rules, 169
    Weihong Huang and Richard H. Day
    The Model, 170
       –Investors, 170
       –Investors, 171
       Market–Makers, 172
       The Price Adjustment Equation, 173
    Market Churning, 174
    Constructing Price Densities, 175
    The Dependence of Market Price Dynamics on Behavioral Rules, 177
    Discussion of Theorem 2, 179
    Notes, 181
    Bibliography, 181

13. The Robustness of Bubbles and Crashes in Experimental Stock Markets, 183
    Ronald R. King, Vernon L. Smith, Arlington W. Williams,
    and Mark Van Boening
    Summary of Previous Experiments, 184
    Experimental Evaluation of Environmental and Policy Treatments
       for Moderating Price Bubbles, 185
    Short Selling, 186
       Experiment 265; Nine Inexperienced Subjects, 187
       Experiment 266; Nine Once–Experienced Subjects, 188
       Experiment 267; Nine Twice–Experienced Subjects, 188
    Margin Buying, 188
    Equal Endowments, 189
    A Fee for Each Exchange, 190
    Informed Traders, 190
       Experiment 229; 6x,3i, 191
       Experiment 233; 6x,3i, 192
       Experiment 278; 9x,3i, 193
       Experiment 282; 9,3i, 193
    Limit Price Change Rule, 194
    Effect of Using Corporate Executives, or Stock Market Dealers, as Subjects, 196
       Experiment 280; 15, 196
       Experiment 293; 6, 3i, 196

Regression Analysis of Treatments, 199
Conclusions, 199
Notes, 200
Bibliography, 200

14. Intraday Nonlinear Behavior of Stock Prices, 201
Melvin J. Hinich and Douglas M. Patterson
Data, 202
Empirical Results, 204
Treatment of Weekends and Missing Days, 204
Evidence of Nonlinearity in Daily Sampled Returns, 205
Linearity Test Applied to Individual Days of the Week, 207
Bibliography, 213

V PROBLEMS OF ESTIMATION AND INFERENCE, 215

15. Searching for Economic Chaos: A Challenge to Econometric Practice
and Nonlinear Tests, 217
Ping Chen
Distinguishing between Deterministic and Stochastic Processes, 218
Phase Space and Phase Portrait, 218
Long-Term Autocorrelations, 218
The Numerical Maximum Lyapunov Exponent, 221
The Correlation and Fractal Dimensions, 222
Pitfalls in Statistical Testing for Chaos, 222
The Discrepancy between Mathematical Theory and Numerical Experiment, 223
Limitations of Statistical Inference, 227
Testing Economic Chaos in Monetary Aggregates, 231
Data Processing and Path Smoothing, 232
Detrending Methods and Attractor Models, 232
Empirical Evidence of Deterministic and Stochastic Processes, 233
A Continuous Time Model of Growth Cycles with Delayed Feedback and Bounded
Expectations, 238
Deviations from Trend and Time Delay in Feedback, 239
What Can We Learn from the Model, 240
Linear Approximations of a Nonlinear Model, 243
Brief Summary and Future Directions, 244
Appendix A. A Direct Test for Determinism in Monetary Time Series, 246
Appendix B. Testing Correlation Resonances in Searching for Chaos, 248
Note, 249
Bibliography, 249

16. Has Chaos Been Discovered with Economic Data?, 254
William A. Barnett and Melvin J. Hinich
The Maintained Hypothesis, 255
The Hinich Bispectral Approach, 256
Definitions and Background, 256

The Test Method, 257
Computation of the Test Statistics, 257
The Data, 260
Results, 260
Conclusions, 262
Notes, 262
Bibliography, 263

17. Inference and Forecasting for Deterministic Nonlinear Times Series Observed
with Measurement Error, 266

John Geweke

A Simple One-Dimensional Noninvertible Map, 267
The Likelihood Function, 271
Inference, 278
Signal Extraction and Forecasting, 281
Unanswered Questions, 285
Notes, 286
Bibliography, 287

18. A Multicriteria Approach to Dynamic Estimation, 288

Robert Kalaba and Leigh Tesfatsion

Multicriteria Estimation: An Illustrative Example, 290
Standard Treatment of the Problem, 294
Generalizations, 298
Concluding Remarks, 299
Notes, 300
Bibliography, 300

VI HONORARY LECTURE, 301

19. My Erratic Progress Toward Economic Dynamics: Remarks Made at Banquet,
Tuesday, April 18, 1989, 303
Richard M. Goodwin

VII ROUND TABLE DISCUSSION, 307

20. Round Table Discussion, 309
Editors' Note, 324

Author Index, 325

Subject Index, 329

Contributors

Peter M. Allen
Cranfield Institute of Technology

Brian Arthur
Stanford University

William A. Barnett
Washington University, St. Louis

Mark Van Boening
University of Mississippi

Robert Boyd
University of California, Los Angeles

William Brock
University of Wisconsin

Ping Chen
The University of Texas at Austin

John Conlisk
University of California, San Diego

Richard H. Day
University of Southern California

Giovanni Dosi
University of Rome

John Geweke
University of Minnesota
and The Federal Reserve Bank of
Minneapolis

Richard M. Goodwin
Universita di Siena

Robert Herman
The University of Texas at Austin

Melvin J. Hinich
The University of Texas at Austin

Weihong Huang
University of Singapore

Robert Kalaba
University of Southern California

Ronald R. King
Washington University, St. Louis

Erik Reimer Larsen
The Technical University of Denmark

Jacques Lesourne
Le Directeur, *Le Monde*

Richard Lipsey
Canadian Institute for Advanced
Research

Michael Mackey
McGill University

Erik Mosekilde
The Technical University of Denmark

Richard Nelson
Columbia University

Douglas M. Patterson
Virginia Polytechnic Institute & State
University

Ilya Prigogine
International Institutes of Physics and
Chemistry (Solvay)
and The University of Texas at Austin

Peter J. Richerson
University of California at Davis

W. W. Rostow
The University of Texas at Austin

Peter Schwefel
University of Dortmund

Vernon L. Smith
University of Arizona

John D. Sterman
Massachusetts Institute of
Technology

Leigh Tesfatsion
Iowa State University

Jesper Skovhus Thomsen
The Technical University of Denmark

Arlington W. Williams
Indiana University

Sidney Winter
United States General Accounting
Office

Ulrich Witt
University of Freiburg

I

NONLINEAR, EVOLUTIONARY DYNAMICS: ALTERNATIVE PERSPECTIVES

This initial part introduces the central themes of the symposium: nonlinear dynamics, bounded rationality, and economic evolution.

In the first essay Professor Prigogine, a Nobel Laureate in chemistry, draws on physical theory to illuminate the concept of bounded rationality that Simon used to describe decision making in economic organizations. He grounds an explanation of unpredictability in the complex dynamics of nonlinear interaction. His analysis implies that the effective information that current data contain for the future — or for the past — decays exponentially as we project farther forward, or backward, so that "acting in complete accord with nature's laws" is a physical impossibility. Novelty does not disappear nor does equilibrium emerge with the passage of time. New events occur, new structures emerge. The human mind can never rest. It always has much to learn. He suggests that this insight should influence further work in economics.

Formal research on nonlinear economic processes that exhibit chaos and evolution has actually emerged from more than two centuries of effort to understand market adjustments, business fluctuations, and economic growth. In Chapter 2 Professor Rostow reminds us of the classics that seem to have anticipated in nonmathematical terms many of the insights that the new analytical methods are making possible.

In Chapter 3 Richard Day provides a survey of more recent lines of economic research that involve nonlinearity and concepts related to adaptation and evolution. He summarizes some of the mathematical concepts of complex dynamics that are used in this work and in the remainder of the paper illustrates them with an "adaptive, neoclassical model" of growth fluctuations and economic evolution. He concludes by contrasting the adaptive, evolutionary paradigm with that of intertemporal equilibrium and suggests that they should form complementary aspects of a unified dynamic economic theory whose construction should be the primary goal of economic science.

1

Bounded Rationality: From Dynamical Systems to Socio-economic Models

ILYA PRIGOGINE

Today we are witnessing a reconceptualization of science, both in the field of hard sciences and in the field of social sciences. Everywhere the vision of nature is drifting toward the multiple, the temporal, and the complex (Prigogine and Stengers, 1984). The importance of fluctuations, nonlinearity, and chaos is today well recognized. In this chapter I would like to analyze from this point of view the concept of bounded rationality introduced by Herbert Simon. Let me first quote two of his texts:

> The term "rational" denotes behavior that is appropriate to specific goals in the context of a given situation. If the characteristics of the choosing organism are ignored, and we consider only those constraints that arise from the *external situation, then we may speak of substantive or objective rationality* — that is, behavior that can be adjudged objectively to be optimally adapted to the situation. On the other hand, if we take into account the *limitations of knowledge and computing power* of the choosing organism, then we may find it incapable of making optimal choices. If, however, it uses methods of choice that are as effective as its decision-making and problem-solving means permit, we may speak of procedural or bounded rationality. (Simon, 1988)

> The capacity of the human mind for formulating and solving complex problems is very small compared to the size of the problems whose solution is required for objectively rational behavior in the world — or even for a reasonable approximation to such objective rationality. (Simon, 1957)

The concept of rationality has, in fact, changed over the centuries. Classical mechanics was always considered as the prototype of rationality in science where it meant acting according to the laws of "nature" (*Laws of Nature*, 1987). Indeed, in French it is often called "mécanique rationelle." Classical mechanics was for a long time identified with the very laws of reason. As you know, the laws of classical mechanics are deterministic and time reversible. A strong distinction is made between initial conditions, which are *arbitrary*, and the laws of motion, which bring us from the initial condition to the final condition. Classical dynamics assumes that initial conditions and final conditions are essentially equivalent. If you can go from the initial conditions to the final conditions, you can also go from the final conditions to the initial conditions. Classical dynamics is based on the concept of trajectories and on the least-action principle. In the view of classical dynamics, all elements of uncertainty are due to human subjective features. Everybody knows Einstein's saying, "God does not play dice." This is a late echo to Leibniz, who wrote that whatever happens could have been predicted by a being which would be sufficiently well informed. In a recent book, Isabelle Stengers and I have a chapter called "On Gods and Demons" (Prigogine and Stengers, 1988). In fact, the history of science is full of appeals to gods or demons — be it the Laplace demon or the Maxwell demon. The reason for this is a desire to see the world from the outside, from a point of view that would be that of a supernatural being, a god or a demon. It is not astonishing that such a point of view, which tries to go beyond our human weaknesses, has a strong appeal not only in science proper but also in human sciences. Let me quote the economist Weisskopf:

> The Newtonian paradigm underlying classical and nonclassical economics interpreted the economy according to the pattern developed in classical physics and mechanics, in analogy to the planetary system, to a machine and to clockwork: a closed autonomous system ruled by endogenous factors of highly selective nature, self-regulating and moving to a determinate, predictable point of equilibrium. (Weisskopf, 1983)

and also, again, Herbert Simon:

> The social sciences have been accustomed to look for models in the most spectacular of the natural sciences. There is no harm in that, provided that it is not done in a spirit of slavish imitation. In economics, it has been common enough to admire Newtonian mechanics (or . . . the Law of Falling Bodies), and to search for the economic equivalent of the laws of motion. But this is not the only model for a science, and it seems, indeed, not to be the right one for our purposes. (Simon, 1959)

Curiously, since the beginning of the century, we have witnessed a regression of the idea of classical rationality. Newtonian spacetime, independent of its material content, had to yield to the spacetime of relativity. However, both relativity and quantum theory can still be fitted inside an "extended" classical rationality. In this context, to come back to the text of Herbert Simon, the constraints come only from us; there are no external constraints, which would prevent "perfect knowledge." For Herbert Simon, there was a strong distinction to make between external limitations and internal limitations on the nature of the observer. Is this kind of distinction really valid?

Let me start by emphasizing that we are today going through a period of reconceptualization of dynamics. I would like to quote a remarkable text by Lighthill:

> I have to speak on behalf of the broad global fraternity of practitioners of mechanics. We collectively wish to apologize for having misled the general educated public by spreading ideas about the determinism of systems satisfying Newton's laws of motion that, after 1960, were to be proved incorrect. (Lighthill, 1986)

This text deals with a unique event in the history of science. It is quite common for a scientist to make a mistake and to apologize for his mistake. However, it is a unique case that a science that was considered to be the model for three centuries has to be so drastically revised as indicated by Lighthill. Professor Victor Szebehely has also emphasized many times the limits of classical dynamics (Szebehely, 1989). The text of Lighthill refers to the discovery of *unstable* dynamical systems. Everybody always knew that we need exact initial conditions to speak of a well-defined trajectory. However, for many dynamical systems, this is a rather unimportant factor. The novelty is the fact that for unstable dynamical systems, whatever the finite information about the initial conditions, there is a time horizon, we can only speak of probabilities. It is interesting that the idea of bounded rationality as introduced by Herbert Simon is consonant with this evolution of dynamics (I shall return to this topic later). It is an example of the common intellectual climate that is beginning to emerge between hard sciences on one side, such as classical dynamics, and socio-economic sciences on the other.

Let me now indicate two types of dynamical systems that illustrate in a striking way the loss of determinism emphasized by Sir James Lighthill. These are examples of highly unstable dynamical systems. We shall consider two classes. First, K-flows, where K stands for Kolmogorov. These are examples of chaotic systems. The second class, which I shall then consider in more detail, is the class of "large" Poincaré systems (LPS).

Let us start with Kolmogorov systems. Such systems are characterized by the fact that the distance δx between two neighboring trajectories increases exponentially with time (see Figure 1.1). $1/t_L$ is called the Lyapounov exponent. This exponent measures the temporal horizon accessible to the system. Indeed, the concept of

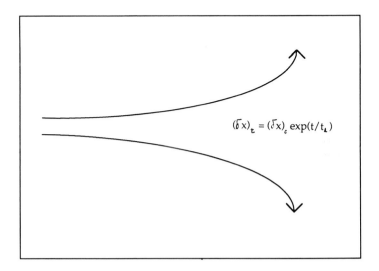

$$(\delta x)_t = (\delta x)_c \exp(t/t_L)$$

Figure 1.1 Divergence of trajectories in K-flows.

a trajectory will be lost for times large in respect to the Lyapounov time. In other words, independently of our computational facilities, there is an intrinsic temporal scale that indicates the period over which the trajectory description is valid. If we wanted to go beyond this period, we would have to increase our accuracy exponentially, and obviously we would rapidly reach a limit whatever the power of our computers.

A very simple example of a K-flow is the so-called baker transformation (Prigogine, 1980). Let me briefly mention its meaning (see Figure 1.2). We take a square, squash it, put the right part above the left, and we go therefore from stage (a) to stage (c). If we repeat this (Figure 1.2β), we fraction the hatched content into two parts. This fractioning is going on every time we repeat the baker transformation. The horizontal direction is the expanding direction. The distances are multiplied by a factor 2 "modulo 1." This corresponds to a Lyapounov exponent $2^n = e^{n lg2}$ and therefore the Lyapounov exponent, or the inverse of the Lyapounov time, is $lg2$. The baker transformation can be expressed in terms of a Bernouilli shift. If we use a binary system of notation, every point x, y can be mapped into an infinite sequence of numbers $\{u_n\}$, each u_n being 0 or 1, and it can be shown (Szebehely, 1989) that the baker transformation corresponds to a simple shift in the order of these digits. The existence of this shift is the reason why this dynamical system is called a Bernouilli shift. In this way, we can easily understand how information is lost as time goes on. Whatever our precision, we have a finite window. For example, we may know the numbers $u_{-3}u_{-2}u_{-1}u_0u_1u_3$, but after a single Bernouilli shift, the number u_{-4} will come in, and since this number is unknown, the concept of a trajectory is already lost as, according to the value of u_{-4}, we can reach two different points. As time goes on, the initial information will be completely lost and the system will be uniformly distributed in its phase space.

This is an interesting model because it explains to us in a very simple way how information that is as "unimportant" as we want can become crucial as time goes on. The weather today is determined by features that, a few days ago, appeared as quite secondary features without any importance. As time goes on, what was important yesterday may become important today. As we lose information, we have to go to a probabilistic description. This leads then to symmetry breaking and to an irreversible approach to equilibrium.

We have recently developed a spectral theory describing the approach to equilibrium. The new feature is that it is a *complex* spectral theory (the imaginary parts are related to the Lyapounov time). But we cannot describe it here, and we refer to the original paper (Petrosky and Prigogine, 1991).

I would like now to go to my second example, which corresponds to large Poincaré systems.

Let me first recall the basic equations of classical mechanics, Hamilton's equations. In the Hamiltonian formulation the energy H is expressed as a function of the momenta p and the coordinates q, and the time change of the p and the q is given by the canonical equations:

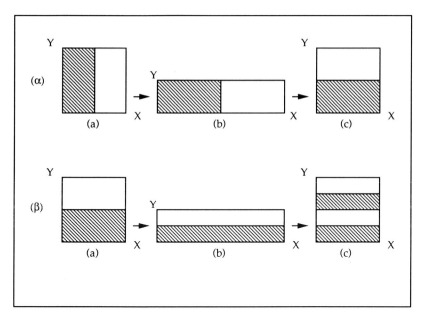

Figure 1.2 The Baker transformation.

$$\dot{q}_i = \frac{\partial H}{\partial p_i},$$

$$\dot{p}_i = \frac{\partial H}{\partial q_i}. \tag{1.1}$$

Classical mechanics studied in great detail "*integrable*" systems. We may then go from the variables p, q to new variables, called angle-action variables, α and J, such that the Hamiltonian would become a function only of the new momenta J, which are the action variables. The canonical equation of motion then becomes

$$\dot{\alpha}_i = \frac{\partial H}{\partial J_i} = \omega_i(J),$$

$$\dot{J}_i = 0, \tag{1.2}$$

which indicates that the angle-variables change with time while the action variables are invariants of motion. The way in which the angle variables change with time is determined by $\omega_i(J)$, called the natural frequencies of the system. Angle-action systems are remarkably simple because they are isomorphic to a system performing independent motions, like a collection of free particles. There also, the total energy is the sum of the kinetic energies of the particles without any potential energy.

Poincaré asked the question: is every Hamiltonian system $H(p, q)$ isomorphic to an angle-action system? To investigate this problem, he considered the class of Hamiltonians such as

$$H = H_0(J) + \lambda V(J, \alpha). \tag{1.3}$$

Here, H_0 is a "free" Hamiltonian, which depends only on the action variable and $\lambda V(J, \alpha)$, a potential energy depending both on action variables and angle variables; λ is a coefficient measuring the strength of interaction. Can we find a transformation that would transform this Hamiltonian into a new Hamiltonian (H, J'), depending only on new action variables (J') that could be expanded in powers of the coupling constant:

$$J' = J_0 + \lambda J_1 + \lambda^2 J_2 \ldots . \tag{1.4}$$

Systems for which this transformation can be performed are called, in Poincaré's terminology, integrable systems.

Are all dynamical systems integrable? Poincaré was able to show that this was not so; that, in general, dynamical systems are nonintegrable. This is a very important result, because if in contrast Poincaré had shown that all dynamical systems are integrable, that would mean that interactions can always be eliminated; that we would essentially live in a noninteracting world, a world that would be isomorphic to a world of free particles floating independently of each other. This would certainly be a quite simple world. However, this would also be a world in which there would be no chemistry, no structure, no life. Poincaré went beyond simply the statement of nonintegrability; he showed *why* systems are nonintegrable. The reason for nonintegrability is the existence of resonances. As indicated before, frequencies ω_i are defined in terms of the unperturbed Hamiltonian by formula (1.2). A resonance appears whenever the relation

$$k_1\omega_1 + k_2\omega_2 + \cdots = 0 \tag{1.5}$$

is satisfied, where the k_i are integers. For example, in the case of two degrees of freedom, this implies that the ratio of the frequencies is a rational number. This rational number depends on the value of the action variables. This leads to a highly complex situation, because for some values of the action variable we may have resonances, for others we do not. In general the ratio of frequencies would be an irrational number, and, as everybody knows, there are "more" irrationals than rationals. Therefore, resonances are, in some sense, rare; on the other hand, they are densely distributed in the phase space. This leads to the situation studied in the famous *KAM* (Kolmogorov–Arnold–Moser) theory — rational points leading to erratic trajectories wandering in the phase space while irrational and nonresonant points leading to periodic trajectories.

For some time, I have been interested in the limit of Poincaré's theorem for large systems, for which I shall use the abbreviation LPS. The important new element is that the condition of resonance (1.5) no longer implies integers, but simply real numbers. As a result, we may now have continuous sets of resonances, and the resonance condition can now be satisfied in almost all points. This leads to the feature that LPS are highly unstable dynamical systems, very similar to K-flows. Again, in contrast with "small" Poincaré systems, now nearly every point is a point of resonance. The interest of LPS is that they are realized in many fields of modern physics, whether in the problem of N-point systems, the interaction between matter and radiation, and in many other problems of basic importance in classical and quantum physics. The LPS correspond really to the type of physical systems that we normally observe around us, whenever we go beyond highly simplified cases such as two-body problems and so on.

Before going to the dynamics of LPS, let us make some qualitative remarks. Let us take an N-body system, for example, a dilute gas. In a dilute gas we have collisions. But collisions are just resonances. In a collision (Figure 1.3a), we have two particles with velocities v_1, v_2, which collide, leading to receding particles with velocities v_1', v_2', energy and momentum being conserved. This conservation of energy and momentum is equivalent to the condition of resonance. We can therefore imagine resonances being essentially "collisions" between the various particles forming the system. Now, collisions lead to correlations.

When we have two particles that collide, they go away from one another after the collision but their motion remains correlated (Figure 1.3b). We are quite sure about that because if we would reverse the velocities, they would come closer again and collide. In other words, the time-inverted motion shows that the two particles were correlated. We have here an example of postcollisional correlation, a correlation that is induced by the collision. We can, of course, also imagine "precollisional" correlation (Figure 1.3c), in which two particles that were correlated before the collision and then recede one from the other. In many-body systems we have a flow of correlations (Figure 1.3d). Two particles collide, giving a binary correlation, but then they collide again with other particles leading to ternary correlation, to correlations involving a larger and larger number of particles. Obviously, when we go to higher order correlations we go to situations that at some point become uncontrollable. We can follow correlations between a small number of particles, but what about correlations between 10, 100, and 1000 particles? This would escape every possible observation.

We should make a clear distinction between correlations and forces. Correlations correspond to a kind of "memory" of a resonance or of a collision. When particles have collided they keep, at least for some time, the memory of their collision through the correlation that has been established. The closest analogue I can give for correlation would be communication. When people meet, they communicate; when they leave, they keep the memory of their encounter. When they again meet other people, this communication is propagated to an ever-increasing number of participants.

The dynamics of LPS has some quite interesting features. I would like to mention two of them. In classical dynamics, direct motion from A to B is considered to be equivalent to the inverse motion from B to A. In LPS this equivalence is broken. Let us indeed consider more closely what happens in direct motion when we start from 0 and go to time t. We suppose the initial condition is expressed in terms of

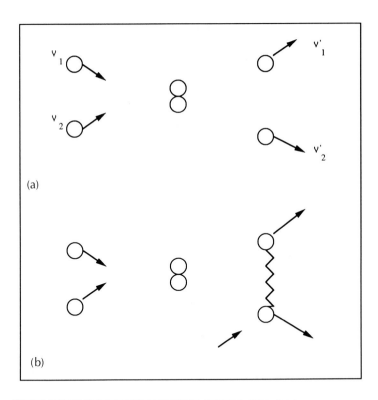

(a)

(b)

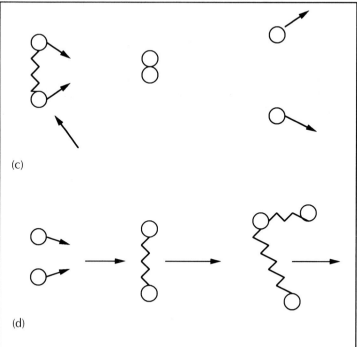

(c)

(d)

Figure 1.3 (a) Binary collision. (b) Postcollisional correlations. (c) Precollisional corre-lations. (d) Flow of correlations.

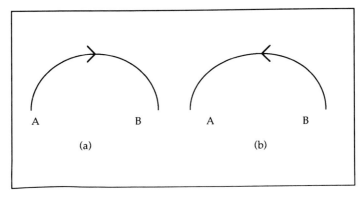

Figure 1.4   Direct and inverse motion.

certain degrees of freedom. We could initially give the velocity distribution of the particles, or we could give the binary correlations between the particles. That is all that we know about the initial condition. As time goes on, we shall witness a flow of correlations, which implies a larger and larger number of particles. This flow of correlation leads both to the creation of disorder (the velocity distribution becomes more and more disordered and tends to a Maxwell–Boltzmann distribution) and also to the creation of order (the spatial distribution that may have been disordered in the beginning will be determined by the intermolecular forces between the particles).

Now let us consider the inverse transformation, going back from t to the initial time as in Figure 1.4. The difference is that we have to recollect the information that has been disseminated during the time $0 \rightarrow t$. It is like the situation after successive conversations between people when we would like to reconstruct the initial conversation that took place. We now need to consider correlations that will compensate the effect of the collisions.

In short, we see now the limitation of classical dynamics. In classical dynamics the "quality" of information is disregarded. This, in a sense, is quite logical if you deal with systems with a finite number of degrees of freedom. For example, we may deal with the system sun–earth–moon. The sun speaks to the moon, the moon speaks to the earth; there is no information escaping from these three actors. But LPS correspond to multiactor systems where the information is transmitted from one degree to another and finally disappears in a sea of highly multiple conditions.

Perhaps a crude analogy can be helpful. From the point of view of the first law of thermodynamics, heat is equivalent to work. But this is no longer true from the point of view of the second law. It is easy to transform work into heat, but it requires more sophisticated devices to transform heat into work. Work is concentrated in a few degrees of freedom, like a moving piston. Heat, however, is disseminated over a large number of particles. In a sense, the transformation $0 \rightarrow t$ is similar to a transformation from work to heat, but the transformation $t \rightarrow 0$ corresponds more closely to the transformation of heat to work.

Let us now consider the dynamics of LPS. The main obstacle, as noticed by

Poincaré, is the occurrence of divergences due to resonances. This is called by Poincaré the principal difficulty of dynamics. We have, however, recently shown how to overcome this difficulty. The divergences are due to the neglect of dissipation, both in classical and quantum theory. As for the Baker transformation, we have developed a complex spectral theory (Hasegawa and Saphir, 1992). The two main characteristics are that it leads to time symmetry breaking, that is, to dissipation, and that it deals with ensembles. It corresponds to a statistical description, which cannot be reduced to trajectories or wave functions.

Instability, probability, and irreversibility are closely related concepts. In classical physics, we had the time paradox. Macroscopic processes were associated with irreversibility, but basic dynamics was ruled by time-reversible, deterministic laws. We have now overcome the time paradox. The fundamental dynamical level corresponds to unstable dynamical systems, which lead to time symmetry breaking. Once we start with unstable dynamical systems (LPS), you have irreversibility. You can then speak about distance from equilibrium at the microscopic level and you can speak about bifurcations, events, chaos, and the generation of "information." Therefore, the basic element for me is really the existence in nature, or the *prevalence* in nature, of unstable dynamical systems. All other remarkable properties (time-symmetry breaking, bifurcation, generation of information) are in some sense consequences of the existence of unstable dynamical systems.

After this excursion to the theory of dynamical systems, let us come back to bounded rationality. The distinction between objective rationality, leading to the external situation and bounded rationality, which takes into account our own limitations, expresses a kind of duality: the duality between the external world and the nature of the observer. In fact, the distinction is not so clear cut. Bounded rationality is imposed on us by the structure of the external world, by the fact that the dynamical structure of the world corresponds to a large extent to unstable dynamical systems. This is a statement of fact, not a statement that corresponds to a deduction from some logical system. It could be conceived that all systems would be integrable and stable; then there would be no need for bounded rationality, but then there would also be no observer, and no one to speak about the world in which the observer is embedded.

The analogy between the basic properties of unstable dynamic systems implying a flow of information with socioeconomic systems is clear. Someone has written "society is talk," and this implies both a flow of information and phenomena of retroaction as in LPS. Of course, society is not *only* talk. There are essential differences between the simple dynamical systems that we have been considering and the behavior of men. In the behavior of human beings, an essential role is played by cognitive maps and especially by the conflict between cognitive maps, which leads to learning. Still, I think there is a remarkable confluence. Human sciences have always looked for models in natural sciences. Classical dynamics of stable dynamical systems is not suitable for this purpose. The dynamics of unstable systems comes much closer to the basic properties of socioeconomic systems.

I have always considered science as a cultural phenomenon that goes beyond the subdivision of science into various disciplines. And from this point of view, the confluence of what happens today is a very interesting example. After all, Simon's ideas of bounded rationality owe nothing to the ideas of Kolmogorov and others about unstable dynamical systems, and vice versa. And still, there is a close relation between the intellectual content of bounded rationality and the implications of unstable dynamical systems. This is perhaps a quite remarkable example of the new cultural and intellectual atmosphere that also infuses this meeting.

Note

I would like to thank my friend Robert Herman, who mentioned my influence. Obviously this influence was a mutual one. He was my mentor in operational research and especially in the theory of traffic flow. That is where I learned the importance of nonlinearity and where I met, perhaps for the first time, a striking bifurcation, one that is observed daily when we go from low-density to high-density traffic. Vehicular traffic is also a field where the mechanism of decision making plays an essential role. Referring to the idea of "bounded rationality" as introduced by Herbert Simon, traffic flow is a good example of a highly bounded rationality, perhaps even of irrationality.

Bibliography

Hasegawa, H.H., and W. Saphir, 1992, "Non-Equilibrium Statistical Mechanics of the Baker Map: Ruelle Resonances and Subdynamics," *Physics Letters A*, 161, 477–482.

Laws of Nature and Human Conduct: Specificities and Unifying Themes, 1987, Proceedings of the Discoveries Symposium, 1985, Brussels: Task Force of Research, Information and Study on Science, Brussels.

Lighthill, J., 1986, "The Recently Recognized Failure of Predictability in Newtonian Dynamics," in J. Mason et al. (eds.), *Predictability in Science and Society, Proceedings of the Royal Society*, 407, 35–60.

Petrosky, T., and I. Prigogine, 1991, "Alternative Formulation of Classical and Quantum Dynamics for Non-Equilibrium Systems," *Physica A*, 175, 146–209.

Prigogine, I., 1980, *From Being to Becoming: Time and Complexity in the Physical Sciences*, Freeman, San Francisco.

Prigogine, I., and I. Stengers, 1984, *Order Out of Chaos*, Bantam, New York.

Prigogine, I., and I. Stengers, 1988, *Entre le Temps et l'Éternité*, Fayard, Paris.

Simon, Herbert, 1957, *Models of Man*, Wiley, New York.

Simon, Herbert, 1959, "Rational Decision-Making in Business Organizations," *American Economic Review*, September.

Simon, Herbert, 1988, "Human Nature in Politics: The Dialogue of Psychology with Political Science," in M. Campanella (ed.), *Between Rationality and Cognition: Policy-Making under Conditions of Uncertainty, Complexity and Turbulence*, Albert Meynier, Torino, 11–34. (First published in *American Political Science Reviews*.)

Szebehely, Victor G., 1989, *Adventures in Celestial Mechanics: A First Course in the Theory of Orbits*, University of Austin Press, Austin.

Weisskopf, W.A., 1983, "Reflections on Uncertainty in Economics," *Geneva Papers on Risk and Insurance*, 9, 335–360.

2

Nonlinear Dynamics and Economics: A Historian's Perspective

W. W. ROSTOW

They could have asked any old peasant woman and she would have told them there is no such thing as equilibrium in man or nature.

ELSPETH DAVIES ROSTOW

In my career as an economic historian I have been especially concerned with aspects of growth and development quite different from balanced, steady growth; aspects that were much on the minds of many of the great economic thinkers through mid-twentieth century, aspects that now are being embodied in nonlinear economic dynamics.

In these brief remarks I shall view this evolution of economic thought and its relation to nonlinear dynamics. Four characteristics of modern (post–1780s) market economies suggest this exercise might be useful.

First, like Edward Lorenz' weather patterns, they have moved forward in "recognizable cycles coming around again and again but never twice the same way."

Second, the overall trend in growth rates is much steadier — and more nearly linear — than the sectoral growth rates that sustain them, notably sectors whose rise and deceleration are closely related to the introduction and diffusion of new technologies.

Third, economies exhibit something akin to structural "phase transitions" as they undergo the creative–destructive process of absorbing new technologies. The most dramatic example of such discontinuity is what I have called the "take-off" and what Simon Kuznets called, "the beginning of modern economic growth." But, as Schumpeter argued, the absorption of any substantial new technology induces positive and negative feedback forces, which, in turn, bring about turbulent direct and indirect structural changes in a society of the kind that are now being incorporated in mathematical models of economic development.

Fourth, corrective feedback forces are provided in competitive economies by changing profit possibilities that have tended to direct capital (including inventive and innovative talent) into "appropriate" channels. The implied feedback has been complicated by two human characteristics: the tendency to envisage the future on the basis of linear projections of the recent past, and a follow-the-leader tendency among those who make investment decisions. These characteristics decreed that the economies systematically undershot and overshot ex post equilibrium conditions, lurching their way through history in perpetual disequilibrium.

A Quick Historical Survey of Nonlinearity in Economics

Let us now consider briefly the past two and half centuries of economic theory in terms of these characteristics.

At the beginning of this period Adam Smith produced a lucid theory that, despite positive dynamic elements, set limits on growth as diminishing returns ultimately prevailed. Subsequently, Malthus and Ricardo opened an explicit debate on deterministic versus nondeterministic methods. Malthus, indeed, was surprisingly conscious of uncertainty, multiple causation, and interaction.

J.S. Mill and Karl Marx — superficially a strange pairing — lived in an era after the Napoleonic wars only dimly perceived as possible by Malthus and Ricardo, a world where technology had become a flow, the rate of population increase was declining in the industrializing countries, and great new sources of food and raw materials were opening up around the world. They sought quite different remedies for the ills of this evidently ongoing and diffusing industrial system; but they both produced analyses in which diminishing relative marginal utility in contrast to diminishing marginal productivity ultimately sets the limit to growth. Karl Marx went further. He also produced a theory of historical stages in which technology at first generates a societal superstructure; but the further progress of technology in time sets up forces and social classes that find the old superstructure excessively restraining. A new order follows after a bloody transition.

Then comes Alfred Marshall. He perceived more clearly than any of his predecessors — and perhaps any of his successors — the dangers as well as virtues of the use of mathematics in economics. He lived through the marginalist revolution and participated in the development of both partial and general equilibrium analysis. But he clearly perceived the inevitably changing technological and societal framework within which economies operated. He argued forcefully that if economics was to be serious, it had to cope with "organic growth" in the face of major technological change and increasing returns. As with the Malthus–Ricardo exchange, the hard-earned conclusions of Marshall bear directly on the central issues of this conference.

During the period from 1870 — a benchmark date for marginalist revolution — to 1939 economics becomes an academic discipline with professors, graduate students, learned journals, and a fragmenting, technical specialization. Several episodes within it, however, carried on a concern with the broad themes inherited from the classics, Marx and Marshall. These include Joseph Schumpeter on innovation; the young Simon Kuznets of *Secular Movements in Production and Prices* (1930) on leading sectors and the overall course of output; the pre-*General Theory* movement toward uniting cycle and growth theory in which Wesley Mitchell and D.H. Robertson were important figures; Harrod's 1939 growth model; and Schumpeter's debate with Alvin Hansen on secular stagnation which followed the sharp depression of 1938 during which unemployment rose in the United States from 14% in 1937 to 19% the next year.

Then came Paul Samuelson's *Foundations*, which sounded a methodological trumpet that was to prevail for some four decades. Samuelson appreciated Marshall's virtuosity as a mathematician, but he underemphasized the limits of mathematics that led Marshall to a biological rather than mechanical approach to the subject. The study of maximizing behavior and the setting up of deterministic behavior in terms of initial conditions, rules of behavior, and parameters — which was the unifying core of Samuelson's method — could not capture the rich legacy inherent in his classical and neoclassical precursors, nor the full complexity of reality.

After 1945 additional approaches to the analysis of economic growth can be identified. First, there were the models of high steady growth rates that enjoyed a lively run from the mid–1950s to the grain and oil price explosions of 1972 and 1973. Second, there were the statistical analyses of the morphology of growth. These were rooted in the pioneering work of Colin Clark that was extended with great industry and valuable results, but the highly aggregated statistical methods required did not permit a firm grasp on the fundamental nonlinear dynamics of growth. Third, there were the development economists, who sought to analyze and prescribe for societies at early stages of growth. Their conclusions are difficult to generalize except for one: *virtually all learned that politics has a powerful influence on economic development; sometimes dampening economic progress (e.g., China, Indonesia), and sometimes reinforcing it (e.g., Taiwan, South Korea).*

Some Tentative Conclusions

Efforts to explore explicitly nonlinear dynamics in its relevance to economic concepts and data have been going on for roughly a decade. Any effort to assess possibly fruitful linkages must, therefore, be highly tentative. Nonetheless, as an economic historian, I am intrigued by these developments and believe it is possible to discern several important insights and several limitations.

I would suggest tentatively three broad sets of implications.

First, *the philosophic impact*. Hans Mark has put forward the hypothesis that, like Newtonian physics, relativity, and quantum mechanics, nonlinear dynamics will have wide ranging consequences for how human beings view nature, societies, and themselves. In substance he concludes: "The basic content of the new science of non-linear dynamics is that one should not be surprised by the astonishing behavior of non-linear systems." Anyone who has observed the instinctive and dangerous tendency of individuals, private institutions, and governments to operate on linear projections of the future will recognize this as an exceedingly substantive conclusion.

The pervasiveness of nonlinearity in economics should not only "heighten sensitivity to surprises" but also dramatize the fact that serious economics is, indeed, a field for nonlinear analysis, which it was — at least in spirit — in its first century or so; that the profession's past obsession with simple dynamics now severely limits — if it does not cripple — the capacity of the discipline to deal effectively with serious problems. It should also dramatize the desirability of reestablishing continuity with the classical and neoclassical ideas that are congruent with nonlinear analysis.

Second, *the technical applicability of nonlinear dynamics.* There are, it appears to me, broadly, *two forms* of application of nonlinear dynamics to economics: *the construction of nonlinear theoretical models* and *the use of nonlinear models for econometric measurement.* At the highest level of aspiration the two methods of analysis are linked by the hope that empirical studies of relatively few time series may reveal the structure of the model that yielded the dynamic pattern established.

To a nonpractitioner, there appear to be three lions in the path of rendering nonlinear economics an instrument for reliable prediction.

1. *The scarcity of accurate, long-time series.* This is a problem by no means confined to economics and the social sciences. Experts on animal populations, for example, confront the same difficulty. As an economic historian I regret to report that long-term, reliable, and uniform economic time series will be hard to come by.

2. *Economic data inevitably contain a great deal of authentic noise* reflecting unpredictable events of considerable magnitude, e.g., wars, revolutions, bad harvests, discontinuous jumps in the oil price brought about by noneconomic events, political decisions. Can nonlinear analysis be developed so that the endogenous forces and exogenous perturbations can be isolated?

3. *Assuming that some adequate series are found or generated, and that endogenous and exogenous forces can be identified, the question arises: will they capture variables of such unambiguous analytic importance that there will be a marked similarity between the dynamics of systems driven by a few variables and those characterized by many variables?* Despite evident difficulties the possibility exists that a few deterministic nonlinear equations and adequate data will, in effect, permit valid prediction — at least over short periods.

Third, *people and celestial mechanics.* My third conclusion concerns people. Nonlinear dynamics is bringing scientists closer together as they explore common nonlinear uncertainties, patterns, and processes. This is a remarkable reversal of the progressive fragmentation and specialization of the physical and social sciences that has been going on for a long time. It would be a salutary development if this interaction could continue. It could help establish linkages between the nonlinear dynamics of human beings and the nonlinear dynamics of the physical world that could enhance our ability to understand and control ourselves and our environment, neither of which is ever at equilibrium.

3

Nonlinear Dynamics and Evolutionary Economics

RICHARD H. DAY

> The very stuff of matter is the product of a highly dynamic evolutionary process . . .
>
> HAROLD FRITZSCH

> Everyday of our lives there occurs in us something of that evolution . . . a chisel stroke, however insignificant, on the eternally unfinished statue of our species.
>
> ERWIN SCHRÖDINGER

It is now widely understood that mathematical dynamics can explain a far wider class of phenomena than Newton and Leibnitz imagined, including even the apparent stochasticity of events and the generation of form that seem to occur everywhere in the natural and social world. Along a different front, advances in evolutionary theory have extended the seminal ideas of Darwin and Wallace beyond the early view that variation and selection would lead to maximum fitness and efficient, ecological equilibria. A more complex picture has emerged, popularized in the writings of Stephen J. Gould, of continuing change, sometimes relatively slow, but interspersed with periods of rapidly unfolding forms. Taken together, these developments are leading to new insights in many sciences, including economics.

Like Professor Rostow, I think this nonlinear, evolutionary perspective is much closer to the great currents of economic thinking than is sometimes recognized; therefore, I want to begin my discussion with some history of thought in economics. Then I will summarize a few key concepts central to nonlinear dynamics and show how they can be applied to an "adaptive neoclassical model" to illustrate how economic growth can be "complex" and have an "evolutionary" character. This model is just an example of a modeling strategy whose general character is outlined in the concluding section. I hope that increasing intellectual resources will be invested in its further development.

Some History of Thought

Equilibrium and Evolution

First, then, let us consider some history of economic thought.

It is not always remembered that classical economic ideas about individual competition and aggregate development formed a part of the intellectual stew within which the biological theories of evolution were synthesized. While economic theorists, like their biological counterparts, often assumed that competition and selection would eventually produce efficient individual and social equilibria, they also recognized the nonequilibrium, developmental aspects of economic change. Rostow has just reminded us of some of these early views, especially those of Marshall who considered individuals to respond to economic opportunities locally with partial adjustments occurring over time. Walras also thought of equilibrium prices as emerging through a sequence of adjustments, and Cournot modeled oligopolistic competition as a chain of temporarily optimal responses to crudely extrapolated expectations. In none of these did the sequence of adjustments as a whole satisfy any overall, intertemporal conditions of optimality or social efficiency.

In a more extreme vision of the market economy theory, Frank Knight argued that people would act *as if* they could make optimal choices even though they did in fact have limited cognitive ability, and that markets worked *as if* they were in equilibrium even though no one knew how to compute such a state. Knight's proposition was made the centerpiece of Friedman's "positive economics." Subsequently, Lucas, took the same step, arguing that economic events can be understood by analyzing models *only* of *intertemporal equilibrium under uncertainty*. In such models, equilibrium is characterized by optimal equilibrium *strategies* that perfectly account for all the interactions in the economy and its environment. In such a state the economy works as if agents have nothing essential to learn, no incentive to modify their rules of behavior, and no need to worry about failures to coordinate their actions.

In a completely different line of work, Schumpeter (1934), who built directly on Walrasian concepts in his first book, *The Theory of Economic Development*, incorporated the psychological realities of bounded rationality, the innovative role of entrepreneur, and the facilitating function of banks, which can make possible a shift of resources to new enterprises out of equilibrium through the medium of credit.[1] He thought that — in the absence of innovation — markets would converge to general equilibrium because "experience taught people what to do." Later, Alchian (1950), who explicitly recognized the use of imitation in contrast to optimizing calculations for guiding much economic behavior, argued that the competitive selection of profitable enterprises would guide a decentralized private ownership economy to a socially efficient equilibrium. Simon and March, Simon, Cyert, and March, and Modigliani and Cohen later emphasized a central role for adaptation in the firm and market. Then Sidney Winter (1964), in a deep methodological examination of the issues raised by Alchian and by Papandreau, showed that economic Darwinism could not be used to justify optimality and equilibrium assumptions in static economic theory. The basic thrust of his insight was that variation and selection need not bring about optimality and equilibrium *even in the long run*, and, consequently, that predictions based on economic equilibrium and comparative statics need not hold even in the absence of innovations!

My own early work on economic dynamics focused on the development of mathematical models that could be calibrated using empirical data, that were amenable to numerical solution, and that could mimic or simulate production, investment, technological change, and resource utilization in agricultural regions and industrial sectors. It was inspired in part by Marshall's idea that economizing does not occur globally over space or time but locally and that investments in long-term projects are based not on detailed expectations of future events but on current profits and quasirents that accrue to current capital stocks and other "quasifixed factors." It incorporated the facts, emphasized by Schumpeter and Simon, that agents experience inertia, that they adjust in response to perceived opportunities with a lag, and that their plans are adapted period by period to experience and new information.

These "recursive programming models" were able to show in specific economic settings and for specific historical periods how collections of individual activities and integrated processes grew and decayed in overlapping waves, how resource utilization might increase or decrease in unbalanced response to economic forces, how the demand for skilled and unskilled labor, for various types of land and for various kinds of capital goods might shift in relative and absolute importance within a system of evolving structures and switching economic regimes (Day and Cigno, 1978). Putting these properties in Darwinian terms, multiple commodity and technological alternatives constitute the "population" whose composition changes over time. Exogenously given innovations in technology at various points in time produce variations. Selection is determined by changing demand, short run profits, and local cost efficiencies.

Nelson and Winter (1982) pioneered dynamic analyses that explicitly incorporated populations of *agents* whose rules of behavior or routines were selected by profit performance with the passage of time and showed how innovations could travel through a population. Iwai (1984) subsequently extended their theory and Gunnar Eliasson (1986) oriented his microanalytic simulation model in a similar direction using empirical data on the Swedish economy. Eliasson's simulations showed how rapid adoption of technological improvements through a population of firms might accelerate growth but might also precipitate subsequent instabilities. Chapters in the present volume by Allen, Boyd and Richardson, Conlisk, Lesourne, and Witt provide models very similar in spirit. A host of other contributions will be found in various collections that include Day and Groves (1975), Day and Eliasson (1986), Batten, Casti, and Johansson (1987), Dosi, Freeman, Nelson, Silverberg, and Soete (1988), and Anderson, Arrow, and Pines (1988).

The latter volume introduces evolutionary models very much along the lines discussed by Nelson and Winter, whose populations consist of behavioral rules that form strings much like genes in a chromosome and that can recombine randomly to produce new behavioral rules. The frequency with which given rules are used depends on their relative performance in a selection and variation process based on Holland's "genetic algorithms." Kaufman (1988) in that volume presents the most elaborate application of this approach and suggests its use as a model of technological discovery and diffusion.

Two Paradigms?

Within this varied literature we can discern two fundamentally distinct characterizations of economic dynamics, both descendants of classical and neoclassical economics,

- one of adapt*ed* equilibrium dynamics and one of adapt*ive* evolutionary dynamics.

In equilibrium dynamics agents' behavior is described by strategies that are optimal with respect to preferences and with respect to all possible future consequences of actions. Agents are optimally adapted to to each other and to their environment. The power of this approach derives from the fact that equilibrium price and output trajectories depend only on preferences and technology (and the shock generating mechanism), and not mechanisms for solving decision problems and generating prices!

We can interpret equilibrium dynamics in several different ways. First, we could think of it as the way an economy works if its agents were to discover — by chance, by adapting or learning in some unspecified way — the optimal equilibrium strategies. Second, and without assuming that the economy is in equilibrium, we could suppose that equilibrium dynamics gives a *useful approximation* of the way the economy works even though it does not describe how it *actually* works. Third, we could suppose, as Lucas (1987) suggested, that the economy always *really works* as if it were in a dynamic equilibrium and cease thinking about disequilibrium theory on grounds that it is a beguiling but ad hoc and misleading temptation (cf. Lucas, 1987, p. 198).

Contrastingly, the adaptive, evolutionary approach focuses on the characterization of the way economies work when they work out of equilibrium and explicitly represents their capacity to change structure, i.e., to evolve or self-organize. It requires far more structure than does the equilibrium approach. Mechanisms that describe *how* agents make decisions, how prices are determined, and how exchanges can take place out of equilibrium must be specified. One can ask if solutions or trajectories exist for such a model and what is their dynamic and economic character. In particular we can ask if any such solutions would have the character of an intertemporal, general equilibrium and under what conditions the adaptive, evolutionary economy would converge to one. The broader problem of generating out-of-

equilibrium dynamics and of characterizing economic evolution itself using disequilibrium theory, in addition to the authors already mentioned, has been considered by
Kaldor, Hayek, Hahn, and Fisher. I have also tried to develop a coherent framework
for this task in a series of papers beginning with my contribution in the Day and
Groves (1975) volume through the most recent version in the Batten, Casti, and Johansson (1987) volume. These, too, are but scratches on a very big surface that has
yet to be thoroughly cultivated.

Nonlinearity and Complex Behavior

The difficulties and pitfalls inherent in such a general intellectual program as that
involved in the adaptive evolutionary view understandably motivate work on simpli-
fications of the economic process more amenable to mathematical analysis. That is
where nonlinear dynamics enters the picture.

Perhaps the first — certainly an early — explicitly nonlinear mathematical analysis of market processes was the "cobweb" theory of competitive markets developed
by Kaldor, Leontief, and many others. Samuelson in his *Foundations* gave a general treatment of types of stability for nonlinear difference equations. But most major mathematical economists, however, e.g., Arrow, Hurwicz, Nikaido, and Uzawa,
tackled the problem of market stability in the alternative form (also framed by
Samuelson) of Walrasian tatonnement, using local linearization in the neighborhood
of equilibria and tracing necessary and sufficient conditions for asymptotic convergence to underlying properties of individual preferences and technology.

Samuelson's formal analysis of the accelerator, like the business cycle studies of
Frisch, Tinbergen, Kalecki, and Modigliani, used linear analysis. Nonlinear aspects
of the business cycle, however, were considered explicitly by Kaldor, Hicks, and especially by Goodwin, who expressed the germ of a fundamental insight, one already
recognized in the early literature of physics and mathematics but noticed by him
in the very different context of economics, namely, that deterministic interactions
among economic sectors can induce nonperiodic behavior, one of the characteristics of what is now widely referred to as "chaos." Others who worked on explicitly
nonlinear macrodynamics included Smythe, Tobin, and Schinasi.

I also explored analytically tractable versions of my own models (1967, 1968)
in the form $x_{t+1} = a + bx_t + cx_t^\gamma$ where a, b, c and γ are parameters derived from
underlying coefficients of technology, time preference, demand, or cost and where
x_t is interpreted either as production in a firm or industry or as capital stock in the
economy as a whole. A bifurcation analysis of these equations showed how stable
stationary states, then 2-period, 4-period, and higher order cycles could emerge.

Contemporaneously, most theorists in the 1960s focused on balanced growth,
understandably because of the exponential trend in the aggregate data over the century and because of the abeyance of pronounced fluctuations following the Great
Depression through the quarter century preceding the 1972 recession. When a new

generation of theorists began to reconsider the business cycle it seemed natural for them to do so within the framework of intertemporal equilibrium and optimality over time that they had inherited from the growth school of the preceding two decades. What emerged was the intertemporal equilibrium, real business cycle school of Lucas, Sargent, Kydland, Prescott, and many others to which I referred previously.

Other important lines of work on dynamics were also pursued in the third quarter of the twentieth century, such as the von Neumann model, dynamic Leontief models, models of adaptive preferences, large scale econometric models, and the overlapping generations approach, originated by Samuelson and subsequently extended by Gale, Diamond, and many others. Only the last of these incorporated nonlinearity theory in any fundamental way, but the *industrial or systems dynamics framework* already described by Forrester in 1956, an example of which will be found in Chapter 5 of this book, had already encompassed both nonlinearity and principles of adaptive adjustment out of equilibrium.

While all this was going on, mathematical understanding of nonlinear dynamics was progressing. In the early 1960s Smale developed techniques for dealing with the global properties of dynamic systems, and Eduard Lorenz discovered nonperodic, turbulent behavior in fluid dynamic models of weather formation. In the mid-1970s May identified similar properties in biological populations. At about the same time a team of collaborators that included Yorke, Pianigiani, Li, Lasota, and Misiurewicz developed an array of constructive, sufficient conditions for the existence of chaotic and ergodic behavior.

When Jess Benhabib and I came across this work in the Fall of 1978, we set about, subsequently with the help of Kazuo Nishimura and Wayne Shafer, to see if these new methods could be used to explore the existence of chaos and the asymptotic statistical distributions of model solutions in a variety of economic settings. I have spent much of the intervening time reconsidering economic growth, business cycle and market adjustment processes from this point of view. Many others have been involved in the same kind of work including among the first to do so, Dana, Grandmont, Malgrange, Montrucchio, Pohjola, Saari, and Stuzer. Many others, too numerous to cite here, are contributing to further developments. On the basis of all this, it can be said that complex dynamics has been shown to arise robustly in

- market adjustment and iterative price mechanisms,
- disequilibrium business cycle theories,
- classical growth theory,
- optimal growth and equilibrium business cycle theory,
- overlapping generations models,
- adaptive optimizing or recursive programming models, and
- system dynamics models.

In short, chaos is generic in virtually any model of a dynamic economic process that retains inherent nonlinearities.

Two Paradigms Again?

In this work on nonlinear dynamic economics we again discern two quite distinct lines of work:

- one that assumes intertemporal equilibrium, and one involving adjustment mechanisms that work out of equilibrium.

To the former belongs the optimal growth, real business cycle, and overlapping generations models. To the latter belong the market adjustment, disequilibrium business cycle, adaptive optimizing, and system dynamics models.

Complex Dynamics

Later in this chapter I will illustrate how some of the character of adaptive, evolutionary processes can be studied using relatively simple nonlinear dynamics. First, however, I need to summarize some of the mathematical concepts that are involved.

I use the term "complex economic dynamics" to designate deterministic economic models whose trajectories exhibit (1) irregular (nonperiodic) fluctuations or (2) endogenous phase switching. The first property includes bounded "chaotic" trajectories that are sensitive to perturbations. The second property means that the equations governing change in system states switch from time to time according to intrinsic rules.

The use of models exhibiting complex dynamics to explain empirical phenomena has been greatly enhanced during the last two decades by advances in nonlinear dynamical systems theory, alluded to above, among which is the discovery that quite simple examples can generate complex behavior qualitatively like real world experience. By "qualitatively" I have in mind the following facts that broadly characterize economic change.

- Individual commodity prices and quantities fluctuate with irregular period and amplitude.
- Aggregate indexes representing the economy as a whole likewise exhibit irregular fluctuations.
- Economic growth does not follow a smooth trend but exhibits fluctuating rates of change.
- Economic activity evolves in overlapping waves, or phases, or stages of consumption, technology and organization.

The work on nonlinear dynamics previously summarized has made it possible to explain these qualitative features in economic terms, either as the outcome of disequilibrium forces or, contrastingly, as a property of efficient equilibrium over time. I now want to summarize briefly, in terms of discrete time, some of the mathematical concepts that make this possible, the case of continuous time being analogous but requiring a dimensionality of three instead of one.

Dynamical Systems

Let (θ, X) be a dynamical system defined by a difference equation in a state variable x_t,

$$x_{t+1} = \theta(x_t) \tag{3.1}$$

with domain X.

A trajectory is a sequence $\tau(x_0) = \{x_t\}_0^\infty$ that satisfies (3.1). We note that $\tau(x) = \{x, \theta(x), \theta^n(x), \ldots, \}$ is a trajectory for $x = x_0$. A periodic fluctuation or cycle is a trajectory in which for some integer $p > 1, x_{t+p} = x_t$ for all t but $x_{t+q} \neq x_t$ for any q with $0 < q < p$. A stationary trajectory is a trajectory for which $x_t = \tilde{x}$ all t for some $\tilde{x} \in X$. A nonperiodic trajectory is one that is neither stationary or cyclic.

Essentially Nonlinear Systems

A nonlinear dynamical system is a dynamical system (θ, X) for which the map θ is not affine. Using terms suggested by Blatt, an *essentially linear* dynamical system is one for which there exists a transformation $f : x \to f(x)$ and an affine map $\lambda : f(X) \to f(X)$ such that

$$(f \circ \theta)(x) = \lambda \left[f(x) \right] \quad \text{all } x \in X. \tag{3.2}$$

An *essentially nonlinear system* is one that is not essentially linear.

For example, consider a simplified version of Solow's model in discrete time,

$$x_{t+1} = \sigma B x_t^\beta, \tag{3.3}$$

where x is the capital/labor ratio, B and β are constants reflecting production, and σ is the savings ratio. Let $f(x) = \log x$. Then $f(x_{t+1}) = \sigma + B + \beta f(x_t) = \lambda[f(x_t)]$. Therefore, (3.3) is essentially linear. Suppose, however, there are absolute diseconomies that change (3.3) to

$$x_{t+1} = \sigma B x_t^\beta (k - x_t)^\gamma \tag{3.4}$$

where $k > 0$ is an upper bound on possible capital/labor ratios and γ a positive coefficient. Then (3.4) is essentially nonlinear.

Chaos in the Sense of Li and Yorke

Sensitivity to initial conditions or perturbations is sometimes defined to mean that two trajectories depart exponentially, but such departure is local in systems that are globally stable. Another criterion of sensitivity is that for given initial conditions $x, y \in X$ then

$$\limsup_{t \to \infty} |\theta^t(x) - \theta^t(y)| > 0. \qquad (3.5)$$

This means in effect that no matter how close y is to x, and no matter how close points $\theta^t(x)$ and $\theta^t(y)$ might come at time t, they will move apart a finite distance. If y is a cyclic point and x is not, then (3.5) means that the trajectory $\tau(x)$ must move away from any cycle no matter how close it may come to one. Condition (3.5) is therefore a strong instability property.

If nonperiodic trajectories are bounded in X, they may fluctuate "around one another," perhaps coming close from time to time. If they almost touch infinitely often, we have

$$\liminf_{t \to \infty} |\theta^t(x) - \theta^t(y)| = 0. \qquad (3.6)$$

Li and Yorke and later Li, Misiurewicz, Pianigiani, and Yorke presented constructive conditions for the existence of an uncountable *scrambled set* $S \subset X \subset \mathcal{R}^1$ such that for all $x, y \in S$, (3.5) and (3.6) are satisfied, and for all $x \in S$ and for any periodic y, (3.5) is satisfied. Trajectories that satisfy these conditions are called "chaotic in the sense of Li and Yorke" and systems that generate them are said to possess *topological chaos*.

If there exist periodic trajectories in X with stationary cyclic initial conditions, then nonperiodic trajectories could wander near some or even all of them. In particular, suppose y is a cyclic point and x is nonperiodic. If

$$\liminf_{t \to \infty} |\theta^t(x) - y| = 0 \qquad (3.7)$$

then the trajectory beginning at x will come close to the periodic point y infinitely many times (in principle) so that even if (3.5) holds, $\tau(x)$ may for a time approximate the cycle that emanates from y, especially if the period of y is fairly small.

Ergodic Behavior

A type of nonperiodic behavior also called chaotic and discussed already in the mid-nineteenth century, arises when the values in a nonperiodic trajectory can be characterized in the long run by a stable probability distribution that gives the relative frequencies (or fraction of time) a system may enter a given subset of states. Modern existence proofs originate with Birkhoff and von Neuman in the 1930s. More recently Lasota, Li, Pianigiani, Misiurewicz, and Yorke provided constructive conditions for existence and techniques for deriving the density functions themselves.

I will call the dynamical system (θ, X) strongly *ergodic* on the set S if there exists a unique absolutely continuous invariant measure μ represented by the density f, such that $\mu(A) = \int_A f dm$ for all $A \subset S$.

That $f(\cdot)$ is absolutely continuous means that it is positive on a set of intervals and that θ is nonperiodic for almost all initial conditions in these intervals. Let $g(\cdot)$ be an integrable function, then

$$\lim_{T \to \infty} \frac{1}{T} \sum_{t=0}^{T-1} g\left[\theta^t(x)\right] = \int_S g(x)f(x)dx \qquad (3.8)$$

and in particular

$$\lim_{T \to \infty} \frac{1}{T} \sum_{t=0}^{T-1} \chi_S\left[\theta^t(x)\right] = \int_S fdx \qquad (3.9)$$

where $X_S(x) = 1$ if $x \in S$ and zero otherwise. These equations mean that one can deal with the expected value of a function of the state variable in the same manner that one would for a random variable *even though it is generated by a deterministic process*.

Evidently, strongly ergodic systems have some characteristics very much like stochastic processes, not only in being representable by density functions, but also in additional properties that follow, such as various laws of large numbers and the central limit theorem.

Deceptive Order

If a system (θ, X) is strongly ergodic, then it can usually be shown that for some integer m the system (θ^m, X) is topologically chaotic in which case cycles of all orders $mn, n = 1, 2, 3, \ldots$ exist as well. For such systems, all nonperiodic trajectories that belong to the support of μ are sensitive to initial conditions in the sense of (3.5) and all nonperiodic trajectories in support of μ possess *deceptive order* in the sense of (3.7). They pass close to periodic trajectories infinitely often but in a nonperiodic way! An example is the tent map on the interval $[0, 1]$ whose limiting distribution is the rectangular or uniform distribution.

Statistical Equilibrium

A strongly ergodic economic system possesses a kind of statistical equilibrium in contrast to a stationary or steady-state equilibrium. In the statistical equilibrium a stationary density function of states replaces the stationary or steady state. Just as it is helpful for some purposes to derive an equilibrium theory and to compare equilibria, so it is also helpful for other purposes to derive density functions and to compare how they might change as parameters of the system change.

Multiple Phase Systems

Let $X_i, i \in \mathcal{I} = \{0, 1, \ldots, n\}$ be a partition of a state space $X \subset \mathcal{R}^n$ and let $\theta_i, i \in \mathcal{I}$ be a collection of maps, $\theta_i := X_i \to X$. By a (discrete time) multiple phase dynamical system, I shall mean the following difference equation:

$$x_{t+1} = \theta(x_t) := \theta_i(x_t) \quad \text{if } x_t \in X_i. \tag{3.10}$$

The sets $X_i \in \mathcal{I}$ are called *phase zones*, the maps, θ_i, *phase structures*, and the pairs (θ_i, X_i) *regimes*. The phase indicated by $i = 0$ is called the *null phase* and has the property that $\theta_0(x) \in X_0$ all $x \in X_0$. In applications it represents a state in which the system under investigation cannot work or breaks down.

Multiple phase systems are essentially nonlinear even though individual regimes may be governed by linear maps.

Frequency in Phase

If (θ, X) is a strongly ergodic multiple phase dynamical system, and if the ergodic set S intersects more than one phase zone, then one can give the "probability" of visiting various regimes and the conditional probabilities of switching from one regime to another. In this case we are permitted to speak quite rigorously about *frequency in phase* for each phase zone will be "visited" with a frequency in proportion to its measure.

Escape and Evolution

For the broader purposes of studying economic development, it would seem to be important to account for structural change and irreversible developments that are not encompassed by the idea of a statistical equilibrium. To capture this idea within the framework of a multiple phase dynamics, we need not assume ergodic behavior but only that escape from one regime to another is possible and that the reversion to previous regimes is eventually blocked for some initial conditions chosen with positive measure; that is, for every regime there is a regime that can be reached with positive measure from which a reversion to the given regime cannot occur.

Using the techniques of ergodic theory, one can sometimes derive probability statements about various kinds of phase switching, the possibility of continuing evolution or for getting stuck with positive probability or of doing one or the other "almost surely." I am going to illustrate how this can be done in an economic model in the next section. For a more detailed survey of these ideas, see Day and Pianigiani (1991) and Day and Walter (1989).

Economic Theory

Models of complex economic dynamics bring these concepts of nonlinear mathematics together with economic theory to show how the economic variables can display the complex empirical characteristics of change listed previously on the basis of internal forces alone, with no resort to unexplained outside influences. To illustrate the theory of complex economic dynamics, I am going to consider first the aggregate real growth model in an intertemporal equilibrium format. Then, drawing on work with Lin, an adaptive neoclassical variant will be described that generates non-periodic growth fluctuations. Finally, a new version of this model that incorporates evolving structure will be outlined. It illustrates a modeling strategy whose general features are outlined in the concluding section of the chapter.

Optimal Economic Growth

Begin with the equation of capital accumulation

$$k_{t+1} = \frac{1}{1+n}[(1-\delta)k_t + y_t - c_t] \tag{3.11}$$

where $s_t = (y_t - c_t)$ is savings of the tth generation, y_t is income, c_t consumption, k_t the capital stock, all in per capita terms, and δ is the depreciation rate.

Let $y = f(k)$ be the production function and supposing that capital stocks cannot be consumed. Then we have the constraints

$$f(k_t) - c_t \geq 0, \quad c_t \geq 0. \tag{3.12}$$

Now let $u(c_t)$ be the utility of consumption in period t. The utility of the entire consumption stream $c_t, c_{t+1}, \ldots,$ is

$$U(c_t, c_{t+1} \ldots) = \sum_{i=5}^{\infty} \alpha^{i-t} u(c_i). \tag{3.13}$$

where $u'(c) > 0, u''(c) < 0$, and $\alpha < 1$.

An *optimal intertemporal equilibrium growth path* emanating from a fixed capital labor ratio k_t is a consumption stream $c_t, c_{t+1}, \ldots$ and a sequence of capital stocks $k_t, k_{t+1}, \ldots$ which maximizes (3.13) subject to (3.11) and (3.12) for $t, t+1, \ldots$.

Using Bellman's principle of optimality, an optimal consumption strategy $c = h^{**}(k)$ satisfies the functional equation

$$V(k) = \max_{0 \leq c \leq f(k)} \{u(c) + \alpha V[(1-\delta)k + f(k) - c]\} \tag{3.14}$$

for all k, where

$$V(k_t) := \max \sum_{i=t}^{\infty} \alpha^{i-t} u(c_i), \tag{3.15}$$

subject to (3.11) and (3.12) for any k_t. A sequence $(c_n, k_n), n = t, t+1, \ldots$ such that

$$c_n = h^{**}(k_n) \tag{3.16}$$

is an optimal intertemporal equilibrium growth path.

It is well known that for this model, the optimal trajectories are monotonic, Pareto optimal, and consistent, that is, a trajectory beginning at generation t will contain consumption levels for each generation that would be optimal in the above sense from the perspective of that generation when its turn comes. Moreover, all trajectories converge to a unique steady-state k^{**}.

This is the neoclassical core from which the contemporary real business cycle has evolved. By adding random shocks to the function $f(\cdot)$ or to the utility function $u(\cdot)$, the model yields an extrinsic explanation of persistent fluctuations. The shocks provide the impulses that buffet output, or utility, or both, and the dynamic structure given by (3.11)–(3.13) provides the propagating mechanism in the manner described long ago by Frisch.

The functional equation (3.14) that embodies Bellman's principle of optimality is based on a backward recursion from the future to the present, which in turn is derived from a complete knowledge of how each successive state of the economy emerges from its predecessor given by equation (3.11). The optimal growth trajectory that it generates is supported by a sequence of competitive equilibrium prices, which if known by the agents will induce them to behave period after period in a manner consistent with the equilibrium consumption and capital stream. This requires an assumption that the pricing half of the primal–dual quantity-value problem *is already solved* by the process of expectation formations and market price adjustment. It is for this reason that the real intertemporal equilibrium business cycle theory invokes the rational expectations assumption. See Lucas (1987) for a nontechnical exposition and Stokey and Lucas (1989) for a thorough treatment.

An Adaptive, Neoclassical Growth Model

An alternative to this intertemporal equilibrium approach that I shall call an adaptive neoclassical model was originally formulated somewhat earlier by Leontief. It is similar in spirit, though technically much simplified, to the more general Hicksian, temporary equilibrium approach advanced by Benassy and Grandmont (see Day, 1969; Lin, 1988; Lin, Tse, and Day, 1992). It uses the same underlying ingredients (3.11)–(3.13), but does not assume intertemporal optimality but only temporary equilibrium. Behavior at each point in time is based on anticipations that depend on current experience which in turn derives from the feedback effect of *past* production and capital accumulation. Expectations are not perfect but crudely proximate, and though they are adjusted in response to what actually happens, the trajectory of the system as a whole does not satisfy the principle of optimality except (possibly) at a steady state. The model, therefore, explicitly incorporates Simon's principle of bounded rationality and assumes adaptive expectations instead of perfect foresight.

Reconsider the intertemporal utility function (3.13) and suppose that instead of an infinite stream in which consumption must be thought about now for each and every date, a two period function

$$u(c) + W(c^1) \tag{3.17}$$

is imagined in which the first term is the utility of current consumption as before, c^1 is a sustainable level of well being in perpetuity and $W(c^1)$ is the utility to current decision makers of this future potentiality. Thus,

$$W(c^1) = \sum_{n=t+1}^{\infty} \alpha^{i-n} u(c^1) = \gamma u(c^1) \tag{3.18}$$

where $\gamma = \alpha/(1 - \alpha)$.

It can be shown that the sustainable consumption level is

$$c^1 = w^1 + \rho^1[y - c + (1 - \delta)k], \tag{3.19}$$

where w^1 is the anticipated future wage level and ρ^1 the anticipated net rate of return

$$\rho^1 := \frac{r^1 - (n + \delta)}{1 + n}, \tag{3.20}$$

and where r^1 is the anticipated gross rate of return to savings. The currently most preferred combination of present consumption and future sustainable consumption (c_t, c_t^1) maximizes (3.17) subject to (3.11)–(3.12) and (3.18)–(3.20).

In this model a given generation cannot foretell the future, nor does it understand the mechanism that generates it. It uses adaptive expectations and, to keep the model simple, we assume here that these take the naive form $r^1 := f'(k)$. That is, the expected gross rate of return from saving is the current marginal product of capital. Then it can be shown that the *adaptive optimizing* or *temporarily optimal strategy*, $c_t = h^*(k_t)$, which maximizes (3.17) subject (3.11)–(3.12) and (3.18)–(3.20), is given by

$$c_t = h^*(k_t) = \begin{cases} c(k_t), & \rho > 0 \\ f(k_t), & \rho \le 0. \end{cases} \tag{3.21}$$

where $c(k)$ is a function that satisfies the Lagrangian conditions. Then

$$k_{t+1} = \frac{1}{1+n} \left[(1 - \delta)k_t + f(k_t) - h^*(k_t) \right] \tag{3.22}$$

which can be reexpressed as

$$k_{t+1} = \theta(k_t) = \begin{cases} \theta^s(k_t) := \frac{1}{1+n}[(1 - \delta)k_t + f(k_t) - h^*(k_t)], & k_t \in K^s \\ \theta^d(k_t) := \frac{1-\delta}{1+n}k_t, & k_t \in K^d. \end{cases} \tag{3.23}$$

where

$$K^s := [0, k^s), \quad K^d := [k^s, \infty), \tag{3.24}$$

where k^s is the unique value of k such at $f(k) = h(k)$.

This is a multiple-phase dynamic model. In the first regime, (θ^s, K^s), the anticipated net rate of return is positive, net savings is induced, and capital stock grows. In the second regime, (θ^d, K^d), the anticipated net rate is negative so capital is allowed to depreciate without replacement.

It can be shown that there exists a unique steady state, k, for this model that is asymptotically stable for a large set of n, δ if γ is small enough and that for a unique value of γ this steady state, $k = k^{**}$, the intertemporally optimal balanced growth path. It can also be shown, however, that for a continuum of δ, n values, trajectories are unstable and ergodic for any sufficiently large γ (see Day and Lin, 1992).

Simple and Complex Dynamics

The adaptive path first lies above the optimal path for any initial condition below $\tilde{k}$ but, when the steady state $\tilde{k}$ is unstable, fluctuations emerge and are perpetuated. These can be periodic, converging to periodic cycles, or nonperiodic and nonconvergent to any periodic behavior. In this case model generated time series are erratic but will approximate cycles of various orders, repetitively but for erratically varying lengths of time. This is the phenomenon of "deceptive order" previously mentioned.

In the ergodic case the frequency of regimes with growth and with excess capacity can in principle be given. Thus, if $\mu(\cdot)$ is the absolutely continuous invariant measure, then $\mu(K^s)$ gives the relative frequency of upswings and $\mu(K^d)$ that of downswings.

A model with specific functional forms has been simulated.[2] A bifurcation diagram for γ, the "future weight" in (3.18), is shown in Figure 3.1, given fixed n, δ, and β. Cycles occur at about $\gamma = 12$ with the cascade of period doubling cycles occurring as γ increases until zones of chaos appear. Some of these appear to be ergodic. The numerical histogram of capital labor ratios is shown in Figure 3.2. The measure $\mu(K^s)$ is the shaded area, while the measure $\mu(K^d)$ is the unshaded area. These results occur robustly, i.e., for a continuum of parameter values.

Fluctuations for the intertemporal equilibrium model of (3.11)–(3.16) are possible only if shocks continually perturb the system. In the asymptotically stable adaptive neoclassical model the same is true. In effect, agents eventually learn the steady-state rate of return. However, when the underlying parameters yield instability, then the expected rate of return on savings is not realized but over- or underestimated, and these errors do not die out. Agents do not learn the steady-state value. Each generation revises the consumption stream planned for it by its predecessors and *an intrinsic, possibly chaotic, real business cycle emerges* driven by forecasting errors indefinitely. In econometric work it would be appropriate to add a shock term in the usual manner to account for all the variations in the data unexplained by the model. Then fluctuations would be caused by a mixture of intrinsic and extrinsic forces.

It is interesting to note that instability occurs when the future weight γ is relatively large; that is, when the time discount is relatively small. This result, *which differs from the optimal growth results*, occurs because when the future matters a lot, errors of forecast have a greater impact on present choice than they would otherwise.

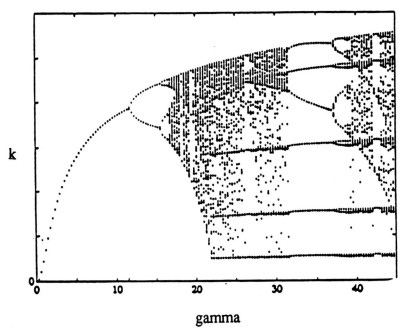

k

gamma

Figure 3.1　Bifurcation diagram for the future weight.

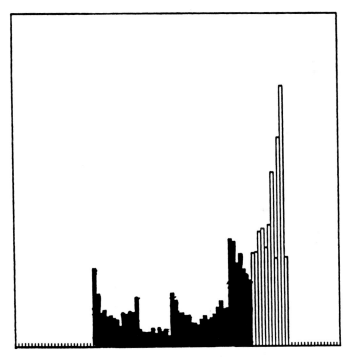

Figure 3.2　A histogram of model generated GNP values. The shaded area is the measure of K^s. The unshaded area is the measure of K^d.

Endogenous Structural Change

To show how nonlinear dynamics can capture some of the character of evolution, I am going to draw on my early work with Walter and more recent studies of Zou, and extend the above model by assuming the existence of several technological "stages." Each stage is represented by a production function

$$y = \begin{cases} 0, & 0 < k < k_i' \\ f_i(k; k_i'), & k \geq k_i'. \end{cases} \tag{3.25}$$

The index i is an index identifying the technological stage. We can let T be the set of such indexes. The capital labor ratio k' is a *threshold of productivity*, which has the following interpretation. For any given workforce L, capital stock must exceed $\bar{K} := k'L$ before the technology is productive. $\bar{K}_t$ can be thought of as *the capital infrastructure*. The (K, L) space for a given technology is shown in Figure 3.3. If the production function is homogeneous in the first degree in the terms L and $K - \bar{K}$, then we can obtain (3.25).

We shall now assume that a given generation chooses a production function that maximizes per capita income, given its current capital/labor structure $k_t = K_t/L_t$, that is

$$y = f(k) = \max_{i \in T} \{f_i(k)\}. \tag{3.26}$$

In all other regards we carry forward the assumptions of the previous model.

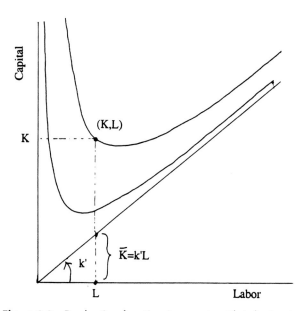

Figure 3.3 Production function isoquants with infrastructure.

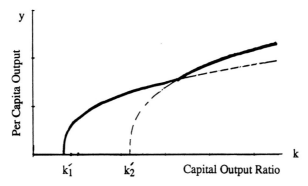

Figure 3.4 Overlapping production functions. The multiple regime production function is the upper envelope given by the solid line.

When the stage thresholds, k_i' exhibit increasing magnitudes

$$k_{i+1}' > k_i'. \tag{3.27}$$

The production function (3.25) has a "curved step" profile such as that shown in Figure 3.4.[3]

The phase diagram has a "mountainous" profile with the discontinuities at the switch points that separate the regimes. An example is shown in Figure 3.5.

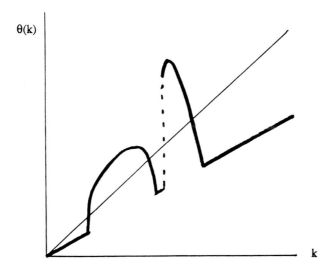

Figure 3.5 The mountainous transition map.

Alternative Developmental Scenarios

Depending on the height of each "peak" relative to it successor and the depth of each "gorge" relative to its predecessor, a great variety of possible developmental scenarios are possible. If ceteris paribus succeeding peaks are high enough, a trajectory can exhibit monotonic growth in a given stage, enter a period of fluctuating growth — a real business cycle, if you will — and then jump to the next higher stage where growth can continue. This possibility depends on the chance of escape which depends on the endogenous "probabilistic" properties of all the potential regimes.

Growth, turbulence, and phase switching could continue as long as there are succeeding stages. However, if the "peak" of a given stage is not high enough, the system could get stuck in a given stage, with growth continuing there. Or, if a given "gorge" is deep enough, a reversion could occur.

A numerical example based on specific functional forms illustrates this process of turbulent evolution.[4] In Figure 3.6 a model generated trajectory in capital–labor space is given. In Figure 3.7a a simulated picture of the capital/output ratio is shown. Also shown in Figure 3.7b is an empirical picture of the capital labor ratio for the U.S. economy. Not too much should be made of such a casual comparison, but the qualitative similarity seems to me to be striking, both in the fluctuations and in the apparent shift in structure that must have occurred in the U.S. economy.

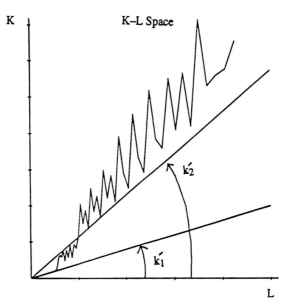

Figure 3.6   A trajectory in capital/labor space.

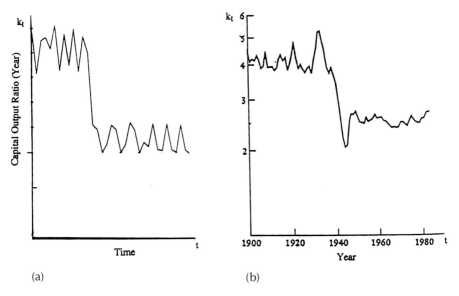

Figure 3.7 The capital/output ratio. (a) Model-generated data. (b) U.S. economy data.

Some General Reflections on Economic Adaptation and Evolution

Toward a General Modeling Approach

The adaptive neoclassical model just outlined represents decision making as a proximate problem whose solution determines current action based on expectations for the future that are adapted to unfolding experience. Plans, at the time they are made, specify the best actions within the current frame of reference. When expectations are not fulfilled — as in general they are in fact not — the plans turn out not to be best. Too much or too little investment occurs because the anticipated rate of return is too high or too low. Plans are revised and a new step into the unknown economic future prepared.

When different technological possibilities are present, structural change can occur, but only if a sufficient level of capital stock has been attained. When fluctuations induced by errors in anticipation occur, such a discrete advance can occur only when the endogenous chance of "escape" is positive. Then the system passes through sequences of stages that consist of growth interspersed with turbulent or chaotic fluctuations. Technological reversions and reswitching are also possible. The time path as a whole does not satisfy an intertemporal optimality condition and, because of expectation errors, each step along the way can involve an inefficient use of capital and labor. But, although production may be inefficient, it may be precisely the excessive build-up of capital that can push growth into a new regime with greater demands on the infrastructure.

This model has not yet been tested with empirical data, and to do so, several additional variables, such as continuous technical advance or learning by doing, should be added. Consequently, it is not offered as an explanation of development in any particular place or for any particular time span. Rather, it is presented here as an illustration of *how intrinsic economic forces can produce the underlying conditions for the emergence of new organizations and how the evolution of structure in a deterministic model can take on a qualitative character somewhat like historical experience.*

The particular model just described is an example of a general approach to modeling, which I called "recursive programming" to distinguish it from dynamic programming. It might better be called "adaptive economizing with feedback" or "adaptive economizing with evolving structure." It represents behavior by cautious, local optimizing subject to stock and flow constraints, to constraints that may delimit a "local" region of flexible response, and in which the constraints depend recursively on past behavior of the agent and other agents in the environment in a way that represents the accumulation and decumulation of stocks and the effects of learning and adaptive adjustments as in the preceding example. The solution of such a model typically exhibits changing modes of behavior, nonperiodic fluctuations and sensitivity to perturbations in initial conditions and parameter values, and *changing sets of utilized activities and tight constraints. When these latter sets switch, the variables and equations governing the evolution of the system switch, in effect bringing in a different set of causal structures.*

Observed over a sequence of periods, such models exhibit a history of specific activities that were and were not pursued, of specific technologies and resources that were and were not utilized, of specific constraints that were or were not binding. In the course of this process, the consumption and/or production activities actually utilized change, or the constraints actually impinging on choice and actions switch. Some variables that appear relevant will no longer appear so; other variables that once seemed of no importance at all will now appear to play an active role in development; some technologies may be abandoned, different ones taking their place; some once plentiful free resources become scarce and valuable; still other resources, once crucial in the production transformation, are abandoned, perhaps even before they are exhausted, again becoming free. Viewed in the aggregate, waves of growth or decline in productivity and fluctuation in output and value will occur and, in the long run, various "epochs" or "ages" will appear, dominated by characteristic activities and resources.

These are salient features of this general modeling approach and also, I think, of the real world.

Viability and Evolving Populations of Agents

Eventually in the process of simulating such a model, some of the feasibility conditions for a given "model agent" will be violated. To restore viability a mechanism must be introduced by the modeler that allows for the formation of new "model agents" to whom the resources associated with disappearing agents are transferred. Alternatively, a new organizational form can be installed that will transfer resources so as to maintain individual agent feasibility and overall systems viability as an analog of "Chapter Eleven" proceedings, unemployment insurance, and welfare payments.

Such *viability creating mechanisms* are the analog of equilibrium "existence" proofs, but in the out-of-equilibrium setting. They are required to guarantee the existence of a continuing "solution" to the system in terms of feasible actions for all of its constituent model components. When they are explicitly represented, then not only the population of production processes evolve, *but also the population of agents, organizations, and institutions.*

Institutional Innovation and Policy Analysis

The study of dynamic systems with this character should be particularly relevant for analyzing government policy. New institutions in reality are, after all, most often invented in response to economic pressures caused by unemployment, bankruptcy, poverty, and other problems of inviability experienced by individuals and organizations. Models that can generate similar phenomena could provide a realistic environment for experiments with alternative policy strategies. They might provide better "engines for discovering the truth," and they might help formulate more effective mechanisms for steering the economy away from precipitous hazards and along less bumpy paths. The prospective payoff for investing more intellectual effort in such research would seem to me to be rather high.

Notes

1. See especially p. 41, *et seq.*
2. The following common functional forms were used:

$$u(c) := \log c, \quad W(c^1) := \gamma \log c^1, \quad y = f(k) := Bk^\beta.$$

The "adaptive economizing strategy" (3.21) is

$$h^*(k) = \frac{1}{1+\gamma} \left[(1-\delta)k + Bk^\beta + \frac{(1+n)(1-\beta)Bk^\beta}{\beta Bk^{\beta-1} - (n+\delta)} \right].$$

See Lin, Tse, and Day (1992).

3. All the function forms are the same as in Note 1 except the production function. The function for the *i*th stage is

$$f_i(k) := B_i(k - k_i')^{\beta_i}.$$

The simulation was performed by Zigang Wang. The adaptive optimizing strategy is somewhat more complicated. It is

$$h_i(k) = \frac{1}{1+\gamma} \left[y + (1-\delta)k + \frac{(1_\mu)(1-\beta)f_i(k)}{\frac{\beta y}{k'-k} - (n+\delta)} + \frac{\beta(1+n)k_i'f_i(k)(h-k_i')}{\beta f_i(k) - (n+\delta)(k-k_i')} \right].$$

There are certain other complicating details that we omit here.

4. Various significant economic differences between the present and the usual neoclassical model emerge with the addition of the thresholds and multiple regimes. Probably the greatest is that the marginal product of labor can be *negative*. Hence, as a descriptive matter that hypotheses could not always hold at the macro level. An average product, traditional share scheme, or some other viable scheme would have to exist.

Bibliography

Alchian, Armen A., 1950, "Uncertainty, Evolution and Economic Theory," *Journal of Political Economy*, 58, 211–222.

Anderson, Phillip, Kenneth J. Arrow, and David Pines, 1988, *The Economy as an Evolving Complex System*, Addison Wesley, Redwood City, CA.

Batten, David, J. Casti, and B. Johannsson (eds.), 1987, *Economic Evolution and Structural Adjustment*, Springer-Verlag, Berlin.

Conlisk, John, 1980, "Costly Optimizers versus Cheap Imitators," *Journal of Economic Behavior and Organization*, 1, 275–293.

Conlisk, John, 1988, "Optimization Costs," *Journal of Economic Behavior and Organization*, 9, 213–228.

Cyert, Richard, and James March, 1963, *A Behavioral Theory of the Firm*, Prentice Hall, Englewood Clifts, NJ.

Day, Richard H., 1967, "A Microeconometric Model of Business Growth, Decay, and Cycles," *Unternehmensforschung*, Band 11, Heft 1, 1–20.

Day, Richard H., 1969, "Flexible Utility and Myopic Expectations in Economic Growth," *Oxford Economic Paper*, 21, 299–311.

Day, Richard H., 1987, "The General Theory of Disequilibrium Economics and of Economic Evolution," Chapter 3 in D. Batten, J. Casti, and B. Johansson (eds.), *Economic Evolution and Structural Change*, Springer Verlag, Berlin.

Day, Richard H., and Alessandro Cigno (eds.), 1978, *Modelling Economic Change: The Recursive Programming Approach*, Elsevier North-Holland, Amsterdam.

Day, Richard H., and Gunnar Eliasson (eds.), 1986, *The Dynamics of Market Economies*, Elsevier North-Holland, Amsterdam.

Day, Richard H., and Theodore Groves (eds.), 1975, *Adaptive Economic Models*, Academic Press, New York.

Day, Richard H., and Tsong Yau Lin, 1992, "An Adaptive, Neoclassical Model of Growth Fluctuations," in N. Dimitri and A. Vercelli (eds.), *Alternative Approaches to Macroeconomics*, Oxford University Press, New York.

Day, Richard H., and Giulio Pianigiani, 1991, "Statistical Dynamics and Economics," *Journal of Economic Behavior and Organization*, 16, 37–83.

Day, Richard H., and Jean-Luc Walter, 1989, "Economic Growth in the Very Long Run: On the Multiple Phase Interaction of Population Technology and Social Infrastructure," with W. Barnett, K. Shell, and J. Geweke, *Economic Complexity: Chaos, Sunspots, Bubbles and Nonlinearity*, Cambridge University Press, Cambridge.

Dosi, Giovanni, Christopher Freeman, Richard Nelson, Gerald Silverberg, and Luc Soete, 1988, *Technical Change and Economic Theory*, Pinter Publishers, London.

Eliasson, Gunnar, 1986, "Microheterogeneity of Firms and the Stability of Industrial Growth," in R. Day and G. Eliasson (eds.), *The Dynamics of Market Economics*, North-Holland, Amsterdam.

Fisher, Franklin, 1983, *Disequilibrium Foundations of Equilibrium Economics*, Cambridge University Press, Cambridge.

Fritzsch, Harald, 1984, *The Creation of Matter*, Basic Books, New York.

Iwai, Katsuhito, 1984, "Schumpeterian Dynamics: An Evolutionary Model of Innovation and Imitation," *Journal of Economic Behavior and Organization*, 5, 159–190.

Kaldor, Nicolas, 1986, *Nonequilibrium Economics*, Yale University Press, New Haven, CT.

Kaufman, Stuart A., 1988, "The Evolution of Economic Webs," in P. Anderson, K.J. Arrow, and D. Pines (eds.), *The Economy as an Evolving Complex System*, Addison Wesley, Redwood City, CA.

Lin, Tsong Yau, 1988, *Studies of Economic Instability and Irregular Fluctuations in a One-Sector Real Growth Model*, Ph.D. Dissertation, University of Southern California, Los Angeles.

Lin, Tsong Yau, Raymond Tse, and Richard H. Day, 1992, in Dimitri Papadimitrious (ed.), *Profits, Deficits and Instability*, Macmillan, Riverside, NJ (forthcoming).

Lucas, Robert E., 1987, *Models of Business Cycles*, Basil Blackwell, Oxford.

Lorenz, E. N., 1963, "Deterministic Nonperiod Flow," *Journal of the Atmospheric Sciences*, 20, 120–141.

March, James G., and Herbert A. Simon, 1958, *Organizations*, John Wiley, New York.

Modigliani, Franco, and Kolman J. Cohen, 1961, *The Role of Anticipation and Plans in Economic Behavior and Their Use in Economic Analysis and Forecasting*, Bureau of Economic and Business Research, University of Illinois.

Nelson, Richard R. and Sidney G. Winter, 1973, "Toward an Evolutionary Theory of Economic Capabilities," *American Economic Review*, 63, 440–449.

Nelson, Richard R. and Sidney G. Winter, 1982, *An Evolutionary Theory of Economic Change*, Harvard University Press, Cambridge, MA.

Nicolis, G., and Ilya Prigogine, 1977, *Self Organization in Nonequilibrium Systems: From Dissipative Structures to Order Through Fluctuations*, John Wiley, New York.

Papandreau, A. G., 1952, "Some Basic Problems in the Theory of the Firm," in B.F. Haley (ed.), *A Survey of Contemporary Economics*, Volume II, Richard O. Froin Co., Homewood, IL.

Schrödinger, Erwin, 1964, *My View of the World*, Cambridge University Press (First English Edition), Reprinted Oxbow Press, Woodbridge, CT, 1983.

Schumpeter, J., 1934, *Theory of Economic Development*, Harvard University Press, Cambridge, MA.

Simon, Herbert A., 1957, *Administrative Behavior*, 2nd ed., The Free Press, New York.

Stokey, Nancy L., and Robert E. Lucas, Jr., 1989, *Recursive Methods in Economic Dynamics*, Harvard University Press, Cambridge, MA.

Winter, Sidney G., 1964, "Economic Natural Selection and the Theory of the Firm," *Yale Economic Essays*, Spring, 4, 225–272.

Winter, Sidney G., 1971, "Satisficing, Selection and the Innovating Remnant," *Quarterly Journal of Economics*, 85, 237–261.

Winter, Sidney G., 1975, "Optimization and Evolution in the Theory of the Firm," in R.H. Day and T. Groves (eds.), *Adaptive Economic Models*, Academic Press, New York.

Winter, Sidney G., 1981, "Attention Allocation and Input Proportions," *Journal of Economic Behavior and Organization*, 2, 31–46.

Winter, Sidney G., 1986, "Schumpeterian Competition in Alternative Technological Regimes," Chapter 8 in R. Day and G. Eliasson (eds.), *The Dynamics of Market Economies*, Elsevier North-Holland, Amsterdam.

Zou, Gang, 1991, *Growth and Development*, Ph.D. Dissertation, University of Southern California, Los Angeles.

the contributions of the other, but, in my view, they are complementary and, when unified, extraordinarily powerful. For these reasons I like to think of my model as a Marx–Keynes–Schumpeter (MKS) system.

To be realistic, the conditions I require of the model are that it must exhibit an unstable equilibrium; that it must be globally stable; that it must endogenously generate morphogenesis in the form of structural change; that it does so in cyclical form, albeit erratically or aperiodically; that it generates both short and long waves; and, finally, that these waves are growth, not stationary, waves.

When Schumpeter said that the cycle is simply the form growth takes, his intuition was a generation ahead of his contemporaries, i.e., the equilibrium theorists, the cycle analysts, the growth men. His perception of reality was also, alas, totally unrelated to his sadly deficient mathematical capability. I tried to teach him how to use linear cycle theory, but he never succeeded in being able to deploy it. When he came to make his final statement on economic development, he opted for 3 cycles: 3 Kitchins to a Juglar, 6 Juglars to a Kondratiev. The very short cycle is important, well understood, but involves no innovation, so I shall omit it as a detail. The Juglars and Kondratievs cannot be treated in such a fashion; each is bound to be influenced by the other. Even if they were linear cycles, they would be coupled oscillations and, hence, both would contain both cycles. With a more complicated, nonlinear dynamic it is possible to fuse them into a unified model.

Schumpeter, an admirer of the earlier work of Keynes, astonishingly, totally rejected the *general theory*; for this he may have had two reasons, one bad and one good. He believed in market clearing, including the labor market; the second reason was the formulation of Keynes in terms of aggregate demand, output, and income. The first seems a grave error and the second poses a basic difficulty. Schumpeter rightly insisted that innovative technical progress is specific to particular industries: hence, aggregation masks and can even falsify the consequences of structural change. Therefore, the analysis should be in large, multidimensional systems, but, alas, I am forced to present an aggregative model, since I am not able to deal with large nonlinear systems of the kind I shall be using. My only defense is that the problem and the model are complicated and that a simple version does effectively illuminate much of the dynamical structure. Also, it is relevant that precisely aggregate demand is the potent agent of self-organization. Innovations are many and different as to timing and duration of integration into the economy. Consequently, for Schumpeter's theory, the innovative "swarms" would be so many, so disparate in timing, amplitude and duration, that his cycle would tend to be nearly invisible. But because the level and growth rate of demand play so great a role in productive decisions, especially in the case of new and risky projects, various innovations are launched and/or rapidly expanded in a rising market: then the requisite investment required further accelerates the already buoyant market. A lot of unrelated decisions are thereby forced to march in step. Thus, the Kahn–Keynes multiplication of expansive and contractive demand furnishes a crucial missing link for Schumpeter's innovative theory of technological evolution.

The central motive force is the seminal conception of a "swarm" of innovations. There is considerable agreement that the archetypical innovation begins very weakly; then gradually proves its worth, becomes better known, along with improved design and adaptation to diverse uses; finally, it decelerates gradually as it is completely integrated into the economy. Thus, it tends to have a quadratic trajectory, happily represented by the logistic.

The Model

Now, a survey of the functioning of the model. Initially, the economy is in or near equilibrium — equilibrium defined so as to isolate the role of innovations from the effects of all other exogenous variables, such as government, foreign trade, etc. Underlying the model is a pair of first order linear differential equations with parameters giving rise to an unstable oscillation. The two variables are ratios, hence independent of scale, thus permitting a growth cycle. To this is added a third, non-linear differential equation which defines a dynamical control parameter, which determines a bounded region in state space within which, after a time, all trajectories of the first two variables are contained. The first variable, v is the ratio of employment, L, to total available labor force, N, taken as constant to emphasize the other relations (though it is not difficult to introduce a constant or slowly varying growth rate of N). The second variable, u, is the share of wages (including salaries, hence average earned income) in gross product, q and u is unit cost of labor, i.e., $u = wa$, where a is employment per unit of output. Net product consists solely of wages and profits; all wages and no profits are consumed, a simplification that can be removed at the cost of moderate complication.

Structural change and growth are introduced by a logistic "swarm," k, of 50 years duration. Schumpeter perceived the basic nature of the problem (cyclical growth) but did not succeed in arriving at a satisfactory formulation, having simply assumed full employment with the higher productivity output. To implement structural change, there must first be investment; the investment increases demand and output, including demand for labor. An increase in employment accelerates demand and output in two ways: more employment increases demand and it also increases the real wage, thus generating a twofold increase in demand. The investment is undertaken to lower cost, primarily labor cost: innovation acts in two opposed directions on employment; by raising output it increases employment, but by technological change it lowers employment per unit of output (higher productivity). The rate of decrease of labor input (increase of productivity) is taken to be proportional to the rate of increase of innovational capacity, k/k. The real wage (average earnings) is assumed to increase faster than productivity when $v > v^*$ and to increase less rapidly when $v < v^*$ (v^* being taken as 0.90, i.e., 10% unemployment). When $v > (v^* + c)$, with $c = 0.04$, i.e., 6% unemployment, the dynamic control parameter, z, increasingly decelerates v, and with $v < 0.94$, it increasingly accelerates v. Thus, the pair v and u are dynamically unstable, but in economics this constitutes no problem since full employment is an impenetrable barrier, implemented here as approaching full employment when $v > (v^* + c)$. There is first the existing limit of capacity, but that can, given time, be overcome. What cannot be extended is the maximum available labor force. As v goes above $v^* + c$, it becomes rapidly more difficult to recruit labor and hence increase output.

To understand the nature of the system dynamic it is helpful to see it as a simplified variant of the Lotka–Volterra predator prey model, with wages as the predator and profits the prey. Setting $v^* = 0$, thus reckoning in deviations from equilibrium, the system is a linearized version of Lotka–Volterra with zero constants. Also, it is independent of scale and hence not limited to a stationary average level. The central dynamic is given by $\dot{v} = -du$ and $\dot{u} = +hv$, d and h positive. To the first equation must be added a term fv, $f > 0$, which makes the model structurally stable and dynamically unstable, thus answering Kolmogorov's criticism of Volterra's structurally unstable formulation. The term can represent the accelerator or any other aspect of the economy deriving from the simple fact that high and expanding demand leads to further increase in demand and output.

Given an unstable cycle, the usual solution, following Poincaré, is to assume upper and lower nonlinearities, yielding global stability and at least one closed limit cycle, a single equilibrium motion. Just as Poincaré generalized the closed curve to a closed region, in which an astonishing variety of aperiodic motions can occur in a seemingly erratic fashion, I shall use a variant of the Rössler Band, as the chaotic attractor most comprehensible and applicable to economics.[1] Instead of defining an upper and lower bound to a variable, one posits a control parameter that provides a growing downward pressure beyond a given high (positive) value and a growing upward one for low (negative) values. The control parameter is specified by

$$\dot{z} = b + gz(v - c).$$

This effectively stabilizes the system globally and leaves it free to perform wildly erratic motion locally around the zero equilibrium. This is such a breathtaking generalization of the notion of a stable equilibrium which originally suggested absence of change as partially to negate it. The concept of a system stable to an equilibrium fixed point has thus been generalized from a point to a closed curve and now to a bounded region.

Within the region endogenously deterministic variables can move in a seemingly arbitrary and unpredictable way. It is for this reason that this recent discovery is so relevant to economics. If one takes the time series generated by such a model and tries to determine the mathematical structure which generated it, one would find that to get a correct estimate of the system there is as yet no technique available, and there may never be. If, however, one knows from other sources the model, then one can extract its contribution, leaving the irregularity due to random exogenous shocks in the statistic. It is significant that the discovery of chaos was made in application to forecasting weather; a system highly deterministic but with a bad record for prediction, which should be some consolation to economists for their own performance.

In my view, the implications of chaos for economics are serious. Economic statistics are pervasively irregular: this has always been ascribed to exogenous shocks. In the behavior under consideration there are no exogenous elements; the erratic element is entirely endogenous. Therefore, in the future it is necessary to adopt the hypothesis that there are two distinct sources of irregularity in economic statistics, the exogenous and the endogenous. This seems to me to require a reformulation of some econometric procedures.

These three differential equations with only one nonlinearity, determine the behavior of the economy in deviations from the exogenous effects, and, in particular, from the effects of innovatory technical progress. To this basic transmission mechanism, which is independent of scale, must be added the accumulation of innovative capacity as the mechanism of structural change and growth. Also, there must be added an equation for the determination of output, as it is affected by innovative investment and as it in turn affects employment, v, and as that in turn affects the share of labor, with its vital effect on consumption demand.

With a constant labor force,

$$\dot{v}/v = \dot{L}/L = \dot{q}/q + \dot{a}/a$$

with the result that

$$\dot{q}/q = \dot{v}/v - \dot{a}/a.$$

The rate of change of productivity is taken to be proportional to the accumulation of innovative capacity, thus $m\dot{k}/k = -\dot{a}/a$. Given historically is a 50 year logistic of innovation:

$$\dot{k} = jk(1 - sk)$$

with the investment reaching a peak in 25 years and approaching zero as $k \to 1/s$. The complete model then becomes

$$\dot{v} = -du + fv - ez$$

$$\dot{u} = hv$$

$$\dot{z} = b + gz(v - c)$$

$$\dot{q}/q = (-du + fv - ez)/(v + v^*) + mj(1 - sk)$$

$$\dot{k} = jk(1 - sk).$$

Numerical Example

The model is not very robust for single parametric changes, but is quite robust for economically plausible related parameter variations. A wide variety of behaviors

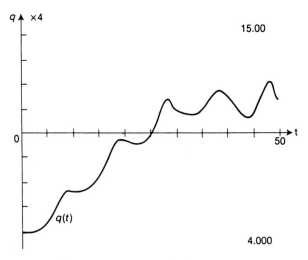

Figure 4.1 Output in the basic model.

can be generated, generically similar to the picture shown in Figure 4.1 for output over 50 years.[2] In my view, it represents the joint insights of Schumpeter and
Keynes, and represents what the former wanted to say but could not formulate. He
maintained that at the end of a Kondratiev there would necessarily be a higher output
since there would always be full employment at a higher productivity. After Keynes,
one can no longer accept that; there can be those unemployed by labor-saving technology, along with a possibly lower or only moderately higher output and income.

Here there is no assumption of full employment and yet there is a guarantee of
a higher average level of output. The problem is posed by the gradual end of the
logistic with investment approaching zero. Without further assumptions, barring arbitrary exogenous investment or public policy (unemployment payments are ignored
in the interest of sharpness of the issue), there will be a decline of output to its original level, or even lower, because of labor saving. Here the problem is solved by the
realistic (un-Marxian) assumption that the competition of producers for given supplies of labor raises the real wage. With the Keynesian approach, i.e., that demand
determines output, the investment demand raises output, this increases employment
and demand further, and in a twofold way, since it also means higher demand per
employee. This securely confirms the lowered demand for labor will be more than
compensated for.

The Kondratiev peak at a half century is explained by the uni-modal, quadratic
investment function. The rising wave substantially erases the first cycle; then as the
Kondratiev levels off at the peaks, the cycle slowly reemerges and gradually completely takes over as the innovations cease. This downside of the Kondratiev is crucial: employment is being cut, though at a decreasing rate, investment demand is
rapidly declining. What has happened is that the equilibrium level of output has

been shifted upward through the operation of the labor market. In the middle the employment ratio is biassed above its equilibrium; this raises demand and the level of wages. Then as the upward motion decelerates, the equilibrium level of employment remains at 10% unemployment of a constant labor force with higher productivity and corresponding real wage and hence demand.

Thus, Schumpeter's "vision" is confirmed: there are only slightly less than five cycles including one large one; the real wage, or average earnings, has risen as has output; structural change has been accomplished but in a cyclical form. What he did not say, but no doubt would have agreed with, is that each cycle is individual, is different from all the others, and not only because of innovations. He confidently asserted that once one Kondratiev was completed, a new wave would get under way. If the new wave is the same as the old, the result recapitulates the process on a large scale, but close attention will show that each cycle is different between the two periods. In this form the Kondratiev brings history into economics and it is an attractive feature of the model that each successive long wave can be as different as time and technology choose to make it. By varying the parameter, s, one makes the innovative capacity greater or smaller; by varying j correspondingly one determines the rate of growth of productivity; by altering m one makes the economic effect (through the capacity–output ratio) greater or smaller. A related fact is that, for historical reasons, some economies grow fast, e.g., Japan, and others grow slowly, e.g., Great Britain. I have given numerical examples elsewhere that illustrate these cases.[3]

Endogenous Innovation

This model can be elaborated in varying ways but one particular change is especially important. The logistic innovative function should be bilaterally, not unilaterally, coupled with output, i.e., investment heavily influences demand and output, but is in turn made subject to their influence. Therefore, instead of assuming a constant growth rate, j, of new innovative capacity, we may assume a linear dependence on the employment ratio (the state of demand), thus

$$\dot{k} = (j + nv)k(1 - sk),$$

and

$$\dot{q}/q = (-du + fv - ez)/(v + v^*) + m(j + nv)(1 - sk).$$

In this form we have a truly unified, single theory of growth with fluctuation whose erratic quality is given a clear indication in Figure 4.2.

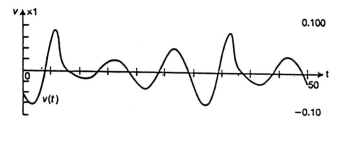

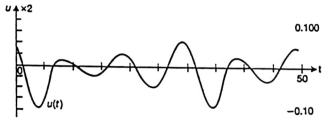

Figure 4.2   Output when innovation is bilaterally coupled with output.

Compensatory Fiscal Policy

The dynamic control parameter, z, which produces various versions of the irregularity characteristic, can be considered as a concrete embodiment of public expenditure. It is well known that the normal governmental budgetary behavior has a markedly stabilizing effect on economic performance. In sharp contrast to the behavior of producers and consumers, a large part of government expenditure is substantially invariant to the short run changes in receipts. Thus, public expenditure on the armed forces, administration, police, etc., is not directly related to current tax receipts, and may even vary inversely, e.g., unemployment benefits and other public assistance.

Compensatory fiscal policy may appropriately be regarded as a simple type of dynamic control implemented at discrete time intervals. It aims, or should aim, to diminish the amplitude of fluctuations in economic activity. As a result of somewhat disappointing postwar performance, there has been a decline in the expectation of major improvements from fiscal policy, and no hope of holding a steady degree of employment. Compensatory fiscal policy has proved to be a somewhat flawed instrument, one which has not fully realized the great hopes placed on it. There are a number of evident reasons for this. First, there is the time lag involved in collecting and processing the information necessary to judge the state of the economy. Then there must ensue considerable time to analyze the results and to agree on a desirable policy, a process that may involve both the executive administration and the legislature, or an effective combination of the two. Finally then, given the dynamical nature of the generation of income and output, still more time has to elapse before the full consequences of any policy are actually realized. The result is that a policy may be

outdated by the time it is fully effective, so that it may happen that it is even coun-
terproductive: such procedures are capable of making fluctuations worse instead of
better. Since it is not possible simply to decide what output and employment should
be and then proceed to place the economy in that position, what is required for a satisfactory, effective policy is instruments of control which are continuously variable
so as to produce a gradual approach to any desired state. By contrast with static control parameters the Rössler dynamic control parameter, z, represents in simple form
just such a procedure.

With z zero, the fixed points for both u and v are zero. To illustrate normal government practice, let $V^* = 0.90$, so that the employment ratio, v is then measured in
deviations from 10% unemployment, with the level of u unspecified. The parameter
z can then be taken to represent the variations in net public deficits and surpluses:
the effects on v being negative, z negative represents a deficit with a positive effect
on employment and output, and a conversely for a surplus. If the value of c is 0.05,
then when unemployment is less than 5%, public surpluses are increasing thus producing a progressive fall in employment and output. When unemployment is greater
than 5%, the government deficit is increasing thus contributing to a rising rate of employment. The real wage (or average earnings) is increasing faster than productivity
whenever v is positive, i.e., $> v^*$, and it is increasing less rapidly than productivity
when v is negative.

Taking these values as representative of the effects of government budget in
the absence of a compensatory policy, the behavior of the employment ratio over
a 50 year period is shown in Figure 4.3, for a given setting of the several parameter
values.[4] Unemployment in this example reaches a maximum of about 12% and a
minimum of 1% over the half century.

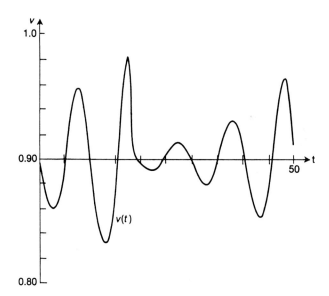

Figure 4.3 The employment ratio.

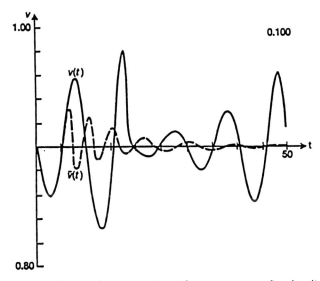

Figure 4.4 The employment ratio with compensatory fiscal policy.

If the government policy forming body aims to reduce the amplitude of fluctuations by instituting a compensatory policy, it should investigate the consequence of altering the government budget when v is above and below smaller and smaller values of c. Keeping all parameters and initial values the same, for smaller and smaller values of c from 0.05 to 0.01, they would find successively smaller phase portraits for v and u, indicating smaller and smaller fluctuations to nearly constant employment and output. Very large scale interventions are required in the early years but they rapidly diminish as the policy becomes effective. The nature of the achievement of such a policy is clearly demonstrated in Figures 4.4 and 4.5, where the two types of behavior for $v(t)$ and $u(t)$ are plotted simultaneously. The potent interventions, not unnaturally, initially alter the course of events by adding new shorter waves but ones of a much smaller amplitude. As the policy succeeds, the amplitudes steadily diminish, so that after 25 years they are only 10 to 15% of their former size.

The model is then extended to include a 50 year Kondratiev in logistic form. The equally impressive effects on output are exhibited in Figure 4.6, compensated $\bar{q}(t)$ is compared with uncompensated $\tilde{q}(t)$. The dynamic control adds initially some wild short waves but in such a way as to smooth the longer term trajectory. Then toward the end of the long wave, the controlled behavior becomes monotonic, approximating the impressed logistic, whereas, the uncontrolled behavior reverts to vigorous wave motion. Thus, the flexible dynamic control has its triumph toward the end by entirely erasing the three final oscillations.

That such a fiscal policy can be, in principle, astonishingly successful is thus demonstrated. And that such result is highly desirable is also clear. However, this happy result has been achieved by stabilizing at 10% unemployment, which is not highly desirable. What is required after the early, sharp interventions is successive,

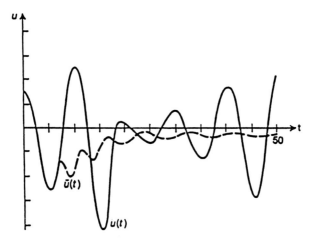

Figure 4.5 The effect of compensatory fiscal policy on output.

independent increases in public expenditure to raise the fixed point of v by succes-sive small amounts, so that after 20 or 30 years, the equilibrium level of unemploy-ment has fallen from 10% to 1, 2, or 3%. This becomes in effect an exogenous disturbance and would increase the necessary dynamical control, but with such a powerful tool, this could be tamed.

The much more serious problems of implementing such a program lie in the re-quired magnitude and rapidity of the interventions. If, however, it were once agreed

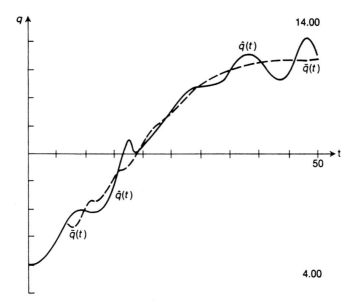

Figure 4.6 The effect of compensatory policy on the long wave.

that such spectacular gains might accrue, then it is conceivable that the necessary, elaborate plans for increased and decreased government expenditure could be formulated and agreed to in advance, so that when the need arises, they could be rapidly made operational. It has to be admitted that, on the basis of past experience, there is, politically, a very strong asymmetry between deficits and surpluses of government budgeting: for obvious reasons surpluses seem to be politically poisonous! The enormous potential advantages of some such difficulties notwithstanding. The example elaborated here is quite abstract, overly simplified, and as such impractical, but what is not impractical is the basic logic of compensatory fiscal policy.

Wages, Leisure, and Growth: The Policy Options

This chapter, being concerned with chaotic growth through structural change, has followed Schumpeter's unneoclassical, semi-Marxian vision of growth driven by the search for ever renewed profit through technical change. However, he inverted Marx by maintaining a rising real wage with profit in the stationary state, equal to zero but kept positive by continual, cost reducing innovations leading to cyclical growth. In spite of some theoretical difficulties, he had a quite realistic insight into how private capitalism works; he was, no doubt, helped by his disastrous experiences as Finance Minister and private banker.

If I may in turn invert Schumpeter, on a basis of no realism whatsoever, imagine a society based on the lust, not for wealth, but for power; a society that is as efficient as managerial capitalism and as devoted to technological innovation. Being politically democratic and equalitarian, it would seek to maximize, not growth of output, but the overall well being of it citizenry. This should be defined and measured by the free choice between work and leisure, but a free choice undistorted by the media of the press, TV, radio, etc. In private capitalism these media are directed to increasing output and profit.

In such a utopian community there could be free individual choice between getting and spending and all the other activities, interests, or pursuits of people. Such a result, being difficult, there would probably have to be a democratically arrived at, common decision setting number of hours of work per week or per year. In that case, the supply of labor becomes a decision variable, even for a constant population, and must be measured in man-hours not number of workers. Given such a decision, then the problem becomes one of determining output subject to a declining supply of labor, consequent on a rising productivity and a rising average earning. Since $v = aq/n(t), \dot{v}/v = \dot{q}/q + \dot{a}/a - \dot{n}/n$. With productivity growth of $g_a = m\dot{k}/k$, and that of $n(t)$ as $g_n, \dot{q}/q = \dot{v}/v + g_a + g_n$. The economy, through the free market, is subject to some sort of perspective control, the aim of which might be monotonic, not cyclical motion; hence with $\dot{v} = 0$. Research, being heavily subject to state subsidy and controlled with the aim of steady-state growth, would be implemented so as to give exponential rather than logistic behavior. With a 2% growth rate of productivity,

there could be two extreme cases. With no change in the working week, output grows at the rate of productivity, e.g., from 10 to 27.2 in 50 years with an equal growth in average earnings. This probably makes little sense for late capitalism where there is no longer any need for accumulation of capital, only substitution of newer equipment for the existing. The other extreme would be output constant with $g_n = -2\%$, so that in 50 years a working week of 40 hours could be reduced to 14.7 hours. To see the effects and relevance of such a choice one need think only of the consequences for the environment and natural resources. By varying the proportions of these two policies, all combinations in between these two extremes would be available.

Notes

This lecture is a brief summary of material that has been incorporated in Chapters 7–10 of my recent book, *Chaotic Economic Dynamics* (Oxford University Press, 1990). The diagrams given here are taken, somewhat modified, from that source. Thanks are due the publisher for permission to reproduce this material here.

1. I would like to acknowledge the crucial importance of the assistance I received from Professor Rössler in my amateurish efforts to understand chaos.

2. The following set of parameters is chosen solely as a plausible illustration: $d = 0.50, e = 0.80, h = 0.50, f = 0.15, b = 0.005, g = 85.0, c = 0.048, m = 0.16, j = 0.17, s = 0.14, v^* = 0.90$. Initial conditions are 0.020, 0.030, 0, 5.0, 0.045, with $0 < t < 50$ years.

3. By altering the parameter j from 0.17 to 0.22 and s from 0.14 to 0.10, one gets the high growth Japanese case, and by altering j to 0.15 and s to 0.25, one gets the low growth with a middle result given by the unaltered values. See my book, cited above, Chapter 8.

4. They are d 0.50, f 0.15, e 0.30, h 0.050, b 0.01, g 85.0, c 0.05, with initial conditions 0, 0.03, 0.02, 5.0, and 0.025.

5

Mode Locking and
Nonlinear Entrainment
of Macroeconomic Cycles

ERIK MOSEKILDE, ERIK REIMER LARSEN,
JOHN D. STERMAN, and
JESPER SKOVHUS THOMSEN

Economists have long noted that industrial economies generate several distinct oscillatory modes including the short-term business cycle, with a period of 3–7 years (Mitchell, 1927; Gordon, 1951; Moore, 1961; Zarnowitz, 1985), the 15–25 year construction or Kuznets cycle (Hoyt, 1933; Riggleman, 1933; Long, 1940; Kuznets, 1973), and the Kondratiev cycle or economic long wave, with a period of 45–60 years (Kondratiev, 1935; Rostow, 1978; van Duijn, 1983; Bieshaar and Kleinknecht, 1984; Sterman, 1986). Schumpeter (1939) suggested it was the coincidence of downturns in these three cycles that could explain the severity of the Great Depression. But why should these cycles have commensurate periodicities so that their downturns may coincide? Why should the periods of the cycles be separated by such wide margins? More fundamentally, why should there be any coherent periodicities in the economy at all?

Some answer such questions by arguing that economic fluctuations do not exhibit enough regularity to establish the existence of distinct modes at widely separated periodicities; there are no "cycles" at all but gradual adjustments to random shocks. But the economy is not a pendulum clock — a system deliberately designed to produce a single, uniform mode of behavior by isolating the mechanism from external disturbances and building it of stable materials. Indeed, given the diversity of geographic, social, and political characteristics; given the variation in technologies, markets, and other situational factors from firm to firm and nation to nation; given the flux in these factors and the continuous bombardment of the economy with shocks both large and small, it is puzzling not why economic cycles are variable in their period and amplitude but why there are aggregate cyclical movements at all.

The durability of the business cycle over two centuries of industrialization, despite complete transformations of virtually every component of the economic, political, and social system, speaks to the existence of a deep structure whose dynamics are robust to major shocks and changes in parameters. The evidence for longer cycles is necessarily less abundant than that for the shorter business cycle. Nevertheless, there is a large body of evidence supporting the existence of the construction cycle and long wave, as well as growing theoretical understanding of the processes that produce these modes (see references above). Thus Schumpeter's question remains important: Why are there cyclical movements at the aggregate level? And how might cycles of different frequencies interact to accentuate or attenuate changes in aggregate economic activity?[1]

Linear models have dominated theoretical approaches to these questions. But linear theory is not an appropriate foundation for the study of economic cycles. Economic systems distinguish themselves from most systems considered in the natural sciences by the prevalence of positive feedback loops. Well known examples include the accelerator and multiplier loops of Keynesian business cycle theories. Other positive loops operate through self-fulfilling expectations, agglomeration effects, increasing returns, the effect of inflation expectations on real interest rates and thus aggregate demand, speculation and financial crises, and synergies and standards formation among and within the technological bases of society (Sterman, 1986; Graham and Senge, 1980; Arthur, 1988; Minsky, 1982; Semmler, 1989). Such positive feedbacks create the possibility of strongly nonlinear behavior: the positive loops may destabilize otherwise convergent processes of adjustment, which then grow in amplitude until constrained by various nonlinearities. Such phenomena cannot be understood by means of linear or nearly linear models. In particular, it is not possible to treat different modes independently of one another.

More fundamentally, in a linear world the different parameters characterizing the physical structure and decision-making processes of different firms would cause them to oscillate with different frequencies and phases. If the economic system were linear, these modes would evolve independently of one another and the total behavior would be the linear superposition of the independent modes. While individual firms might exhibit fluctuations, the aggregate of many independently oscillating firms might be quite constant. There would be no business cycle as a macroeconomic phenomenon. The most common explanation is that such linearly independent firms are driven by common sources of external variation, either government monetary and fiscal policies, changes in aggregate demand, or highly correlated shocks and expectations (Burns, 1969; Mitchell, 1927; Zarnowitz, 1985 provides a survey).

Modern nonlinear theory offers another explanation: nonlinear mode locking. In nonlinear systems, superposition does not hold. Instead, the periodicities of coupled oscillators may adjust to one another to achieve a rational ratio, or winding number. Mode-locking has recently attracted considerable interest in the natural sciences, particularly since it has been established that the phenomenon possesses a number of universal features independent of the particular system under study (Jensen, Bak, and Bohr, 1983, 1984). The same processes of entrainment have thus been observed, for instance, in paced nerve cells (Colding-Jorgensen, 1983), in externally stimulated heart cells (Glass, Shrier, and Belair, 1986), in fluid dynamics (Glazier et al., 1986), and in coupled thermostatically controlled radiators (Togeby, Mosekilde, and Sturis, 1988). Mode locking provides an explanation for the entrainment of economic fluctuations that is more robust than prior explanations, and predicts the possibility of nonlinear phenomena such as period-doubling bifurcations, simultaneous multiple periodic solutions, deterministic chaos, and the 'devil's staircase', an unusual fractal structure we describe below.

We begin with a few empirical examples of nonlinear interactions in various industries. We then introduce a model of the economic long wave, and show how it produces an endogenous fluctuation of approximately 50 years. The behavioral rules in the model have been subjected to extensive econometric and experimental test (Sterman, 1989a,b). We demonstrate how the model can exhibit mode-locking and other highly nonlinear phenomena. Mode locking and related phenomena are shown to arise through the interaction of basic macroeconomic feedback processes and fundamental nonlinearities such as nonnegativity and capacity constraints. Though Forrester (1977) proposed nonlinear entrainment as the explanation for the apparent mode-locking among macroeconomic cycles, a formal investigation of such macroeconomic entrainment processes with modern nonlinear theory does not appear to have been attempted before. The paper provides an explanation for the existence of a small number of related oscillatory modes, as well as tools which can be used to study nonlinear phenomena in other economic settings.

Illustrations

At the level of microeconomic structure, the nonlinear character of economic systems is fundamental (Forrester, 1987): Output suffers diminishing returns as individual factors of production are increased relative to others; gross investment remains nonnegative no matter how much capacity exceeds orders; shipments are determined primarily by orders when warehouses are full but must drop to zero as inventories are depleted; the cash position of a firm normally has little influence on capital investment or employment decisions, but in a severe liquidity crisis dominates all other considerations; nominal interest rates do not become negative no matter how rapid deflation may be; and so on. Every significant economic process and institution involves nonlinearities, though much of the history of economic theory in general and business cycles in particular has been an attempt to work around nonlinearity for reasons of analytic tractability (Richardson, 1991; Zarnowitz, 1985, p. 540).

Time series data from many different sources provide clear evidence that such nonlinearities make a difference to the dynamics of economic systems. As an example, Figure 5.1a shows the variation in the spot rate for oil tankers from 1950 to 1990. Spot rates are characterized by a series of sharp peaks and deep valleys at 3- to 5-year intervals, separated by periods of 10 to 15 years in which rates are lower and much less volatile. During the peaks, which often last for only a few months, spot

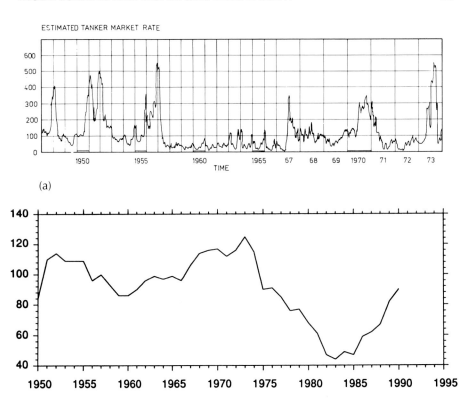

(a)

(b)

Figure 5.1 (a) Oil tanker spot rates, 1950–1990 (worldscale units for medium size vessel, single voyages Arabian Gulf – West Europe, monthly); (b) capacity utilization of world fleet (100% utilization = normal = 70% of theoretical capacity, annual data). Periods of large, rapid price fluctuations alternate with long periods of low prices and small fluctuations. The behavior of spot rates is caused by nonlinear interaction of the 3–5 year business cycle in the demand for oil shipment with the 15–25 year endogenous construction cycle in the shipping capacity (seen in utilization). Source: Bakken (1990).

rates of more than 500 are attained as compared with rates as low as 40–60 during the intervening periods. Rostow (1990) documents these cycles as far back as the 1800s.

The variation depicted in Figure 5.1a reflects the interaction of a tanker construction cycle with a period of 15–25 years and the ordinary 3–5 year business cycle. The construction cycle, visible in capacity utilization of the world fleet (Figure 5.1b) is endogenous to the ship-building industry and results from the bounded rationality of tanker investors, who order new ships during periods of high prices, even after sufficient capacity is under construction to restore equilibrium prices (Randers, 1984; Bakken, 1990). After delivery, excess capacity pushes spot rates below normal and new orders fall. The long lifetime of ships accounts for the extended periods of

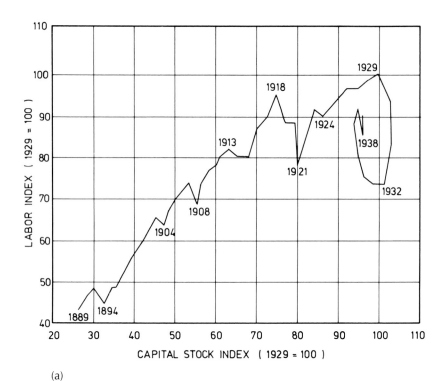

(a)

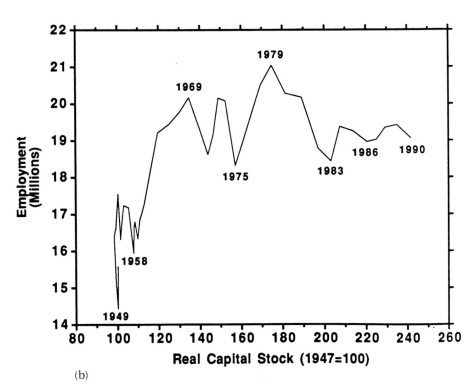

(b)

excess capacity and depressed prices. The short-term business cycle creates fluctuations in oil demand that perturb the system. In periods of surplus tanker capacity, such as between 1958 and 1967 and 1974–1990, tanker rates are low and relatively insensitive to changes in the demand for oil. Shipment demand fluctuations are absorbed by changes in the utilization of the excess capacity. In periods of high fleet utilization, small variations in demand created by the business cycle cause dramatic fluctuations in prices. Thus the parameters governing the market's response to high-frequency signals depend nonlinearly on the state of the low-frequency construction cycle. Similar examples of nonlinear coupling at the industry level can be found in the paper and timber industries, the commercial real estate industry, and agricultural commodities, among others.

The examples suggest the importance of nonlinearity in modulating the amplitude of the business cycle in different phases of a market's evolution. The focus of the present analysis is the role of nonlinear entrainment in the economic long wave or Kondratiev cycle. The long wave is characterized by successive waves of overexpansion and decline of the economy with a periodicity of approximately 40–65 years. Most scholars agree that the historic depression periods were the 1830s and 40s, the 1870s through late 1890s, the 1920s and 1930s, and the period from about 1974 through the present (Sterman, 1986; Forrester, 1977; van Duijn, 1983). One of the difficulties in developing and testing theories of long economic fluctuations is the relative paucity of data for such a long-term phenomenon. However, a large number of empirical, theoretical, and even experimental studies now lend strong support to the theory (Vasko, 1987; Sterman, 1986; Forrester, 1977; Sterman, 1989a; Goldstein, 1988; Rasmussen, Mosekilde, and Holst, 1989).

The amplitude of the business cycle appears to be modulated nonlinearly by the phase of the long wave. During long wave upswings, economic growth rates are above the long-run average, unemployment is low and capacity utilization is generally high. In consequence, the business cycle appears to have a small amplitude — recessions are mild and short, as in the early 1900s and again in the post-World War II boom. As the economy enters the downturn of the long wave, excess capacity develops, and the amplitude of the business cycle appears to increase recessions are deeper and longer, as in the period from 1873 to 1897, and, more recently, since 1970 (Sterman, 1986). Figure 5.2a shows the evolution of the capital/labor mix in U.S. manufacturing during the last complete long wave cycle (from about 1900 to

---

Figure 5.2 Historical data for the variation in labor/capital mix in United States manufacturing over the long wave. (a) 1889–1939 (Sterman, 1986). Note stagnation of employment growth and amplification of the business cycle after 1918. (b) 1947–1990. Similar behavior is observed in the postwar long wave, with large swings in employment over the business cycle since 1970 (employment in manufacturing: Bureau of Labor Statistics, annual average; capital stock index: calculated from Department of Commerce data for deflated expenditures on plant and equipment for manufacturing industries by perpetual inventory method using 20 year average lifetime and exponential depreciation).

1939). The initial upswing is characterized by joint expansion of employment and capital stock with relatively small business cycle fluctuations. As full employment is approached, however, firms substitute capital for labor, and at the same time a destabilization of the business cycle appears to take place. Between 1918 and 1929 output growth was caused primarily by increased capital intensity while employment experienced significant fluctuations (compare the decline between 1918–1921 and 1929–1933 with the small recessions between 1900 and 1918).

Figure 5.2b shows the same variables for the post-war period. Again, employment growth is rapid and relatively smooth in the upswing period, as both labor and capital expand. Since its 1969 peak, employment in manufacturing has declined on average while experiencing severe fluctuations. Thus there appear to be nonlinear interactions between long wave and business cycle. During long wave expansions the amplitude of the business cycle seems to be reduced, sometimes leading economists to suggest the business cycle has disappeared (Bronfenbrenner, 1969). However, as the economy moves into the downswing of the long wave, the severity of recessions seems to increase substantially. Similarly, downturns of the long wave have been hypothesized by some to coincide with severe recessions or downturns in the construction cycle (Long, 1940).

Such coincidences are perhaps not accidental but suggest mode-locking among these cyclic processes. The intrinsic periodicities of the different cycles may adjust as they interact such that each long wave spans a full number of Kuznets cycles, and each Kuznets cycle a full number of business cycles. We next consider these possibilities through a formal model of the long wave.

The Model

The model analyzed here captures a subset of the long wave theory developed in the System Dynamics National Model (Forrester, 1977; Sterman, 1986). The model portrays the economy as a disequilibrium system in which agents have bounded rationality. The full long wave theory relates capital investment, employment and work force participation, aggregate demand, monetary and fiscal policy, inflation and debt, innovation and productivity, and even social and political change. At the core of the long wave theory emerging from this project are a set of positive feedbacks that destabilize processes of capital accumulation, converting what would otherwise be a damped oscillation of some 15–25 years duration into a limit cycle of approximately 40–60 years (Sterman, 1986). One critical positive feedback arises from the capital investment multiplier, that is, from the fact that the capital producing sector depends on its own output to expand its production capacity. The model used here focuses on these investment dynamics and has been subjected to extensive testing and validation (Rasmussen, Mosekilde, and Sterman, 1985; Sterman, 1989a,c).

The model represents a two-sector economy with capital producing and goods producing sectors and a single factor of production, capital plant, and equipment (Figure 5.3). The model includes an explicit representation of the capital acquisition delay (construction lag) and the capacity of the investment goods sector. As a result, orders for and acquisition of capital are not necessarily equal, and at any moment there will typically be a supply line of capital under construction. For simplicity, the demand for capital of the goods-producing sector is exogenous, and there is no representation of the consumption multiplier. The full model constitutes a set of three coupled nonlinear differential equations.

The model allows for variable utilization of the capital stock. Thus production

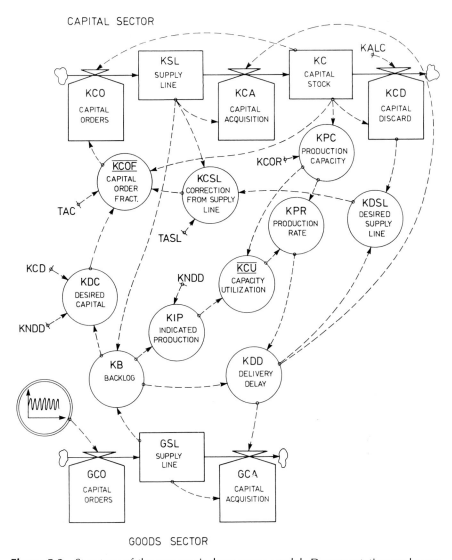

Figure 5.3 Structure of the economic long wave model. Documentation and equations are provided by Sterman (1985). Focusing on the positive feedback produced by the investment accelerator, the model can generate 45–60 year self-sustained oscillations with realistic parameter values.

of capital KPR is given by production capacity KPC multiplied by the rate of capacity utilization KCU. Utilization is a nonlinear function of the ratio of indicated production KIP to production capacity. Capacity is proportional to the capital stock, with a constant capital/output ratio KCOR. The capital stock of the capital sector KC is augmented by acquisitions KCA and diminished by depreciation KCD. The average lifetime of capital is a constant given by KALC; the discard process is first-order exponential decay. The acquisition of capital by both the capital and goods sectors depends on the supply line of unfilled orders each has accumulated and the current delivery delay. The explicit representation of capacity constraints and the construction process means that the lag in acquiring capital may be variable. If capacity is greater than or equal to the desired rate of production, the delivery delay for capital is normal and capital is received at the desired rate. If capacity is insufficient, utilization reaches a maximum, production is less than the desired amount, and the delivery delay lengthens. Shipments to each sector fall in proportion to the shortfall.

The critical behavioral formulation in the model is the decision rule for capital orders placed by the capital sector KCO. The decision rule assumes three motives for ordering capital. New orders are placed to (1) replace discards, (2) adjust the actual capital stock KC toward the desired stock KDC, and (3) adjust the supply line of unfilled orders toward the desired supply line KDSL. The desired capital stock is given by the desired rate of production and the capital/output ratio. Since capital is not received immediately but only after a delay representing the planning, construction, and delivery process, it is necessary to provide for the supply line of capital which has been ordered but not yet received. The longer the average delay in receiving new capital or the larger the required throughput, the larger the supply line must be in order to ensure that capital will be received at the desired rate. In the model the desired supply line is determined by the average delivery delay in acquiring new capital and the rate of discards (the equilibrium throughput). The parameters time to adjust capital (TAC) and time to adjust supply line (TASL) determine the amount of capital ordered each period for a given discrepancy between the desired and actual capital stock and supply line, respectively. The sum of the replacement, stock adjustment, and supply line adjustments relative to existing capacity determines the required order rate as a fraction of existing capital stock; the actual capital order fraction KCOF is a nonlinear function of the indicated rate. The nonlinearities prevent gross investment from becoming negative and also capture physical and financial constraints to excessively high investment.

The decision rule for capital investment used in the model has been tested extensively both econometrically and experimentally. Econometric analysis shows it provides a better account of postwar U.S. data for a variety of industries than the neoclassical investment function, and is theoretically preferable on behavioral grounds (Senge, 1980). Experimental tests of the model (Sterman, 1989a) and related systems (Sterman, 1989c) show that the investment decisions of subjects, including experienced managers, are captured well by the rule and correspond to well-documented psychological processes for decision making in complex environments. The complete equations are presented and discussed in Sterman (1985).[2]

The equilibrium of the model is unstable. When any small disturbance is introduced, coherent oscillations begin, growing in amplitude until constrained by the nonlinearities. The steady state behavior with the base case parameters is a limit cycle with a periodicity of 47 years (Figure 5.4). At about $t = 20$ years, the capacity of the capital producing sector becomes inadequate, and the capital sector increases its orders for capital. Rising orders soon cause desired production to exceed capacity, however, and the desired capital stock therefore exceeds the current capital stock, causing orders to rise above replacement. As orders increase, the total demand for capital increases still further through the positive feedback loop of capital self-ordering. Also, since orders increase earlier than capacity, the backlog of unfilled orders rises and delivery times increase, leading to further orders as the required supply line grows. Eventually, the capital stock catches up to demand, and the backlog peaks. Capacity must continue to increase in order to work off the backlog of unfilled orders. However, as the capacity shortfall is filled and as delivery times fall the need for new capital drops, and orders fall. Falling demand now means that desired capacity drops, further reducing orders. The remaining backlog is quickly worked off, and production falls soon after orders peak, opening a large margin of excess capacity. With so much excess capacity, the capital producers cut their investment nearly to zero, and capital stock begins to decline. The long lifetime of capital,

Billion units/year

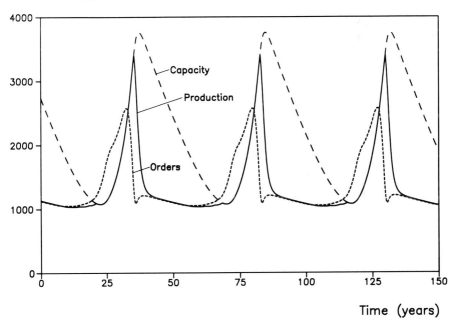

Figure 5.4 Steady-state behavior of long wave model without external forcing. Shown: the order rate for capital (dotted curve), the rate of production of capital (solid line), and capital sector production capacity (broken curve). The period of the cycle is 47 years.

however, dictates a period of depression lasting several decades. Eventually capital stock becomes inadequate once again, orders rise, and the next cycle begins.

The cycle is produced endogenously by the investment behavior of the capital producing sector — the demand for capital derived from the consumer goods sector is constant throughout. The long wave arises from basic characteristics of the macroeconomic system: the fact that capital is an input to its own production, the long construction delays, and the bounded rationality of investment decision making by each firm. Sensitivity analysis (Sterman, 1985) shows the limit cycle behavior is not particularly sensitive to wide variations in the parameters.

Mode Locking

To study the entrainment of the long wave with the Kuznets and business cycles we now perturb the system by imposing a sinusoidal fluctuation on the demand for capital derived from the consumer goods sector. For nonlinear systems the principle of superposition does not apply. In the presence of a periodic disturbance the behavior of the long wave changes, adjusting to the period and amplitude of the forcing cycle. Typically, the behavior adjusts to lock the two cycles into an overall periodic motion in which the oscillations have commensurate periods with the long wave completing q cycles each time the external forcing completes p cycles, where p and q are integers. Thus, if the model is perturbed by a signal with a period different from but relatively close to its natural period, the interaction between the two modes may cause the period of the long wave to change until the modes oscillate synchronously. Similarly, if the period of the external signal were close to the fraction $1/n$ of the undisturbed long wave period the model tends to adjust such that the long wave completes precisely one cycle each time the external signal completes n cycles. Thus the process of mode-locking can cause the downturns of different cycles to coincide over a wide range of parameter values. Mode-locking might explain the apparent rational ratios of the periods of the different cycles without requiring unlikely combinations of parameters. In the real economy, the business and Kuznets cycles will also adjust to the long wave. Entrainment and mode locking are therefore likely to be even stronger in reality than here where the high frequencies are modeled by external forcing rather than endogenous economic structures.[3]

As an example of such entrainment, Figure 5.5 shows the results obtained when the model is perturbed by a sinusoidal modulation of orders for capital placed by the goods sector (GCO) with amplitude $A = 0.20$ of the equilibrium value. The period of the external signal is $P = 22.2$ years, in the range of the Kuznets cycle. Relative to the unforced simulation (Figure 5.4), the long wave has increased its period by nearly 40% so as to accommodate precisely three periods of the external signal. Moreover, within the interval 19.9 years $< P <$ 24.8 years, a change in the period of the external signal causes a precisely proportional shift in the period of the long wave

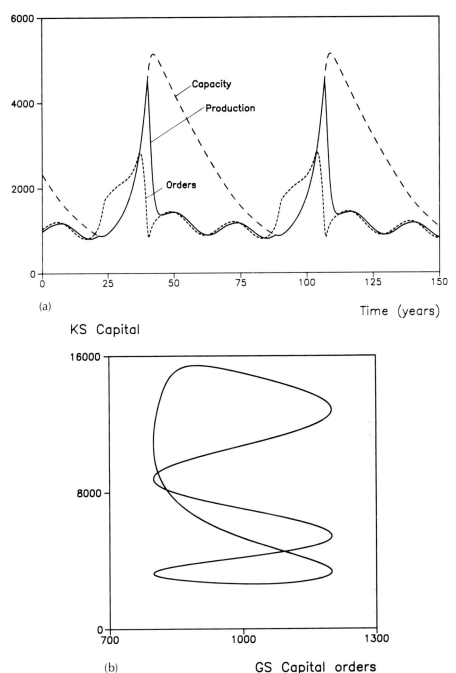

Figure 5.5 Simulation results obtained with sinusoidal forcing in orders for capital placed by the goods sector. Here the amplitude $A = 20\%$ and the period of the external signal $P = 22.2$ years, in the range of the Kuznets cycle. The period of the long wave has changed by almost 40% so as to accommodate precisely three Kuznets cycles. (a) Time domain; (b) phase space projection showing capital sector capital stock (KS capital) and goods sector orders for capital (GS capital orders).

such that the 1:3 entrainment is maintained. If P is reduced or increased beyond these limits, abrupt qualitative shifts in the behavior of the model occur.

The periodic nature of the mode-locked solution is clearly illustrated in phase-space projections of the steady-state behavior. Figure 5.5b shows such a projection corresponding to the temporal variation depicted in Figure 5.5a. We have here plotted contemporaneous values of capital sector capital stock (KC) and goods sector capital orders (GCO) over many long wave oscillations. The horizontal axis thus represents the external forcing, and the vertical axis the response of the model. Inspection of the figure shows production capacity in the capital sector builds up and decays precisely once for each three swings of the external signal. Figure 5.6 shows the results obtained with the same amplitude of the external signal ($A = 0.20$), but with a modulation period $P = 4.6$ years. In this case, representing interaction between the economic long wave and the ordinary business cycle, we find 1:10 entrainment. The long wave completes precisely one cycle each time the business cycle completes 10 oscillations. The 1:10 mode-locked solution exists in the interval from $4.47 \leq P \leq 4.70$ years. Near the interval of 1:10 entrainment we find intervals with entrainment at ratios of 1:9, 1:11, 2:19, and 2:21.

The interval in which a particular mode-locked ratio occurs is a measure of the strength of the nonlinear interactions in the model. The interval tends to widen with increasing amplitude of the modulating signal, as larger excursions of system states forces the model more strongly into its various nonlinearities. The interval also depends on the winding number, i.e., the ratio of the periods of the two interacting modes. Entrainment between modes with simple winding numbers and with winding numbers of the order of unity is more pronounced than entrainment between modes with more complicated ratios. 1:1 and 1:3 entrainment thus occur over a wider range of P than does, for instance, 1:10 or 4:9 entrainment.

To illustrate the variety of different behaviors which can result from relatively weak perturbations of the long wave model, the following figures show simulation results obtained with $P = 29.5$ years (Figure 5.7) and $P = 34.6$ years (Figure 5.8), respectively. The amplitude of the external signal has now been reduced to $A = 0.05$. Both figures show temporal variation over an extended simulation period (600 years) together with the corresponding phase-space projection. The first simulation shows a 2:3 mode-locked solution in which the long wave peaks in production capacity alternate between a high value and a somewhat lower value. Only after two complete long wave cycles (and three cycles of the perturbing signal) does the model repeat itself. Figure 5.8 shows the 3:4 mode-locked solution existing for $P = 34.6$ years. The model now performs three long wave cycles for each four cycles of the external signal. Such 3:4 entrainment only occurs in a relatively small interval for P.

In principle, the system mode-locks at all rational winding numbers. Between the intervals with mode-locked behavior, quasiperiodic and chaotic solutions can be observed. These are behaviors in which the trajectory never repeats itself, but continues to find new paths in phase-space. Quasiperiodicity corresponds to irrational values for the winding number. The quasiperiodic trajectory thus winds around a

Billion units/year

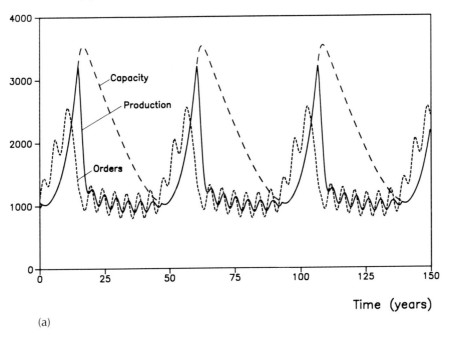

(a)

KS Capital

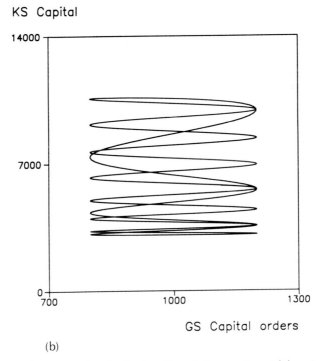

GS Capital orders

(b)

Figure 5.6 Simulation results obtained with a 4.6 year sinusoidal variation in the orders for capital to the goods sector, corresponding to a typical business cycle. To mode-lock with the external signal, the long wave has adjusted its period from 47 to 46 years. (a) Time domain; (b) phase diagram.

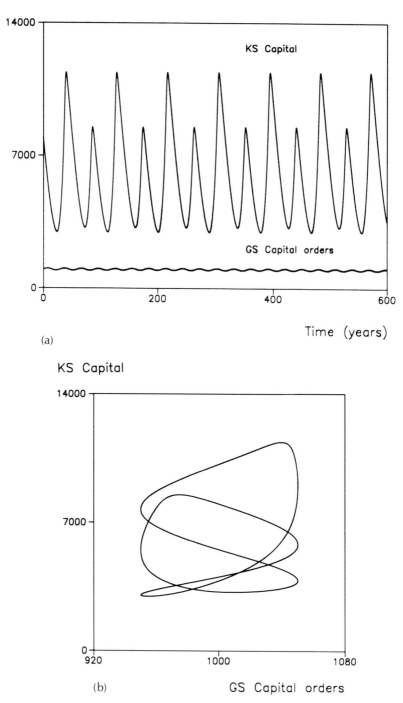

Figure 5.7 Temporal variation (a) and phase plot (b) for the 2:3 mode-locked solution obtained for $P = 29.5$ years and $A = 0.05$. The long wave alternates between high and low peaks, and only after two complete long wave cycles (and three periods of the external signal) does the trajectory repeat.

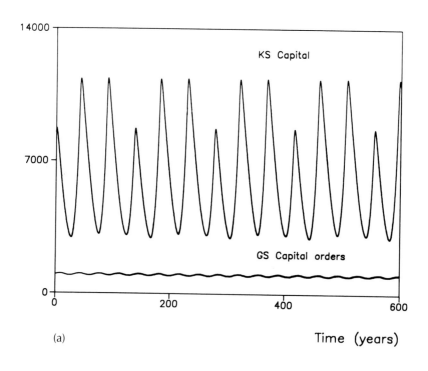

(a)

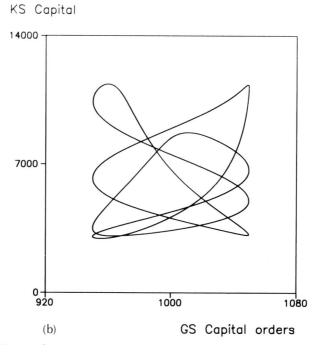

(b)

Figure 5.8 Temporal variation (a) and phase plot (b) for the 3:4 mode-locked solution that exists for $P = 34.6$ years and $A = 0.05$.

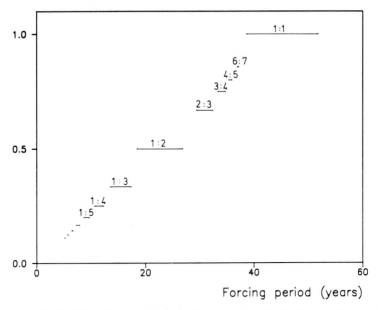

Figure 5.9 The devil's staircase. Mode locking at rational winding numbers exists in finite intervals of the forcing period (the horizontal steps of the staircase). Between the steps, solutions with other commensurate winding numbers exist (inset) with characteristic fractal self-similar structure at ever-finer scales. The steps are separated by quasiperiodic and chaotic solutions with irrational winding number.

torus without ever returning to the same point. Quasiperiodic solutions, which occur for $A < 0.025$, are distinguished from deterministic chaos by their lack of sensitivity to initial conditions (the largest Lyapunov exponent in a quasiperiodic system is 0 rather than positive for a chaotic system). Usually, the phase-space projection of a quasiperiodic solution also shows a much more orderly behavior than that of a chaotic solution. For $A > 0.025$, the intervals of some of the mode-locked solutions may overlap the intervals of other solutions. In these cases, several periodic solutions can exist simultaneously. Initial conditions or subsequent perturbations then determine which solution the trajectory approaches (thus small amounts of external noise may have large qualitative effects on the system dynamics).

A more complete picture of the entrainment process is obtained by plotting the winding number as a function of the forcing period (Figure 5.9). The period of the external signal has here been varied from 2 to 60 years while keeping the amplitude constant at $A = 0.05$. The figure shows a series of $1:n$ mode-locked solutions. Between these solutions, solutions with other commensurate wave periods are observed. In the region from $P = 29$ years to $P = 37$ years, we thus find intervals with 2:3, 3:4, 4:5, and 6:7 entrainment. For $A = 0.025$ we have identified 3:8, 2:5, 7:17, 3:7, 4:9, and 6:13 mode-locking between the regions of 1:2 and 1:3 entrainment.

By refining the calculations one continues to find more and more resonances covering narrower and narrower intervals. For small values of A, i.e., below the critical value where the mode-locked intervals start to overlap, the intervals of mode locking have a self-similar structure in which the intervals of mode-locking at rational winding numbers are separated by solutions with incommensurate winding number (quasiperiodicity) ad infinitum on smaller and smaller scales of P. In practice, noise washes out the finer details, that is, the random exogenous events which continuously bombard the economy will not allow the trajectory to settle down in the neighborhood of the more complicated winding numbers. Simpler examples of mode-locking such as, for instance, 1:3 and 1:4 are much more likely to be observed in the real economy.

The structure exhibited in Figure 5.9 is known as a devil's staircase (Mandelbrot, 1977; Bak and von Boehm, 1980). The devil's staircase has a universal character that transcends the particular system in which the dynamics are realized (Jensen et al., 1983). Essentially the same devil's staircase can be observed in the behavior of paced nerve cells (Colding-Jorgensen, 1983), periodically stimulated heart cells (Glass et al., 1986), and coupled thermostatically controlled radiators (Togeby et al., 1988). Universality has a most important consequence, namely, that the main aspects of our results are independent of the details of the model. All models in which economic fluctuations are characterized by self-sustained oscillation can be expected to exhibit similar mode-locking behavior. For a particular class of systems, the universality is quantitative in the sense that these systems all possess the same fractal dimension for the set of quasiperiodic solutions at the critical line (Jensen et al., 1983).

Amplitude Dependence of Entrainment: Structure of the Arnol'd Tongues

If the amplitude of the driving signal is changed, the intervals of entrainment also change. An overview of this variation is provided by the phase diagram in Figure 5.10, which maps some of the principal mode-locked zones as a function of A and P. These zones are commonly referred to as Arnol'd tongues (Jensen et al., 1984). For $A = 0$ there can, of course, be no entrainment at all. As A is increased, however, wider and wider intervals of mode-locked behavior develop. As long as A is relatively small, quasiperiodic modes, distributed with the characteristic fractal dimension for the devil's staircase, exist between the tongues.

The widths of the tongues cannot continue to grow, however. At a certain point they begin to overlap, and quasiperiodic behavior then ceases to exist. Overlap occurs at approximately $A = 0.025$. Above the critical value, the trajectory is either periodic or chaotic. Multiple periodic solutions coexist where the Arnol'd tongues overlap, for example in the region around $P = 32$ years and $A = 0.07$, where the 1:1 and the 2:3 tongues cross. In such cases initial conditions determine which solution the system chooses. Note the bumps on the left side of the tongues where they

Forcing amplitude

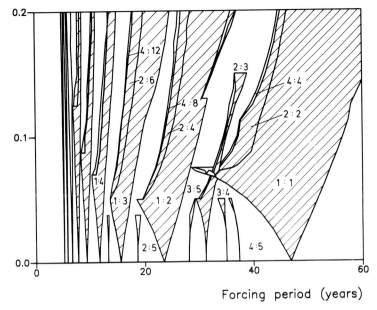

Forcing period (years)

Figure 5.10 Phase diagram showing the regions of some of the main mode-locked solutions. These regions are known as Arnol'd tongues. Note the bumps on the tongues where they approach one another. Above the bumps, period-doubling bifurcations occur along the edges of the tongues.

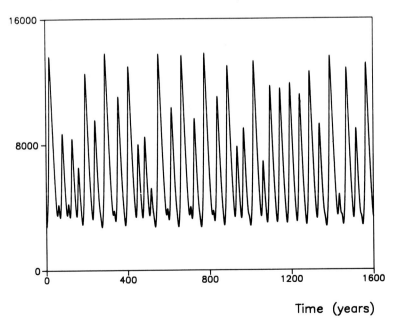

KS Capital

Time (years)

Figure 5.11 Deterministic chaos caused by external perturbation of period $P = 16.1$ years and amplitude $A = 0.20$. Chaotic behavior is characterized by a positive value of

overlap. While absent in some experimental studies of mode-locking in physical systems, Cumming and Linsay (1987) observed similar bumps in a driven nonlinear electronic oscillator. Deterministic chaos may arise via period-doubling bifurcations (Feigenbaum, 1980), frustration (Jensen et al., 1984), or other possible routes. In frustration chaos the trajectory switches unpredictably between two or more periodic solutions lying nearby in phase space. Figure 5.11 shows a typical chaotic solution.

Lyapunov Exponents and Lock-In Time

The Lyapunov exponents, of which there are as many as there are state variables in the system, measure the long-term average rates of divergence or convergence of nearby trajectories, and are extremely useful in characterizing the dynamics of the system (Bennetin et al., 1980; Wolf, 1986).

A positive value of the largest Lyapunov exponent signals sensitivity to the initial conditions and deterministic chaos. For driven nonlinear systems, a negative value of the largest Lyapunov exponent indicates a periodic orbit, while a quasiperiodic orbit is characterized by a vanishing value. Bifurcation points correspond to orbits of marginal stability, and are also characterized by vanishing values of the largest Lyapunov exponent.

For periodic orbits, the reciprocal of the magnitude of the largest Lyapunov exponent measures the time scale over which transients die out and the system locks into its cyclic motion. The lock-in time provides a good measure of the stability of the orbit with respect to (small) disturbances. To calculate the Lyapunov exponents of the periodically driven long wave model we have utilized the method described by Wolf (1986). Figure 5.12 shows the variation of the largest Lyapunov exponent as a function of the period P of the external signal, with amplitude $A = 0.05$. For comparison, we have also shown the devil's staircase depicted in Figure 5.9. The steps of the staircase correspond to regions with negative values for the largest Lyapunov exponent. Particularly for low forcing periods, the Lyapunov exponent becomes positive between the steps, where the winding number is irrational, indicating the presence of deterministic chaos. The finite resolution of the forcing frequency scan and calculations limit the amount of detail seen in the trace of Lyapunov exponents.

The mode-locked behaviors seen in the model are, for rational winding numbers, perfectly regular, unlike the fluctuations in the actual economy, where the periods of different cyclical modes are only approximately commensurate. The mode-locked behavior discussed here refers to the steady-state behavior of the sys-

---

the largest Lyapunov exponent, and thus sensitivity to initial conditions. Two simulations with initial conditions differing by as little as 10^{-15} will diverge exponentially so that after about 15–20 cycles the difference reaches macroeconomic significance.

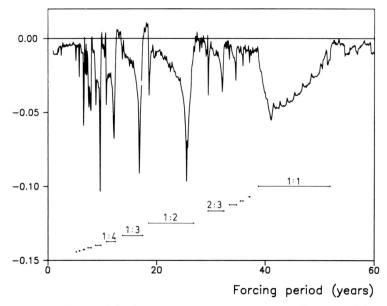

Figure 5.12 Variation of the largest Lyapunov exponent as a function of the period of the external signal, with $A = 0.05$. To help identify regions in which mode-locked solutions exist, we have also plotted the corresponding devil's staircase. In intervals where the largest Lyapunov exponent is positive, the model exhibits chaotic behavior.

tem, after transients have died out. The dynamics are more complex when the system is excited by random events. Each disturbance will knock the system away from its stationary orbit and, at least for sufficiently small shocks, a new approach to the orbit will then begin. The time constant of approach, or lock-in time, is equal to the reciprocal of the magnitude of the largest Lyapunov exponent. Figure 5.13 shows the lock-in time as a function of the period of the external forcing. The amplitude $A = 0.05$. The time constant for entrainment into one of the primary solutions (simple winding numbers) is on the order of 10–20 years, while time constants of the order of 20–50 years are found for more complex winding numbers. Thus entrainment is likely to be observed in the economy only at the primary resonances. The system will never have time enough to settle down into one of the more complex mode-locked solutions before a new external excitation again knocks it away from the steady-state mode-locked orbit.

The lock-in time depends upon the amplitude of the forcing signal. Figure 5.14 shows the minimal lock-in times for the 1:1, 1:2, 1:3, and 1:4 mode-locked solutions as functions of amplitude. For small amplitudes the minimal lock-in time decreases rapidly with increasing A. Above the critical amplitude, however, the lock-in time

Lock—in time (years)

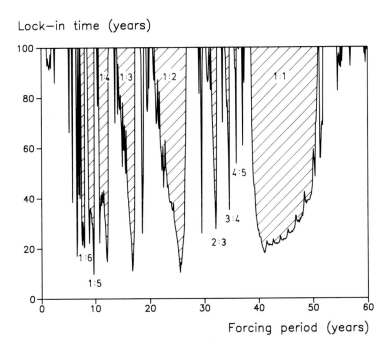

Forcing period (years)

Figure 5.13 Variation of the lock-in time with the forcing period. The lock-in time is a time constant characterizing the rate at which the model locks onto the various periodic solutions. The amplitude of the external signal is $A = 0.05$. Entrainment at fundamental winding numbers such as 1:2 and 1:3 occurs in 10–20 years; 20–50 years are required for the system to entrain at less fundamental ratios.

varies only little with A. For $A < 0.06$, mode-locking occurs most rapidly for the 1:3 and 1:2 solutions.[4]

Even for the primary mode-locked solutions, lock-in times on the order of a decade are long in relation to the frequency of external shocks to which the macroeconomic system is subjected. It should be recalled, however, that we have only considered the adjustment of the long wave to more rapid fluctuations, which in turn were modeled by exogenous forcing. If the business and Kuznets cycles were modeled endogenously, we would observe reciprocal adjustment of these cycles to the long wave and entrainment would most likely be more pronounced. Still, lock-in times are likely to be nontrivial relative to the frequency distribution of random shocks in the economy. Such a system would exhibit *approximate* mode-locking, in which the different cycles were locked into one of the simpler winding numbers (1:1, 1:2, 1:3, etc.) on average but exhibit as well variations in the relative amplitudes, phasing, and character of individual orbits as random shocks continually displace the system from its steady-state behavior. Such approximate mode-locking is what we actually observe in the economy.

Minimal Lock—in time (years)

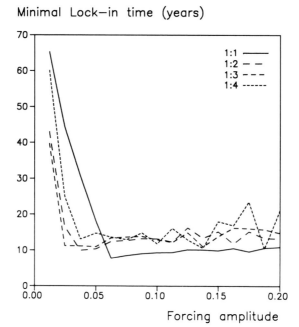

Forcing amplitude

Figure 5.14 Dependence of the minimal lock-in time for some fundamental mode-locked solutions on the amplitude of the external signal. For small amplitudes, the lock-in time decreases rapidly with A, but saturates at a minimum above the critical line.

Conclusion

Nonlinear entrainment can cause different oscillatory processes with approximately similar periods to move in phase at a single frequency, producing aggregate business fluctuations. Thus oscillatory tendencies of similar periodicity in different parts of the economy are drawn together in 1:1 entrainment to form a single mode, and each mode is separated from the next by a wide enough margin to avoid entrainment at the same period. Hence the economy exhibits clearly distinguishable modes economic historians have dubbed the business cycle, the Kuznets cycle, and the economic long wave.

Even with relatively wide separation in periodicity, the interaction between modes may be strong enough to lock them together such that they have commensurate periods. Nonlinear interactions may thus pull the Kuznets cycle and business cycle into phase with the long wave and accentuate its peaks or downturns. Additionally, since mode-locking at a given rational winding number is stable over a finite range of individual cycle periods, mode-locking is robust with respect to variations in the parameters governing the individual cycles, allowing entrainment to persist over long time periods despite technological and institutional change, perturbations, and other sources of variation in economic life.

Notes

Richard Day and Michael Radzicki provided many helpful comments on earlier versions. We thank Ellen Buchhave for her assistance in preparation of the manuscript.

1. As Zarnowitz (1985) notes, theoretical work on economic cycles itself varies cyclically. During the great post-WWII boom business fluctuations received less and less attention, and it was widely argued that cycles were becoming a topic of economic history. Since 1970 the business cycle has reasserted itself, and interest in cycles has increased. As argued below, such variations in the amplitude of the business cycle may be endogenous.

2. In the original model the capital sector's orders for capital could fall to zero during the contraction phase of the long wave as excess capacity dominated the replacement and supply line motivations for ordering. As a result, the supply line KSL approached zero. This behavior does not seem reasonable for a macroeconomic system with diverse types of and needs for capital. It also creates numerical difficulties in calculating the Lyapunov exponents. The model used here has thus been modified to constrain investment to a small but nonzero quantity. There are no significant differences in the behavior of the revised and original models.

3. Additionally, since the forcing cannot respond to the endogenous dynamics of the model, and no disturbances are introduced, the model's behavior is more uniform than that of the real economy. In a fully endogenous system with variations in parameters and external shocks, the model would generate, in addition to the clock-like mode-locked behavior seen in these simulations, local perturbations in coherence, periodicity, and amplitude, as observed in the data. More importantly, the process of mode locking itself can generate erratic behavior, through period doubling bifurcations, quasiperiodicity caused by incommensurate winding number, frustration chaos caused by overlapping regions of mode-locked behavior at different winding numbers, and sensitive dependence of the chaotic trajectories on initial conditions and perturbations.

4. The fluctuations in calculated lock-in-time, particularly for the 1:4 entrainment, are primarily caused by inaccuracies in the calculation of the very sharp minimum for the largest Lyapunov exponent.

Bibliography

Arthur, W. Brian, 1988, "Self-Reinforcing Mechanisms in Economics," in P. Anderson, K. Arrow, and D. Pines (eds.), *The Economy as an Evolving Complex System*, Addison-Wesley, Reading, MA.

Bak, P., and J. von Boehm, 1980, Ising Model with Solutions, Phasons, and the Devil's Staircase," *Physical Review B*, 21, 5297–5308.

Bakken, B., 1990, "Transfer of Learning in Cyclical Markets: An Experimental Approach," Working paper D–4166, System Dynamics Group, Sloan School of Management, MIT, Cambridge, MA.

Bennetin, G., L. Galgani, and J.-M. Strelcyn, 1980, "Lyapunov Characteristic Exponents for Smooth Dynamical Systems and for Hamiltonian Systems," *Meccanica*, 15, 9–20.

Bieshaar, H., and A. Kleinknecht, 1984, "Kondratiev Long Waves in Aggregate Output? An Econometric Test," *Konjunkturpolitik*, 30, 279–303.

Bronfenbrenner, M., 1969, *Is the Business Cycle Obsolete?*, John Wiley, New York.

Burns, A., 1969, *The Business Cycle in a Changing World*, National Bureau of Economic Research, New York.

Colding-Jorgensen, M., 1983, "A Model for the Firing Pattern of a Paced Nerve Cell," *Journal of Theoretical Biology*, 101, 541–568.

Cumming, A., and P.S. Linsay, 1987, "Deviations from Universality in the Transition from Quasiperiodicity to Chaos," *Physical Review Letters*, 59(15), 1633–1636.

Feigenbaum, M., 1980, "Universal Behavior in Nonlinear Systems," *Los Alamos Science*, 1, 4–27.

Forrester J.W., 1977, "Growth Cycles," *De Economist*, 125, 525–543.

Forrester, J.W., 1987, "Nonlinearity in High-Order Models of Social Systems," *European Journal of Operational Research*, 30, 104–109.

Glass, L., A. Shrier, and J. Belair, 1986, "Chaotic Cardiac Rhythms," in A.V. Holden (ed.), *Chaos*, Nonlinear Science: Theory and Applications, Manchester University Press, England.

Glazier, J., M. Jensen, A. Libchaber, and J. Stavans, 1986, "Structure of Arnold Tongues and the f(a) Spectrum for Period Doubling: Experimental Results, *Physical Review A*, 34(2), 1621–1624.

Goldstein, J., 1988, *Long Cycles: Prosperity and War in the Modern Age*, Yale University Press, New Haven.

Graham, A., and P. Senge, 1980, "A Long Wave Hypothesis of Innovation," *Technological Forecasting and Social Change*, 17, 283–311.

Gordon, Robert A., 1951, *Business Fluctuations*, Harper & Row, New York.

Hoyt, H., 1933, *One Hundred Years of Land Values in Chicago*, University of Chicago Press, Chicago.

Jensen, M.H., P. Bak, and T. Bohr, 1983, "Complete Devil's Staircase, Fractal Dimension, and Universality of Mode-Locking Structure in the Circle Map," *Physical Review Letters*, 50, 1637–1639.

Jensen, M.H., P. Bak, and T. Bohr, 1984, "Transition to Chaos by Interaction of Resonances in Dissipative Systems. I. Circle Maps," *Physical Review A*, 30, 1960–1969.

Kondratiev, N.D., 1935, "The Long Waves in Economic Life," *Review of Economic Statistics*, 17, 105–115.

Kuznets, S., 1973, "Modern Economic Growth: Findings and Reflections," *American Economic Review*, 63, 247–258.

Long, C.D., Jr., 1940, *Building Cycles and the Theory of Investment*, Princeton University Press, Princeton, NJ.

Mandelbrot, B.B., 1977, *Fractals: Form, Change and Dimension*, Freeman, San Francisco.

Minsky, H., 1982, *Can "It" Happen Again? Essays on Instability and Finance*, M.E. Sharpe, Armonk, NY.

Mitchell, W.C., 1927, *Business Cycles: The Problem and Its Setting*, National Bureau of Economic Research, New York.

Moore, G.H. (ed.), 1961, *Business Cycle Indicators*, National Bureau of Economic Research, Princeton University Press, Princeton, NJ.

Randers, J., 1984, "The Tanker Market," Working Paper 84/9, Norwegian School of Management, Oslo.

Rasmussen, S., E. Mosekilde, and J.D. Sterman, 1985, "Bifurcations and Chaotic Behavior in a Simple Model of the Economic Long Wave," *System Dynamics Review*, 1, 92–110.

Rasmussen, S., E. Mosekilde, and J. Holst, 1989, "Empirical Indication of Economic Long Waves in Aggregate Production," *European Journal of Operational Research*, 42, 279–293.

Richardson, G., 1991, *Feedback Thought in Social Science and Systems Theory*, University of Pennsylvania Press, Philadelphia.

Riggleman, J.R., 1933, "Building Cycles in the United States, 1897–1932," *Journal of the American Statistical Association*, 28, 182.

Rostow, W.W., 1978, *The World Economy: History and Prospect*, Macmillan, London.

Rostow, W. W., 1990, *Theorists of Economic Growth from David Hume to the Present*, Oxford University Press, New York.

Schumpeter, J.A., 1939, *Business Cycles*, McGraw-Hill, New York, 173.

Semmler, W. (ed.), 1989, *Financial Dynamics and Business Cycles: New Perspectives*, M.E. Sharpe, Armonk, NY.

Senge, P., 1980, "A System Dynamics Approach to Investment Function Formulation and Testing," *Socio-Economic Planning Sciences*, 14, 269–280.

Sterman, J.D., 1985, "A Behavioral Model of the Economic Long Wave," *Journal of Economic Behavior and Organization*, 6, 17–53.

Sterman, J. D., 1986, "The Economic Long Wave: Theory and Evidence," *System Dynamics Review*, 2(2), 87–125.

Sterman, J., 1989a, "Misperceptions of Feedback in Dynamic Decision Making," *Organizational Behavior and Human Decision Processes*, 43(3), 301–335.

Sterman, J., 1989b, "Deterministic Chaos in an Experimental Economic System," *Journal of Economic Behavior and Organization*, 12, 1–28.

Sterman, J., 1989c, "Modeling Managerial Behavior: Misperceptions of Feedback in a Dynamic Decision Making Experiment," *Management Science*, 35(3), 321–339.

Togeby, M., E. Mosekilde, and J. Sturis, 1988, "Frequency-Locking in a Model of Two Coupled Thermostatically Controlled Radiators," Proceedings of the Winter Annual Meeting of the American Society of Mechanical Engineers, paper 88-WA/DSC–14.

van Duijn, J.J., 1983, *The Long Wave in Economic Life*, George Allen and Unwin, London.

Vasko, T. (ed.), 1987, *The Long Wave Debate*, Springer-Verlag, Berlin.

Wolf, A., 1986, "Quantifying Chaos with Lyapunov Exponents," in A.V. Holden (ed.), *Chaos, Nonlinear Science: Theory and Applications*, Manchester University Press, England.

Zarnowitz, V., 1985, "Recent Work on Business Cycles in Historical Perspective: A Review of Theories and Evidence," *Journal of Economic Literature*, 23, 523–580.

6

From Micro Behavior
to Macro Dynamics:
The Case of Vehicular Traffic

ROBERT HERMAN

Approaching the problem from the point of view of classical physics, this chapter explains the aggregate properties of vehicular traffic from a specification of the local interaction of neighboring vehicles on a highway, which exemplifies the more general problem, so important in economics, of establishing a connection between the way individuals behave and the macro-dynamic properties of the collection of individuals as a whole. Moreover, it demonstrates that even in the sphere of human behavior there are problems which can be illuminated — in spite of their complexity — by theoretical methods based on relatively simple dynamic principles and that can be substantiated empirically.

We began by considering the dynamics of a platoon of vehicles on a single lane of highway, with no passing, in terms of human behavior. The initial hypothesis was that the acceleration response at the time t plus a time lag T of a driver in a platoon of vehicles is proportional to the relative speed, with respect to the nearest neighbor vehicle ahead at the time T, multiplied by a gain factor, λ, which, for example, can be taken equal to a sensitivity coefficient divided by the spacing between the two vehicles. The sensitivity coefficient is a measure of how large a response is generated by the driver when confronted with an external stimulus, namely, a finite relative speed. It is assumed that the driver wishes to keep up with the car ahead.

While it is an oversimplification to assume that the complex car-following task can be described properly only in terms of a continuous differential-difference equation, this approach has led to very useful results.

One of the main interests in any dynamic theory is to determine its steady-state flow characteristics and its stability properties. With respect to stability it can be shown for a wide range of cases that the car-following task is unstable. Observational data have been represented quite well by means of a relatively simple car-following equation of the form

$$\frac{d^2x_n(t+T)}{dt^2} = \lambda \left[\frac{dx_{n-1}(t)}{dt} - \frac{dx_n(t)}{dt} \right] \qquad (6.1)$$

For this simple stimulus–response model with λ = constant, the asymptotic stability criterion is found to be

$$2\lambda T \leq 1, \qquad (6.2)$$

which shows that the stability of a platoon of vehicles depends on human behavior as specified by two parameters, a sensitivity coefficient and a time lag. Moreover, the theory yields a relation between the flow and the concentration of vehicles which interestingly has a maximum when the traffic is moving at an average speed equal to the sensitivity coefficient. This again shows the intertwining of an overall macroscopic traffic effect with micro-human behavior. The spirit of our work at that time was to create a theoretical model, to design and conduct experiments to validate the model, and particularly to obtain data to learn what real experience was saying.

One might ask, how do we compare theory with experiment and observations? Let us examine this question for the simple car following case where the acceleration of the following vehicle is proportional to the relative speed between it and the nearest forward neighbor as in equation (6.1). We arranged that a lead driver would go through some programmed speed maneuvers and also that the following driver would follow in a normal safe manner. Using appropriate instrumentation, it was possible to record in detail the time histories of the dynamical variables for the two vehicles involved in this car following exercise. This data provided us with the position, speed, acceleration and relative speed, all as a function of time, for each of the vehicles.

It was then possible to perform a linear correlation analysis using the above mentioned simple linear car following equation, equation (6.1), in which T is the time lag and λ a constant gain factor, which tells us how much a driver does in response to a given relative speed stimulus. The idea is to determine the correlation coefficient between the acceleration of the following vehicle and the relative speed between the two vehicles for selected values of the time lag. When this is done for a series of time lags, the correlation coefficient has a maximum at some particular time lag which is taken as the time lag of the following driver. The statistical procedure also tells us that the coefficient λ is equal to the maximum correlation coefficient multiplied by the ratio of the standard deviations of the acceleration and the relative speed, i.e.,

$$\lambda = r_{\max} \frac{\sigma(a)}{\sigma(u_{\text{rel}})} \qquad (6.3)$$

In this manner it is possible to obtain the time lag and the sensitivity coefficient for various drivers in a real world situation. Interestingly, it turns out that the drivers of passenger cars have values of this pair of parameters that imply they are driving on the margin of stability. In contradistinction the values of these same parameters for drivers of heavy vehicles, such as buses in similar car following experiments, imply that these drivers are generally driving well within the region of stability and are infrequently close to the instability bound. This result in itself is fascinating *in that it shows that human beings often push to the limits of a given task.*

Moreover, when we refine the model and take into account that λ varies inversely as the intervehicle spacing as in

$$\lambda = \frac{\lambda_{1,0}}{x_{n-1}(t) - x_n(t)} \tag{6.4}$$

we are able to obtain a relation between the flow and the concentration of the traffic. The flow, q, can be expressed in terms of the concentration, k, and the speed, u, as follows:

$$q = uk = -\lambda_{1,0}k \ln(k/k_j) \tag{6.5}$$

where k_j is the maximum or so-called jam concentration. This equation yields the result that the maximum flow is achieved when the average speed of the traffic is equal to the sensitivity coefficient $\lambda_{1,0}$. It is extremely interesting that the average value of the sensitivity coefficient, which is actually a microquantity different for different people, provides information about the collective macroquantity flow. Thus, we have a connection between the micro and macro traffic worlds showing that the detailed behavior of people in the car following mode, for example on a single lane of a tunnel with no passing, determines the condition under which there will be maximum flow.

All of these ideas have been verified by experimentation and observation; the reader is referred to thorough discussions that can be found in the various papers cited in the selected bibliography appended to this chapter.

When I next turned my attention to the problem of vehicular traffic on a multilane highway as opposed to a single lane, it was not clear how to take into account the influence of the time lag. It was then that I discussed the problem with Ilya Prigogine who quickly became interested even though many of my physicist colleagues had already argued that problems in vehicular traffic would unquestionably lead to a statistical morass. They were wrong.

It is exciting, many years later, to recall that Prigogine suggested a model which was based on a Boltzmann-like equation to describe the evolution of the speed distribution function of the cars on a multilane highway. This is a nonlinear integrodifferential equation in the unknown distribution function in which the average speed and concentration of the vehicles depend implicitly on the distribution function itself. This kinetic theory of vehicular traffic describes the evolution of the speed–distribution function of traffic on multilane highways in terms of a number of important processes: a relaxation or speeding up process, which expresses the attempts of drivers to achieve their own desired speeds, i.e., microgoals, by passing slower cars; an interaction or slowing down process, which arises in the conflict between a faster driver and a slower driver; and an adjustment process that reduces the variance around the local mean speed. On the other hand, we tried to avoid examining many specific details, for example, the detailed description of all the vehicles in queues and the dynamical details of passing maneuvers.

The model, simple though it is, already had rather realistic features embedded in it, such as a regime in which drivers, to some extent, could act independently to achieve their microgoals, and another, a collective regime, in which the behavior of the traffic no longer depends on the desired speeds of the individual drivers, thus revealing a phase transition. In this collective regime the average speed of the cars depends only on the concentration, as well as on the probability of passing, and the relaxation time (both of which are themselves functions of the concentration). It was also possible to show that the first order deviations from the linear portion of the flow–concentration curve at very low concentrations are determined by the dispersion of the desired speed distribution function and are proportional to the cube of the concentration. This high power dependency is, of course, the result of collective effects. The model was subsequently more fully developed and tested successfully years later for multilane traffic on the New Jersey turnpike.

Subsequently our kinetic theory of vehicular traffic has been extended to describe in a similar overall fashion the traffic in towns, i.e., traffic circulating on an extended urban street network. The extensive data available revealed remarkable regularities in the speed distribution function as a function of concentration, the variance of the speed and the variance of the acceleration as functions of the speed, and between the observed stop time per unit distance and the trip time per unit distance for a vehicle circulating in an urban street network.

To explain these regularities Prigogine and I drew on a "two-fluid model" of town traffic that we had already used in our kinetic theory of multilane highway traffic 20 years earlier when the transition to the so-called collective flow regime was achieved at sufficiently high vehicular concentrations. In this case we found that the average speed depends on the fraction of the cars that are "immobilized." At the collective transition in the case of highway traffic, the speed distribution for cars splits into two parts — one corresponding to moving vehicles and the other to vehicles that are stopped as a consequence of congestion, traffic signals, stop signs, and barricades, but not in the parked condition.

During the past 10 years we have applied these ideas to traffic in many cities around the world and have been able to verify the theoretical basis with observations as well as experiments carried out in various urban street networks. This work has enabled us to make quantitative assessments of the relative quality of the traffic and the traffic systems in a large number of cities in the United States and abroad, a most practical consequence of these theoretical ideas. What is perhaps most important in this connection is that here again we have a nonlinear problem of great complexity with many variables which can be organized by recognizing certain relatively simple properties of the system.

Notes

Various aspects of the work touched on in this paper were carried out during a period of about 35 years. It is natural that much of it was done in collaboration with many co-workers. I am indebted to a number of colleagues, to Ilya Progogine and the late Elliot W. Montroll, who played principal roles in the evolution of the research. In addition are other important colleagues and friends: Siamak Ardekani, University of Texas at Arlington, Man-Feng Chang and Leonard Evans, General Motors Research Laboratories, the late Leslie C. Edie, formerly of the Port of New York and New Jersey Authority, Denos C. Gazis, IBM, Tenny Lam, University of Hong Kong, Renfrey B. Potts, University of Adelaide, and Richard Rothery, University of Texas at Austin, with all of whom it has been a great pleasure to be associated. The complete text of my talk presented at the Austin Conference, which gives important mathematical details necessarily deleted here, has been published in Herman (1991).

Bibliography

Ardekani, Siamak, and R. Herman, 1985, "A Comparison of the Quality of Traffic Service in Downtown Networks of Various Cities Around the World," *Traffic Engineering and Control*, 26, 574.

Ardekani, Siamak, and R. Herman, 1987, "Urban Network-Wide Traffic Variables and Their Relations," *Transportation Science*, 21, 1.

Chandler, R.E., R. Herman, and E.W. Montroll, 1958, "Traffic Dynamics: Studies in Car Following," *Operations Research*, 6, 165.

Chang, Man-Feng, and R. Herman, 1978, An Attempt to Characterize Traffic in Metropolitan Areas," *Transportation Science*, 12, 58.

Chang, Man-Feng, and R. Herman, 1981, "Trip Time Versus Stop Time and Fuel Consumption Characteristics in Cities," *Transportation Science*, 15, 183.

Edie, Leslie C., R. Herman, and T.N. Lam, 1980, "Observed Multilane Speed Distribution and the Kinetic Theory of Vehicular Traffic," *Transportation Science*, 14, 55.

Gazis, Denos C., R. Herman, and R.B. Potts, 1959, "Car Following Theory of Steady State Traffic Flow," *Operations Research*, 7, 499.

Gazis, Denos C., R. Herman, and R.W. Rothery, 1961, "Nonlinear Follow-the-Leader Models of Traffic Flow," *Operations Research*, 9, 545.

Herman, Robert, 1966, "Theoretical Research and Experimental Studies in Vehicular Traffic," *Proceedings of the Third Conference of the Australian Road Research Board*, 3, 25.

Herman, Robert, 1982, "Remarks on Traffic Flow Theories and the Characterization of Traffic in Cities," in W.C. Schieve and P.M. Allen (eds.), *Self Organization and Dissipative Structures*, University of Texas Press, Austin, 260.

Herman, Robert, 1991, "Traffic Dynamics Through Human Interaction: Reflections on Some Complex Problems," *Journal of Economic Behavior and Organization*, 15, 303–311.

Herman, Robert, and S. Ardekani, 1984, "Characterizing Traffic Conditions in Urban Areas," *Transportation Science*, 18, 101.

Herman, Robert, and I. Prigogine, 1979, "A Two-Fluid Approach to Town Traffic," *Science*, 204, 148.

Herman, Robert, E.W.Montroll, R.B. Potts, and R.W. Rothery, 1959, "Traffic Dynamics: Analysis of Stability in Car Following," *Operations Research*, 7, 86.

Prigogine, Ilya, and Robert Herman, 1971, *Kinetic Theory of Vehicular Traffic*, American Elsevier, New York.

III

ADAPTATION, LEARNING, AND SELF-ORGANIZATION

This section contains five studies concerning various aspects of adaptation, learning, and self-organization in evolving economic processes. In Chapter 7 Ulrich Witt, an economist, explores the implication of novelty, which is an essential aspect of innovation and technological diffusion, explaining the fundamental limit it imposes on the use of difference and differential equations. In Chapter 8 Peter Allen, a physicist by training, summarizes his work on dynamic models that incorporates individual deviations or perturbations to average behavior in a population of interacting agents. The perturbations create diversity, which results in an "evolutionary drive" to learn. He illustrates this with a review of his work on spatial economic development and on the economics of fisheries.

In Chapter 9 John Conlisk, an economist, describes a model with a population of innovators and imitators. Innovators must invest in superior knowledge, planning, research and development, and so on, and obtain a reduction in their production costs as a result. Imitators save on the investment in innovation but can adopt improved practices only with a lag. The model generates a mix between the two groups. If innovation costs are substantial, then both types coexist in the long run.

In Chapter 10 Boyd and Richardson, who are ecologist/anthropologists, introduce tradition into economic theory by assuming that prior beliefs are initially obtained by imitating role models in the family, community, occupation, etc. They then assume that further decision making updates these prior beliefs in the usual Bayesian way. They show in a manner somewhat analogous to Conlisk that the population will generate a mix of individuals who optimize and individuals who imitate, thus establishing and maintaining tradition.

In Chapter 11 Jacques Lesourne presents three models in which organizations form or restructure in an adaptive response to the unfolding interactions of their participants' behaviors. One model mimics the endogenous formation of a worker's union within a labor market. The second model generates the evolution of a labor market when individuals can acquire higher levels of competence. The third model considers a labor market with populations of workers and firms whose spatial distributions evolve.

7

Emergence and Dissemination of Innovations: Some Principles of Evolutionary Economics

ULRICH WITT

The Basic Concepts

Although there is a large variety of contributions now to what has come to be labeled evolutionary economics little agreement has been achieved as to what the basic features of this approach are. The present chapter therefore proposes some basic standards by generalizing what might be considered the methodological and epistemological key concepts of any evolutionary theory. Out of the vast number of definitions of evolution a very simple one will be chosen to start with: *evolution can be defined as the self-transformation over time of a system under investigation.* The system may be the gene pool of a population as in biology, a collection of interacting individuals as in an economy or some of its parts (Nelson and Winter, 1982; Day, 1987; Allen, 1988), or even the set of ideas produced by human mind (Popper, 1987). Theories on evolution as defined above have to satisfy some general standards in order to be able to explain self-transformation over time. They must

1. be dynamical,
2. deal with nonconservative systems, i.e., irreversible processes,
3. cover the generation and the impact of novelty as the ultimate source of self-transformation.

Criterion (1) is certainly not controversial. It rules out any kind of static analysis. Criterion (2) rules out all dynamical theories that describe stationary states, closed orbits, or equilibrium movements. What still remains are dynamical theories that focus on all kinds of transient behavior: convergence, divergence, or irregular patterns, e.g., chaotic movements. However, as conditions (1) and (2) together are necessary but not sufficient, what is furnished by the latter nonstationary, dynamical theories — although sometimes labeled "evolutionary" — is not yet a complete explanation for evolution. For this to be achieved the role of novelty has to be clarified, hence criterion (3). Unfortunately, novelty is an amorphous concept. By definition, the informational content, the meaning and the properties of what newly emerges, cannot be anticipated. It is therefore sometimes thought that theoretical constraints cannot be imposed on the infinite realm of possible novelty, which thus implies that novelty must be treated as exogenous. Yet, this view is unnecessarily restrictive.

It is true that theory cannot positively anticipate the results of evolution. On the other hand, hypotheses can always be developed that *exclude* certain kinds of novelty from occurring. This implies empirically meaningful, testable predictions even though they may be rather weak ones.[1] Theoretical considerations of the latter kind will be called here *prerevelation* analysis. As criterion (3) also demands an inquiry into the effects of novelty on a given system under the assumption that no further novelty intervenes, a similarly important domain of evolutionary theory is *postrevelation* analysis. As will become apparent in the next sections, this domain is already better understood and includes, as special case, most of the traditional economic adjustment models.

Let us now relate the notions of novelty and innovation to one another and define: *innovation is an action that has not been carried out earlier*, i.e., *involving novelty*. The role assigned to novelty here contrasts with conventional Schumpeterian views. Schumpeter (1934) considered the carrying out of ideas already around for a while and commonly known but not yet tried as innovation. He confined the emergence of novelty to the realm of invention which he clearly distinguished from innovation and deemed irrelevant for economics. However, his distinction is counterfactual. All experience shows that novelty is continually discovered in all phases of the trial and error process reaching from invention to the carrying out of innovative action. For this reason, a vast number of recent models of "innovation races" (Reinganum, 1985; Baldwin and Scott, 1987), which follow Schumpeter in his distinction rest on shaky foundations. To be able to apply the optimization algorithm they presuppose systematic knowledge on the part of the decision makers concerning the properties of innovations — knowledge which simply does not exist in the prerevelation context.

Despite their rather trivial nature the methodological implications of the nonanticipatability condition are sometimes violated. For instance, stage theories of evolution, historical determinism, and extrapolation of innovative trends obviously do presuppose positive anticipation of future novelty. The common verdict that evolution increases the complexity of the affected system is another case in point. A problem is also the use of differential and difference equations in evolutionary theories. Where the solutions are irregular and nonanticipatable an interesting homomorphism to the problem of novelty revelation may be encountered (Witt, 1992, Chapter 1). Unfortunately, mathematics has as yet little to say on these cases. Where, by contrast, the solutions are uniquely determined by the specification of the functions and the initial conditions and known, these equations are of little use for evolutionary theory. They can only be applied at the postrevelation level, since otherwise they would clearly interfere with the nonanticipatability condition. It is no accident that these latter forms of differential equations have originally been developed for applications in astronomy, i.e., for analyzing physical systems not subject to the emergence of novelty and, hence, to evolution.

Emergence of Innovations — Prerevelation Analysis

Prerevelation analysis can help to understand how novelty is generated, what novelty arguably can*not* be expected to emerge, and when innovations are more and when less likely to occur. Let us take up the three aspects in turn. In biology, the question of how new genetic information — mutation — comes about has received considerable attention. The basic mechanism seems to be understood well as a random recombination "error" in copying genetic material in the process of reproduction (Eigen, 1973). In the realm of deliberate human behavior, where novelty takes the form of new mental constructs, the creation of these constructs may also be considered as a recombination. More basic cognitive configurations stored in the memory are recombined, possibly compounded by incoming perceptions, so that they merge into a new pattern or *gestalt* (Barnett, 1953; see also Day, 1987). It seems quite likely that these processes represent phase transition as they are well known from nonlinear phenomena in various other fields (Prigogine, 1976; Andersson, 1987; Weidlich, 1991).

The recombination model of imaginative thinking allows some restrictions to be imposed on the realm of possible novelty. What newly emerges in a recombinatorial *gestalt*-switch must be constrained by the information base on which it builds: on the one hand the "tacit knowledge" (Polanyi, 1967) the individual has come to accumulate in the past and, on the other hand, the current information to which the agent's environment draws her/his attention. New ideas that are entirely unrelated to earlier interpretations and problems are unlikely to occur, although it may often be difficult to reconstruct the existing relationships.

The role of tacit knowledge, of the knowledge base, of technological paradigms, etc. has also been emphasized in the research on technological innovations (Sahal, 1981; Freeman, 1982; Chapter 4.2; Dosi, 1988). It has been argued that a "technological trajectory" can be deduced with regard to the further impact of innovations on technological development. Such a view is obviously difficult to reconcile with the epistemological position taken in the previous section. At best, predictions like these can be derived from a selection hypothesis (which belongs to the postrevelation analysis to be discussed below) according to which no newly detected possibility of action is considered relevant unless it solves a given problem. What actually emerges will grow out of the current context, but it cannot be theoretically constrained to take some particular path. The outcome may, for instance, be the discovery of a more general problem that renders the original one obsolete without really solving it. Furthermore, if the distinction between relevant and irrelevant novelty is made by the researcher rather than the innovative individual spillover effects may arbitrarily be ignored and the true breadth of the innovative process underrated.

In any case it is worth noting that the mere possibility of new mental constructs being created challenges the deep-rooted practice in economics of representing the individual agent by a given, closed set of alternatives among which the best choice, or, in a dynamical setting, the optimal adjustment has to be made. The "everything given" interpretation excludes from the theory of economic behavior the dimension in which the individual uses his imaginative power to create possibilities of action that have not been there before. Notice that this is a more basic conceptual problem than the one of uncertainty which may be accounted for by introducing (subjective) probabilities.[2]

The Question of When Innovations Are Likely to Occur

The human brain seems to spontaneously produce recombinations of mental constructs more or less continually. Of course, not all of these are related to action knowledge and even those which are, are not necessarily considered of interest for actual decisions. Two different aspects are involved here: relevance and reliability of new ideas. (In many cases new mental constructs emerging from brain activity may simply be of no relevance to economic behavior.) Where new information is not spontaneously provided the agent may deliberately search for relevant new action knowledge. When will this happen? Furthermore, if apparently relevant but still only vaguely understood new ideas have been generated, the individual may want to invest time and effort to inquire into their preconditions and consequences. When will this be done?

The answers to these questions require explaining the motivation for search for as yet substantially unknown action possibilities. The optimization model can be considered an acceptable approximation only as far as the experience of new action knowledge and novelty is the immediate purpose of the activity and as long as it is something positively valued in itself, i.e., as long as there is a preference for doing something new. Phenomena such as curiosity and excitement gained from previously unexperienced stimuli (Scitovsky, 1976) may indeed explain one — permanent — source of motivation. However, where search for new possibilities of action is instrumental and of little or no intrinsic value, the optimization hypothesis is of little help. This is because it presupposes a positive knowledge of the consequences of the alternative actions among which to choose — something not available as far as novelty is concerned.

The motivation to search for action knowledge can be explained by the satisficing model suggested by Simon (1955) and March and Simon (1958). The major components of the model are the following three theses. First, as long as the outcome of the best *known* alternative of action does not satisfy the current aspiration level of the individual, the search for not yet known, better alternatives and the testing of their consequences, goes on. Second, the greater the discrepancy between aspiration level and status quo, i.e., the best known alternative, the more intensive is the search effort. Third, a favorable search outcome tends to increase the aspiration level — hence it does not necessarily eliminate the motivation for further search — while persistent failure to find satisficing solutions curbs the aspiration level and the motivation to search.

Consider, for example, an agent who, due to some exogenous influences, is confronted with a deterioration of her/his choice set. The previously chosen alternative is no longer feasible. The agent suffers a significant decline in the individual utility level, if he/she adapts to the best remaining alternative. In such a situation it is straightforward to identify the previous achieved utility level with the current aspiration level. The dissatisfaction from not attaining the aspiration level (frustration, anger-notions that have no role to play in the neoclassical world) creates, according to the first thesis, the motivation to search for extensions of the choice set.

Indeed, a vast number of historical examples, including natural disasters, resource depletion, petering out of prevailing techniques, economic or political deprivation, can be given which create "problem pressure" and search motivation in the form just described (Hagen, 1964). Following the second thesis, the deviation of the aspiration level from the actual level can be taken as a monotonic measure of the motivation to search for novelty. Since the aspiration level is *assumed* to be adaptive over time — the third thesis — the agent's search effort will, depending on what results are achieved in search, either fade away over time and the deterioration will definitely be accepted or a new, satisficing possibility of action will be found and chosen.

The discussion so far suggests the following personality factors as fostering innovativeness: creativity, imagination (two factor that accounts for a large part of the interindividual variance of inventiveness), and perseverance (indicating a rather slow downward adjustment of the individual aspiration level). Other personality factors that have been identified in the literature as contributing to innovativeness are self-control, diligence, and achievement motivation (Schumpeter, 1934; also Gilad, 1986 for an extensive listing).

Environmental factors also play a role with regard for both the how and when of emerging novelty. For instance, environmental conditions may be decisive in placing the people with the right personality at the right place and ensuring that their creative skills are fully utilized — an intricate problem in the attempt to design a "creative organization" (Steiner, 1965). Furthermore, the formation of specialized R&D staff can be seen as an investment toward building up a knowledge base and a coherent search tradition that increases the likelihood of creative recombinations. As far as the exploitation of innovations systematically creates competitive advantages, this kind of investment may be particularly attractive to large corporations that can also try to realize economies of scale in the commercialization of new knowledge (Rosenberg, 1985).

Different sorts of environmental factors that may "channel innovativeness" are institutions, rules, and the responses to innovativeness by other individuals (Witt, 1987). A generally hostile response of the individual's environment — reflecting a corresponding rule or institutions grossly threatening innovative behavior — discourages search for novelty. Facing such a response whatever novelty an agent comes up with is a prospect likely to curb the motivation to search for novelty. On the other hand, a conducive environmental response to innovative behavior may have the opposite effect, i.e., increase search motivation.

Indeed, in many stationary, traditional societies innovativeness is heavily negatively sanctioned in productive activities and social interactions while it is tolerated or even encouraged in others, e.g., the arts, play, or warfare. In modern, liberal societies innovativeness in the economy is by and large appreciated and can thus be expected to soar. More frequent innovative activity raises competitive pressure, which, in turn, may induce even more search — those agents affected by tighter competition may suffer a decline so that their aspiration levels are no longer satisfied. This potentially self-reinforcing tendency again points to a kind of bifurcation phenomenon implied by the alternative environmental attitudes toward innovative behavior.

Dissemination of Innovations — Aspect of Postrevelation Analysis

Once the informational content of novelty has been revealed the effects it has throughout the economy can be explored in ways that come closer to conventional economic analysis. Two questions seem of particular importance. First, how do individuals respond when being exposed to novelty — when is the newly offered action possibility likely to be adopted; second, what kind of interactive dynamics underlie sequences of adoptions — diffusion processes — and what are the effects on the coordination of economic activities?[3] Not much progress has been made so far in answering these question. Many empirical studies have investigated the diffusion of innovations (Griliches, 1957; Rogers, 1983; Dosi, 1988), yet, hardly any robust and coherent empirical regularities have been found. The only exception seems to be the prevalence of frequency-dependency effects, i.e., an already familiar pattern from nonlinear dynamics.

Different from the situation of an agent discovering a possibility of action never tried by someone before, which was discussed in the previous section, potential later adopters face a comparatively better structured decision problem. Observation of the pioneering innovation provides a "social model" (Bandura, 1977) that can be imitated. The more precedents, the more information becomes available that can be used for assessing the consequences of adopting a new possibility of action. Thus, in postrevelation analysis the preconditions for "optimal" decision making seem more likely to be met. At the same time the increasing adoption frequency may, as a matter of conformity or of competition, turn into a subjectively felt adoption pressure so that relative adoption frequency itself may become an important environmental

factors. It is not difficult to imagine the modeling steps to be taken in order to de-
duce the empirically often observed logistic diffusion curve from the systematically
changing frequency-dependency effect (see Witt, 1989). Furthermore, the influence
of standardization problems, network externalities, technological "lock in" (David,
1987; Arthur, 1988) on diffusion paths fits perfectly here — these are all special
forms of a frequency-dependent decision making.

The preconditions for optimal decision making emerging, the sequences of
adoption decisions can be paraphrased as being governed by "the pursuit of self-
interest" in the sense of the classics. As is well known, Adam Smith and the Scot-
tish moral philosophers suggested that the pursuit of self-interest in the market does
not prevent an outcome that is to the mutual benefit of the involved parties (Hayek,
1967b). It may now be asked whether, and if so how, the classics' view of market
coordination is to be modified when innovative activities occur. In the case of simple trade, from which the mutual benefit conjecture started, the argument relies on
the prerequisites of the market: property explaining the motivation, freedom of trade
and competition explaining the mutually imposed constraints. If some of these prerequisites are systematically attenuated in the case of innovations, then it may be
doubted whether the conjecture still applies.

Indeed, there seem to be two different sources of attenuation: those induced by
innovations and those created by attempts to constrain innovativeness as has often
been historically observed. With respect to the former the Schumpeterian hypothesis (Nelson and Winter, 1982, Part V for its various aspects) associates innovative
activities with the power and/or the motive to restrain competition. While this hypothesis is hard to evaluate empirically, it can perhaps generally be agreed on that the
process of creative destruction, however imperfect with respect to competition, has
after all improved the "standard of living of the masses" (Schumpeter, 1942, Chapter
7). This, at least, does not contradict the mutual benefit conjecture. In fact, the evolutionary perspective tends to emphasize the potentially welfare increasing effects of
competition by innovation (Hayek, 1978; Buchanan and Vanberg, 1990).

Why then the attempts to constrain competition by innovation as they can be
observed in the history of many societies? Since individually advantageous new
action knowledge may be harmful to some or even many members of the polity there
may be an incentive to organize collective action in order to restrain other agents
from pursuing innovations. As has been discussed elsewhere this has been attempted
by aggressive behavior, threat, moral proscriptions, or even legal measures (Witt,
1987). The point here is that the success of these measures once more depends on a
frequency effect, i.e., a typical nonlinear feature of potential dynamical transitions as
it has already been identified several times above. In this case it is a critical relative
share of supporters which the enforcement of the measures requires that may or may
not come about (or, looked the other way round may break down). It can easily be
imagined that the consequence of measures that curb innovativeness, if successful, is
a much slower pace of economic evolution. The society runs the danger of becoming
"locked in" in a relatively unproductive form of coordination by socially controlled

customs and traditions (see also Day, 1992). One of the challenging tasks for an evolutionary theory in economics is to improve our understanding of the historical transition from these apparently stationary conditions in the past to the presumably self-reinforcing high pace of technological and institutional development of modern societies.

Notes

The ideas in this paper have been developed over the years in many discussions. I wish to thank in particular H. Albert, R. Day, M. Faber, F.A. Hayek, and E. Hoppmann who may not be aware of the impact they have had and who certainly are not responsible for any shortcomings. Financial support by the Deutsche Forschungsgemeinschaft is gratefully acknowledged.

1. This has been pointed out by Hayek (1967a) in generalizing common practice in the neo-Darwinian, synthetic evolutionary theory in biology. Neo-Darwinian theory does not predict the properties of future mutations. But it excludes imaginable mutations such as dogs eventually being given birth to which lack a forepaw after the forepaw of several parent generations has been amputated — a drastic example of what would be a Lamarckian transmission of hereditary traits. In economics conditions may be more complicated. The perpetuation and transmission of learned behavior, where new action knowledge can conceivably enter, clearly display Lamarckian features so that the possible sources of novelty multiply.

2. It is not the uncertain influences to which the agent's choice are subject that matter here, but the fact that the creative power of the individual may endogenously change the choice set as well as the state space, as it is subjectively perceived. This is precisely the argument which Shackle (1958, p. 102, 1983) and other subjectivists, notably the Austrian school of economic thought, have forwarded as a long-standing criticism against traditional choice theory.

3. In evolutionary economics a reinterpretation of these problems using the Darwinian concepts variation, selection, and replication is sometimes attempted, e.g., in Matthews (1984). It should be noted, however, that selection in the realm of human innovations seems to follow a different and apparently more complex logic than in the genetic sphere. Inclusive genetic fitness is a clear-cut, globally valid concept of neo-Darwinian theory which produces a uniform explanatory pattern for highly diverse empirical phenomena in biology. A comparable concept governing selection within the human economic sphere could not be found; see Winter (1964).

Bibliography

Allen, P.M., 1988, "Evolution, Innovations and Economics," in G. Dosi, C. Freeman, R. Nelson, G. Silverberg, and L. Soete (eds.), *Technical Change and Economic Theory*, Pinter, London, 95–119.

Andersson, A.E., 1987, "Creativity and Economic Dynamics Modelling," in D. Batten, J. Casti, and B. Johansson (eds.), *Economic Evolution and Structural Adjustment*, Springer, Berlin, 27–45.

Arthur, W.B., 1988, "Competing Technologies: An Overview," in C. Freeman, R. Nelson, G. Silverberg, and L. Soete (eds.), *Technical Change and Economic Theory*, Pinter, London, 590–607.

Baldwin, W.L., and Scott, J.T., 1987, *Market Structure and Technological Change*, Harwood, New York.

Bandura, A., 1979, *Social Learning Theory*, Prentice Hall, Englewood Cliffs, NJ.

Barnett, H.G., 1953, *Innovation: The Basis of Cultural Change*, Alfred Knopf, New York.

Buchanan, J.M., and Vanberg, V.J., 1990, "The Market as a Creative Process," mineo. Center for the Study of Public Choice, George Mason University, Fairfax, VA.

David, P., 1987, "Some New Standards for the Economics of Standardization in the Information Age," in P. Dasgupta, and P.L. Stoneman (eds.), *Economic Policy and Technological Performance*, Cambridge University Press, Cambridge, 206–239.

Day, R.H., 1987, "The Evolving Economy," *European Journal of Operations Research*, 30, 251–257.

Day, R.H., 1992, "Bounded Rationality and the Coevolution of Market and State, " in R. Day, G. Eliasson, and C. Wihlborg (eds.), *The Market for Innovation, Ownership and Control*, North-Holland, Amsterdam.

Dosi, G., 1988, "Sources, Procedures, and Microeconomic Effects of Innovation," *Journal of Economic Literature*, 26, 1120–1171.

Eigen, M., 1973, "The Origin of Biological Information," in J. Mehra (ed.), *The Physicist's Conception of Nature*, Reidel, Dodrecht, 594–632.

Freeman, C., 1982, *The Economics of Industrial Innovation*, 2nd ed., Pinter, London.

Gilad, B., 1986, "Entrepreneurial Decision-Making: Some Behavioral Considerations," in B. Gilad, and S. Kaish (eds.), *Handbook of Behavioral Economics*, Vol. A, JAI Press, Inc., 189–208.

Griliches, Z., 1957, "Hybrid Corn: An Exploration in the Economics of Technological Change," *Econometrica*, 25, 501–522.

Hagen, E.E., 1964, *On the Theory of Social Change: How Economic Growth Begins*, Tavistock, London.

Hayek, F.A., 1967a, "The Theory of Complex Phenomena," in F.A. Hayek, *Studies in Philosophy, Politics, and Economics*, Routledge & Kegan Paul, London, 22–42.

Hayek, F.A., 1967b, "Dr. Bernard Mandeville," *Proceedings of the British Academy*, Vol. 52, Oxford University Press, London.

Hayek, F.A., 1978, "Competition as a Discovery Procedure," in F.A. Hayek, *New Studies in Philosophy, Politics, Economics, and the History of Ideas*, Chicago University Press, Chicago, 179–190.

March, J.G., and H.A. Simon, 1958, *Organizations*, John Wiley, New York.

Matthews, R.C.O., 1984, "Darwinism and Economic Change," in D.A. Collard, D.R. Helm, M.F.G. Scott, and A.K. Sen (eds.), *Economic Theory and Hicksian Themes*, Clarendon Press, Oxford, 91–117.

Nelson, R.R., and S.G. Winter, 1982, *An Evolutionary Theory of Economic Change*, Harvard University Press, Cambridge, MA.

Popper, K., 1987, "Natural Selection and the Emergence of Mind," in G. Radnitzky, and W.W. Bartley, III (eds.), *Evolutionary Epistemology, Rationality and the Sociology of Knowledge*, Open Court, La Salle, IL, 139–155.

Polanyi, M., 1967, *The Tacit Dimension*, Doubleday, Garden City, NY.

Prigogine, I., 1976, "Order Through Fluctuations: Self-Organization and Social System," in E. Jantsch and C.H. Waddington (eds.), *Evolution and Consciousness: Human Systems in Transition*, Addison-Wesley, London, 93–133.

Reinganum, J.F., 1985, "Innovation and Industry Evolution," *Quarterly Journal of Economics*, 50, 81–99.

Rogers, E.M., 1983, *Diffusion of Innovations*, 3rd ed., Free Press, New York.

Rosenberg, N., 1985, "The Commercial Exploitation of Science by American Industry," in K.B. Clark, R.H. Hayes, and C. Lorenz (eds.), *The Uneasy Alliance*, Harvard Business School Press, Cambridge, MA.

Sahal, D., 1981, *Patterns of Technological Innovation*, Addison, New York.

Schumpeter, J.A., 1934, *The Theory of Economic Development*, Harvard University Press, Cambridge, MA.

Schumpeter, J.A., 1942, *Capitalism, Socialism and Democracy*, Harper, New York.

Scitovsky, T., 1976, *The Joyless Economy*, Oxford University Press, Oxford.

Shackle, G.L.S., 1958, *Time in Economics*, North-Holland, Amsterdam.

Shackle, G.L.S., 1983, "The Bounds of Unknowledge," in J. Wiseman (ed.), *Beyond Positive Economics?* Macmillan, London, 28–37.

Simon, H.A., 1955, "A Behavioral Model of Rational Choice," *Quarterly Journal of Economics*, 69, 99–118.

Steiner, G.A., ed., 1965, *The Creative Organization*, Chicago University Press, Chicago.

Weidlich, W., 1991, "Physics and Social Science — The Approach of Synergetics," *Physics Reports*, 204, 1–163.

Winter, S.G., 1964, "Economic 'Natural Selection' and the Theory of the Firm," *Yale Economic Essays*, 4, 225–272.

Witt, U., 1987, "How Transaction Rights Are Shaped to Channel Innovativeness," *Journal of Institutional and Theoretical Economics*, 143, 180–195.

Witt, U., 1989, "The Evolution of Economic Institutions as a Propagation Process," *Public Choice*, 62, 155–172.

Witt, U., 1992, *Individualistic Foundations of Evolutionary Economics*, Cambridge University Press, Cambridge.

8

Evolution: Persistent Ignorance from Continual Learning

PETER M. ALLEN

The basis of scientific understanding has been the mechanical model based on the action of causal links between the components. By classifying these components into categories, and by supposing that mechanisms of interaction may be treated on average, a set of deterministic equations can be obtained which govern system behavior. However judicious the choice of variables, parameters, and interaction mechanisms, these only concern *average* behavior. Underneath the "model" or "reduced description" there will always be the greater particularity and diversity of reality. But real systems evolve, that is they add and subtract mechanisms, components, and interactions over time, whereas the deterministic model does not. Evolutionary change therefore must result from what has been "removed" in the reduction to the average description from the complete system. Determinism has been bought at the expense of structural change.

In a series of recent studies (Allen and McGlade, 1987a, 1989) it has been shown that when nonaverage perturbations are reintroduced, there is an "evolutionary drive" that selects for populations with the *ability to learn*, rather than for populations with *optimal behavior*. This corresponds to the selection of "diversity creating" mechanisms in the behavior of populations. In human systems decisions reflect the different expectations of individuals, and it is the interaction (competitive and cooperative) of these that actually creates the future. When the expectations of actors are not fulfilled they may modify either their values or their understanding of the world, or, alternatively simply remain perplexed. Evolution in human systems is therefore a continual, imperfect learning process, spurred by the difference between expectation and experience, but rarely providing enough information for a complete understanding.

In the models that I have developed, the evolutionary pathway of the system that actually occurs will depend on the accidents of history and on the contextual and nonaverage details. The future of any such system will be due to two kinds of terms: changes brought about by the deterministic action of the typical behavior of its average components, and structural qualitative changes brought about by the presence of *nonaverage* components and conditions within the system. We find a dialogue between the "average dynamics" of the chosen description (a process that results in what we may call selection) and the exploratory, unpredictable "nonaverage" perturbations around this that results from the inevitable occurrence of nonaverage events and components (a search or exploration process that generates information about other behaviors).

Spatial Evolution of Urban Systems

As has been pointed out in the preceding chapters, ideas of nonlinearity and evolution have a long history in economics. Progress in synthesizing dynamics and economic theory has greatly accelerated in recent years. During this exploratory phase in economics, the theory of dissipative structures in physics and chemistry was being developed by Prigogine and the Brussels School (Nicolis and Prigogine, 1977; Prigogine and Stengers, 1987). Already in 1976 I began to use this approach to understand change in human systems. Initially, the models concerned most directly the question of the evolution of spatial economic structure. They demonstrated the key ideas of the discussion today: the existence of multiple paths into the future, the role of historical accident, and the importance of dealing with a system in disequilibrium.

A nonlinear dynamic system of equations expressing the supply and demand of different products was made to evolve by the random occurrence of entrepreneurs at different points and times in the system (Allen and Sanglier, 1978, 1979). The supply side was characterized by a nonconvex production function for different economic activities, and consumer demand was assumed to reflect relative prices. The "random parachuting of entrepreneurs onto the plain of potential demand" resulted in the gradual emergence of a stable market structure and pattern of settlement.

Just as in the well known case of "technological lock-in" (Arthur, 1983) here too we found that the system could get itself locked into a somewhat unsatisfactory market structure, as a result of a particular history. Basically, a very large number of possible stable structures could result from the experiment, involving different numbers of centers in different locations, and necessarily not offering the same level of efficiency.

Even in this very preliminary form the models already showed many important principles: many final states are possible, precise prediction in the early stages is impossible, approximate rules appear (centre separations etc.) but always with considerable deviation and local individuality present. The results are affected by the particularities of the transportation system, as well as by information flows affecting the mental maps of consumers. Also, the evolution of structure as a result of changing technology, transportation, resource availability etc. can be explored, as the changing patterns of demand and supply affect each other in a complex dynamic spatial process.

The fundamental basis for the models is the decisions of the different types of individual actors considered, which reflect their values and functional requirements. These are represented by very simple rules. However, the spatial dynamics gives rise to very complex patterns of structure and flow, and to a structural emergence and evolution at the collective level. In such systems the microscopic and macroscopic levels are not related in a simple fashion. It is not true that the large structure is simply the small writ large. This is because macroscopic structure emerges, and this affects the circumstances of the microscopic parts, as they find themselves playing a "role" in a larger, collective entity. Each actor is *coevolving* with the others.

These models have been continuously developed from these early simulations in order to provide realistic tools for understanding regional and urban evolution, in which the patterns of structure and flows are the result of an on-going evolutionary process of self-organization (Allen and Sanglier, 1981; Allen, 1988; Sanglier and Allen, 1989).

Evolution in Natural Resource Systems

I have also used this approach to develop dynamic models for the management of natural resources. In particular the simulation of fishing activities proved to be extremely fruitful (Allen and McGlade, 1986) because it illustrates all the essential aspects of the evolutionary problem in a strikingly simple way. This work has been discussed elsewhere in detail, but it is worth summarizing briefly some of the main conclusions.

The essential point that emerged was that success in fishing, as in life, requires two almost contradictory facets of behavior. First, the ability to organize one's behavior so as to exploit the information available concerning "net benefits" (to be rational), which we have called "Cartesian" behavior. More surprisingly, however, a second ability is required, that is to be able to ignore present information and to "explore" beyond present knowledge. We have called these kinds of fishermen "Stochasts." The first makes good use of information, but the second generates it! At the root of creativity is always this second type.

In the short term it is always true that the more "rational" actor must outperform the less, and therefore that for example taking steps to *maximize present profits* must, by that yardstick, be better than not doing so. Nevertheless, over a longer period the best performance will not come from the most rational but instead from behavior that is some complex compromise. For example, a fleet of Cartesians that goes where available information indicates highest profits will in fact lock into zones for much too long, remaining in ignorance of the existence of other, more profitable zones simply because there is *no information available* concerning other zones: "You don't know what it is you don't know."

New information can come only from boats that have "chosen" not to fish in the "best" zones, or that do not share the consensus values, technology, or behavior, and hence that generate information. They behave like risk takers, but may or may not see themselves as such. They may act as they do through ignorance, or through a belief in some myth or legend. Whatever the reason, or lack of it, they are *vital* to the success of the fishing endeavor as a whole. It is their exploration that probes the value of the existing pattern of fishing effort, and lays the foundations for a new one.

As information is generated concerning the existence of new, rich fishing grounds, so the value of this starts to fall as the news spreads, and exploitation rates increase there. We see a cyclic pattern in the discovery of value in a zone, the spread of information and with it the saturation or exhaustion of the discovery, calling for fresh explorations (Allen and McGlade, 1987b,c).

This approach can be inverted. Instead of supposing that we know, from observation, the parameters that characterize the fishing strategies of different fleets, we can use the model to *discover robust fishing strategies for us.*

To do this, we can run many fleets simultaneously (our current software will run up to 8) from identical initial conditions. The fleets differ, however, in the values of the parameters governing their fishing strategy, and whether or not they spy on, and copy some other fleets. Our model will reinforce the more effective strategies, and gradually eliminate the others, and by including a stochastic change in strategies for losing fleets, our model will gradually evolve sets of compatible behaviors. Each of these will be effective in the context of the others, not objectively optimal. In addition, such a system can adapt to changed external circumstances, and could be used to show us "robust heuristics" for the exploitation of renewable natural resource. This is clearly similar in aim to the work on "learning algorithms" (Holland, 1986; Miller, 1988).

The same approach is being used to explore the characteristics of successful behavior in financial and economic systems, and for exploratory development policies. The models provide an interdisciplinary integrating framework for considering the mutual interaction of the ecological, economic, social, and demographic aspects of any particular development policy, strategy, or project.

Evolutionary Drive

The learning process just described illustrates the concept of "evolutionary drive" developed in Allen and McGlade (1987a, 1989). It shows that evolution selects for populations with the *ability to learn*, rather than for populations with *optimal behavior*. This corresponds to the selection of "diversity creating" mechanisms in the behavior of populations, initially involving genetics, and later cognitive processes.

The model was based on a two-dimensional adaptive landscape illustrated in Figure 8.1 for the most simple population equation possible:

$$dx/dt = bx(1 - x/N) - mx$$

The landscape considered was one of some "characters" or "strategies" of the population that affected the values of b, the birth rate, and m, the mortality rate.

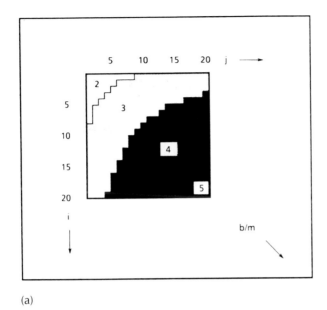

(a)

(b)

Figure 8.1 (a) The adaptive landscape of the logistic equation. (b) Errors in reproduction lead to offspring being produced in neighboring cells of character space.

Evolutionary progress corresponds to diagonal movement towards the lower right hand corner of Figure 8.1a, as both the birth rate and the longevity of the population x increase. But how does "progress" occur? Do populations "improve," and if so, how?

Into the dynamics of the logistic equation, we have introduced the possibility of *error making* in reproduction, where the parental character that corresponds to a particular value of b and m is not reproduced faithfully enough in an offspring, which therefore appears at a different point in the b/m landscape. In accordance with common sense, we have further supposed that random errors in reproduction of a complex organism give rise much more frequently to a lower performance than to a higher one.

The occurrence of errors over successive generations therefore results in an initially homogeneous population occupying a single cell in b/m space gradually spreading into a cloud of populations, mostly located lower on the hill than the initial position. However, the populations that are lower down reproduce slower and have a higher mortality rate than those higher up, and so gradually the cloud slides *up the hill* as the differential performance of the populations present leads to the apparent movement of the cloud up the hill. This influence of error is shown in Figure 8.2. We may look at this result and interpret it as being due to the forces of *selection*, but it is important to realize that there is no "intervention" from outside, deciding which types should be retained and which rejected. The system runs itself with a diffusive spread due to error making and a differential selection resulting from the dynamical equations.

The model was used to examine the most effective amount of error making for climbing a hill of a given slope, and also how easy or difficult it was to "invade" a system with a new population. However, the main point raised was that any particular population considered would always in fact be sitting within an ecosystem, with prey, predators, parasites, and competitors all using a similar mechanism of "search" and "differential reinforcement" to further their own success. Therefore, for any real population, b and m concern the relative performance of the population studied with respect to the others in the ecosystem — *who will also be evolving* — which means that instead of a hill that can be climbed, we have a "down escalator" on which "climbing" is necessary just to stay at the present level! This leads to a view very similar to the Red Queen Hypothesis of Van Valen (1973), but we have here quantitative models that can be used to examine it.

An important question that was considered concerned the manner in which evolution can itself adjust the degree of error making and variability that is leading to evolutionary change. By supposing that the fidelity of reproduction was an hereditary property that could itself be passed on imperfectly it was shown how the dynamics of such systems gave rise to an apparently "willful" reaction wherein a population increased its error making quite violently in order to climb an adaptive slope, and then increased its fidelity when it had succeeded. This is illustrated in Figure 8.3.

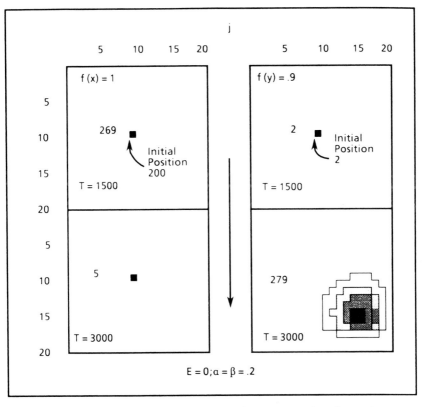

Figure 8.2 Evolution selects for imperfect reproduction even though at any moment it would always be better not to make errors.

This work has been further extended in some joint research together with M. Lesser (Allen and Lesser, 1989). First, a different dimension of evolution was explored by considering the effects of "error making" on a term of positive feedback that enhances the reproduction of a particular character or type. In other words, we examined what would happen if a character or strategy existed that would *increase the reproduction of that particular character or strategy.*

$$dx/dt = bx(1 + pf \cdot x)(1 - \text{tot pop}/n) - mx$$

If we consider an adaptive space of the b and pf, then for a population that is initially at the lowest point, depending on the relative slopes of the b and pf dimensions, the population evolves to a certain value of pf, and then is unable to move further. It is "locked in," being able neither to increase its own positive feedback nor to climb the slope of improved reproduction. The mechanism of self-reinforcement expressed by pf becomes so dominant that it outweighs the advantages in improved birthrate that deviants may detect.

We have called this phenomenon the Positive Feedback Trap.

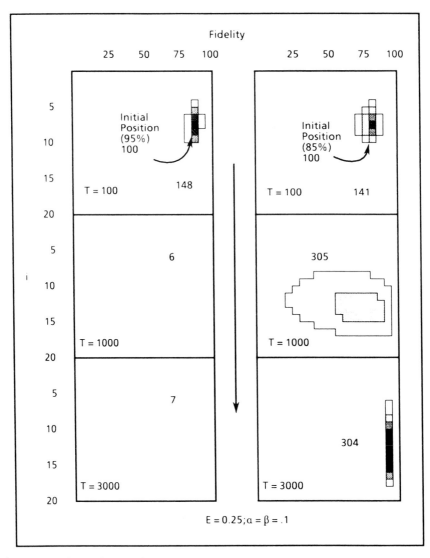

Figure 8.3 The evolution of two competing populations when the fidelity of reproduction is itself an hereditary property subject to errors and evolutionary adjustment.

It suggests that although in many dimensions evolution will lead to error making and adaptability enabling agents to adjust to their changing circumstances, some characteristic or strategy could exist involving mutual recognition and cooperativity for example, which would result in positive feedback enhancing this type and trapping it. An example of this from biology is the "Peacock's tail," where a gene produces the beautiful tail in the male, and makes such a tail attractive to the female. In sexual reproduction, anything that enhances the probability of mating produces a positive feedback on its own population dynamics, and fixes itself. However, it is at the expense of functionality with respect to the external environment that Peacock's tails are not an aid to finding its food better, or escaping predators, but only a characteristic marker of a positive feedback trap — the real origin of species.

In human systems, such positive feedback systems abound. Much of culture may well be behavior that is fixed in this way. Imitative processes, positive feedback mechanisms par excellence, cannot be eliminated by the evolutionary process, and so fashions, styles, and indeed cultures rise and decline without necessarily expressing any clear *functional advantages*. Indeed, "culture" can be viewed as being an expression of ignorance of other ways of doing things. Similarly, academic disciplines offer almost perfect examples of such autocatalytic, self-adulatory systems, where theorems and proofs are rewarded with prestige and medals, even though it is quite clear to outside observers that there is no contact with reality. So much of human preoccupation is with playing a role in such groups where values are generated internally, and the physical world outside is largely irrelevant. Evolutionary drive tells us that there is a tendency for the growth of "internal games" in any organization, and that these can even dominate over the external interactions.

In some further experiments the models of evolutionary change were extended to consider how ecologies evolve. In character space it seems reasonable to suppose that populations which are most alike are most in competition with each other, since they can feed of the same resources, and suffer from the same predators. From this, one may also suppose that there is some "distance" in character space, some level of dissimilarity, at which two populations do not compete with each other.

Such an idea can be expressed in a two-dimensional character space by modifying the competition term in the "logistic" bracket so that it expresses the decay of niche overlap with increasing separation in character space. Our equations now express simply the dynamics of populations that reproduce imperfectly in this two-dimensional character space, diffusing to nearest neighbors. We start a simulation with a single, well-defined population at the center of the surface.

Initially, this population grows until it reaches the limits set by the competition for underlying resources. At this point, there is a payoff for error makers, because of the negative feedback due to competition. We could say that although initially there was no "*hill*" to *climb*, the population effectively digs a valley for itself through growth, until there is a "hill" to climb on either side of the present character centroid. However, over some distance in this space the small numbers of error populations cannot multiply, because they are still in the "competitive shadow" of the original population, and so they diffuse in small numbers up the slope away from the original type.

After a certain time, however, small populations arise that are sufficiently different from the original type that they can grow and multiply on the basis of some other resource. In its turn, the population increases until it too is limited by internal competition for the limiting resource, and once again there is a payoff for deviants, particularly for those on the "outside" of the distribution, as they climb another self-made hill toward unpopulated regions of character space. In this way, well-defined

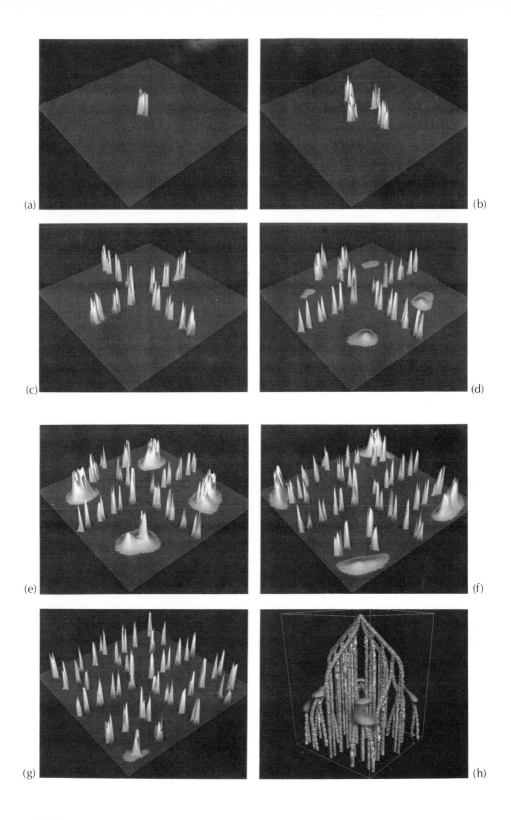

populations appear successively, and colonists diffuse out from each of them as they reach a competitive limit, gradually filling character space with a set of populations separated approximately by some distance which is characteristic of the resource diversity that can be tapped.

From a single population our model generates a simple ecology (as shown in Figure 8.4), and a dynamic one since the identity of each population is maintained by the balance between a continual diffusion of deviants outward into character space, and the differential reproduction and survival that are due to the presence of the other populations. Random events that occur during the "filling" process will affect that populations arise, and so it is not true that the evolution represents the *discovery of pre-existing "niches."*

Conclusions

Instead of viewing evolutionary dynamics as the progress of a population up a given (if complex) landscape, our models show how the landscape itself is produced by the interacting populations, and how the detailed history of the exploration process itself affects the outcome. Evolution is not just about populations solving optimization problems, but also about the optimization problems they *pose*. It is the emergence of self-consistent "sets" of populations, both posing and solving the problems and opportunities of their mutual existence that characterizes evolutionary dynamics.

In economics, this corresponds to the idea that production and demand functions are *not given independently of one another*. They emerge, and the chance details of the process of emergence alter what is finally "revealed." Supply affects demand, and vice versa, and what really occurs is that there are potentialities of positive and negative feedbacks — economies of scale, learning by doing, imitation, etc. are positive, while competition for market and for resources are negative.

Innovation occurs because of nonaverage individuals and initiatives, and whenever this leads to an exploration into an area where positive feedback outweighs negative, then growth will occur. We assign "value" afterward. It is only when we wish to *rationalize* about what we see that we insist that there was some preexisting demand which was revealed by the supply. Just as for biological evolution — in fact *there is no hill*. Hills and hill climbing are a rationalization of dynamic changes that have been observed, and this becomes clearer when we attempt to imagine what the vertical axis of such a hill could be? In some "product/service" space, if it means potential demand, then in fact there is no unique "hill" or "surface" before the "hill climbing" occurs? Once we admit even just the presence of imitative mechanisms, of fashion, then the potential demand for something is a *dynamic* variable which itself depends on the unfolding of events.

Figure 8.4 In a two-dimensional character space, incomplete information at the individual level creates a simple ecology of populations. The final picture shows the evolutionary tree generated endogenously by the process.

Ignorance of the future and differing opinions allow exploration to occur, and hence permit discoveries, or more accurately "creations" to occur. But, as this happens, the system is changed, and there is fresh uncertainty about the future. Ignorance permits learning, but learning creates new ignorance. This offers a much more realistic picture of the complex game that is being played in economic and financial systems, and one which our models can begin to quantify and explore.

Bibliography

Allen, Peter M., 1988, "Evolution: Why the Whole is Greater Than the Sum of Its Parts," in *Ecodynamics*, Springer-Verlag, Berlin.

Allen, Peter M., and M. Lesser, 1989, "Evolution: Cognition, Ignorance and Selection." Presented at International Symposium on Evolution and Cognitive Maps, Bologna, Italy, May 13–19, 1989. To be published in *The Evolution of Cognitive Maps: New Paradigms for the 21st Century*, Gordon and Breach, New York.

Allen, Peter M., and J.M. McGlade, 1986, "Dynamics of Discovery and Exploitation: the Scotian Shelf Fisheries," *Canadian Journal of Fishery and Aquatic Science*, 43 (6) 1187–1200.

Allen, Peter M. and J.M. McGlade, 1987a, "Evolutionary Drive: The Effect of Microscopic Diversity, Error Making and Noise," *Foundations of Physics*, 17 (7), July, 723–738.

Allen, Peter M., and J.M. McGlade, 1987b, "Modelling Complex Human Systems: a Fisheries Example," *European Journal of Operations Research*, 30, 147–167.

Allen, Peter M., and J.M. McGlade, 1987c, "Managing Complexity: a Fisheries Example," Report to the United Nations, University, Tokyo.

Allen, Peter M., and J.M. McGlade, 1989, "Optimality, Adequacy and the Evolution of Complexity," in P.L. Christiansen and R.D. Parmentier (eds.), *Structure, Coherence and Chaos in Dynamical Systems*, Manchester University Press, Manchester.

Allen, Peter M., and M. Sanglier, 1978, "Dynamic Models of Urban Growth," *Journal of Social and Biological Structures*, 1, 265–280.

Allen, Peter M., and M. Sanglier,1979, "Dynamic Model of Growth in a Central Place System," *Geographical Analysis*, 11 (3), 256–272.

Allen, Peter M., and M. Sanglier, 1981, "Urban Evolution, Self-Organization and Decision Making," *Environment and Planning* A, 167–183.

Arthur, Brian, 1983, "Competing Technologies and Lock-In by Historical Events: The Dynamics of Allocation Under Increasing Returns," IIASA Paper WP, 83–90, Laxenburg, Austria.

Holland, J., 1986, "Escaping Brittleness: The Possibilities of General Purpose Machine Learning Algorithms Applied to Parallel Rule Based Systems," in R.S. Michalski et al. (eds.), *Machine Learning: An Artificial Intelligence Approach*, Vol. 2, Kaufmann, Los Altos, CA.

Miller, J.H., 1988, "The Evolution of Automata in the Repeated Prisoner's Dilemma," Santa Fe Institute, Working Paper No. 89-003.

Nicolis, G., and I. Prigogine, 1977, *Self-Organization in Non-Equilibrium Systems*, Wiley Interscience, Chichester.

Prigogine, Ilya, and I. Stengers, 1987, *Order Out of Chaos*, Bantam Books, New York.

Sanglier, M., and P.M. Allen, 1989, "Evolutionary Models of Urban Systems: an Application to the Belgian Provinces," *Environment and Planning*, A, 21, 477–498.

Van Valen, L., 1973, "A New Evolutionary Law," *Evolutionary Theory*, 1, 1–30.

9

Adaptive Firms and Random Innovations in a Model of Cyclical Output Growth

JOHN CONLISK

The goal is a model of cyclical output growth driven by the randomly occurring innovations of individual firms. Each firm in each period is thought of as making and implementing a production plan. At random, a firm's plan may work well or poorly. A plan that works particularly well may become an innovation that is picked up by other firms and that serves as a basis for cumulating further innovations. There are two types of firms, "innovators" and "imitators." Innovator firms are technologically progressive, but pay an "innovation cost" for that advantage. Imitator firms are technological followers, but do not pay the innovation cost. The numbers of innovators and imitators evolve according to profit-based entry and exit rules.

The model generates the mix of innovator and imitator firms, the long run growth rate of the economy, the mix between deterministic trend and nonstationary drift in growth, and cyclic patterns of growth, including the possibility of Schumpeterian cycles. The relation between the innovator–imitator mix and the growth of the economy is important. For example, an increase in certain innovation parameters increases the growth rate of the model as a direct effect and increases the relative number of innovators as an indirect effect (since innovators absorb innovations faster than imitators and thus gain in fitness when innovation is faster). The increase in the relative number of innovators in turn reinforces the growth rate increase. As another example, an increase in the model's innovation cost parameter reduces the relative number of innovators as a direct effect and reduces the growth rate of the model as an indirect effect; again the effects reinforce each other.

Though firms in the model will hire labor according to simple marginal conditions, firm behavior is largely adaptive rather than optimizing. The entry and exit rules are relatively simple trigger rules; and imitator strategy regarding technical change is overtly adaptive. Innovators display greater apparent astuteness than imitators regarding technical change, but they have to pay a cost to do so. Bounded rationality is the premise underlying these specifications.

Bounds on human problem-solving ability mean that this ability is a scarce resource, suggesting that it be treated like other scarce resources—as available to agents only at a cost. The usual unbounded rationality postulate in effect treats a scarce resource as if infinitely plentiful, which should seem peculiar to economists. In the model, the innovation cost paid by innovator firms represents the cost of superior production planning, of study of the practices of other firms, of absorption of scientific discoveries, and so on. It might seem sensible at first glance to suppose that a firm selects an optimal level of problem-solving effort. However, such an assumption involves a logical circularity. If a firm cannot costlessly solve an initial problem, how can it costlessly solve the typically more complicated problem of how much problem-solving effort to devote to the original problem? Adaptive rather than optimizing behavior seems to be the only way out of this circularity.

The general case for treating rationality as bounded and for treating adaptation as a more fundamental behavioral rule than optimization has been persuasively argued by numerous economists. A good entry to the literature is the conference volume *The Behavioral Foundations of Economic Theory*, published as a special issue of the *Journal of Business* (1986). The volume contains wide-ranging discussions by Kenneth Arrow, Robert Lucas, Herbert Simon, Sidney Winter, and others, including many references to earlier discussions. The circularity issue in particular has been emphasized in Conlisk (1988), which contains other references to the issue. For the specific model below, the main intellectual debt is to Nelson and Winter (1982). Some of the particular specifications in the model are like those in Conlisk (1980, 1989). Segerstrom (1991) and Jovanovic and MacDonald (1990) present models of technical change with innovator and imitator firms. Their models are substantially different from the model here. Segerstrom analyzes a steady state involving no aggregate fluctuations; Jovanovic and MacDonald analyze a single transitory wave of innovation; and both models treat firms as unboundedly rational rather than adaptive.

In the model, innovator firms are able to display a higher degree of apparent decision-making astuteness than imitator firms, and thus are able to look more like the unboundedly rational firms of mainstream economic theory. If the innovation cost is small enough, innovators quickly drive imitators out of business, an outcome somewhat in the spirit of economic selection justifications for the unbounded rationality postulate. However, if the innovation cost is not small, imitators coexist profitably with innovators in the long run; and the innovator–imitator mix is dependent on all model parameters. In this sense, the average degree of decision-making astuteness in the economy is endogenously determined.

In more detail, the coexistence mechanism works as follows. Imitator firms copy other firms' technological practices. When innovators dominate in relative number, imitation is well rewarded because most firms, by undergoing the expense to be legitimate technological leaders, are worth imitating. Hence profit-seeking entry and exit lead to an increase in the relative number of imitator firms. When imitators dominate in relative number, imitation is poorly rewarded because most firms, by refusing the expense to become technological leaders, are not worth imitating. Hence entry and exit lead to a decrease in the relative number of imitator firms.

The model invokes many simplifying assumptions; it is intended to be suggestive rather than realistic. Nonetheless, the nonlinear random dynamics put the model beyond analytic solution (at least beyond my ability at analytical solution). However, since the model is not far beyond analytic solution, a fairly clear picture of model behavior will follow from partial analysis and from simulation.

A Benchmark Static Model

It is convenient to start with a benchmark static model and then to superimpose the dynamics on it. Let there be n firms, indexed $i = 1, \ldots, n$. Assume that the ith firm has production function $Y_i = TL_i^\alpha$. Here Y_i and L_i are the output and labor employed by the firm; T is a level of technology multiplier common to all firms; and the exponent α is a parameter common to all firms, with $0 < \alpha < 1$. Assume that the firm's profit level, denoted Π_i, is given by $\Pi_i = Y_i - wL_i - kT$. Here w is the wage and kT is a fixed cost proportional to the level of technology, with k the proportionality parameter. Assume competition among firms for labor, and assume a fixed supply of labor L. These assumptions lead to the following benchmark model.

$$Y_i = TL_i^\alpha, \quad \Pi_i = Y_i - wL_i - kT, \quad w = \alpha TL_i^{\alpha-1}, \quad L_1 + \cdots + L_n = L. \quad (9.1)$$

The third equation is the competitive condition that firm i demands labor to the point where the wage equals the marginal product of labor; and the fourth equation equates labor demand to labor supply. Since i runs from 1 to n, model (9.1) has $3n + 1$ equations. They determine the n outputs Y_i, the n labor forces L_i, the n profits Π_i, and the wage rate w, all as functions of the given magnitudes T, α, k, L, and n.

Since model (9.1) treats firms symmetrically, they will share the same values for Y_i, L_i, and Π_i. The solution $L_i = L/n$ is immediate, and the other solutions follow quickly:

$$L_i = L/n, \quad Y_i = T(L/n)^\alpha, \quad \Pi_i = T[(1 - \alpha)(L/n)^\alpha - k], \quad w = \alpha T(L/n)^{-(1-\alpha)}. \quad (9.2)$$

The ith firm's profit rate is $\Pi_i/(kT)$. If the number of firms n is determined by free entry instead of being given, and if firms will not produce at a profit rate less than a reservation rate r, then

$$n = \left(\text{largest integer no greater than } \{(1 - alpha)/[k(1 + r)]\}^{1/\alpha} L \right). \quad (9.3)$$

The algebraic expression on the right can be gotten by solving $\Pi_i/(kT) = r$ and equations (9.2) for n. The solution (9.2)–(9.3) has the optimality property that it maximizes total output net of fixed cost and net of required profit $\sum_i (Y_i - kT - rkT)$.

The dynamic model to follow can be thought of as an elaboration of this static model. In the dynamic model, each firm will have its own technology level T_i instead of a common technology level T. The various technology levels will evolve through a partly random technical change assumption. Innovator firms will pay a cost to achieve more up-to-date technology, while imitator firms will follow along through imitation. Profit-motivated entry and exit will assure a dynamic analog of the reservation profit rate condition and will determine the evolution of the mix between innovators and imitators. Two algebraically convenient properties of the static solution of (9.2)–(9.3) will carry over, roughly speaking, to the dynamic model. First, the property that output, profit, and wage levels in (9.2) are proportional to T will appear in the dynamic model as the property that these levels will grow equiproportionately with technology levels in the long run. That is, the model will have a balanced growth property traceable in part to the algebraic assumptions which make Y_i, Π_i, and w proportional to T in (9.2). Second, the property that the number of firms in (9.3) does not depend on T will appear in the dynamic model as the property that the number of firms is trendless in the long run.

The Dynamic Model

Time will be discrete, indexed by t. The technology level of firm i will be denoted $T_i(t)$. At the beginning of period t, the relevant history of the model will be summarized mainly by the lagged technology levels $T_i(t-1)$, by the types (innovator versus imitator) of the existing firms, and by their profit histories. There will be no capital stock in the usual sense. However, at the beginning of each period, firms will pay technological maintenance costs. It is possible to interpret $T_i(t)$ as a composite of knowledge and physical capital, in which case the maintenance cost can be interpreted as a physical capital cost. The absence of a capital stock distinct from $T_i(t)$ simplifies the model considerably, but is not critical to the issues under discussion.

The Timing of a Period

Given the history, the timing of events for a typical firm in period t is this. At the beginning of the period, the firm plans its technology for the period, pays a technological maintenance cost, and signs on workers. In addition, if the firm is an innovator, it pays an innovation cost. Between the beginning and end of the period, the firm produces its output and experiences its technology shock. At the end of the period, the firm distributes its output as wages to workers and as profits to itself. Also, at the end of the period, entry and exit take place.

Behavior of an Innovator Firm

The following five equations summarize the behavior of the ith innovator firm. The equations are explained immediately below.

(production)
$$Y_i(t) = T_i(t)L_i(t)^\alpha \tag{9.4}$$

(definition)
$$T^{\max}(t) = \max \left[T^{\max}(t-1), \{T_j(t) \,|\, j\, in\, J(t)\} \right] \tag{9.5}$$

(technical change)
$$T_i(t) = T^{\max}(t-1) \exp[\lambda + \varepsilon_i(t)] \tag{9.6}$$

(profit)
$$\Pi_i(t) = Y_i(t) - w(t)L_i(t) - kT_i(t-1) - cT^{\max}(t-1) \tag{9.7}$$

(labor demand)
$$L_i(t) = [\alpha e^\lambda T^{\max}(t-1)E^{\mathrm{IN}}(e^\varepsilon)/w(t)]^{1/(1-\alpha)} \tag{9.8}$$

Equation (9.4) is the production function for firm i. It is the function $Y_i = TL_i^\alpha$ from the static model with a firm subscript added to T and with time indices added. So $Y_i(t), T_i(t)$, and $L_i(t)$ are the output, technology level, and employment level of firm i in period t. The parameter α obeys $0 < \alpha < 1$.

Equation (9.5) defines a best-ever technology indicator. Let $J(t)$ denote the set of indices of all firms (innovators and imitators) existing in period t; so $\{T_j(t)\,|\,j\, in\, J(t)\}$ is the list of all firm technology levels for period t. Equation (9.5) thus defines $T^{\max}(t)$ as the best technology level ever achieved by any firm up through period t.

Equation (9.6) is the technical change assumption for firm i. λ is a nonnegative parameter. The $\varepsilon_i(t)$ are white noise disturbances, assumed to have zero means, to be independent across firms i and over time t, and to have the same distribution for all innovator firms. There will be $\varepsilon_i(t)$ disturbances for imitator firms also. They will also have zero means, independence across firms i and time t, and a common distribution for all imitator firms. However, the ε-distribution for innovators may differ from the ε-distribution for imitators. The expectation $E\{\exp[\varepsilon_i(t)]\}$, assumed to be finite, will appear in equations for both innovators and imitators. For short, this expectation will be denoted $E^{\mathrm{IN}}(e^\varepsilon)$ for innovators and $E^{\mathrm{IM}}(e^\varepsilon)$ for imitators.

At the start of period t, an innovator firm makes a production plan for the period. Equation (9.6) recognizes two sources of good technological practice—past practice throughout the economy and the firm's own current ideas for improvements. Past practice is represented by the $T^{\max}(t-1)$ factor on the right of (9.6). Since $T^{\max}(t-1)$ is the best past practice, the assumption is that an innovator firm, in return for paying the innovator cost, is able to scan the economy, to note innovations of other firms, and to incoporate those innovations fully into their own practices by the following period. The firm's own current ideas about improvements are represented by the factor $\exp\lambda + \varepsilon_i(t)$], where the disturbance $\varepsilon_i(t)$ represents the fact that ideas may work out well or poorly. The algebra of (9.6) is such that $\lambda + \varepsilon_i(t)$ represents a proportional increment to $T_i(t)$, given $T^{\max}(t)$; so $\lambda + \varepsilon_i(t)$ is a component of the growth rate of $T_i(t)$.

Implicit in (9.11) is the assumption that an imitator firm cannot freely observe whether other firms are innovators or imitators; otherwise the imitator firm would imitate only the innovators. The spirit of this assumption is that a real economy, being vastly more complicated than the simple model here, does not easily reveal the particular technological character and decision-making astuteness of individual firms. Thus, when an imitator firm passively follows prevailing practice, it cannot pick and choose the best objects of imitation.

A convenient way to contrast the technical change assumption (9.6) for innovators to the technical change assumption (9.11) for imitators is to take logarithms of each and to subtract $\log T_i(t - l)$ from both sides of each. The resulting equations are

(innovator)
$$\Delta \log T_i(t) = \lambda + [\log T^{\max}(t - 1) - \log T_i(t - 1)] + \varepsilon_i(t) \qquad (9.14)$$

(imitator)
$$\Delta \log T_i(t) = [\log \bar{T}(t - 1) - \log T_i(t - 1)] + \varepsilon_i(t) \qquad (9.15)$$

Here Δ denotes a first difference, so that $\Delta \log T_i(t) \equiv \log T_i(t) - \log T_i(t - 1)$ is the growth rate of $T_i(t)$ between $t - 1$ and t. The two equations give the technology growth rates of the two types of firm. An innovator's advantage is in the parameter λ (if it is positive) and in the presence of $T^{\max}$ rather than $\bar{T}$ in the bracketed term.

Equation (9.12) is the ith imitator firm's profit function. It is like the innovator profit function (9.7) except that there is no innovation cost. Equation (9.13) is the ith imitator firm's labor demand. It gives the amount of labor that maximizes expected profits for period t, conditional on the wage and conditional on information available at the end of period $t - l$. The derivation is like the derivation for an innovator firm (last paragraph of the preceding section) except that the expected technology level for an imitator is $\bar{T}(t - 1)E^{\text{IM}}(e^{\varepsilon})$ instead of $e^{\lambda}T^{\max}(t - 1)E^{\text{IN}}(e^{\varepsilon})$. Thus, imitator labor demand (9.13) is like innovator labor demand (9.8) except that $\bar{T}(t - 1)E^{\text{IM}}$ replaces $e^{\lambda}T^{\max}(t - 1)E^{\text{IN}}$.

Labor Market Clearance

The labor market is assumed to be well behaved in the sense that firms and workers are price takers and in the sense that the wage $w(t)$ for period t equates supply and demand. Supply is fixed at L, as in the benchmark static model. The market clearance condition is

$$\sum_{i \in J(t)} L_i(t) = L. \qquad (9.16)$$

If there were no entry or exit, and if the disturbance distributions were given, the equations would now give a complete description of how the variables evolve from one period to the next. For each innovator firm, there are four current variables $[Y_i(t), T_i(t), \Pi_i(t), L_i(t)]$ and four corresponding equations $[(9.4), (9.6), (9.7),$

(9.8)]. For each imitator firm, there are the same four variables, and there are four corresponding equations [(9.9), (9.11), (9.12), (9.13)]. In addition, there are three economy-wide current variables $[T^{\max}(t), \bar{T}(t), w(t)]$ and three corresponding equations [(9.5), (9.10), (9.14)]. The number of current unknowns matches the number of equations; and it is easy to show that there is a unique solution. However, this solution must be modified by entry and exit.

Entry and Exit

Innovator decisions are generally superior to imitator decisions. However, innovator firms pay a cost for their better decisions. If the benefit of being an innovator exceeds the cost, then innovators have a higher "fitness" than imitators, and sensible assumptions about entry and exit should lead to an increase in the relative number of innovators. Under the opposite condition, the relative number should decrease. Simple entry and exit rules will be specified to create such a mechanism. It will be shown that under appropriate parameter restrictions, entry and exit will act to equalize the fitnesses of innovators and imitators, which will in turn lead to coexistence of innovators and imitators in the long run. The particular entry and exit specifications were chosen to have two main characteristics, consistency with bounded rationality and simplicity in a modeling sense.

Regarding bounded rationality, the idea of the entry and exit specifications is to make firms behave as if, like real firms, they face a reality too complex to understand except vaguely. In this spirit, firms will not be supposed to know how the model operates. Rather they will react in simple ways to profit experience. High profits will trigger entry; low profits will trigger exit. It will be assumed that the profit histories of all firms are known, but that firm types (innovator versus imitator) are not known [as discussed in connection with (9.11) above].

An entry and exit specification must include an assumption about how many firms can enter or exit simultaneously. This issue will be evaded here by restricting analysis to an economy with a relatively small population of firms, typically 50 or fewer in the simulations, and by assuming that there is no more than one entry and no more than one exit per period. The restriction to a small population is primarily to economize on computer time in the simulations. However, interest in the small number case might also be justified by appeal to the one-industry character of the model economy. In a real economy, profitability and innovation have substantial independence from one industry to another. Thus, for a one-industry model, it can be argued that an industry-sized population is natural.

Given the small-numbers emphasis, the one-per-period restriction on entry and exit seems natural. The idea is that with a small population and with plausibly moderate fluctuations, firms will not have an incentive to enter or exit more rapidly than one at a time. For example, suppose that three firms with unacceptable profit records are contemplating exit. When the firm with the worst record exits, the economy will be perceptibly less crowded (given the small population); hence the profits of the other two firms may pick up enough that they need not exit. A similar argument can be made about entry.

As the discussion is beginning to suggest, there are many entry and exit specifications that might be entertained, with no compelling reason to select one over another. However, the qualitative behavior of the model is likely to be robust to a variety of changes in the entry and exit rules.

Turning to specifics, the entry and exit rules will depend on the profit histories of firms, as represented by cumulative profit rates, denoted $\pi_i(t)$. These profit rates and their average are defined by the following four equations, explained immediately below.

(for i an innovator)
$$\pi_i^+(t) = \Pi_i(t)/[kT_i(t-1) + cT^{max}(t-1)] \tag{9.17}$$

(for i an imitator)
$$\pi_i^+(t) = \Pi_i(t)/[kT_i(t-1)] \tag{9.18}$$

$$\pi_i(t) = \delta\pi_i(t-1) + (1-\delta)\pi_i^+(t) \tag{9.19}$$

$$\bar{\pi}(t) = [\text{average of}\{\pi_i(t) \mid i \text{ in } J(t)\}]. \tag{9.20}$$

Recall that the ith innovator firm pays maintenance and optimization cost $kT_i(t-1) + cT^{max}(t-1)$ at the beginning of period t and that it receives profit $\Pi_i(t)$ at the end of period t. Thus, the ratio $\Pi_i(t)/[kT_i(t-1) + cT^{max}(t-1)]$ is a rate of profit on invested funds. Equation (9.15) thus defines the current profit rate $\pi_i^+(t)$ for the ith innovator firm. Equation (9.16) defines a similar current profit rate for the ith imitator firm. Equation (9.17) then defines (for either type of firm) the cumulative profit rate $\pi_i(t)$ as a weighted average of the current profit rate and the lagged cumulative profit rate. The weight δ is assumed to obey $0 \le \delta < 1$. The size of δ will reflect the emphasis placed on past as opposed to current profit experience in entry and exit decisions. Equation (9.18) defines $\bar{\pi}(t)$ as the average cumulative profit rate over all firms.

The entry and exit rules will depend on comparisons between cumulative profit rates and a benchmark rate of return, denoted r. Subject to qualifications below, profit rates above r will trigger entry, and profit rates below r will trigger exit. Thus, r represents investors' reservation price for tying up their capital. In a fuller model, the benchmark rate r would be determined within the model; but it will be taken as a given constant here. It is easier to describe the entry and exit rules in words than in mathematical notation. Start with exit. The rule supposes that the firm with the most unsuccessful profit history, fearing a continuation of that history, will be the one to consider exit.

Exit rule. At the end of period t, the firm with lowest cumulative profit rate $\pi_i(t)$ (with ties broken at random) will exit if that rate is less than r. Otherwise there will be no exit.

Next consider entry. Subject to two qualifications, the idea is that a potential entrant uses $\bar{\pi}(t)$ as if a profit forecast and thus enters if the inequality $\bar{\pi}(t) > r$ is satisfied. The two qualifications are adjustments to the two sides of the inequality. First, the potential entrant is assumed to adjust $\bar{\pi}(t)$ downward to account for the fact that one more firm in the economy will squeeze profits. The exact adjustment is to replace $\bar{\pi}(t)$ by the smaller amount $[1 + \bar{\pi}(t)]\{n(t)/[n(t) + 1]\}^{\alpha} - 1$, where $n(t)$ is the number of firms in the economy. This adjustment, based on a static model approximation, is explained in the Appendix. Second, the potential entrant is assumed to have special entry costs which it needs to recover; hence it adjusts the benchmark rate r upward by an amount ρ. With these two adjustments, the trigger inequality $\bar{\pi}(t) > r$ becomes $[1 + \bar{\pi}(t)]\{n(t)/[n(t) + 1]\}^{\alpha} - 1 > r + \rho$. Both adjustments to the trigger inequality make entry more conservative. Entry is in fact still more conservative because the inequality does not allow for the fact that an exit may occur simultaneously and may thus make the economy less crowded.

If the inequality is met, a new firm enters. The new firm must choose a management type, innovator or imitator. It is assumed that the decision is made at random, as if by a fair coin flip. After entry, a new firm's future will be dictated by the various difference equations of the model. Thus, the new firm will need an unused index, say m; and it will need various starting values for period t to generate its values for $t + 1, t + 2$, and so on. Specifically, a new firm will need starting values for $T_m(t)$ and $\pi_m(t)$. The entry rule specifies these values.

Entry rule. Let $n(t)$ be the total number of firms in existence during period t. At the end of period t, if $[1 + \bar{\pi}(t)]\{n(t)/[n(t) + 1]\}^{\alpha} - 1 > r + \rho$, then one firm will enter. If there is an entry, then: The new firm will choose its type (innovator or imitator) at random as if by fair coin flip. The new firm will be assigned an unused index m and starting values $T_m(t) = \bar{T}(t)$ and $\pi_m(t) = [1 + \bar{\pi}(t)]\{n(t)/[n(t) + 1]\}^{\alpha} - 1$.

The coin flip assumption is convenient in its simplicity, is consistent with bounded rationality, and ensures that there is always some willingness in the economy to experiment with both types of firm management (innovator and imitator). The coin flip does not allow an entrant, in choosing its type, to compare profit rates of existing innovators and imitators. This property of the entry rule is required by the assumption that firm types are not observable.

The numbers of innovator and imitator firms may change only through entry and exit. No switching of type by an existing firm is allowed. The idea behind the no-switching simplification is that choice of management type involves major commitments (in terms of personnel hired, research lab investment, planning procedures, and so on). Such commitments are costly; hence abandonment of one management type and inauguration of the other is much like an exit followed by an entry. Since exit and entry are already in the model, a switching mechanism would merely complicate the model without fundamentally altering its behavior.

The entry and exit rules complete the model. An algorithm of model dynamics must of course include updating of the set $J(t)$ of firm indices to account for entry and exit. $J(t + 1)$ must include the elements of $J(t)$, less the index of the exit firm if there is one, plus the index of the entry-firm if there is one. Further, the partition of this set into the set of innovators and the set of imitators must be updated.

Model Behavior

Though the model is too complicated for analytic solution, a fairly clear picture of model behavior is available. Intuition and analytic results for simplified variants of the model suggest hypotheses about behavior. These hypotheses have been confirmed through simulations of the complete model for about 200 parameter settings. A longer version of the paper, available from the author on request, describes in detail the simulations and the analytic results for simplified variants of the model. A summary is presented here.

Stationarity

All properties of the model are easier to analyze if time series generated by the model are stationary. Then means, autocorrelations, and so on are well defined objects for analysis. The algebraic specifications were designed to promote stationarity of ratios among trending variables and to promote stationarity of the growth rates of trending variables. The first chore is to check whether stationarity does in fact apply.

To gain insights, consider the simplified variant of the model gotten by suppressing entry and exit. Then the numbers of innovator and imitator firms are constant. If the numbers are selected to keep profit rates near the benchmark value r, the approximate model may behave roughly like the complete model. It is convenient to put variables into two lists.

Trending variables: $Y_i(t), T_i(t), \bar{T}(t), T^{\max}(t), \Pi_i(t), w(t)$.

Nontrending variables: $L_i(t), \pi_i^+(t), \pi_i(t), \bar{\pi}(t), \varepsilon_i(t)$.

Since the model is a growth model, we expect outputs, technology levels, profits, and the wage all to grow in the long run; hence the first list is labeled "trending." Since the total labor force is fixed, since the disturbances are stationary by assumption, and since the profit rates are ratio variables, we expect the variables on the second list not to trend; hence the second list is labeled "nontrending."

Since the equations of the simplified model are homogeneous of degree one in the trending variables (and their lagged values), the model can be restated in terms of ratios of trending variables. In particular, the simplified model can be restated as a first-order stochastic difference equation

$$X(t) = F[X(t - 1), \varepsilon(t)]. \tag{9.21}$$

Here $X(t) \equiv [X_i(t)]$ is an $n \times 1$ vector of normalized technology levels, defined by $X_i(t) \equiv T_i(t)/T^{\max}(t)$; $\varepsilon(t)$ is the $n \times 1$ disturbance vector $\varepsilon(t) \equiv [\varepsilon_i(t)]$; and F is an $n \times 1$ vector of continuous functions. Since each $X_i(t)$ must obey $0 \leq X_i(t) \leq 1$, (9.19) causes $X(t)$ to trace out a random path within a bounded set. This system can be viewed as a continuous state Markov chain. Under mild assumptions on the ε-distributions, it can be shown that (9.19) implies a unique stationary equilibrium for $X(t)$. Any of the variables listed above as nontrending, and any ratio between two variables listed as trending, are stationary since they can be expressed as a function of $X(t)$ and its lags. Further, let $Y(t) \equiv \sum_{i \in J(t)} Y_i(t)$ denote aggregate output. The algebra of the model allows growth rates of trending variables, such as $\Delta \log Y(t)$ and $\Delta \log T^{\max}(t)$, to be expressed as functions of $X(t)$ and its lags; hence growth rates are also stationary.

The question is whether the stationarity properties of the simplified model carry over to the full model with entry and exit. The full model is still a Markov process. However, it is much more complex, and it defies my ability to provide analytic solution. Nonetheless, there is reason to expect stationarity to carry over. Despite entry and exit, technology growth should not lead to long run trend in the number of firms since the outputs of individual firms increase along with technology. Thus, we might expect stationarity in the number of firms $n(t)$; and, given stationarity in $n(t)$, we might expect stationarity of ratios and growth rates to carry over from the fixed-n case.

One major complication of entry and exit is the possibility of multiple equilibria. Consider an example. Suppose that randomness in technology is suppressed by setting all $\varepsilon_i(t)$ equal to zero; and suppose that there are three innovator firms and two imitator firms. If all five firms have profit rates above r but below $r + \rho$, then neither entry nor exit will occur; and the model is in equilibrium. Now reverse the relative numbers so that there are two innovators and three imitators. It is possible that all five profit rates will still be above r and below $r + \rho$, in which case there is a second equilibrium. Such multiple equilibria can survive in the presence of disturbances also, so long as the $\varepsilon_i(t)$ distributions are sufficiently constrained (say uniform distributions with small variances) that no strings of bad and good luck by the various firms will be enough to drive any profit rates out of the interval from r to $r + \rho$. In Markov chain terms, each of these equilibria is a trapping set. Within a given trapping set, however, we might expect stationarity in ratios and growth rates.

These considerations lead to the following specific hypotheses about model behavior. There may be multiple trapping sets for the model. Within a given trapping set, the following series will all be stationary: the number of firms $n(t)$, the ratio of innovator firms to total firms, the ratio $T^{\max}(t)/Y(t)$ of the best practice technology to total output, the growth rate $\Delta \log T^{\max}(t)$ of best practice technology, and the growth rate $\Delta \log Y(t)$ of aggregate output.

The simulation results confirmed these hypotheses. Further, multiple trapping set cases seemed to be aberrant cases. They occurred only when parameters would support only a small number of firms and when there was so little random variation that the economy could "get stuck" in a small region.

Economic Properties of the Growth Path

The remainder of the discussion will presume stationarity and will thus discuss means, autocorrelations, and so on as well-defined magnitudes. To provide a numerical example, consider a particular specification, where the time unit is a year. Call it the "benchmark specification":

$$L = 1000, \alpha = 0.75, c = 0.31, k = 2.8, \delta = 0.4, r = 0.1, \rho = 0.01.$$

$$\varepsilon_i(t) = \varepsilon_{1i}(t) + \varepsilon_{2i}(t).$$

For all i : $\varepsilon_{1i}(t)$ is uniformly distributed over $[-u, +u]$.

For i an imitator: $\varepsilon_{2i}(t) = 0$.

For i an innovator: $\lambda + \varepsilon_{2i}(t) = b$ with probability p,

$$= 0 \text{ with probability } 1 - p.$$

$$u = 0.01, b = 0.04, p = 0.02.$$

The disturbance components $\varepsilon_{1i}(t)$ and $\varepsilon_{2i}(t)$ are assumed to be independent of each other and to be independent over i and t. To interpret the $\varepsilon_i(t)$ specification, recall that $\varepsilon_i(t)$ is a component of the ith firm's technology growth rate. Here $\varepsilon_i(t)$ has been specified in two pieces. The first disturbance component $\varepsilon_{1i}(t)$ can be thought of as pure noise; it has the same distribution for both types of firm. The second component $\varepsilon_{2i}(t)$ is always zero for imitator firms and is specified for innovator firms as part of the sum $\lambda + \varepsilon_{2i}(t)$. This sum is a component of the technology growth rate of innovator firm i. The sum can be thought of as an attempted innovation. With large probability $1 - p = 0.98$, the attempted innovation yields nothing; but, with small probability $p = 0.02$, the attempted innovation yields the substantial growth rate boost $b = 0.04$. Thus, innovations are rare but substantial when they occur. To give $\varepsilon_{2i}(t)$ a zero mean, λ must equal $pb = 0.0008$. Now consider various features of model behavior.

Coexistence

For a wide range of parameter values, imitator firms coexist with innovator firms in the long run in the sense that the average number of imitator firms is substantial and in the sense that imitator firms are on average as profitable as innovator firms. For the benchmark specification, the long run average numbers of imitator and innovator firms are approximately 13 and 20. The key parameter for coexistence is the innovation cost parameter c. If it is large enough, given other parameters, then imitation is well rewarded behavior because imitators avoid a substantial cost. Coexistence then occurs. If it is small enough, new imitator firms are soon driven out of business; and the long run average profit rate of imitator firms is below that of innovator firms. Coexistence then fails. Insight about coexistence and other issues can be gotten by analyzing the deterministic variant of the model when all disturbances $\varepsilon_i(t)$ are suppressed, when L is large enough to carry a large population of firms, and when entry and exit are tight in the sense that $\rho = 0$. Then the condition for coexistence is simply $c > k[e^{\lambda\alpha/(1-\alpha)} - 1]$.

Steady Growth, Balanced Growth, and Cointegration

In growth theory terminology, stationarity of the growth rates $\Delta \log Y(t)$ and $\Delta \log T^{\max}(t)$ means steady growth; and stationarity of ratios such as $T^{\max}(t)/Y(t)$ means balanced growth. In time series terminology, $\log Y(t)$ and $\log T^{\max}(t)$ are cointegrated; see Engle and Granger (1987). A stylized empirical fact about many pairs of trending macroeconomic variables is that they are cointegrated; the model suggests a possible reason why. In view of balanced growth, the series for $\Delta \log Y(t)$, $\Delta \log T^{\max}(t)$, and other growth rates of trending aggregates must all have the same long run mean. That is, there is a single long run growth rate characterizing the growth performance of the economy. For the benchmark specification, it is 0.015 per year.

Deterministic Trend versus Nonstationary Drift

There is a controversy over the question of whether trending macroeconomic variables display deterministic trend with stationary deviations (the older view), or whether trending variables display nonstationary drift (the newer view). Nelson and Plosser (1982) stimulated the controversy; see Blanchard and Quah (1989) for a recent contribution and for further references. The model here allows either possibility separately, or a mix of the two. Thus, the model provides a possible microeconomic story (innovations of firms) to illustrate the (supply side of the) macroeconomic issue.

   To get an example of pure deterministic trend with stationary deviations, set parameters as follows. For innovator firms, suppress the disturbances but create steady innovation by setting λ positive. For imitator firms, allow nonzero disturbances, but make them small enough that an imitator firm never achieves an improvement in best practice technology. The results will be deterministic trend at growth rate λ (due to innovator firms) and stationary deviations about that trend (due to imitator disturbances).

   To get an example of pure nonstationary drift, consider the following innovators-only case. Set $c = 0$ so that there is never an advantage in being an imitator. Select a positive value of λ and a bounded innovator ε-distribution such that $\lambda + \varepsilon_i(t)$ is always positive. At $t = 0$, let there be n_0 innovator firms and no imitator firms; and rig the entry and exit parameters so that there will be never be entry or exit. In this case,

$$\Delta \log T^{\max}(t) = \lambda + \max \{ n_0 \text{ draws from innovator } \varepsilon \text{ distribution}\}.$$

That is, $\Delta \log T^{\max}(t)$ will be white noise. It follows that $\log T^{\max}(t)$ itself is a random walk with drift, the classic example of nonstationary drift. Since $\log Y(t)$ follows $\log T^{\max}(t)$, then $Y(t)$ must also display nonstationary drift.

More typically, as in the benchmark specification, the model will display a mixture of deterministic trend and nonstationary drift. The presence of nonstationary drift means that disturbances have permanent as opposed to transitory effect. In the model, a disturbance $\varepsilon_i(t)$ will have a permanent effect if and only if the ith firm has an innovation in t that raises the best practice technology. In many models with nonstationary drift, a particular disturbance term either always has a permanent effect or always does not. In this model, in contrast, only one disturbance term at a time can have a permanent effect, and its location will randomly jump from firm to firm.

Schumpeterian Cycles

In a typical simulation for what appear to be plausible parameter values, there is slight variation over time in the total number of firms $n(t)$, but long and wide swings in the mix of innovator and imitator firms. For example, the benchmark specification was simulated for 775 periods. The total number of firms remained in the narrow interval $31 \le n(t) \le 34$, with few periods at 31 or 34. However, the number of innovator firms, call it $n^{IN}(t)$ varied over the wide interval $5 \le n^{IN}(t) \le 23$; and the swings were long, as indicated by an autocorrelation of 0.97 for $n^{IN}(t)$. Since innovators are technologically progressive, the average output growth rate was higher during peak intervals of the $n^{IN}(t)$ cycle.

The long swings in $n^{IN}(t)/n(t)$ result from a tension between a "spillover mechanism" and a "coexistence mechanism." Recall that an innovation by one innovator is picked up within one period by all other innovators. So all innovators feed on the success of any one. But an increase in the number of innovators implies a higher probability that at least one substantial innovation will be found in any given period. Thus, there is a spillover mechanism tending to increase the fitness of innovators as their numbers increase (and decrease their fitness as their numbers decrease). This spillover mechanism tends to push the innovator share $n^{IN}(t)/n(t)$ toward the extremes. Countering this is the coexistence mechanism described above. Imitation tends to be better rewarded as the number of innovators gets relatively larger. Though the coexistence mechanism dominates at the extremes in the sense that $n^{IN}(t)/n(t)$ does stay away from the extremes (under appropriate parameter conditions), the spillover mechanism nonetheless causes wide drifts in the middle.

All this has a Schumpeterian flavor. A long upswing in $n^{IN}(t)/n(t)$ occurs when an initial run of innovative good luck engenders an expanding wave of further innovation. During the wave, innovators push imitators out of business with a resultant upward push on the growth rate $\Delta \log Y(t)$.

Table 9.1 Equilibrium Elasticities
for the Benchmark Specification

	$(n^{IN}/n)^*$	$(\Delta \log Y)^*$
c	-1.14	-.65
u	0.72	0.68
p	1.20	1.05
b	1.24	1.53
L	1.93	1.51
α	12.12	4.16
k	1.63	0.29
δ	-0.02	-0.13
r	0.01	-0.08
ρ	0.12	0.07

Sensitivities

Two central indicators of model behavior are the long run equilibrium means of the innovator share $n^{IN}(t)/n(t)$ and the output growth rate $\Delta \log Y(t)$. Let these equilibrium means be denoted $(n^{IN}/n)^*$ and $(\Delta \log Y)^*$; they are functions of model parameters. $(n^{IN}/n)^*$ measures the model economy's average degree of innovative astuteness (a "degree of rationality" of sorts), and $(\Delta \log Y)^*$ measures overall economic growth performance. Each measure is fully endogenous in the sense that it is sensitive to all model parameters. The two measures represent the two main components of the model—the bounded rationality component and the random innovations component. The two components interact in important ways.

Table 9.1 illustrates. It displays elasticities of $(n^{IN}/n)^*$ and $(\Delta \log Y)^*$ to the parameters. The table assumes the benchmark functional forms for the ε–distributions and evaluates the elasticities at the benchmark numerical specification. The interaction of the bounded rationality and random innovations components of the model is illustrated by the senstivities in the top panel of the table (the first four rows). The signs of these sensitivities were the same for all numerical trials.

Consider the first row. An increase in the innovation cost parameter c represents the degree to which rationality is bounded. As a direct effect, an increase in c reduces innovator fitness and thus reduces the relative number of innovators. As a secondary effect, the growth rate declines with the number of innovators. The message is that bounded rationality may be important in analyzing growth.

Consider the next three rows. As a direct effect, an increase in one of the innovation parameters (p, b, u) stimulates growth by increasing the frequency and magnitude of innovations. (In the case of u, an increase spreads the ε–distributions and thus increases the probability of large positive drawings.) An increase in one of the innovation parameters also stimulates growth indirectly through the bounded rationality mechanism. Faster innovation increases the relative number of innovators (since innovators absorb innovations faster than imitators and thus gain in fitness when innovation is faster), and more innovators means more innovations. Again the message is that bounded rationality may be important in analyzing growth.

Appendix. Profit Rate Effect of an Additional Firm

No exact solution is available for the profit rate effect of an additional firm. However, an approximate formula can be based on the benchmark static model. Let π_n denote the profit rate for the static model (9.1) when there are n firms. From (9.2), $\pi_n \equiv \Pi_i/(kT) = (1 - \alpha)(L^\alpha/k)n^{-\alpha} - 1$. It follows that

$$(1 + \pi_{n+1})/(1 + \pi_n) = [n/(n + 1)]^\alpha.$$

That is, for the static model, the proportional reduction in the profit factor $1 + \pi_n$ caused by one additional firm equals $[n/(n + l)]^\alpha$. The entry rule incorporates this adjustment.

Note

Helpful comments were provided by Paul David, Richard Day, Curtis Eaton, Ronald Heiner, Murray Frank, Richard Nelson, Harald Uhlig, Sidney Winter, and other participants in the International Symposium on Evolutionary Dynamics and Nonlinear Economics.

Bibliography

Blanchard, O.J., and D. Quah, 1989, "The Dynamic Effects of Aggregate Demand and Supply Disturbances," *American Economic Review*, 79, 655–673.

Conlisk, John, 1980, Costly optimizers versus cheap imitators, *Journal of Economic Behavior and Organization*, 1, 275–293.

Conlisk, John, 1988, "Optimization Cost," *Journal of Economic Behavior and Organization*, 9, 213–228.

Conlisk, J., 1989, "An Aggregate Model of Technical Change," *Quarterly Journal of Economics*, 104, 787–821.

Engle, R.F., and C.W.J. Granger, 1987, "Co–Integration and Error Correction: Representation, Estimation and Testing," *Econometrica*, 55, 251–276.

Hogarth, R.M., and M.W. Reder (eds.), 1986, "The Behavioral Foundations of Economic Theory," Special Issue of *Journal of Business*, 59.

Jovanovic, B., and G.M. MacDonald, 1990, "Competitive Diffusion," manuscript.

Nelson, C.R., and C.I. Plosser, 1982, "Trends and Random Walks in Macroeconomic Time Series: Some Evidence and Implications," *Journal of Monetary Economics*, 10, 139–162.

Nelson, Richard R., and Sidney G. Winter, 1982, *An Evolutionary Theory of Economic Change*, Harvard University Press, Cambridge, MA.

Segerstrom, P.S., 1991, "Innovation, Imitation, and Economic Growth," *Journal of Political Economy*, 99, 807–827.

10

Rationality, Imitation, and Tradition

ROBERT BOYD and PETER J. RICHERSON

When the quality of information is poor, people often rely on tradition in making economic decisions. What is the best retail markup percentage? When should one refinance one's home? What is the right safety factor in designing a building? Retailer, homeowners, and engineers typically make such decisions using traditionally acquired rules-of-thumb. This tactic has both advantages and disadvantages. It can be useful because solving problems from scratch is difficult and costly. On the other hand, the uncritical adoption of traditional solutions to problems can lead people to acquire outmoded or even completely unfounded beliefs. Peasants sometimes resist beneficial innovations proffered by development agencies and retain traditional agricultural practices; many contemporary Americans maintain the unfounded belief that there are innate differences between the members of different ethnic groups.

The fact that tradition is sometimes reliable and other times misleading creates an interesting problem for economists. Traditions often work; when they do, they are useful because they reduce the costs of acquiring information and lower the possibility of making errors. However, if everyone were to depend exclusively on traditional rules, what would cause traditional rules to be modified in response to changes in the environment, and what would initially cause useful and reliable behaviors to become traditions?

Conventional economic theory is not helpful in answering this question (Conlisk, 1980). Economists have adopted the Bayesian theory of rational choice as the natural extension of the utility maximizing view of human behavior when there is uncertainty, and use it as a positive theory to predict people's behavior in a wide variety of contexts (Hirshleifer and Riley, 1978). Within the context of this theory, a person's beliefs about the world are represented as a subjective probability distribution. Once this distribution is specified, the theory tells us how rational people should behave, and how they should modify their beliefs in accord with their experience. The theory does not tell us why people initially come to have the beliefs that they do, but simply takes them as given.

The role of traditional knowledge has been discussed by some economists, but the processes that lead to sensible traditions seem to have been largely ignored. Hayek (1978) believes that limited knowledge and cognitive abilities force people to rely on traditional beliefs and values, and argues that traditions are sensible because groups with favorable traditions survive longer, and attract more members. Proponents of evolutionary models of firms (Alchian, 1950; Nelson and Winter, 1982) assume that beliefs, values, and other determinants of firm behavior are transmitted within firms, and that these beliefs are shaped by the natural selection of firms. The only formal theoretical treatment of tradition seems to be the interesting paper of Conlisk (1980) in which the individuals who optimize compete with individuals who acquire their behavior by imitation. If optimization is costly, Conlisk shows that imitation can persist in the population.

In this chapter, we introduce tradition into conventional theory by assuming that people acquire their initial subjective probabilities by imitating their parents, relatives, teachers, business associates, and friends, but otherwise behave as classical Bayesian rationalists. Several lines of empirical evidence support the assumption that people acquire their beliefs about the world by imitation and similar processes. Psychologists have shown that children readily acquire behavioral traits from moral beliefs to rules of grammar by imitating adult models (Bandura, 1977; Rosenthal and Zimmerman, 1978). Data collected on familial resemblances show high parent–offspring correlations for a wide variety of cognitive traits (I.Q., Scarr and Weinberg, 1976), behaviors (child abuse, alcoholism, Smith, 1975), and indicators of beliefs (religious and political-party affiliation, Fuller and Thompson, 1960). A wealth of anthropological data suggests that human groups possess considerable cultural inertia; members of groups with different cultural histories behave quite differently even when living in similar environments (e.g., Edgerton, 1971). There is also evidence that individuals acquire new beliefs by imitation when they enter organizations such as business firms (Van Maanen and Schein, 1979), and that this process causes distinct cultures to develop in different organizations. (This body of evidence is reviewed in more detail in Boyd and Richerson, 1985: 38–60.)

The assumption that people acquire their beliefs by imitation leads to models that keep track of the processes that change the frequency of alternative beliefs in a population of decision makers. To understand why a particular person acquires a particular set of beliefs, we must know to what kinds of behavior naive individuals are exposed. This in turn will depend on the distribution of beliefs (and thus behaviors) that exist in the population. A person in a village in which many people have adopted modern farming practices is more likely to acquire the beliefs that underlie such practices than a person exposed only to traditional lifeways. To predict the distribution of beliefs in the population at some future time, we must know the present distribution of beliefs, and account for all of the processes that change that distribution through time. Here we present several such models of cultural change. For a more extensive exposition of our views, see Boyd and Richerson (1985), and for related work, see Pulliam and Dunford (1980), Cavalli-Sforza and Feldman (1981), Lumsden and Wilson (1981), and Rogers (1989).

These models are different from Conlisk's in two important ways: (1) Conlisk regards imitation as an alternative to optimization; individuals are either imitators or optimizers. We assume that imitation is a precondition for optimization; everyone must acquire beliefs about the world before they can optimize. (2) Conlisk simply posits dynamical relations between variables that describe a whole population of decision makers; we are more concerned to show how the details of individual imitation and decision-making processes lead to the dynamics of the distribution of beliefs in a population through time. As we shall see, the optimal behavior in these models is usually for individuals to mix imitation and individual decision making, depending on how the temporal dynamics work out.

We think that there are three lessons to be drawn from our theory of traditions: First, there are plausible circumstances in that it is optimal to depend nearly completely on tradition at equilibrium. Second, there are plausible genetic and cultural mechanisms that could cause people to achieve this equilibrium. Third, when people do depend largely on tradition, processes other than individual choice may have important effects on why people behave the way they do. We will begin by modeling a reference case in which people acquire their initial subjective probabilities by imitation and then modify them in accordance with their own experience in a uniform and constant environment. This model indicates that when beliefs are transmitted culturally, greater reliance on tradition always leads to higher expected utility. We will then add environmental variability to the model. When the optimal behavior varies because individuals encounter different environments, there is an optimal level of dependence on tradition. If there is a substantial chance that individuals and the people that they imitate experience the same environment, and if the information available to update priors is poor, it can be an evolutionary equilibrium to rely almost completely on tradition. In the simplest model, a population of such individuals will, on the average, behave almost as if they were perfect-information optimizers. However, in such a population other processes, which can lead to both beneficial (but poorly understood) beliefs or deleterious superstitions, may also be important. Finally, we will argue that there are cultural processes that may cause people to be characterized by an optimal reliance on tradition.

The Basic Model

In the first and simplest model there are only two processes that affect the distribution of beliefs in a population of decision makers. First, individuals use available information to update their subjective probability distributions. Second, the frequency of different beliefs is changed by the transmission of these beliefs to another generation. The model has three parts: a description of how single individuals modify their beliefs in light of their experience (a process we refer to as "individual learning"), a consideration of how individual learning affects the distribution of beliefs in a population of individuals, and a mechanism for passing one generation's beliefs to the next.

Consider the following very simple decision problem. An individual decision maker has the following utility function:

$$u(y, z) = -u_0(z - y)^2. \tag{10.1}$$

where z is a decision variable under his control, y is a variable that represents the state of the world, and u_0 is a constant. While the quadratic form of this utility function is unconventional in the theory of the consumer, it is a mathematically convenient representation of the usual view of individual choice. To see this, consider the following example: suppose that the decision maker is a young professional just beginning his or her career, and that z represents the amount of time devoted to career advancement. The remainder of the young professional's time, t, is devoted to family and recreation. Then t and z are arguments of a personal "production function," which gives amounts of various "commodities," for example, income and marital happiness, produced for each combination of t and z. The consumption of these commodities in turn generates utility. By using the constraint that total time is fixed and assuming that the young professional's personal production and utility functions have the appropriate convexity properties, one could derive a unimodal function giving utility as a function of z. The optimum value of this function, y, would depend on the properties of the personal production function, which in turn will depend on the state of the world. For example, the relationship between time devoted to work and income might depend on what kind of firm the young professional has entered. While the utility function so derived is unlikely to be exactly quadratic, this functional form is a reasonable caricature of a more general unimodal function. In fact, one could think of it as the first two terms of a Taylor's series expansion of an arbitrary utility function in the neighborhood of the optimum. Because we have not specified how commodities map onto utilities, this model can represent any degree of risk preference.

The individual does not know the value of y with certainty, but his or her beliefs about the likelihood that y takes on various values conform to a normal probability distribution with mean $\hat{y}$ and variance L. Note that y is not a random variable; in a given environment there is an optimum amount of time devoted to career. The probability distribution describes the decision maker's subjective beliefs about what value of z is optimum.

Before making his or her choice, the decision maker has the opportunity to review a certain amount of evidence about the state of the world. For example, by observing the effects of time devoted to work on career advancement and home life, the young professional could get an estimate of the optimal amount of time to devote to work. Because our young professional's initial rate of advancement and domestic satisfaction might depend on a variety of factors other than the amount of time devoted to work, this estimate will be imperfect. Suppose that this evidence can be quantified by the variable x. The decision maker believes (correctly) that the value of x is normally distributed with mean y and variance V_e. After using this evidence and Bayes' law, the decision maker's updated subjective probability distribution is normal with mean $\hat{y}'$ where

$$\hat{y}' = \frac{V_e \hat{y} + Lx}{V_e + L} \tag{10.2}$$

To simplify the development here, assume that the decision maker does not update the variance of his or her subjective probability distribution.

The decision maker uses the updated distribution to calculate his or her expected utility as a function of z

$$E\{u(z, y)|\hat{y}', x\} = -u_0 \left[(z - \hat{y}')^2 + L\right] \tag{10.3}$$

and, thus the value of z that maximizes his or her expected utility, z^* is

$$z^* = \hat{y}' \tag{10.4}$$

That is, the optimal behavior is the individual's posterior estimate of the most likely state of the environment.

Now, suppose that there is a large population of decision makers. The individuals who make up this population differ in only two respects: (1) they have different prior beliefs about the most likely state of the world, and (2) they are exposed to different evidence about the state of the world. To formalize the first assumption we assume that the frequency distribution of $\hat{y}$ in the population before the subjective probability distributions have been updated, $Q_t(\hat{y})$, is normal with mean M_t and variance B_t. Notice that this is a description of the population, not a probability density. To formalize the second assumption, we assume that the value of x experienced by each different individual is an independent random variable with the density $p(y)$, which has a mean equal to the true state of the world, y, and variance V_e. Otherwise, all individuals are identical; in particular they all have the same utility function and their subjective probability distribution is characterized by the same value of L.

Let us now consider how the use of Bayes' law by individuals to modify their beliefs changes the frequency distribution of $\hat{y}$ in the population. The distribution of $\hat{y}$ in the population of decision makers after updating, Q'_t, is

$$Q'_t(\hat{y}) = \int \int h(\hat{y}|\hat{y}', x) Q_t(\hat{y}') p(x) \, d\hat{y}' dx \tag{10.5}$$

where $h(\hat{y}|\hat{y}', x)$ is the conditional density of an individual's belief after updating, given that the individual had beliefs characterized by $\hat{y}'$ before updating and observed x. Then $Q'_t(\hat{y})$ is normal with mean

$$M_t' = \frac{M_t V_e + yL}{V_e + L} \tag{10.6}$$

and variance

$$B_t' = \frac{B_t V_e^2 + V_e L^2}{(V_e + L)^2}. \tag{10.7}$$

Thus, after updating, the mean value of $\hat{y}$ moves closer to the correct value, y; the variance may either increase or decrease depending on the magnitudes of $B_t, V_e,$ and L.

So far, we have followed the usual practice of taking the decision maker's initial subjective probabilities as given. We are now in a position to consider the effect of the transmission of these beliefs to another "generation" of decision makers by imitation. For example, suppose that the young professionals advance in their firm, and are eventually replaced by a new cohort of entry level professionals, who form a new population of decision makers and face the same decision problem that their predecessors faced. Initially the individuals in this second "generation" are naive; they have no beliefs of any kind about how much time should be devoted to work. However, each naive individual has been able to observe n models of behavior of the previous generation of professionals. Based on the behavior of their models, naive individuals are able to infer what each model believes about how much time should be devoted to one's profession. Then each of the naive individuals adopts the mean of the n inferred values of $\hat{y}$ that characterize their models as the mean of their own subjective probability distributions. We assume that the variance, L, remains constant at the same value as in the previous generation.

With these assumptions the distribution of $\hat{y}$ in the population just before up-dating in generation $t + 1$, $Q_{t+1}(\hat{y})$, is normal with mean, $M_{t+1} = M_t'$ and variance, $B_{t+1} = (1/n)B_t'$. Because the distribution of $\hat{y}$ remains normal, the state of the population of decision makers at any time can be specified by the mean and variance of $\hat{y}$. If the environment remains constant, the values of the mean and variance in the population will eventually reach a unique stable equilibrium, $\hat{M}$ and $\hat{B}$, where

$$\hat{M} = y \tag{10.8}$$

and

$$\hat{B} = \frac{V_e L^2}{n(V_e + L)^2 - V_e^2} \tag{10.9}$$

Equations (10.6) and (10.8) say that the effect of the repeated application of Bayesian inference and accurate imitation on the mean value of $\hat{y}$ is unambiguous: the average of the best guesses about the state of the environment in the population converges monotonically to the actual state of the environment. According to (10.7) and (10.9), however, the variance of $\hat{y}$ is affected by competing processes. New variation is introduced each generation by errors in individual learning; this process acts to increase $\hat{B}$. On average, however, inference causes beliefs about the environment to become more accurate, and this decreases $\hat{B}$. Finally, if $n > 1$, imitation itself acts to decrease the variance of $\hat{B}$ in the population.

The Evolutionary Stable Amount of Tradition

The relative importance of tradition and individual learning is determined by the relative magnitudes of the width of each individual's initial prior probability distribution (L) and the quality of the information available to individuals (V_e). If L is small compared to V_e, young professionals' work habits will be mostly determined by the beliefs that they acquire by imitation. If L is large, the information that individuals gather for themselves will be more important.

In this section we determine the evolutionary stable, or ESS, value of L. To do this we find the value of L that when common in a population has higher expected utility than slightly different values of L. One way to justify the ESS approach is to assume that L is a genetically variable character, and that utility is monotonically related to fitness. The ESS value of L is the value that prevents the rare genotypes from invading under the influence of natural selection. Some models of cultural transmission have very similar properties to genetic ones, and for our immediate purposes we can think of L as evolving under the influence of either process. Clearly, cultural and genetic transmission also differs in important ways, for example, in the time scale over which they are relevant. Variations in reliance on tradition among contemporary societies likely require a cultural explanation, while a genetic model would be appropriate for studying the evolution of humans from apes. The penultimate section of the chapter will address several explicitly cultural mechanisms that can lead to the ESS.

Consider a population in which most individuals have a learning rule characterized by the parameter value, L, and that has reached the associated equilibrium values $\hat{M}$ and $\hat{B}$. The expected utility of an individual whose learning rule is characterized by parameter L' is

$$E\left\{u(\hat{y},x)\right\} = -U_0 \frac{V_e^2}{(V_e+L)^2}\left[(y=\hat{M})^2 + \hat{B}\right] + \frac{L^2 V_e}{(V_e+L)^2}. \qquad (10.10)$$

One can show that this expression for expected utility is concave with a global maximum at the value of $L, L^{\dagger}$,

$$L^{\dagger} = (y - \hat{M})^2 + \hat{B}. \qquad (10.11)$$

The term $(y - \hat{M})^2 + \hat{B}$ measures the closeness of the population's beliefs about the state of the world to its actual state; V_e measures the accuracy of the information gained by each individual through his own experience. Relation (10.11) [together with (10.1)] says individuals should rely on imitation in proportion to the accuracy of the distribution of beliefs. If $(y - \hat{M})^2 + \hat{B}$ is large compared to V_e, individuals should rely mainly on their own experience; if $(y - \hat{M})^2 + \hat{B}$ is small compared to V_e, then it is optimal to depend mainly on imitation. This expression does not depend on the assumption that the population is in equilibrium, nor that the environment is constant.

Now, suppose that natural selection, or an analogous cultural process, favors L, which increase expected utility. Then because $\hat{B}$ is a function of L, the population will eventually reach an ESS value of L, L^*, such that $L^* = \hat{B}(L^*)$. Using the expression for $\hat{B}$ given in equation (10.9), one can show that the ESS amount of imitation is $L^* = 0$. At equilibrium individuals will depend completely on tradition and totally disregard the evidence presented by one's own experience.

This result has an intuitive explanation. At equilibrium, the relative merit of tradition and learning depends on the relative "noisiness" of the two sources of information. Learning has two effects on the variance in the population. On average, learning causes individual's estimates of y to move toward the correct value and thus acts to reduce the variation in the population. However, errors made during learning increase the variation of the population. Once the population reaches equilibrium in a constant environment, the net effect of learning is to maintain erroneous beliefs in the population. Decreasing L always decreases $\hat{B}$. Thus, any process that acts to change L so as to increase expected utility will reduce L until experience plays no role in determining individual beliefs.

Heterogeneous Environments

There are good reasons to doubt the robustness of the conclusion of the previous section. So far, we have assumed that (1) every member of the population experienced the same state of the world, (2) the state of the world did not vary from generation to generation, and (3) all individuals had the same utility function. Relaxing any one of these assumptions reduces the usefulness of tradition. For example, consider a heterogeneous environment in which different individuals experience different states of the world, but in which there is some chance that individuals in one environment draw models from other environments. In a given environment, people's beliefs will tend toward the optimum in that environment, but drawing models from diverse environments will reduce the likelihood that an individual acquires beliefs that are appropriate to its own environment. The models in this section show that a substantial reliance on tradition may still be evolutionarily stable in a heterogeneous environment or in a population in which utility functions vary. We have shown elsewhere that this conclusion also holds true in an environment that changes through time (Boyd and Richerson, 1983, 1985: Chapter 4).

The essential feature of a heterogeneous environment is that different individuals in the population experience different states of the world, formalized in terms of the value of y. Such variation might arise for many reasons. For example, different young professionals might work in different firms, practice different professions, or live in different regions. We will model heterogeneous environments by assuming that the probability that an individual in the population experiences the environment specified by the value y is given by a normal density function, $f(y)$, with mean 0 and variance H. Setting the mean to 0 can be done without loss of generality since it sets only the origin from which different environments are measured. The variance, H, is a measure of the amount of environmental variation.

Suppose that in the environment characterized by the value y, the frequency of individuals with a subjective probability distribution characterized by a mean $\hat{y}$ before updating is normal with mean $M_t(y)$ and variance $B_t(y)$. Then the mean and variance after updating in that environment are given by equations (10.6) and (10.7) with the appropriate value of y. Further, suppose that there is a probability $1 - m$ that given models experience the same environment that their naive imitators will experience, and a probability, m, that models are drawn at random from the population as a whole. Thus, for example, some of a particular young professional's models might be drawn from another firm in which more (or less) dedication is required to succeed. This model also applies to a population of individuals who live in a uniform environment but whose utility functions have different optima.

With these assumptions, one can derive recursions for the mean and variance of the distribution of prior beliefs in each environment. One can show that the equilibrium mean in habitat y is

$$\hat{M}(y) = \frac{(1 - m)yL}{mV_e + L} \tag{10.12}$$

Equation (10.12) says that in a heterogeneous environment on average individuals have incorrect beliefs about their environment. The mean value of $\hat{y}$ in any environment y results from the balance of two forces. The Bayesian learning process tends to move the mean toward the correct value for that environment, but the exposure to models drawn from other environments moves the mean toward the mean for the entire population, 0. To find the equilibrium variance we proceed exactly as in the previous section.

By averaging the expressions for the equilibrium mean and variance over all habitats, and using the expression for the ESS value of L given by equation (10.11), one can calculate L^* in a heterogeneous environment. The results of this calculation are shown in Figure 10.1, which plots the relative importance of imitation in determining behavior, $V_e/(L^* + V_e)$, as a function of V_e for several values of m. This figure indicates that the equilibrium optimum amount of imitation increases as the quality of the information available through individual experience declines, and as the probability that models are drawn from foreign environments decreases.

These results make sense. The amount of imitation favored by evolutionary processes depends on the relative quality of two sources of information, the information available to individuals through their own experience and through observing the be-

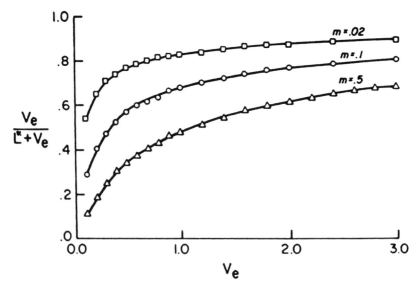

Figure 10.1 Plot of the fractional importance of tradition in determining behavior when the propensity to rely on tradition is at its equilibrium value $[V_e/(L^* + V_e)]$ as a function of the quality of information available to individuals (V_e) assuming a heterogeneous environment, $n = 1$ and $H = 1.0$. Increasing values of m represent increasing amounts of mixing of models among different environments.

havior of their models. As V_e increases, the quality of the information available to individuals through experience declines. As m decreases, the probability that an individual's models will exhibit behavior that is appropriate in the local environment increases. Thus, both increasing V_e and decreasing m cause the equilibrium value of L to increase.

These results suggest that the conclusions of the first section are not entirely misleading. When the amount of mixing between environments is not too large and information is of low quality, individuals achieve the highest expected utility by relying mainly on tradition. We think that this combination of circumstances is not uncommon. The world is complicated and poorly understood and the effects of many decisions are experienced over the course of a lifetime. In deciding how much time to devote to their families, young professionals must not only estimate the immediate effect on their careers and homelives, but the long run effects on the development of their children's adolescent behavior. In such cases the information available to individuals may be very poor indeed, and it is plausible that they are best off relying almost entirely on traditional beliefs. Also notice that Figure 10.1 is a worst case for tradition because it assumes that there is only one model ($n = 1$). As n increases, the equilibrium variance within environments decreases, and, therefore, tradition is relatively more reliable.

It is important to note that even when the amount of individual learning is small, it plays an important role in the evolutionary dynamics of the population.

Some individual learning is necessary if traditional beliefs are to remain utilitarian in local environments in the face of imitation of experienced individuals from other environments. However, a relatively small amount of individual learning is sufficient to keep traditional behaviors on average reasonably near utilitarian optima, so long as mixing between heterogeneous environments is not too great.

Biased Imitation

To this point, we have assumed that individuals adopt a simple unbiased average of the beliefs of the models to which they are exposed. This may not be the most sensible procedure. It would seem better to preferentially imitate models whose behavior has been successful. Young professionals might imitate models who are particularly accomplished in their work and content in their private lives. More generally, naive individuals may imitate prosperous models, contented models, prestigious models, or devout models. By doing this, naive individuals will be more likely to acquire beliefs that lead to prosperity, devotion, contentment, or prestige. In this section we show how this form of biased cultural transmission can increase the frequency of correct beliefs in a population, even when individuals do not understand the causal connection between beliefs and their consequences.

Suppose that instead of simply averaging the beliefs of their models, naive individuals weight models according to their utility-models achieving higher utility having a greater influence on a naive individual's initial belief than individuals with lower utility. There are many plausible observable correlates of utility, such as level of consumption. It seems likely that by imitating individuals with higher levels of consumption, naive individuals might increase their chances of acquiring beliefs that lead to higher utility. In particular, suppose that the initial value of $\hat{y}$ acquired by a naive individual exposed to models with the utilities $u_1, \ldots, u_n$, and beliefs $\hat{y}_1, \ldots, \hat{y}_n$, is

$$\hat{y} = \frac{\sum_{i=1}^{n} \hat{y}_i (1 + bu_i)}{\sum_{i=1}^{n} (1 + bu_i)} \tag{10.13}$$

where b is a positive constant small enough that terms of order b^2 can be ignored.

With this assumption, it can be shown (Boyd and Richerson, 1985) the mean in the population after transmission is

$$M_{t+1} = M_t' + (1 - 1/n)B_t'E\{\text{Reg}[\hat{y}, u(\hat{y})]\} \tag{10.14}$$

where $E\{\text{Reg}(\hat{y}, u(\hat{y})\}$ is the regression of utility on $\hat{y}$ averaged over all possible sets of models. According to equation (10.14), the change in the mean due to biased transmission depends on two factors: the amount of variability within sets of models

$[(1 - 1/n)B_t']$ and the extent to which beliefs about the world are predictably related to utility $[E\{\text{Reg}[\hat{y}, u(\hat{y})]\}]$. Variability within sets of models is important because biased transmission is a culling process that works because some models are more attractive than others. If all models are identical, biased transmission can have no effect. The regression of utility on $\hat{y}$ is a measure of the average effect of a change in an individual's beliefs on his or her utility. If it is positive, individuals with larger values of $\hat{y}$ will have higher utility and, therefore, be more likely to be imitated. This will cause the mean value of $\hat{y}$ in the population to increase. Both the sign and the magnitude of $E\{\text{Reg}[\hat{y}, u(\hat{y})]\}$ depend on the distribution of $\hat{y}$ in the population. If M_t is less than the optimum value (y), larger values of $\hat{y}$ will on average lead to higher utility, and the regression will be positive. The reverse will occur if $M_t < y$. This means that biased transmission will leave the mean unchanged only if it is at the optimal value.

Biased transmission is of interest because it can explain the existence of "folk wisdom," beneficial but poorly understood customs. The preferential imitation of successful people will tend to increase beliefs and practices that lead to success; there is no need for individuals to understand the causal connection between traditional practice and success, even on the part of the individuals who invent the practices.

Natural Selection

So far we have assumed that the probability that a naive individual is exposed to models who are characterized by given beliefs (i.e., a given value of $\hat{y}$) is equal to the frequency of that kind of individual in the previous generation. There is good reason to suppose that this assumption is often violated. For example, the probability that young professionals are advanced in their firm is likely to depend on how much time they devote to work. Underachievers are likely to be fired and overachievers to be promoted. Thus, models who are available for imitation within a firm may represent a biased sample of the original population. More generally, if the behaviors that are shaped by the beliefs acquired by imitation are important, they may affect many aspects of individuals' lives: whom they meet, how long they live, how many children they have, or whether they get tenure. All of these factors could affect the probability that an individual becomes available as a model for others. This means that individuals characterized by some values of $\hat{y}$ will end up being more likely to be imitated than individuals with other values. All other things being equal, it is intuitive that this process, which we will term "natural selection" because of its close resemblance to the biological process, will increase the frequency of the variants most likely to "survive" to enter the pool of models. For a more extensive discussion of the natural selection of culturally transmitted behaviors, see Boyd and Richerson (1985: 173–203).

To formalize this idea, we suppose that the probability that an individual who chooses behavior z becomes available as a model, $W(z)$, is

$$W(z) = \exp\{-(z - w)^2/2K\} \tag{10.15}$$

w is behavior that maximizes the probability of being in the model pool and $1/K$ is a measure of the intensity of the selection process. Note w need not equal y; for example, individuals who devote more than the utility maximizing amount of time to their work may be more likely to be promoted within the firm.

Using (10.15) one can show that the mean value of $\hat{y}$ in the population of models (after selection), M_t'', is

$$M_t'' = \frac{M_t'K + wB_t'}{B_t' + K}. \tag{10.16}$$

Thus, selection moves the mean value of $\hat{y}$ in the population toward the value that maximizes the probability of entering the pool of models, w. One can also show that it reduces the variance of $\hat{y}$ in the population. The strength of both these effects is proportional to the variance in $\hat{y}$ in the population, and the intensity of the selection process.

Natural selection is important because it explains how a reliance on tradition can lead to erroneous or deleterious beliefs. Many social and economic processes affect the kinds of individuals available as models. Some of these processes act on the level of the individual as in the case of the young professional. Others affect whole firms or institutions. For example, firms composed of overachievers may be more likely to survive and expand than firms composed of utility maximizers. When culturally acquired beliefs are important in determining people's behavior, these selective processes will affect what kinds of people are available for imitation, and therefore what beliefs will characterize the population. Since there is no reason to believe that such selective processes always favor utility maximizing behavior, selection may cause the most common beliefs in a population to be deleterious. Nonetheless, if information is imperfect and costly to acquire, it may still be sensible to rely on tradition; a modest systematic error may be preferable to a larger random error.

As an aside, we could also interpret the case of a naive manager being socialized by overachievers as the acquisition of a new utility function by considering that preferences are transmitted by tradition and modified by evolutionary processes such as selection. Such a model would allow a more general account of the relationship between learning and tradition than the Bayesian framework used here permits in order to reflect other models of the decision-making process (e.g., Nelson and Winter's, 1982, evolving "routines"). To enlarge on these problems is, however, outside the scope of this paper. Here we want to emphasize that the standard, and normatively appropriate, Bayesian model is incomplete without a theory of tradition.

Cultural Mechanisms Leading to the ESS Amount of Imitation

So far we have assumed that natural selection acting on genetic variation or an analogous cultural process causes the value of L to change in the direction of increasing expected utility. In this section we consider such cultural processes in more detail. Suppose that the relative dependence on tradition versus own experience itself is a cultural transmitted trait. Then each of the three mechanisms we have just studied can, under the right circumstances, act like natural selection to change L in the direction that increase expected utility.

First, however, it is important to clarify why, within the context of the model outlined so far, it is not possible for individuals to choose directly the appropriate value of L. An essential assumption of this chapter is that the information available to individuals is limited; they know the results of their own direct experience, and the observable behavior of the individuals whom they had available to imitate, but they do not know the optimum behavior, y. From equation (10.11), the optimal amount of imitation is given by the term $\hat{B} + (\hat{M} - y)^2$. Individuals can estimate $\hat{B}$ and $\hat{M}$ from their sample of models, and under some circumstances this information might be sensibly used to modify L. They cannot choose the optimum value of L, however, because that value depends on how close the mean belief in the population is to the optimum, y.

How do people acquire their attitudes toward tradition? Assume that people acquire their value of L by imitation during an earlier episode of social learning. With this assumption, any of the processes that change the frequency of a culturally transmitted trait could affect the evolution of the mean value of L in the population:

1. *Ordinary Learning.* Individuals might acquire an initial value of L by imitation or teaching, and then modify it in accordance with their experience. For example, during enculturation individuals must acquire many different beliefs and behaviors. They might experiment with different values of L during early episodes of learning, retaining the value that seems to yield the best results. This process would change the mean value of L among members of the population in the direction that increased average utility.
2. *Biased Transmission.* Suppose that available models are variable, some of them relying on tradition to a greater degree than others. Moreover, suppose that naive individuals can observe some behavior of their models that serves as a useful index of the model's utility. Then if naive individuals are predisposed to imitate successful models, the mean value of L in the population will move toward the optimum. Notice that this can be true even if, as we have assumed, individuals have no understanding of why certain beliefs lead to higher utilities.
3. *Natural Selection.* Once again assume that individuals vary in their attitudes

toward tradition. Individuals with different values of L will, on average, behave differently. If an individual's behavior affects the probability that he or she becomes a model, natural selection will change the mean value of L in the direction that increases the chance of acquiring behaviors that make an individual likely to become a model. To the extent that there is a correlation between the utility associated with a behavior, and the probability that an individual with the same behavior will become a model, natural selection would modify L in a utility maximizing direction.

To see how these processes might work, consider how attitudes toward tradition might change as a society undergoes industrialization. It is often thought that in preindustrial agricultural societies people rely heavily on tradition. If one supposes that in such societies information is costly, then their reliance on tradition is sensible according to our model. Now, suppose that during industrialization, technical and institutional change makes information less costly. According to the model, people would be better off if they relied more on their own experience and less on tradition. This might come about by any of the three processes mentioned above. To some extent, individuals might have been able to infer from their own experience that a lower reliance on tradition improved their lot. More plausibly, during industrialization people with a tendency to rely more on their own experience and less on traditional beliefs might more readily acquire nontraditional skills that lead to wealth and other kinds of observable markers of success. If successful individuals are more likely to be imitated, biased transmission would decrease average reliance on tradition. Or less traditional individuals might simply be more successful at becoming teachers, managers, and bureaucrats in modernizing societies. The natural selection mechanism could have favored a reduced dependence on tradition through differential achievement of roles that are important in socialization.

Invoking processes that affect earlier episodes of imitation to understand the nature of a subsequent episode clearly creates a problem of explanatory regress. Each of the three processes mentioned depends on some aspect of the imitation process, which then must be explained. In the case of ordinary learning, individuals must have some way of weighting the importance of the value of L that they acquired by imitation against the value that their experience indicates is best. Do they rely on their experience or on imitation? In the case of biased transmission, individuals must have some criteria of success — Do they imitate wealthy individuals? Content individuals? Even natural selection will differ in its effects depending on whom naive individuals are prone to imitate. Are they disproportionately affected by their parents, or are other individuals important?

Ultimately, these are questions about human nature. The answers must be sought in the long-run processes that govern the interactions of cultural and genetic evolution in our species. This topic has been discussed at length by ourselves (Boyd and Richerson, 1985) and others (Pulliam and Dunford, 1980; Lumsden and Wilson, 1981; Durham, 1978). Our work supports two generalizations that are relevant here:

1. If there is genetic variation that affects the tendency of people to imitate, natural selection will tend to modify this tendency so that it maximizes genetic fitness. Thus, to the extent that people prefer fitness enhancing outcomes, selection would increase average utility.

2. There are a variety of conditions in which the fitness maximizing values of L are near 1. Thus, it is plausible that even the earliest episodes of imitation are not directly subject to genetic influences.

Discussion

The economic theory of rational choice under uncertainty is incomplete because it is silent about the source of people's initial beliefs about the world. People are not immortal; sometime between birth and adulthood they acquire a set of beliefs about the world. Because rational behavior, including the rational response to new information, depends on the nature of an individual's prior beliefs, virtually any behavior can be rational, and therefore explicable, given some set of prior beliefs. A peasant's initial resistance to a beneficial innovation is explicable if one supposes that he believes that traditional ways are superior to modern ones. His ultimate rejection of modern practices may also be rational if his beliefs are described by "tight" priors.

In this chapter we have extended the economic theory of choice under uncertainty by assuming that individuals acquire their initial subjective probability distribution by imitation. In particular, we supposed that each naive individual observes the behavior of a number of experienced models sampled from a larger population, induces the belief that led to the observed behavior, and then adopts an average of those beliefs as his own initial beliefs. Then to understand why people acquire the initial beliefs that they do, we must understand why the population is characterized by a particular distribution of beliefs. This means that models that allow for imitation must account for all of the processes that will arise from individual learning and decision making, while others result from social and economic processes that have different effects on people with different beliefs.

This amendment to economic theory is not proposed as a behavioral alternative to the usual assumption that people are rational optimizers. Whether they are optimizers or not, mortal individuals must acquire their initial beliefs from others. It well may be that the particular model of imitation we have chosen is incorrect, that Bayesian optimizing is a poor model of how humans make choices, or that genetic inheritance is important in determining people's behavioral predispositions. In any case, we believe that a complete theory of human behavior would have a similar structure to the models outlined here; it would keep track of the dynamics of a population of decision makers by accounting for the processes that change the distribution of beliefs or other predispositions in the population. Some of these processes will result from people's attempts at improving their lot, while others will result from what happens to them because they hold the beliefs that they do.

There are two lessons that can be drawn from the models presented here: First, they suggest that a strong reliance on tradition may indeed be sensible. At equilibrium, individuals may rely almost entirely on traditional knowledge and ignore any other information that may be available to them. When (1) the quality of information available to individuals is low and improving it is costly, and (2) there is a good chance that the individuals' models experienced the same environment that they experience. Traditional solutions to problems may be much closer to the optimal behavior, on the average, than the solutions that individuals could devise on their own.

The theory also suggests, however, that when traditions are substantially more important in determining people's beliefs than their own experience, a variety of processes other than individual learning may affect the commonness of different beliefs. When tradition is important, it acts like a system of inheritance to create heritable variation within and among groups. Processes like biased transmission and natural selection can then affect the frequency of different beliefs by making it more likely that some beliefs will be transmitted from one generation to the next. When the effect of individual experience is small, it is plausible that such processes may have an important effect on the way that people behave.

Some of these processes, such as biased transmission, may increase the frequency of utility enhancing behaviors. This fact is of interest because it may explain "folk wisdom," that is, the fact that people hold beneficial traditions that they do not understand. The most striking examples of folk wisdom comes from anthropological research. For example, in many parts of the New World native peoples treated maize as a strong base to produce foods such as hominy or masa as part of their traditional cuisine. Katz et al. (1974) have shown that such treatment makes more of the amino acid lysine available (lysine is the least plentiful amino acid in maize). They have also shown that there was a strong negative correlation between the use of alkali treatment and the availability of protein from sources other than maize. Given that many factors influence nutrition, and that only small, uncontrolled samples were available, it is difficult to see how individuals in these cultures could have detected the effect of the treatment. Indeed, although Africans have been using maize as a staple for a few centuries, alkali cooking has not yet developed there. It seems more likely that it could spread because eating treated maize made people more successful or more likely to survive, and, therefore, more likely to be imitated. Folk wisdom also plays a role in the economic thinking. Hayek (1978) argues that traditional beliefs and institutional arrangements reflect wisdom beyond the ken of any individual, and he bases many political and economic prescriptions on this view. Similarly, proponents of an evolutionary view of the firm (e.g., Alchian, 1950; Nelson and Winter, 1982) argue that inherited decision rules that determine a firm's response to market conditions may be sensible in ways that nobody in the firm understands.

However, for other processes that affect the frequency of alternative beliefs in a population, such as natural selection, there is no guarantee that utility maximizing behaviors will be favored. This may explain the existence of behavior that seems paradoxical under the usual assumption of individual rationality. In our example of natural selection on behaviors transmitted in the workplace, people could come to work harder than they would desire. Such behaviors could remain in a population because on average the traditions transmitted within a firm are more useful than alternative behaviors individuals could acquire by their own efforts. In other words, a reliance on tradition causes individuals to trade systematically suboptimal behaviors transmitted within the firm for the randomly suboptimal ones that can be discovered by individual effort. Elsewhere we show that processes other than natural selection can have this general effect (Boyd and Richerson, 1985).

Finally, models of the kind described here may also be useful in clarifying the relationship between human evolution and contemporary human behavior. Hirshleifer (1977) has argued that one of the attractive features of sociobiological theory is that it provides an independent way to derive utility functions; namely, human preferences have been shaped by natural selection so that, at least in the context of a hunter–gatherer society, they enhanced genetic fitness. While we are sympathetic to this general approach, we have argued (Boyd and Richerson, 1985) that many human preferences are difficult to explain on this basis. For example, many contemporary professionals seem to sacrifice genetic fitness by delaying marriage, reducing family size, and limiting time devoted to child care in order to gain professional success. Such behavior is explicable, however, if one imagines that individuals who value professional accomplishment for its own sake are more likely to rise to positions of influence than those with more "sociobiological" values. To take another example, humans cooperate in large groups of unrelated individuals to provide public goods (such as victory in warfare) in a way that seems difficult to reconcile with individual fitness maximization. In the work cited above, we have shown how some forms of cultural transmission, permitting selection on culture at the level of groups, can arise from attempt to use traditions to enhance the ends of genetic fitness. To take advantage of the economies of information acquisition that tradition offers requires a measure of blind trust of traditional wisdom. Such weak rational control on tradition by its users may be sensible, but at the same time allow culture to respond to blind evolutionary processes unique to the cultural system of inheritance. These processes may ultimately have important effects on what individuals prefer as well as on what they believe.

Note

We thank Robert Brandon, John Conlisk, Jack Hirshleifer, Richard Nelson, Eric A. Smith, John Staddon, Robert Seyfarth, Joan Silk, Michael Wade, and John Wiley for providing comments on an earlier version of this manuscript; we also thank John Gillespie and Ron Pullman for crucial insights about modeling environmental variation and learning, respectively. As tradition dictates, we stipulate that any errors are our own.

Bibliography

Alchian, A.A., 1950, "Uncertainty, Evolution and Economic Theory," *American Economic Review*, 58, 219–238.

Bandura, A., 1977, *Social Learning Theory*, Prentice Hall, Englewood Cliffs, NJ.

Boyd, Robert, and Peter J. Richerson, 1983, "The Cultural Transmission of Acquired Variation: Effect on Genetic Fitness," *Journal of Theoretical Biology*, 100, 567–596.

Boyd, Robert, and Peter J. Richerson, 1985, *Culture and the Evolutionary Process*, University of Chicago Press, Chicago, IL.

Cavalli-Sforza, L.L., and Feldman, M.W., 1981, *Cultural Transmission and Evolution*, Princeton University Press, Princeton, NJ.

Conlisk, John, 1980, "Costly Optimizers Versus Cheap Imitators," *Journal of Economic Behavior and Organization*, 1, 275–293.

Durham, W.H., 1978, "Toward a Coevolutionary Theory of Human Biology and Culture," in A. Caplan (ed.), *The Sociobiology Debate*, Harper & Row, New York.

Edgerton, R.B. (with W. Goldschmidt), 1971, *The Individual in Cultural Adaptation: A Study of Four East African Peoples*, University of California Press, Berkeley.

Fuller, J.L., and R.W. Thompson, 1960, *Behavior Genetics*, Wiley, New York.

Hayek, F.A., 1978, *The Three Sources of Human Values*, L.T. Hobhouse Memorial Trust Lecture 44, London School of Economics and Political Science, London.

Hirshleifer, Jack, 1977, "Economics From a Biological Viewpoint," *Journal of Law and Economics*, 20, 1–52.

Hirshleifer, Jack, and J. Riley, 1979, "The Analytics of Uncertainty and Information: An Expository Survey," *Journal of Economic Literature*, 17, 1375–1421.

Katz, S., M. Hediger, and L. Valleroy, 1974, "Traditional Maize Processing Techniques in the New World," *Science*, 184, 765–773.

Lumsden, C., and E.O. Wilson, 1981, *Genes, Mind, and Culture*, Harvard University Press, Cambridge, MA.

Nelson, Richard R., and Sidney G. Winter, 1982, *An Evolutionary Theory of Economic Change*, Harvard University Press, Cambridge, MA.

Pulliam, R., and C. Dunford, 1980, *Programmed to Learn*, Columbia University Press, New York.

Richerson, Peter J., and Robert Boyd, 1978, "A Dual Inheritance Model of the Human Evolutionary Process I: Basic Postulates and a Simple Model," *Journal of Social Biological Structure*, 1, 127–154.

Rogers, A., 1989, "Does Biology Constrain Culture," *American Anthropologist*, 90, 819–831.

Rosenthal, T., and B. Zimmerman, 1978, *Social Learning and Cognition*, Academic Press, New York.

Scarr, S., and R.A. Weinberg, 1976, "I.Q. Performance of Black Children Adopted by White Families," *American Psychology*, 31, 726–739.

Smith, S.S., 1975, *The Battered Child Syndrome*, Butterworths, London.

Van Maanen, J., and E.H. Schein, 1979, "Toward a Theory of Organizational Socialization," *Research on Organization and Behavior*, 1, 209–263.

11

Self-Organization as a Process in Evolution of Economic Systems

JACQUES LESOURNE

Over these past 15 years the industrial process has exhibited economic renewal or decline of regions or nations, progressive polarization of geographic space, sclerosis or success of enterprises, conditions for the emergence of dominant firms, discovery and diffusion of innovations, perenniality of the dynamic differentiation of markets, and change in sociological, economic and political modes of regulation. These movements suggest a self-organizing process that consists of the forming of behavior, the establishing of relations between actors, the creation of rules, and the building of institutions, that is, the emerging of an eventual order, its adaptation, its transformation, and its dissolving into chaos.

Using this observation as a starting point, I have developed with the team from the Econometrics Laboratory at the Conservatoire National des Arts et Métiers (Paris) a series of models of self-organization in economics, which shows how systems acquire new properties by organizing or reorganizing themselves. We set ourselves the task of building precise models inspired by microeconomic theory and based on explicit hypotheses.

To illustrate this work, I shall summarize three of these models:

- a model that emulates the endogenous forming of a workers' union within the labor market;
- a model that analyzes the differentiation of a labor market into two distinct markets following training phenomena that are produced throughout the dynamic adaptation of supply and demand; and
- a model that describes the irreversible dynamics of the localization of workers confronted with a geographically dispersed labor market.

I hope that these three examples will enable readers to share three convictions that are at the base of our research program:

1. It is possible in economics to devise models of self-organization that account for the process of evolution without starting from arbitrary analogies borrowed from other sciences.

2. It is conceivable to reinsert progressively the essential part of the contributions of neoclassic microeconomics into the larger paradigm of evolutionary self-organization. Within this new framework, the traditional results will appear as particular cases engendered by specific adaptation behaviors of actors and by the simplicity of the environment (the absence of irreversibility, for example). But a much richer group of results will be brought out. They will allow the theoretic interpretation of a large number of phenomena that economic observations have detected but that current economic theory does not satisfactorily take into account, having as a consequence a reorientation of reflections on desirable microeconomic policies.

3. By emphasizing the fact that an economic system can, by starting from the same initial situation, knows different evolutions depending on the uncertainties of its history, the paradigm of evolutionary self-organization proposes a coherent vision of the future, undetermined but engendered by a mixture of necessity, chance, and will power: the necessity of heavy trends that can be modified only slowly, the random nature of scientific discovery, the appearance of exceptional figures or the conjunction of situations, and the desire of individuals or social groups to incorporate incompatible projects into reality.

The Birth of a Labor Union[1]

Imagine a labor market consisting on the one hand of individuals having identical professional skills, offering one unit of work each but differing in the minimum salary that they will accept, and on the other hand consisting of enterprises each needing a unit of work from the preceding individuals, but differing in the maximum salary that they are willing to pay. The minimum and maximum salaries define, respectively, a "demand curve" and a "supply curve." Their intersection determines the equilibrium salary and the level of employment in the absence of a labor union.

The dynamics of such a market may be studied by supposing that enterprises and workers commit themselves by contract for a period and that during each period contracts for the following period are signed, the signing of the contracts putting a triple process into play:

- a search process (during each period the workers appear in random order on the market and draw a random sample of companies which they visit);
- a process of negotiation (workers try to obtain employment from the company that they know and that offers them the best conditions); and
- a process of adaptation of demands (workers tend to increase their demands when they are employed and lower them when they are out of work, while companies adjust the salary offered depending on whether or not the position is filled).

It can be demonstrated (Lesourne-Laffond, 1979; Laffond-Lesourne, 1981) that the dynamics of such a market leads in a finite period of time with probability 1 to a stable state, which is none other than the static equilibrium.

But what happens to the preceding dynamics when the workers are able to form a union? And how can such a union come into being? To study this question let us suppose that there exists a single "embryo" of a union who could be an individual who during each period takes precise initiatives towards the workers and the firms.

What structures of the market, of the decision-making processes, of the adaptation of demands of the actors and the union, will allow the union to develop and survive?

The Market

The market proceeds through a series of successive periods, $t \in \mathcal{N}^+$ standing for both the tth period and the starting date of that period. Present on the market all through the evolution will be

1. a set M of individuals, each individual $k(1 \leq k \leq m_0)$ being characterized by the reservation salary $w(k)$ below which he or she refuses to work under any circumstances; the individuals are classified by rising order of demands, $k' > k$, implying $\lambda w(k) < w(k')$;
2. a set N of companies, each company $i(i \leq i \leq n_0)$ being characterized by the maximum salary $\bar{v}(i)$ above which it prefers that the position remain vacant under any circumstances; these companies are ranked in descending order of demands, $i' > i$ implying $\bar{v}(i)' < \bar{v}(i)$. If there were no union, a single salary would emerge in such a way that K individuals would be employed and K positions filled.

At each date T, the union embryo formulates a salary demand σ_t that verifies the two following conditions:

$$\forall t \in \mathcal{N} \sigma_t \geq s_0 \quad \text{with} \quad \sigma_1 > s_0 \tag{11.1}$$

$$\text{if } \exists T \in \mathcal{N} \text{ such that } \sigma_T = s_0 \quad \text{then } \forall t > T \sigma_t = s_0 \tag{11.2}$$

- The first condition states that the salary demanded is at least equal to the salary in an equilibrium state without a union, the initial union salary demand always being greater than the equilibrium salary.
- The second condition means that the union has lost its power and thus disappears from the moment it has to bring its salary demand down to the level of the equilibrium salary on a market without a union.

When there is a union, two markets coexist during period t:

- *an organized market* on which operate the set N_t of companies having signed with the union for the period T and the set M_t of individuals who are members of the union; m_t and n_t will be used to designate the cardinals of these two sets;

- *a free market* on which operate the other companies and other individuals; on this free market, the confrontation between supply and demand defines an equilibrium salary s_t (there may in fact be a range of salaries but then, for the sake of hypothesis, the highest one is taken as the equilibrium salary).

During each period, it is assumed that the free market converges towards a stable state characterized by the salary s_t and by the associated consequences as to the individuals employed and the positions occupied. At the end of the period t all the economic actors are supposed to know the salary s_t.

The Individual Decision-Making Process

During each period, a contract is offered by the embryo to each of the workers. According to the terms of the contract, the worker promises to work only for companies that sign with the union.

Each worker naturally makes the decision to accept or refuse the contract based on individual past experiences and present knowledge. More particularly, each individual is supposedly characterized at period t by an indicator $a_t(k)$, which we call the worker's *amount of attraction for the union*. It is in relation to the level of this indicator that the individual decides to become a member of the union or not:

1. If $a_t(k) \leq 0$, the individual does not join the union, $k \notin Mt$
2. If $a_t > 0$ and $a_{t-1}(k) \leq 0$ the individual joins the union with a probability $p(k)$ $[0 < p(k) < 1]$ $a_{t-1}(k) > 0$ the individual joins the union with probability 1.

In other words, the amount of attraction must be positive for two consecutive periods for the individual to become with certainty a member of the union.

We shall see a bit further on how the amount of attraction is determined.

The Company Decision-Making Process

On the strength of the number m_t of its members and their commitments, the union sets σ_t and contacts the companies in random order. It suspends its offers when the number of enterprises having accepted reaches m_t or, if this number is not reached, when all the companies have been contacted.

Each firm is free to accept or to refuse the union's proposition on the basis of its past experience and present knowledge. Each knows, in particular, that if it rejects the union's propositions, all of the members will refuse to work for the firm. More particularly, each firm is supposedly characterized by a *threshold $b_t(i)$ of negotiation with the union*, the building of which will be explained in the following paragraph. This threshold has the dimension of a salary.

The company contacted

1. refuses the union propositions if $b_t(i) < \sigma_t$

2. signs a protocol of agreement with the union if $b_t(i) \geq \sigma_t$; it then becomes part of the group N_t^p of potential contractors.

After signing a protocol, a potential contractor has the right to cancel the contract with a certain probability at the period t. For the sake of convenience, we shall use the term *betrayal* to designate this situation.

When betrayal occurs, we shall assume that the union retaliates by forbidding its members to work for any company during that period. At that point, the entire group of enterprises will find itself back on the free market.

The result of the preceding is that

$$N_t = N_t^p \quad \text{or} \quad N_t = \emptyset \qquad (11.3)$$

and that $n_t \leq m_t$.

The Adaptation of the Demands of the Actors and of the Union

The problem of adaptation of demands affects the individuals, the companies, and the union alike.

The Individuals

Every member of the union is assumed to have the same probability of being recruited by the signing companies:

$$\pi_t = n_t/m_t. \qquad (11.4)$$

The average income that individual k obtains (or could obtain) at period t as a member of the union is

$$h_t(k) = \pi_t \sigma_t + (1 - \pi_t)w(k) \qquad (11.5)$$

The individual compares this average income to the salary on the free market and in consequence adjusts his amount of attraction for the union. He increases the amount if $h_t(k) > s_t$ and reduces it in the opposite case. The rule of adaptation drawn is the following:

$$a_{t+1}(k) = a_t(k) + \mu[h_t(k) - s_t] \qquad (11.6)$$

in which $\mu(\cdot)$ is a strictly increasing function such that $\mu(0) = 0$.[2]

The Companies

The model distinguishes between several cases depending upon whether the company refuses the union offers, accepts and then betrays them, or transforms the protocol into a firm contract.

1. If the company refuses the union offers, three situations are possible:
   a. $s_t > \sigma_t$: the company seeing that the salary on the free market is high, is ready to make concessions to sign with the union at period $(t + 1)$; it increases its threshold by one unit unless it has already reached $\bar{v}(i)$.
   b. $s_0 \leq s_t \leq \sigma_t$: the company does not modify its attitude towards the union.
   c. $s_t < s_0$: the company hardens its position in negotiating and reduces the threshold by at least one unit.
2. If the company has contracted then betrayed, two situations are possible:
   a. $s_t \geq \sigma_t$; the company does not modify its attitude and will again be ready to sign at the following time period if the union does not modify its offer.
   b. $s_t < \sigma_t$; the company lowers its negotiating threshold to just below the union offer; it will only be ready to negotiate at the following period if the union lowers its offer.
3. If the company has signed a firm contract, the threshold of negotiation remains unchanged.

It is assumed that a company cannot take the initiative of a betrayal for two consecutive periods.

The Union

It naturally seeks to increase the salary demanded, but it must also consider the risk of lowering the number of companies that will agree to work with it.
   The following rules express this behavior:

$n_t > 0$
    If $x_t > \sigma_t$, the union increases its offer by one unit.
    If $x_t \leq \sigma_t$, the union maintains its offer or increases it with a certain probability.

$n_t = 0$
    If $s_t > \sigma_t$, the union maintains its offer.
    If $s_t \leq \sigma_t$, the union lowers its offer by a unit (unless there are potential candidates, in which case it leaves it as it is).

Finally, we assume

- that at period $0, n_t - 0$, the salary being at its equilibrium level s_0;
- that the enterprises have at the start negotiation thresholds that are positive; and
- that the individuals do not necessarily know about the union at Period 1 (if $\tau_k > 0$ is the date from which the individual k knows about the union, one will set down a $\tau_{k-1} = -\infty, \alpha\tau_k \in \mathcal{N}$).

The model possesses several characteristics that are crucial in understanding its dynamics:

- The actors do not adjust their demands abruptly. Instead, their behavior depends on the past history of events they have experienced.

- The salary on the free market tending to be lower than that on the organized market, an enterprise would always benefit from betrayal if it were the only one on the market. The result is that if enterprises betray separately and in turn one would witness a gradual destruction of the union, the single salary s_0 prevailing on the market. This phenomenon does not take place in the model because of the conjunction of the two following linkages;
  a. as soon as a company betrays, the union members refuse to work and do not leave the union immediately, and
  b. from that point on, the influx of an additional demand for work on the free market causes the salary to rise abruptly on that market and enterprises can see that it is not in their interest in the short term to betray the union.
- The actors never give up trying to improve their situation. Thus, when $\sigma_t \geq s_t$ and $n_t > 0$, the union increases its demand with a probability, which is not nil. In the same way, an enterprise that did not betray at the preceding period and that signed a potential candidate protocol annuls its contract nonetheless with a positive probability.

Long Run Dynamic Behavior

During any one period, the state of the system may be defined using the following triplet:

$$e_t = \{\sigma_t, M_t, N_t\} \tag{11.7}$$

which we shall call a *configuration*.

We shall call *connected union of m size and σ salary* the union formed by the m first individuals ranked in order of the decreasing $w(k)$ and for which $w(k) \leq \sigma$.

It is therefore possible to demonstrate the following proposition:

Proposition 1. *Starting with an initial configuration, there exists a date T such that one of the following properties shall be verified:*

- *the union dies before T,*
- *$\forall_t > T$ the union exists and is connected.*

In this case the labor market presents the following characteristics:

1. *there exist σ and $\bar{\sigma}$ such that $\sigma_t \in [\sigma, \bar{\sigma}]$;*
2. *there are two subsets of enterprises not necessarily connected N and $\bar{N}$ such that $N \subset Nt \subset \bar{N}$;*
3. *the set of individuals may be separated into five connected groups:*
   a. *two groups, possibly empty, of individuals never belonging to the union, one composed of individuals having very low minimal demands, the other composed of individuals having minimal demands superior to $\bar{\sigma}$;*

b. *two groups, possibly empty, of individuals belonging intermittently to the union; and*

c. *a group not empty,* M *of individuals belonging to the union at all times.*

The groups M, N *and* $\bar{N}$, *the salaries* σ *and* $\bar{\sigma}$, *depend on the past history of the market.*

This model helps to understand how, from a system in which only unrelated individuals and enterprises are present, a new institution may be formed, grouping the workers and separating the labor market into two submarkets: an organized market with an imposed salary and a free market on which the salary results from the confrontation of supply and demand.

But for the union embryo to be transformed into a stable union, two conditions seem necessary. On the one hand, the individuals and enterprises do not abruptly modify their attitude toward the union; the individual who notices that belonging to the union was not advantageous during the last period reduces the amount of attraction but does not necessarily quit the union; the company that notices that the salary on the free market is lower than the union salary does not abruptly lower the threshold of negotiation to the level of the salary on the free market. On the other hand, the companies linked to the union, by presenting themselves on the free market, test the advantage of continuing to sign with the union, but the union members refusal to work creates an arrival of enterprises on the free market, pushes the salary on that market up to the union salary level, and brings the companies back to an agreement with the union.

Moreover, the size and the salary the union demands are a function of the past history and not only of the initial conditions.

It should also be noted that the outcome of market evolution is not predetermined, and that self-organization is imperfect since there remains a group of individuals and companies whose behavior is unstable, and that for an indefinite period of time.

We shall now approach another phenomenon of self-organization that results from the interaction of the evolution of the labor market and the training of individuals.

The Creation of Professional Skills by the Labor Market[3]

The model that we are going to describe deals with a labor market that is, in the beginning, identical to that of the preceding description. The individuals are assumed initially to be unskilled workers (workers for short). During the course of market evolution certain workers may acquire the skills. The companies may now choose between organizations based on unskilled workers or skilled technicians. A second more-or-less sizable labor market may therefore appear. Depending on its past history, the economy may use the whole of its human resources, making technicians of those workers who are potentially capable of such, or it may be trapped in an end state rendering sterile a greater or lesser fraction of its human capital.

The Market

The market, as before, goes through a series of successive periods.

The *individuals* are introduced in the same manner except that their competence is not identical. Some have competence 1 (worker), others have competence 2 (technician). $m_\alpha(\alpha \in 1, 2)$ designates the set of individuals capable of occupying a technological position α. By hypothesis, all of the individuals can occupy a technological position 1, but only technicians can occupy a technological position 2. In other words,

$$M = M_1 M_2 \subset M_1 \tag{11.8}$$

The *enterprises* $(1 \leq i \leq n)$ are also treated as before, but each of them chooses a technology α and employs an individual with at most competence α. If it pays a salary s, it makes a profit $\bar{v}_\alpha(i) - s$, the $\bar{v}_\alpha(i)$ taking on integer values.

Shall be designated by

$i_t(k)$ the enterprise that, during period t, employs individual k [by agreement $i_t(k) = 0$ means that individual k is unemployed];

$s_t(i)$ the salary paid by enterprise i during period t if its position is occupied;

$s_t(k) = s_t[i_t(k)]$ the salary received by individual k during period t if he is employed during this period;

$\alpha_t(k)$ the competence of individual k at moment t;

N_t and M_t the sets of positions occupied and individuals employed during period t;

N_t^1 and N_t^2 the sets of enterprises (whose positions are occupied during period t) that have recourse respectively to technologies 1 and 2.

The Dynamics of the Model with Invariant Competence

Let us first discuss the demands of the actors. For each individual k, there is, throughout period t, an integer $w_{t+1} \geq w(k)$ that defines his or her minimum salary demand for the period $(t + 1)$.

The same as for each enterprise i, there is, throughout period t an integer $x_{t+1}(i)$ that defines the minimum profit demanded for the period $(t + 1)$. Under these conditions, the maximum salary offer for this enterprise for an individual of competence α in period $(t + 1)$ is

$$v_{t+1}^\alpha(i) = \bar{v}_\alpha(i) - x_{t+1}(i) \tag{11.9}$$

During period t, the individuals appear in turn on the market; each individual then draws at random — all of the positions having a nonzero probability of being discovered — a subset $I_t(k)$ of positions of whose offers he or she observes $[i_t(k) \in I_t(k)]$. Let us suppose that k be the τth individual who appears on the market.

Each enterprise i makes that individual an offer of employment at salary $z_\tau^\alpha(i)$ for the work category α and period $(t + 1)$. These offers are firm offers. We must then describe how the company chooses $z_\tau^\alpha(i)$ and how the individual k chooses among the offers that are made. Let NN_τ be the set of enterprises that has found an employee for $(t + 1)$ before the appearance of k on the market $[z_\tau^\alpha(i) = 0$ if $i \in NN_\tau]$.

Individual k considers the offers of the companies in subgroup $I_t(k)$ not belonging to NN_τ. He classifies them by decreasing salary and considers the positions associated with the maximum salary. If the set is empty or if the maximum salary is inferior to $w_{t+1}(k)$, the individual is unemployed for period $(t + 1)$. If the maximum salary is above or equal to $w_{t+1}(k)$, the individual chooses to remain in the same company if he or she can or takes any one of the possible positions.

As for the offer of company i, it is equal to $v_{t+1}^\alpha(i)$ if the individual k is different from $k_t(i)$ and to the salary of period t if $k = k_t(i)$.

But how do the actors readjust their demand from one period to another? For the companies, two cases may be imagined according to whether the position is occupied or not during period t.

1. In the first case, the company tries to increase its profit by one unit when the passage from period t to period $(t + 1)$ is made.
2. In the second case, the company reduces by a unit its profit demands (and thus increases its salary offers). For the individuals, there are also two cases according to whether they are employed or not during period t.
   a. If employed, they maintain their demands.
   b. If unemployed, they reduce them by a unit.

More general assumptions on demand adjustments made by the actors may be introduced without troubling the convergence of the market towards a stable state, but the preceding ones have the advantage of being simple.

A state e_t of the market is a triplet,

$$e_t = \{i_t(\cdot), s_t(\cdot), \alpha_t(\cdot)\}. \tag{11.10}$$

It is stable if for every $t' \geq t, e_{t'} = c_t$.

The following proposition can then be demonstrated.

Proposition 2. *With the given hypotheses, the market converges in probability toward a stable state in a finite period of time. This state has the following properties:*

- *The salaries prevailing for unskilled workers (and for technicians, respectively) differ by one unit at the most.*
- *For each active enterprise, there is no better technology than that which it employs.*

- *For each inactive enterprise, neither of the two technologies is profitable.*
- *Any unemployed individuals have minimal demands that are too high considering their skills.*

The Dynamics with Modification of Individual Competence

The new phenomenon is the following: certain individuals who at the beginning of the process are of competence level 1 can randomly and in function to their history acquire competence 2. This acquisition is assumed to be irreversible.

One may, for example, suppose that individual k of competence 1 employed at period t by company i (therefore in a competence 1 position) acquires for the period $(t + 1)$ competence 2 with the probability p_{ki}. This probability depends on the individuals: some are more gifted and more motivated than others. It also depends on the companies: certain positions provide more training than others. Naturally, the probability p_{ki} may be nil for certain k regardless of the company and for certain i regardless of the individual k. It is supposed that the competence that individual k will have in period $(t + 1)$ is known before the search for employment starts for that period.

The definition of a stable state now brings another condition into play: for every $t' \geq t$, the competence of the individuals must remain the same.

Under these circumstances, with the new hypotheses drawn, the market always converges toward a stable state in a finite period of time.

But this extension of the preceding proposition hides a very different economic reality. To analyze it, we shall define a *promotable individual* to be any individual k for whom there exists a date t and a succession of market states $e_0, e_1, \ldots, e_t$, for which the probability that the individual rise to competence 2 in $(t + 1)$ is positive (we shall denote M_p the set of promotable individuals), and a *promoted individual* any promotable individual for whom there exists a date t at which he will have risen to competence 2 following the effective functioning of the market.

Granted, the market does converge toward a stable state, but this stable state is not unique and *depending on the stable state* reached, the individuals promoted are not the same.

Let us imagine a market that functions in such a way that at date t all promotable individuals are promoted; from t on, the market will converge toward a stable state in which all the *efficient* individuals (and only the efficient ones) will be employed.[4] Let M_e stand for the set of these efficient individuals.

Let us then consider an ordinary functioning of the market. This functioning will lead to a *stable state*, which can be qualified as "*finished*" if that stable state is such that all individuals $k \in M_e \cap M_p$ have been promoted. In this case, the functioning of the market has revealed all the existing usable apprenticeship potential in the economy. It has engendered no loss of human resources. But there naturally exist *unfinished stable states* in which the economy may, in a way, find itself entrapped as a result of an evolution that has rendered sterile a part of the potential human resources. Hence, the fundamental question: *under what conditions does the random apprenticeship resulting from the functioning of the market lead to a stable finished state?*

The Characteristics of Stable States

This question being difficult, we shall limit ourselves to two particular cases.

1. that in which all enterprises are formative (if j exists in such a way that $p_{kj} > 0$ for a certain individual k, then $p_{ki} > 0$ regardless of i);
2. that in which all individuals are promotable.

In the *first case*, it can be demonstrated that a sufficient condition for all equilibrium states to be finished is that the most demanding of the employable individuals in a finished state equilibrium be both promotable and willing to work in a competence 1 position if they are not yet promoted. In other words, this is sufficient for the market to lead to full use of human resources that the individuals do not hinder their information with premature demands.

In the *second case*, a sufficient condition for all the equilibrium states to be finished is that in every finished equilibrium state, there exists at least one formative enterprise having recourse to technology 1; this enterprise will work for the collectivity by training individuals of competence 2 until the stock of efficient promotable individuals is exhausted. In other terms, it is essential that not all formative enterprises find it to their advantage to adopt technology 2.

Examining these two particular cases helps to understand the nature of the mechanisms that can trap an economy in a state which makes poor use of its potential human resources.

The Significance of the Results

The model shows how the functioning of the market can engender new markets at random and create, in variable quantities, new resources for the economy. With this model to start from, it is easy to imagine more complex models. Here are just a few:

1. It is possible to introduce more than two categories of individuals, individuals of competence level 2 becoming, through random endogenous training, individuals of competence level 3 (engineers, for example).
2. Only for the convenience of formalization do we suppose that each enterprise employs only one worker. In reality the companies choose their organization in relation to the salaries of different categories of personnel and this organization generally implies recourse to personnel of different categories. The more technologies the company has at its disposal, the fewer the possible combinations of positions requiring diverse skills, or the more the relative salaries are rigid, the greater the risk of rendering human resources sterile.

3. It is reasonable to believe that the end products of the two technologies are different. If such is the case, the economy will produce only level 1 products at first; level 2 products will begin to appear afterward. Their price, very high at first, will diminish progressively as level 2 individuals become more abundant. But the evolution may be blocked if enterprises move too quickly to technology 2 or if the demands of the promoted individuals are too high.

4. The birth of a new activity (computer designing, launching of satellites) may necessitate a minimum stock of individuals with certain skills. At this point, an economy trapped in an unfinished stable state may be incapable of developing certain branches of industry. The functioning of the labor market may therefore, from the same starting point, give rise to economies whose structures will differ more and more.

5. Just as companies reveal individuals to themselves, the latter are capable of incidentally bringing companies to discover technologies. It would be easy to construct a model in which individual k of competence level 2 is capable of suggesting to enterprise i — which employs him in a level 1 position — technology 2 with a probability of g_{ki}.

6. Parallel to the functioning of the labor market, there exists another process intended to modify individual skills: education. According to the situation, this process engenders individuals of superior competence directly or simply increases the probabilities p_{ki}, experience remaining indispensable. Interaction between the two processes has a fundamental influence on the future of an economy.

The self-organization mechanisms brought out by this second model facilitates the understanding of certain essential aspects of the impact of the functioning of the labor market on growth, both in industrial countries as well as in developing countries.

The last model presented will illustrate a third form of self-organization, a form that comes into play in dealing with the concentration of the localization of economic agents.

The Irreversible Structure of Space[5]

This last model also brings in a set M of individuals ($1 \leq k \leq m$) with the minimum demand $w(k)$ and a set N of enterprises ($1 \leq k \leq n$) with the maximum salary $v(i)$, but the positions offered by the companies are geographically dispersed in a fixed manner in a set L of localities. As the individuals on the other hand, can work only in the locality they live in, they are sometimes forced to move. A localization of individuals is a function l_t from M into L defining for each individual k the locality $l_t(k)$ where he or she resides during period t.

The individuals will plan on moving from one locality to another in order to have access to a position. To describe this situation, the usual theory of migrations assumes that individuals compare the present value of their future net incomes with

or without a move, which comes down to considering them capable of solving the most complex stochastic dynamic programs! Consequently, we have assumed more realistically that an individual living in one locality and planning on moving to another directly compares the salaries that are offered to a *cost of anticipated access* linked to moving from the first locality to the second. Such a cost includes not only the monetary and psychological cost of the move, but also the value the individual attaches to future job prospects and salaries in the two cases.

Let α, β, γ, be three localities; we shall use $d_k(\alpha, \beta)$ to designate the cost of anticipated access for individual k in the move from α to β and it shall be accepted that the costs of anticipated access verify the triangular inequality:

$$d_k(\alpha, \beta) \leq d_k(\alpha, \gamma) + d_k(\gamma, \beta). \tag{11.11}$$

These preliminaries having been set forth, it is possible to analyze with this model the notions of optimality and stability, the problem of convergence, and the significance of the results.

The Concepts of Optimality

To introduce them a few definitions are called for:

- We shall designate by the term *assignment* of individuals to positions, a one-to-one function of a part M_x (the individuals employed) of M into a part N_x of N defining for each individual k in M_x the position $x(k)$ that he or she occupies (N_x is the set of occupied positions in assignment x).
- A *state of the market* will be a couple (x, s) in which x is an assignment and s a function that links to each position i the salary $s(i)$ paid [with the agreement $s(i) = \bar{v}(i)$ if i is not occupied]. If l is the localization of individuals corresponding to assignment x, the state of the market can naturally take the form of a triplet (x, l, s).
- Finally, *the collective utility* of a state of the market *from an initial localization l_0 of individuals* will be defined by the relation.

$$U(l_0, x) = \sum_{k \in M_x} \{\bar{v}[x(k)] - w(k)\} - \sum_{k \in M_x} d_k \{l_0(k), \quad L[x(k)]\}. \tag{11.12}$$

The first term may be called *the surplus freed by assignment x*, the second being, accurate to a sign, the sum of costs of anticipated access borne by the individuals who must change localities.

Two concepts of optimality may then be defined:

1. An assignment x is a *differential optimum in relation to a localization l_0* if for any assignment y:

$$U(l_0, y) \leq U(l_0, x). \tag{11.13}$$

The notion of a differential optimum therefore has meaning only in relation to an initial localization l_0.

2. A couple (x, l) of an assignment and of the localization that corresponds to it is a *local optimum* if x is a differential optimum in relation to l.

It is obvious that any differential optimum is a local optimum, but on the other hand, if (x, l) is a local optimum, x is not generally a differential optimum in relation to $l' \neq 1$.

But if one can call on two notions of optimality, an obvious question for an economist is whether there also exist two notions of stability that can be linked to them. The answer is affirmative.

The Concepts of Stability

1. A first notion is that of *local stability*: a state is locally stable if, for any individual, the salary in that state is superior to that offered for any other position, once the deduction is made, if necessary, of the costs of anticipated access. It is easy to demonstrate the following result:

    A couple (x, l) of an assignment and its corresponding localization is a local optimum if, and only if, there exists a function s such that (x, l, s) be a locally stable state of the economy.

2. A second, more subtle notion is that of *differential stability*: a state $e = (x, l, s)$ individually rational on the basis of a localization l_0 is differentially stable in relation to l_0 if, for any couple of an individual k and a position i:

$$r_k - d_k[l_0(k), l'(k)] \geq s(i) - k_k[l_0(k), L(i)] \qquad (11.14)$$

designating by
- r_k the salary of the individual in state (x, l, s)
- $l'(k)$ the localization $l_0(k)$ if $k \in M_x$ and $L[x(k)]$ if $k \in M_x]$.

Two interpretations of inequality (14) may be given:

- From a *tâtonnement point of view* it means that each individual compares the net remuneration $r_k - d_k[l_0(k), l'(k)]$ that the state e procures with $s(i) - d_k[l_0(k), L(i)]$ which the offer of any other job i would bring. In other words, imagining that the individuals select only those states that are differentially stable in relation to the initial localization l_0 is the same as admitting that they are capable of comparing the salary offers in a state e *before that state comes into being*, taking into account the costs of anticipated access starting from l_0. Because when state e comes into being, the differential stability of (x, l, s) in relation to l' is simply written:

$$r_k \geq s(i) - d_k[l_0(k), L(i)]. \qquad (11.15)$$

- From a *cooperative action point of view*, the coalition $[k, i]$ can guarantee to itself from localization l_0:

$$\bar{v}(i) - w(k) - d_k[l_0(k), L(i)]. \tag{11.16}$$

The condition of stability means then that this coalition cannot guarantee to itself, starting from l_0 a result superior to that which state e gives it. A state e differentially stable in relation to l_0 is therefore a state that is not refused based on l_0, by the coalitions of an actor and of a position (condition of stability) and by actors separately (condition of individual rationality).

It is possible to demonstrate the following result:

A couple (x, l) formed by an assignment and the localization linked with it is a differential optimum in relation to localization l_0, if and only if, s exists in such a way that (x, l, s) be a differentially stable state of the market in relation to l_0.

Thus, the traditional optimum — competitive equilibrium equivalence must in fact be divided into two equivalences: *local optimality — local stability* and *differential optimality — differential stability*.

The Problem of Convergence

Let us consider now a dynamic process such that at each stage the individuals appear successively on the labor market in random order and draw at random a selection of positions, each position having a nonzero probability of being discovered. Let it be given that an individual becomes a candidate for a position if the salary offered is superior to the difference between the present remuneration and the cost of anticipated access corresponding to an eventual move. Let us imagine that an unemployed individual eventually lowers his demand [to $w(k)$] and that an employed individual raises it while a firm increases the salary it offers [possibly to $v(i)$] if the position is unoccupied and lowers it in the opposite case.

It is possible to prove that the state of the market converges, with the probability 1, from the initial localization l_0 and in a finite lapse of time toward a locally stable state.

But naturally this state is generally not differentially stable in relation to l_0. The collectivity can be sure of reaching a differential optimum only if it organizes a process of negotiation that allows it to go directly to this differential optimum. Indeed, if the economy is initially in state e_0, then passes to state e_1, the costs of transition from e_0 to e_1 are irreversibly lost, and it is no longer in the interest of the collectivity to seek a differential optimum in relation to e_0 but rather in relation to e_1.

The irreversibility resulting from the existence of costs of anticipated access therefore has two consequences:

1. It makes dependent on the initial state and on the uncertain history of market dynamics the locally stable state to which evolution will lead.
2. It generally makes the market converge toward a state that is not the optimum that the collectivity could reach.

This observation illustrates an important aspect of the geographical evolution of an economy. On the basis of a given geographic and human reality, the economic space can structure itself differently in the course of time, the nature and concentration of the activities resulting in a large part from the uncertainties of intermediate situations. Starting from an initial state, the costs of transition enclose the economy in a state very different from the differential optimum. In other words, when individuals move in order to make an immediate gain superior to their cost of anticipated access, they can keep the market from reaching the differential optimum later on. Therefore, the notion of differential stability is a means of bringing out the amount of cooperation needed between actors in order to avoid this disadvantage.

Notes

1. This model has been developed in cooperation with O. Compte and B. Levy.
2. It must simply be admitted that when no company has contracted with the union — following a collective betrayal, for example — the individual adopts a waiting attitude and does not adjust his or her level of attraction.
3. This model has been developed in cooperation with G. Laffond.
4. We call efficient the individuals of competence 1 or 2 whose minimal requirements are such that they are employed in the static equilibrium of the market.
5. This model has been developed in cooperation with E. Renault.

Bibliography

Allen, Peter, 1980, "Self-Organization in Human Systems," *Problems in Interdisciplinary Studies*, Gover, 104–132.
Allen, Peter, 1981, "Urban Evolution Viewed as a Self-Organizing Nonlinear System," paper presented at the yearly meeting of the British Regional Science Association, Durham.
Braudel, F., 1979, *Civilisation matérielle, économie et capitalisme, XVéme-XVIIIéme siécle*, Armond Colin, Paris.
Caron-Salmona, H., 1985, "Equilibre sur le marché d'un bien en information imparfaite: une analyse de la littérature, *Economie Appliqueée*, XXXVIII, No. 3–4, 637–661.
Caron-Salmona, H., and J. Lesourne, 1987, "Dynamics of a Retail Market," *European Economic Review*, 31, 995–1021.
Laffond, G., and J. Lesourne, 1981, "Market Dynamic and Search Processes with Information Costs," paper presented at the Econometric Society European Meeting, Amsterdam.
Laffond, G., and J. Lesourne, 1985, "Un exemple d'auto-organisation: la création de capacités professionnelles par le marché du travail," *Economie Appliquée*, XXXVIII, No. 3–4, 767–788.
Lesourne, Jacques, and G. Laffond, 1979, "Market Dynamics and Search Processes," paper presented at the Econometric Society European Meeting, Athens.
Nelson, Richard R., and S. Winter, 1982, *An Evolutionary Theory of Economic Change*, Harvard University Press, Cambridge, MA.
Prigogine, Ilya, and I. Stengers, 1988, *Entre le temps et l'éternité*, Fayard, Paris.
Renault, E., and J. Lesourne, 1985, "Auto-organisation et dispersion géographique des marchés," *Economie Appliquée*, XXXVIII, No. 3–5, 703–738.
Williamson, Oliver, *Markets and Hierarchies*, Free Press, New York.

IV

STOCK MARKET DYNAMICS

For obvious reasons stock market behavior has invited explanation in terms of complex dynamics. Most explanations assume that it is driven by random news and other exogenous shocks. As long ago as 1974, however, Christopher Zeeman used a deterministic nonlinear model to explain unstable behavior in stocks. In Chapter 12 Huang and Day introduce a model that incorporates a specific stock price adjustment mechanism based on a stylized model of a stock "specialist," along with two types of investors analogous to Zeeman's "speculators" and "fundamentalists." They provide conditions under which stock prices are ergodic and, for a simple example, derive the density function of stock prices from the underlying parameters of investor and specialist behavior.

The persistence of unstable market behavior is also the subject of Chapter 13 by King, Smith, Williams, and Boening, who report the results of laboratory analyses. They examine the robustness of the strong propensity of laboratory stock markets to yield price bubbles followed by crashes. Previous research shows such bubbles to persist until subjects return for a third market session. Several treatments for dampening bubbles are suggested by rational expectations theory or popular policy reports: short selling, margin buying, brokerage fees, equal endowments, informed insiders, and limit price change rules. None of these treatments significantly reduces the severity of bubbles: short selling, margin buying, and limit price change rules make them worse. The most reliable treatment for eliminating bubbles is to use twice-experienced subjects. Bubbles are no less severe when business persons are the subjects.

In Chapter 14 Hinich and Patterson also address an empirical issue, not whether laboratory markets could generate unstable behavior as in Chapter 13, but whether actual stock market data could be generated by a (unspecified) nonlinear mechanism. A number of investigators have found such evidence, but their tests suffer from certain limitations that Hinich and Patterson hope to have ameliorated by using an improved test (described more fully in Chapter 16) and by giving special attention to weekend and weekday effects. Evidence for nonlinearity remains but appears to have an "episodic" character.

12

Chaotically Switching Bear and Bull Markets: The Derivation of Stock Price Distributions from Behavioral Rules

WEIHONG HUANG and RICHARD H. DAY

Recently, we developed a theory that explains the tendency of stock markets to exhibit alternating periods of generally rising or generally falling prices, so called "bull" and "bear" markets (Day and Huang, 1990). It incorporates a stylized representation of three types of market participants: (1) the α-*investor*, who uses fundamental information sometimes referred to as an "information trader," "sophisticated investor," or "fundamentalist;" (2) the β-*investor*, who uses extrapolative rules, sometimes known as "sheep," "noise trader," or "chartist;" and (3) the *market-maker* or "specialist," who mediates transactions and whose legal function is to "maintain an orderly market."[1]

Market prices equilibrate if α-investor demand is strong relative to β-investor demand. The actual movement in prices is then determined by the equilibrium of supply and demand and exogenous events or "shocks," as in the efficient market theory reviewed by LeRoy (1989). If, however, β-investors have a strong enough role, the market is unstable. Prices then are governed not only by fundamental values, but by the relative demands and supplies of the two types of participants and by the market-maker's price adjustment rule. They may exhibit nonperiodic fluctuations of an essentially stochastic kind and erratic switching between bullish and bearish moves. In such a world portfolio values are always rising above or falling below their fundamental values, wealth in being gained or lost, and random shocks merely add an exogenous source of irregularity to what is already a process that is intrinsically complex.

In this chapter we give the model a piecewise linear form and derive the densities of stock price distributions from the investment strategies and pricing rules. We also show how these distributions change when the underlying parameters are modified. To obtain these results, the market is highly stylized. In spite of this the analysis seems to us to point in a new and fruitful direction for further research.

As for previous work in a similar vein, Zeeman (1974) incorporated a distinction between (what we call) α- and β-investors in a deterministic, nonlinear model of stock price fluctuations. He used catastrophe theory to derive conditions for alternating bear and bull markets. Although our underlying reasoning is roughly similar to his, we base our model on an explicit representation in discrete time of the participants' rules and exploit quite different mathematical tools to give a stronger characterization of market behavior in terms of deterministically generated price distributions. Other authors who have incorporated α- and β-investors (including Zeeman) provide no explicit role for the market-maker. In most cases (excluding Zeeman) they also use linear models and as a consequence bubbles and fluctuations are derived from stochastic shocks rather than from intrinsic market interactions. Although it is reasonable to assume that random events impinge on investor behavior, we abstract from them here. Once we understand the intrinsic, deterministic forces, we can then reintroduce stochastic elements.

The idea that ergodic theory might be useful in economics goes back at least to Benhabib and Day (1982), Grandmont (1985), and Day and Shafer (1985). It has been exploited in various theoretical contexts, for example, by Dana and Montruccchio (1987), Denekere and Pelikan (1987), and Day and Shafer (1987). We have seen no actual constructions of deterministically generated distributions for a general class of maps other than the standard examples of the tent or quadratic maps given, for example, in Lasota and Mackey (1985). For a review of basic concepts and applications in different economic settings, see Day and Pianigiani (1991).

The Model

Suppose p is the current market price of shares, v, is the *current fundamental value* of the stock, which is calculated on the basis of quarterly data such as earnings, dividends, debt–equity ratio, etc. in the most recently issued quarterly shareholder's report, and u is the *investment value*, which is similar to v except that it is calculated on the basis of anticipated future or "long run" considerations and on a judgment about how current news will influence this "investment" value.

α–Investors

Let p^B and p^T be anticipated bottoming and topping prices, respectively, and let p' and p'' be *threshold buying* and *threshold selling prices*, respectively, with

$$p^B < p' < u < p'' < p^T$$

The parameters p' and p'' are sensitivity thresholds that determine when α-investors are active or inactive.

Let $f(p)$ be a weighting function representing the subjectively perceived *chance* of lost opportunity either to fail to buy when the market is low, or to fail to sell when the market is high and assume that

$$f(p) := \begin{cases} \gamma\frac{p'-p^B}{u-p^B}, & 0 \leq p \leq p^B \\ \gamma\frac{p'-p}{u-p}, & p^B \leq p \leq p' \\ 0, & p' \leq p \leq p'' \\ \delta\frac{p''-p}{u-p}, & p'' \leq p \leq p^T \\ \delta\frac{p''-p^T}{u-p^T}, & p^T \leq p. \end{cases} \tag{12.1}$$

The parameter p^B and p^T indicate the prices below (above) which prices are expected to rise or fall almost certainly. When p is close to the topping price p^T, the chance of losing a capital gain and of experiencing a capital loss is great; when p is close to the bottoming price p^B, the chance of missing a capital gain by failing to buy is great. In between p' and p'' the perceived chance of gain or loss is small or zero.

We assume that the excess demand of α-investors can be represented by a function

$$\alpha(p) := k(u - p)f(p) \tag{12.2}$$

where the positive parameter "k" is a measure of the strength of α-*investor response*. Given the chance function, excess α-investor demand has the following character.

When $p \in [p', p'']$, α-investors simply hold their positions; when $p > p''$, they enter the market to sell; when $p < p'$, they enter the market to buy.

To reduce the number of parameters and to simplify the analysis we assume here that $f(\cdot)$ is symmetric. Then

$$\alpha(p) = \begin{cases} A, & p \leq p^B \\ a(p' - p), & p^B \leq p \leq p' \\ 0, & p' \leq p \leq p'' \\ -a(p - p''), & p'' \leq p \leq p^T \\ -A, & p^T \leq p. \end{cases} \tag{12.3}$$

where $a = k\gamma = k\delta$ and $A = a(p^T - p'') = a(p' - p^B)$.

The functions $f(\cdot)$ and $\alpha(\cdot)$ for this symmetric case are shown in Figure 12.1.

β–Investors

The β-investors are individuals whose behavior is based on a belief that it is the market price, *not* estimated future fundamental data that best incorporates the relevant

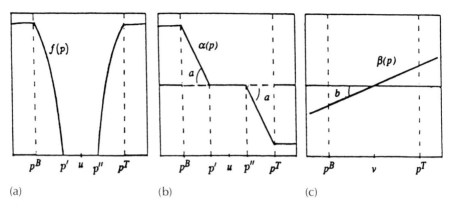

Figure 12.1   Chance and excess demand functions. (a) The chance function. (b) Excess α-investor demand. (c) Excess β-investor demand.

information about the future. Thus, if $p < v$, a bear market is expected, and if $p > v$, a bull market is expected on grounds that the market "knows" that stocks are really worth less (more) than current quarterly fundamental data suggest. Such individuals can be shown to behave in a manner that uses extrapolative price expectations and a uniform chance function. Alternatively, they can be thought of as following a simple technical rule, such as, "buy into a rising market and sell into a falling one." Although their behavior sometimes appears to be irrational, one must take note of the fact that during bear and bull markets, β-investors are correct except at turning points. In this sense, they are right more often then they are wrong. This reinforces their behavior even though on average they lose wealth in the long run.

Assuming a constant chance function and simple linear extrapolative expectations, β-investors' excess demand can be represented by

$$b(p - v) \tag{12.4}$$

where b is a positive constant.

Market–Makers

Market-makers mediate transactions on the market, set the price p in response to excess demand or supply, and at this price supply excess demand from inventory or accumulates inventory when there is an excess supply. Their primary function is to mediate transactions out of equilibrium, that is, to "make the market" in financial parlance, when the demand exceeds supply at the announced price, or vice versa. In our model they are a stylized analog of the New York Stock Exchange specialist or the dealer on the French Bourse. See Bradford and Zabel (1977) and Stoll (1983).

Let p_t be the price in period t and p_{t+1} the new price established by the market-maker. Also, let $e(p_t)$ be aggregate excess demand

$$e(p_t) = \alpha(p_t) + \beta(p_t) \tag{12.5}$$

As in Walrasian tatonnement, the market-maker determines the change in price, $p_{t+1} - p_t$, by a continuous, monotonically increasing function of excess demand $e(p_t)$. For simplicity here we assume that

$$p_{t+1} = \theta(p_t) := p_t + ce(p_t) \tag{12.6}$$

where $c > 0$ is the price *adjustment coefficient*. Also, for simplicity we suppose throughout that

$$u = v. \tag{12.7}$$

This means that expected future and present actual fundamentals are in equilibrium. This does not mean, however, that the market for equities is in equilibrium.

The Price Adjustment Equation

Given these specifications, it follows that prices change according to the following piecewise linear rule:

$$p_{t+1} = \theta(p_t) := \begin{cases} k_1 + \pi p_t, & p_t \le p^B \\ k_2 - \rho p_t, & p^B \le p \le p' \\ k_3 + \pi p_t, & p' \le p \le p'' \\ k_4 - \rho p_t, & p'' \le p \le p^T \\ k_5 + \pi p_t, & p^T \le p \end{cases} \tag{12.8}$$

where the several coefficients are

$$\begin{aligned} \pi &= 1 + cb \\ \rho &= c(a - b) - 1 \\ k_1 &= c(A - bv) \\ k_2 &= cv(a - b) - cah \\ k_3 &= -cbv \\ k_4 &= cv(a - b) + cah \\ k_5 &= c(A + bv). \end{aligned} \tag{12.9}$$

Equation (12.8) is illustrated in Figure 12.2.

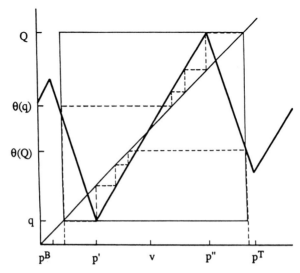

Figure 12.2 The price adjustment equation based on the strong symmetry conditions $[\theta^4(q) = Q]$.

Market Churning

We have assumed that α-investors expect that the investment value is just equal to the current fundamental value ($u = v$). This, of course, would rarely be the case in reality, but is invoked so we can see exactly how the speculative aspect of α-investor behavior, interacting with that of β-investors, causes irregular fluctuations about this long run equilibrium. The stationary long run price is just $\tilde{p} = u = v$, but it is unstable because c and b are both positive. Thus, the behavior of β-investors moves prices away from $\tilde{p}$ whenever they come close, just as in Zeeman's analysis.

Two additional stationary states exist:

$$\tilde{p}^l = \frac{bv - ap'}{b - a} \quad \text{and} \quad \tilde{p}^u = \frac{bv - ap''}{b + a}. \tag{12.10}$$

It should be obvious, however, that bull or bear regimes (*i.e.*, prices above or below v, respectively) cannot persist indefinitely because it would imply unbounded accumulation of stocks by β-investors, and unbounded decumulation α-investors, or vice versa. Consequently, the price mechanism must be unstable at these two values. This will be the case if

$$\theta'(\tilde{p}^l) < -1 \quad \text{and} \quad \theta'(\tilde{p}^u) < -1,$$

which will occur if

$$-\rho < -1 \quad \text{or equivalently} \quad a - b > 2/c. \tag{12.11}$$

To make it possible for bull and bear regimes to switch, we also assume that

$$\theta(q) > v > \theta(Q) \tag{12.12}$$

where

$$q = \theta(p') \quad \text{and} \quad Q = \theta(p''). \tag{12.13}$$

Given these assumptions, the price adjustment map $\theta(\cdot)$ has the appearance shown above in Figure 12.2. The graph shown there is a special case in which

$$p^B < q, \quad Q < p^T. \tag{12.14}$$

It is an expansive map and all price trajectories that begin in the interval $[q, Q]$ remain there, so this interval is a *trapping set*. Using the Lasota–Yorke Theorem (1973) and an argument analogous to that used in our earlier paper that used smooth chance functions, it can be shown that the following properties hold.

Theorem 1. *Given assumptions (12.10)–(12.12) and for randomly chosen initial conditions, we have*

1. *switching regimes: fluctuations switch between bear and bull markets eventually almost surely;*
2. *observability of chaos and ergodicity: the distribution of prices converges to a stable density function, and prices are chaotic almost surely;*
3. *robustness: these results hold robustly, i.e., for all parameters satisfying (12.11)–(12.14);*
4. *law of large numbers: periodic price averages obey the central limit theorem;*
5. *deceptive order: trajectories visit the neighborhoods of infinitely many distinct cycles infinitely often. This means that approximate patterns will appear repeatedly but never in exactly the same way.* □

Constructing Price Densities

Although in general it is difficult or impossible to represent the density function of an ergodic map in analytical form, it can be done in some special cases using techniques discussed in Lasota and Mackey (1985) and illustrated in Day and Pianigiani (1991). The distribution function derived from these special cases can in turn help us to understand the distributional dynamics in general. Huang (1989) carried out a comprehensive study of possible analytic forms of probability distributions for piecewise linear maps like Figure 12.2 when the turning points, p', p'', are cyclic. His results can be used to show that the density function of prices in these cases

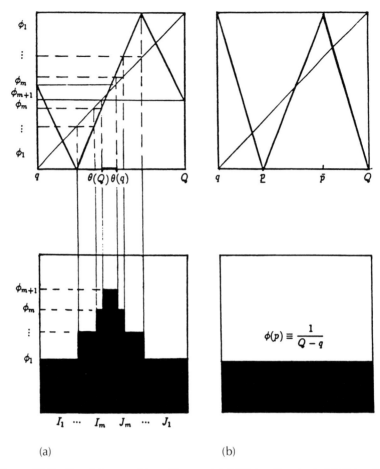

Figure 12.3   Special case of type III map. (a) $\theta^{m+1}(q) = Q$, $m \geq 1$; (b) $\theta(q) = Q$.

1. are symmetric piecewise step functions with steps decreasing below the mean and increasing above it;
2. the mean price is $u = v$;
3. the modal price is not unique but consists of an interval containing v.

Figure 12.3 illustrates these results.

Formally, we have the following theorem whose proof will be given at the end of this chapter.

Theorem 2. *For the price adjustment mechanism defined in (12.8), when conditions (12.11)–(12.14) are satisfied, the price fluctuation is restricted to the trapping set $Z = (q, Q)$, and it can be characterized by a symmetric, piecewise constant probability density function ϕ. In particular, if q, Q belong to a given periodic orbit, i.e., if*

$$\theta^{m+1}(Q) = q \quad [\text{so } \theta^{m+1}(q] = Q), \quad m \geq 1 \tag{12.15}$$

then[2]

$$\phi(p) = \sum_{i=1}^{m} \chi_{I_i \cup J_i}(p)\phi_i + \chi_{[\theta(Q),\theta(q)]}(p)\phi_{m+1}; \tag{12.16}$$

where

$$I_i = [\theta^{m-i+2}(Q), \theta^{m-i+1}(Q)) \quad i = 1, 2, \ldots, m \tag{12.17}$$

$$J_i = [\theta^{m-i+1}(q), \theta^{m-i+2}(q)] \quad i = 1, 2, \ldots, m \tag{12.18}$$

are mutual disjoint subintervals in Z such that

$$\lambda(I_1) = \lambda(J_1) > \lambda(I_2) = \lambda(J_2) > \cdots > \lambda(I_m) = \lambda(J_m) \tag{12.19}$$

and where the $\phi_i, i = 1, 2, \ldots, m$ are positive constants satisfying the inequalities

$$\phi_1 < \cdots < \phi_m < \phi_{m+1}. \qquad \square \tag{12.20}$$

Note that if $\theta^2(q) = Q$ [so $\theta^2(Q) = q$], then $m = 1$ and ϕ is a uniform (rectangular) density (as in the diadic or tent map) and

$$\phi(p) \equiv \frac{1}{Q - q}. \tag{12.21}$$

The proof is given at the end of this chapter.

The Dependence of Market Price Dynamics on Behavioral Rules

It is quite instructive to derive the effect of changes in the various parameters on the densities of stock prices. By way of illustration, consider what happens when the strength of α-investors' response changes. Simulations for various values are shown in Figure 12.4. The effect of a decrease (increase) in a is to decrease the slope ρ leaving the slope π unchanged. This tends to flatten (and fatten) the tails and sharpen the peak of the distribution.

It can also be shown that the smaller c and the smaller the difference $(a - b)$, the more peaked the density function. In general, all three types of participants can influence both the range and peakedness of the price densities.

In particular, the following can be stated.

1. By increasing the price adjustment parameter c, the market-maker can extend the price fluctuation range and decentralize the price distribution.

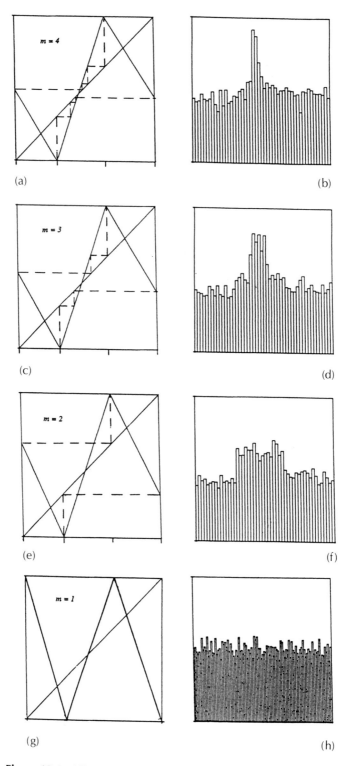

(a)

(b)

(c)

(d)

(e)

(f)

(g)

(h)

Figure 12.4 Histograms of price distributions, ρ fixed, π changes.

2. When the response thresholds p', p'' are fixed, α-investors can induce the switching behavior into the market, and decentralize the price distribution by increasing this intensity of response parameter a. The changes in the distributional pattern that would result are identical to those for the market-maker except that the price fluctuation range does not change.

3. The role of the β-investors is essentially opposite to that of the α-investors. By increasing their intensity of response parameter b, β-investors extend the price fluctuation range, but strongly centralize the price distribution around the fundamental value of the stock.

Discussion of Theorem 2

We conclude by providing a proof of Theorem 2 using the Frobenius–Perron operator approach. This operator, denoted by P_θ for the map θ, is a transformation on the density function ϕ defined by the equation

$$\int_A P_\theta \phi(s) d\lambda(s) = \int_{\theta^{-1}(A)} \phi(s) d\lambda(s), \quad \forall A \in I, \tag{12.22}$$

where λ is Lebesgue measure and I is the state space (assumed here to be an interval). By differentiating both sides of equation (12.22), it follows that

$$P_\theta \phi(x) = \frac{d}{dx} \int_{\theta^{-1}([a,x])} \phi(s) d\lambda(s) \tag{12.23}$$

The Frobenius–Perron operator has an interesting intuitive interpretation in the present setting. Assume the stock price is not known for certain, but its subjective distribution is given by a density ϕ. The trajectory of price starting from any price p at time $t = 0$ is given by $[\theta^t(p)]_{t=0}^\infty$. Then $p_\theta \phi$ is the "posterior subjective" density of prices, and this density evolves in the time. Its evolution is described by $(P_\theta^t \phi)_{t=0}^\infty$, where

$$p_\theta^t \hat{=} \underbrace{p_\theta \circ \cdots \circ p_\theta}_{t \text{ times}} \tag{12.24}$$

If this sequence converges to a stationary density ϕ^*, then ϕ^* satisfies the functional equation

$$p_\theta \phi^* = \phi^*. \tag{12.25}$$

The existence of stationary density functions for expansive maps has been established by several authors. For example, see Lasota and Yorke (1973). And it has been shown that *when the map θ is ergodic, the stationary density function is unique.* As we pointed out in Theorem 1, our map is ergodic so the corresponding stationary density can in principle be constructed.

To do this we take advantage of the fact that the condition $\theta^{m+1}[Q] = q$ [so $\theta^{m+1}(q) = Q$], $m \geq 1$, enables us to divide the trapping set into $2m + 1$ subintervals

$$Z = [q, Q] = \left(\bigcup_{i=1}^{m} I_i\right) \bigcup [\theta(Q), \theta(q)] \left(\bigcup_{j=1}^{m} J_j\right), \tag{12.26}$$

where

$$I_i = \left[\theta^{m-i+2}(Q), \theta^{m-i+1}(Q)\right) \quad i = 1, 2, \dots, m \tag{12.27}$$

$$J_i = \left(\theta^{m-i+1}(q), \theta^{m-i+2}(q)\right] \quad i = 1, 2, \dots, m \tag{12.28}$$

are mutual disjoint subintervals in Z.

Assume that the stationary density is invariant and that it is constant on each subinterval, equation (12.25) gives rise to the following linear system:

$$
\begin{aligned}
\phi_1 &= & \pi^{-1}\phi_1 + \rho^{-1}\phi_2 \\
\phi_2 &= & \pi^{-1}\phi_1 + \rho^{-1}\phi_3 \\
&\vdots & \vdots \\
\phi_m &= & \pi^{-1}\phi_1 + \rho^{-1}\phi_{m+1} \\
\phi_{m+1} &= & \pi^{-1}\phi_1 + \rho^{-1}\phi_{m+1} + \phi^{-1}\phi_{2m+1} \\
\phi_{m+2} &= & \pi^{-1}\phi_1 + \rho^{-1}\phi_{m+1} + \pi^{-1}\phi_{2m+1} \\
&\vdots & \vdots \\
\phi_{2m+1} &= & \pi^{-1}\phi_1 + \rho^{-1}\phi_{m+1} + \pi^{-1}\phi_{m+n}
\end{aligned}
\tag{12.29}
$$

or in matrix form:

$$A_{2m+1}\phi = \mathbf{0} \tag{12.30}$$

where $\phi = (\phi_1.\phi_2, \dots, \phi_{2m+1}^T)$ and

$$
A_{2m+1} = \begin{bmatrix}
1 - \pi^{-1} & -\rho^{-1} & \cdots & 0 & 0 & 0 & \cdots & 0 & 0 \\
\pi^{-1} & 1 \cdots & 0 & 0 & 0 \cdots & & 0 & 0 \\
\cdot & \cdot & \cdots & \cdot & \cdot & \cdot & \cdots & \cdot & \cdot \\
\pi^{-1} & 0 & \cdots & 1 & -\rho^{-1} & 0 & \cdots & 0 & 0 \\
\pi^{-1} & 0 & \cdots & 0 & 1 - \rho^{-1} & 0 & \cdots & 0 & -\pi^{-1} \\
0 & 0 & \cdots & 0 & -\rho^{-1} & 1 & \cdots & 0 & -\pi^{-1} \\
\cdot & \cdot & \cdots & \cdot & \cdot & \cdot & \cdots & 1 & -\pi^{-1} \\
0 & 0 & \cdots & 0 & 0 & 0 & \cdots & -\rho^{-1} & 1 - \pi^{-1}
\end{bmatrix} \tag{12.31}
$$

We can show $|A_{2m+1}| = 0$ and *rank* $A_{2m+1} = 2m$ when the condition $\theta^{m+1}(Q) = q$ is satisfied. So the unique stationary density function exists. Further, symmetry implies that

$$\phi_i = \phi_{2m-i+2} \quad i = 1, 2, \ldots, m. \tag{12.32}$$

It can also be shown that $\rho(1 - \pi^{-1}) > 1$. Note that

$$\phi_{i+1} = \rho\pi^{-1}\phi_1, \quad i = 1, 2, \ldots, m, \tag{12.33}$$

and

$$\phi_2 = \rho(1 - \pi^{-1})\phi_1. \tag{12.34}$$

Therefore, we have $\phi_2 > \phi_1$ because $k_\pi > 1$. We then show $\phi_{i-1} > \phi_i$ is also true for any $1 \leq i \leq m$ by induction. Actually, if we have $i^*, 1 \leq i^* \leq m - 1$ such that

$$\phi_{i^*} > \phi_{i^*-1}, \tag{12.35}$$

then from (12.31),

$$\phi_{i^*+1} = \rho\phi_{i^*-1} - \rho\pi^{-1}\phi_1$$
$$> \rho\phi_{i^*-1} - \rho\pi^{-1}\phi_1 = p_{i^*}, \tag{12.36}$$

so we have the inequalities

$$\phi_1 < \phi_2 < \cdots < \phi_{m-1} < \phi_m < \phi_{m+1}. \qquad \Box \tag{12.37}$$

Notes

1. Gu (1992) contains an extended discussion of the underlying assumptions and empirical evidence concerning the model presented here.
2. Let χ be the characteristic or indicator function defined by

$$\chi_A(p) = \begin{cases} 1, & p \in A \\ 0, & \text{otherwise.} \end{cases}$$

Bibliography

Benhabib, Jess, and Richard H. Day, 1982, "A Characterization of Erratic Dynamics in Overlapping Generations Model," *Journal of Economic Dynamics and Control*, 4, 37-55.

Bradford, James, and Edward Zabel, 1977, "Price Adjustment in a Competitive Market and the Securities Exchange Specialist," Working Paper 77-15, Department of Economics, University of Rochester.

Dana, Rose-Anne, and Luigi Montrucchio, 1987, "Dynamic Complexity in Duopoly Games," in Jean-Michel Grandmont (ed.), *Nonlinear Economic Dynamics*, Academic Press, Boston.

Day, Richard H., and Weihong Huang, 1990, "Bulls, Bears and Market Sheep," *Journal of Economic Behavior and Organization*, 14, 299–330.

Day, Richard H., and Giulio Pianigiani, 1991, "Statistical Dynamics and Economics," *Journal of Economic Behavior and Organization*, 16, 37–83.

Day, Richard H., and Wayne Shafer, 1985, "Keynesian Chaos," *Journal of Macroeconomics*, 7, 277–295.

Day, Richard H., and Wayne Shafer, 1987, "Ergodic Fluctuations in Deterministic Economic Models," *Journal of Economic Behavior and Organization*, 8, 339–361.

Denekere, Raymond, and Steve Pelikan (1987), in Jean-Michel Grandmont (ed.), *Nonlinear Economic Dynamics*, Academic Press, Boston.

Grandmont, Jean-Michel, 1985, "On Endogenous Competitive Business Cycles," *Econometrica*, 53, 995–1046.

Gu, Mu, 1992, "A Behavioral Theory of the Stock Price Formation Process," Ph.D. Dissertation, University of Southern California.

Huang, Weihong, 1989, "Distributional Dynamics for Chaotic Economic Systems," Ph.D. Dissertation, University of Southern California.

Lasota, Andrzej, and Michael C. Mackey, 1985, *Probabilistic Properties of Deterministic Systems*, Cambridge University Press, Cambridge.

Lasota, Andrzej, and James Yorke, 1973, "On the Existence of Invariant Measures for Piecewise Monotonic Transformations," *Transaction of the American Mathematical Society*, 186, 481–488.

LeRoy, Stephen F., 1989, "Efficient Capital Markets and Martingales," *Journal of Economic Literature*, 27, 1583–1621.

Stoll, Hans R., 1983, *The Stock Exchange Specialist System: An Economic Analysis*, Monograph, 1985:2, Monograph Series in Finance and Economics. New York University, Graduate School of Business Administration, New York.

Zeeman, E.C., 1974, "On the Unstable Behavior of Stock Exchanges," *Journal of Mathematical Economics*, 1, 39–49.

13

The Robustness of Bubbles and Crashes in Experimental Stock Markets

RONALD R. KING, VERNON L. SMITH,
ARLINGTON W. WILLIAMS, and
MARK VAN BOENING

Previous research reports the results of 26 asset market experiments in which trading is continuous in each of 15 sequential periods (Smith, Suchanek, and Williams 1988, hereafter SSW). At the end of each period a "dividend" is realized from a probability distribution of dividends (i.i.d.) whose parameters are common information to all N traders. Each trader is given an initial endowment of cash and shares, and at the end of the experiment is paid the sum of his/her initial cash endowment, all dividend earnings, and all capital gains less capital losses. Consequently, the intrinsic (expected) value of a share in each period is well defined as the expected one-period dividend value multiplied by the number of trading periods (dividend realizations) remaining in the horizon. The declining dividend value of a share is represented by the dashed lines shown in the figures.

Briefly, only 4 of the reported 26 experiments yielded prices consistent with intrinsic value over the horizon. Inexperienced subject traders invariably trade in high volume at prices that are considerably at variance from intrinsic value, which we refer to as a bubble. Once-experienced traders yield somewhat smaller price bubbles followed by crashes, and trading volume is smaller compared with inexperienced traders. Although the sample size was small, it appeared that twice-experienced subject groups yield prices tending to follow intrinsic value.

Some interpretations of these results are as follows: (1) common probabilistic dividend information is not sufficient to induce common "priors" or expectations; (2) thus price bubbles are made possible by trader subjective uncertainty about the behavior of other traders; (3) bubbles are a form of myopia (Tirole, 1982) from which agents learn eventually that capital gains expectations cannot be sustained indefinitely; (4) expectations are adaptive and the adaptation over time is to a rational expectations equilibrium as originally defined by Muth (1961).

Summary of Previous Experiments

All of the asset markets discussed in this paper were conducted using a version of the double continuous auction trading institution programmed on the NovaNET computer system. (For details see SSW, pp. 1122–1125.) Under our double-auction asset market rules, traders can switch between buying mode and selling mode by pressing a key on their keysets. Traders in buying mode can enter a bid to buy or accept an offer to sell as long as the trader has cash holdings sufficient to cover the purchase price. Traders in selling mode can enter an offer to sell or accept a bid to buy as long as the trader has a nonzero share holdings. A trading period ends by unanimous consent of all participants, or with the expiration of a preannounced time period (240 seconds). The double-auction markets reported here use a bid–ask spread reduction rule in combination with a "rank-queue" limit-order file; bids to buy below the highest (standing) bid and offers to sell above the lowest (standing) offer are queued in the limit order file rather than being rejected. When a contract occurs, the highest queued bid and lowest queued offer are automatically entered as the new bid–ask spread. Subjects are continuously informed of their position in the limit-order file and can withdraw a price quote from the queue at any time.

To convey a new perspective on the data found in SSW we provide a different summary of their results in Table 13.1. We also include the results of several new replications of SSW.[1] In Table 13.1 we list the means across independent experiments of several indicators of the discrepancy between market price and the rational expectations (RE) dividend value of a share. The most comprehensive measure (column 3) is based on the cumulative absolute deviation of prices from the RE value of a share normalized with respect to the number of shares outstanding, since individual experiments sometimes differed in terms of number of traders and/or their endowments of cash and shares. The volatility of prices in an experiment is measured by the variance of prices over the 15-period life of the asset. This is the most common measure of volatility using field data where fundamental value is not objectively defined. The mean of these variances is listed in column (4). The amplitude of the boom [column (5)] is measured by the maximum (low to high) deviation of mean period prices from the RE value of a share. Duration [column (6)] is the number of periods separating the market low and market high mean price deviations. Finally, column (7) measures turnover: total exchange volume divided by shares outstanding. With the exception of the price variance, the mean of each of these measures declines monotonically with experience level, in accordance with the results reported in SSW.

In SSW regression results are reported that provide an empirical characterization of the price dynamics in their experimental stock markets. The regression equation is

Table 13.1 Summary of Previous Results: Baseline, Mean Measures of Price Bubbles

(1) Experience level	(2) Number of experiments	(3) Normalized absolute price deviation from RE[a]	(4) Price variance	(5) Boom amplitude[b]	(6) Boom duration[c]	(7) Turnover[d]
Inexperienced	10	5.68	1.08	1.24	10.2	4.55
Once–experienced	3	2.77	1.22	0.766	5.67	3.20
Twice–experienced	2	0.279	0.815	0.107	3.00	1.70

[a] Computed from $\sum_{i-1}^{Q_i} |P_i - IV|/NSO_i$, where P_i = price, contract i; IV = intrinsic dividend value in period of contract; Q_i = market volume in experiment i; NSO_i = number of shares outstanding in experiment i.
[b] Change in mean period price deviation (from RE) low to high.
[c] Number of periods from low to high mean price deviation from RE.
[d] Total volume in experiment divided by shares outstanding.

$$\bar{P}_t - \bar{P}_{t-1} = \alpha + \beta(B_{t-1} - O_{t-1}) + \epsilon_t \qquad (13.1)$$

where $\bar{P}_t$ is the mean contract price in period t. B_{t-1} is the number of bids to buy entered by all traders in period $t - 1$, O_{t-1} is the number of offers to sell entered by all traders in period $t - 1$, and ϵ_t is an error term. If the measure of lagged excess bids ($B_{t-1} - O_{t-1}$) is a reliable surrogate measure of excess demand arising from spontaneous capital gains expectations, then $\beta > 0$ while $\alpha = -E(d_t)$ where $E(d_t)$ is the one-period expected dividend value. Thus the change in mean price from period $t - 1$ to period t should be composed of three terms: (1) a decline in price equal to the one-period expected dividend value because of the decline in number of dividend realizations remaining [price will decline less than $E(d_t)$ if subjects are risk averse in dividends], (2) an increase (decrease) in price due to capital gains (losses) expectations, and (3) random variation.

All 14 of the bubble experiments reported by SSW yield estimates $\hat{\beta} > 0$ (estimates are significantly positive). All but one of the estimates $\hat{\alpha}$ are insignificantly different from $-E(d_t)$. A pooled regression, reported in SSW, using closing prices P_t^c rather than the mean prices $\bar{P}_t$ does not alter the qualitative conclusions (mean prices and closing prices are highly correlated).

Experimental Evaluation of Environmental and Policy Treatments for Moderating Price Bubbles

In this study we report a series of experiments designed to evaluate various experimental "treatments" including some proposed policies that offer the potential for preventing or modifying the observed tendency for environments with known probabilistic dividends to produce price bubbles. We examine experimentally the affect of the following:

1. All subjects are endowed with a capacity to sell short.
2. All subjects have a capacity to buy on margin.
3. Every trade is subject to a brokerage fee levied on both buyer and seller.
4. All subjects receive equal endowments.
5. The presence of a subset of subjects that are informed of the content of SSW, and receive data on excess bids each period.
6. Each trading period is subject to a limit price change rule.
7. The subjects are experienced business persons.

Although most of the new research we report here was conducted a year or more before the Great World Crash of stock markets on October 19, 1987, the parallels are evident. These treatments, particularly (1), (2) and (6), are relevant to understanding this phenomenon and to assessing some of the proposed policy remedies.

Short Selling

In seminar presentations of the work reported in SSW, it was often suggested that the observed propensity of these experiments to produce price bubbles would be eliminated or at least moderated if the traders were allowed to sell short. The argument for this outcome rests on the assumption that any trader who expects the bubble to burst can leverage his/her sales by taking a short position. Consequently, a small number of traders who have counter cyclical expectations would be able to offset the ebullient expectations of others.

Hypothesis, H1: The effect of introducing short sales will be to reduce the absolute price deviation, price variance, duration, and amplitude of bubbles; turnover may increase as part of the arbitrage process that shortens and dampens the bubble.

Alternatively, there may be no effect from this treatment if expectations are generally ebullient, and/or an insufficient number of traders are willing to risk taking a short position. In the event that some traders act on their opportunity to sell short, but they short the market too early in the boom stage and make covering purchases while prices are still rising, the effect may be to lengthen the boom.

We report 12 experiments in which we vary subject experience level, and, in addition to the usual endowment of cash and shares, each trader is endowed with two shares borrowed from the experimenter. Borrowed shares must be returned by the end of period 15 or a penalty of one-half the initial dividend value is deducted from total earnings. No dividends are paid on borrowed shares. Four experiments used only inexperienced subjects; in five experiments all subjects were once-experienced, and in three sessions the subjects were twice-experienced. Summary data for all 12

Table 13.2 Short Selling and Margin Buying Experiments: Mean Observation by Treatment

Treatment	Number of experiments	Normalized absolute price deviation from RE	Price variance	Boom amplitude	Boom duration	Total turnover
Short selling						
Inexperienced	4	11.88	2.20	1.61	9.50	6.67
Once–experienced	5	3.90	1.79	0.772	5.80	4.19
Twice–experienced	3	1.23	1.46	0.397	3.67	2.74
Margin buying						
Inexperienced	1	15.3	7.96	3.64	8.00	5.48
Once–experienced	1	2.61	6.15	1.15	2.00	2.33
Short selling and margin buying						
Inexperienced	1	16.3	0.656	0.876	13.0	3.60
Once–experienced	1	9.71	0.326	0.646	11.0	6.89

experiments are shown in Table 13.2. Comparing Table 13.2 with Table 13.1 for each experience level we observe no tendency for short selling to moderate price bubbles. In fact most of the bubble measures are larger with short selling than without.

Three of the 12 experiments are charted in Figures 13.1a–c.

Experiment 265; Nine Inexperienced Subjects

The bell-shaped mean price path over time and the high volume of trading in this experiment are typical of several experiments reported in SSW using inexperienced subjects. Short selling seems to exacerbate the boom in the first seven periods. By

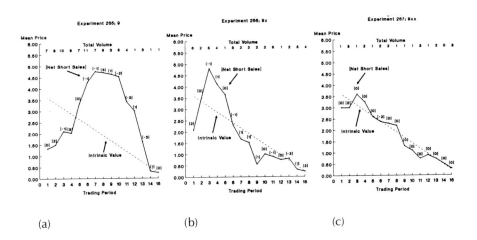

(a)   (b)   (c)

Figure 13.1 Mean price, volume, and net short sales.

period 4 the total short position is four shares, two of which are covered with purchases by period 7. The rate of price increase, relative to dividend value, declines in periods 8 and 9 as the short position rises to six shares. The crash is actually moderated by short covering purchases in periods 10, 11, and 13 by which time the total short position is zero. Trader earnings varied from $3 to $34, although expected earnings was about $13 for each subject.

Experiment 266; Nine Once–Experienced Subjects

Figure 13.1b charts the results for nine experienced subjects, seven of whom participated in experiment 265. The price dynamics are similar to what we observe in other once-experienced groups without short selling, i.e., the price deviations and volume are both smaller than for inexperienced subjects. Again, we observe some procyclical short trades: two sales in period 1 below intrinsic value and a covering purchase at the peak of the boom in period 3.

Experiment 267; Nine Twice–Experienced Subjects

All nine subjects in experiment 266 returned for 267, which is a pure replication of 266 except for subjects' increased experience. Again, short sales, entirely attributable to one subject, are procyclical, and not maximally profitable. But the trader in question performed above average, ranking fourth in overall profitability.

Margin Buying

The argument for the effect of allowing margin purchases is symmetrical with that for short sales. If subjects have the capacity to buy shares on margin this will tend to moderate price bubbles to the extent that traders who expect a bubble leverage their purchases with borrowed money when prices are below dividend value, and then sell from their enlarged inventories of shares when prices are above dividend value.

Hypothesis H2: The effect of introducing the opportunity for each trader to purchase shares on margin will be the same as in **H1**.

Alternatively, if traders' expectations are generally bullish, the effect of providing a margin buying capacity may simply fuel the bubble longer and to greater heights. If we allow margin buying in conjunction with short selling, it follows from H1 and H2 that the effects stated will be the same.

We report four experiments in which each subject is endowed with a capacity to borrow funds (Table 13.2): two experiments allowed margin purchases only; two allowed both margin purchases and short sales; one experiment in each of these classes used inexperienced subjects and one in each used experienced subjects.

Comparisons between Table 13.1 and 13.2 suggest that the effect of margin buying capacity is to increase all measures of the bubble, except duration, for inexperienced traders; for once-experienced subjects the results are more mixed suggesting that with experience the effect of margin buying is nil. The comparisons are similarly mixed when subjects can both short sell and make margin purchases.

We conclude that margin buying does not reduce price bubbles; if anything they are worse for inexperienced subjects.

Equal Endowments

In the experiments reported by SSW there is a pronounced tendency for prices in the first period to be below dividend value, but to rise above dividend value within the first few periods. An examination of first period trades suggests that there is a tendency for the buyers to be those subjects whose endowments are large in cash and small in shares; the reverse holds for sellers. This is consistent with risk aversion, i.e., initially traders use the market to acquire more balanced holdings of cash and shares. Consequently, if early prices are depressed because of liquidity preference sales, and if prices then rise once these preferences are satisfied, this process may help to ignite capital gains expectations.

Hypothesis H3: Equal endowments reduce all measures of the bubble.

The results based on four experiments, reported in Table 13.3, all used inexperienced subjects. All measures in row 1 of Table 13.3 are as high or higher than the corresponding observations in Table 13.1. Equal endowments do not dampen bubbles.

Table 13.3 Equal Endowment and Exchange Fee Experiments:
Mean Observation by Treatment

Treatment	Number of experiments	Normalized absolute price deviation from RE	Price variance	Boom amplitude	Boom duration	Total turnover
Equal endowment						
Inexperienced	4	13.57	2.22	1.87	10.0	6.29
Exchange fee						
Inexperienced	2	3.91	0.526	0.731	10.0	5.55
Once–experienced	3	1.51	0.615	0.631	6.0	1.75

A Fee for Each Exchange

It has been suggested that a contributing factor in the propensity of laboratory stock markets to bubble is the fact that transactions costs are negligible with computerized trading. We examine this hypothesis by introducing an exchange fee of $0.20 on each transaction ($0.10 each on the buyer and seller in every trade).

Hypothesis H4: an exchange fee of $0.20 per transaction will reduce all measures of bubbles.

Clearly, bubbles must be affected if the exchange fee is large enough. A fee of $0.20 represents a cost of $1.20 per share outstanding if turnover is six times total shares. Therefore, a priori, we expected fees of this magnitude to reduce all three measures of a price bubble.

Table 13.3 reports five experiments with an exchange fee: two with inexperienced subjects and three with experienced subjects. Comparing the mean measures with the baselines in Table 13.1, we find negligible effects of an exchange fee on boom duration; the mean amplitude and price variance declines for both experience levels; mean turnover increases for inexperienced subjects, but declines for once-experienced subjects. The summary measure, absolute price deviation from RE, declines for both experience levels.

We conclude that an exchange fee of $0.20 per transaction has a mixed effect in moderating bubble intensity.

Informed Traders

The typical bubble can be characterized empirically by equation (13.1). If some traders are informed of the behavioral characteristics of these markets, including the price forecasting rule provided in equation (13.1), then rational expectations theory predicts that the counter speculative activities of these traders will moderate the bubbles observed for a given level of experience among the non-informed traders.

Hypothesis H5: The effect of informed insiders is to reduce the absolute price deviation, price variance, duration, and amplitude of bubbles. The arbitrage process by which this occurs may increase turnover.

We conducted five experiments each with three informed subjects. In four experiments, these subjects were graduate students at Indiana University and Washington University (St. Louis) and/or the University of Arizona. Each insider subject had been provided a prepublication copy of SSW prior to the experiment, and had been asked to read it in preparation for the experiment. During the experiment, at the end of each period, each informed subject was provided with written (private) information reporting the number of bids, number of offers, and excess bids for that period. The insiders acted independently of each other as do the "public" noninformed traders. A discussion of four of these experiments and their results is provided below.

Experiment 229; 6x,3i

The first experiment used nine traders, six of whom were once-experienced in an asset trading market, and three were insiders informed as described above. The mean price per period is plotted in Figure 13.2a; volume by period is shown at the top

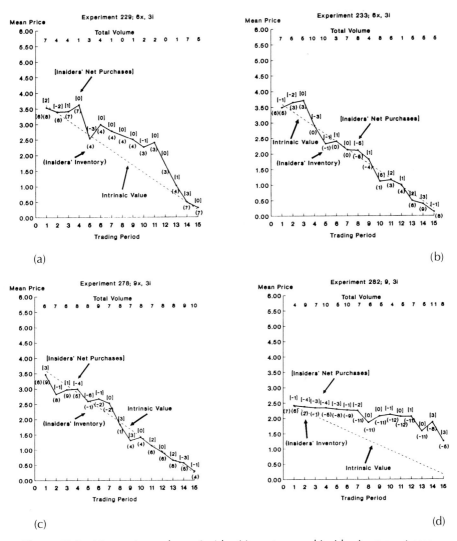

(a)

(b)

(c)

(d)

Figure 13.2 Mean price, volume, insiders' inventory, and insiders' net purchases.

Table 13.4   Informed Insiders, Limit Price Change Rule Experiments: Mean Observation by Treatment

Treatment	Number of experiments	Normalized absolute price deviation from RE	Price variance	Boom amplitude	Boom duration	Total turnover
Informed insiders						
Inexperienced	1	1.61	0.57	0.626	13.0	1.67
Experienced	1	0.691	1.72	0.362	10.0	2.33
Informed insiders, short selling						
Inexperienced	1	3.05	0.192	0.634	13.0	3.68
Experienced	2	1.21	1.23	0.254	4.00	4.92
Limit price change rule						
Inexperienced	2	9.46	0.213	2.50	10.5	4.84
Once–experienced	2	2.12	1.76	1.77	5.5	2.22
Twice–experienced	2	0.390	1.45	0.696	1.5	1.89

of the figure for each period. The series shows a low volume bubble with a duration of 10 periods (beginning in period one and peaking in period 11) measured relative to dividend value. Comparing Tables 13.4 and 13.1, absolute price deviation, price variance, amplitude and turnover are all reduced by informed traders and once-experienced subjects although duration is increased. The most significant feature of this experiment is the fact that two of the three informed traders had exhausted their inventory of shares by period six. Two of the three sold "too soon" while the third waited "too long." Such was the uncertainty they faced. Figure 13.2a also contains the period-by-period net change in the informed traders' position. They made net purchases of two in period 1, net sales of two in period 2, and so on. In period 5 they panicked, accounting for all three sales at depressed prices. If we rank the subjects from one to nine according to total earnings, our informed traders ranked one, four, and eight. Hence, being informed was no guarantee of profitability.

Given the early selling propensity of two of the informed traders it appears that they need to be armed not only with information, but with a capacity to sell short. Our next three experiments corrected this conjectured shortcoming.

Experiment 233; 6x,3i

Six new once-experienced subjects and the same three informed subjects from experiment 229 were recruited for a new experiment. Our three informed traders, in addition to having ownership endowments of 1, 2, and 3 shares, respectively, were each endowed with a capacity to borrow up to four shares. Sales from the four borrowed shares had to be repurchased by the end of period 15 to avoid a penalty of $1.80 per defaulted share borrowed and not returned. In addition to a short plus long selling capacity totaling 18 shares (which is equal to the outstanding stock), our three traders were now once-experienced.

The results are shown in Figure 13.2b. Now we observe a bubble duration of only two periods and small fluctuations thereafter. One or more of the three informed traders were short in 13 of 15 periods, but they had a net short position in only three periods (periods 5, 8, and 9). One was short the four share limit in periods 6–9 and ranked second in total earnings. The three informed traders ranked first, second, and third among all traders in total earnings, which demonstrates the value of being informed combined with an adequate short selling capacity. The high to low mean price amplitude is only 0.254, well below the amplitude of all the once-experienced groups reported in Table 13.1, but above the amplitudes recorded for the two twice-experienced groups. But to moderate the propensity to bubble required a heavy turnover — five times the outstanding stock of shares — higher than for any "natural" experiment with once-experienced subjects listed in Table 13.1.

Experiment 278; 9x,3i

Three new informed insiders were recruited for this experiment. Each had an initial endowment of four borrowed shares plus 1, 2, and 3 owned shares, respectively. There were nine once-experienced noninformed traders rather than six as in the two previous experiments. Consequently, the insiders' potential sales volume (18 units) is now two-thirds of the outstanding stock (24 units). The results in Figure 13.2c show clearly the effectiveness with which informed traders stabilized the market with only minor fluctuations around declining dividend value. Our insiders transactions were very profitable. Rank ordering all traders from first to twelfth in total earnings, the insiders ranked first, second, and third.

Experiment 282; 9,3i

This experiment replicates the previous one except that the nine public traders are inexperienced and the dividend-endowment environment corresponds to the one we normally use to "train" new inexperienced subjects. Dividend value begins at $2.40 in period 1, and declines at the expected dividend rate of $0.16 per period. Informed traders' initial endowment of owned shares is 1, 2, and 4, respectively, and each has a capacity to sell 4 borrowed units. The penalty for defaulting on borrowed shares (failing to cover a short position) is $1.20 per unit borrowed.

The results in Figure 13.2d provide an excellent example in which the ebullient homegrown expectations of the public traders cause the short sellers to be severely squeezed. The latter are not able to contain the bubble relative to dividend value and fail to cover all their short positions. Our three informed traders were net sellers in the first seven periods and in the tenth period. All these sales were in market periods in which there was a positive and growing gap between the mean market price and fundamental value. In this sense our traders acted correctly on the basis of fundamentals. Their timing, however, was less than ideal. In period 8, the market premium over fundamental value narrowed, and our traders held their short position (11 units total). At this point it was reasonable for them to expect the market to crash further based on their knowledge of the behavior of previous experiments. But in periods 9–12 the market recovered, and the premium widened. One venturesome trader sold his last borrowed share short in period 10. Now, all informed traders were short the maximum permissible. In period 13 the market sold off, but the mean price, as in all previous periods was still well in excess of the $1.20 per unit penalty for failing to cover short sales; better to remain short and pay the penalty. In period 14 the market recovered on the highest volume (11 units) in the entire experiment. Our traders, with only two periods remaining in which to cover, bought three short-covering shares, at prices near, or below $1.20. In the final period the expected crash came, but was heavily damped by short covering purchases. The informed traders accounted for 3 of the 8 purchases in period 15. Further short covering purchases simply were not executable at prices below $1.20. A rank ordering of all traders according to total earnings shows that the informed traders' performance was well below average; they ranked eighth, ninth, and tenth. The top two public traders received earnings at least 75% greater than any of our informed traders.

In understanding behavior in this experiment it is well to remember the elementary proposition that the potential profit on short sales is more severely bounded than the potential loss. This is why brokers sharply constrain short sales positions. The experiment demonstrates that (1) short sellers can be right in their fundamental assessments but lose money because the market does not share their expectations; (2) short selling need not prevent market bubbles, and may even exacerbate them.

Limit Price Change Rule

Historically meat and grain futures have been constrained by limit price change rules (LPCR) that suspend trading if the price of the contract rises or falls by a stated amount from the previous day's closing price. These rules generally have not been extended to stock markets or to options and futures indexes for equity shares. Since the world stock market crash in October 1987 several proposals have been offered to institute such rules to prevent "meltdown." The Chicago Mercantile Exchange, under political pressure to make institutional changes in futures index trading, introduced (very wide) LPCRs in some of their futures contracts. Such rules are believed by some to have the effect of suppressing expectations of rapid price changes, thereby imposing a more structured, less volatile price path. The expectations that capital gains may not materialize might then yield prices near intrinsic value.

Hypothesis H6: Imposing a LPCR will reduce all measures of the intensity of price bubbles.

We report six experiments applying a LPCR; two experiments (304 and 307, Table 13.4) use inexperienced subjects, and trading in each period beyond the first is constrained by a price ceiling and price floor equal to plus and minus 32 cents (twice the one-period expected dividend) from the previous period's closing price; two experiments (305 and 308) use once-experienced and two (306 and 309) use twice-experienced subjects and trading is constrained by a LPCR plus and minus 48 cents from the previous close. Comparing the LPCR experiments in Table 13.4 with the baselines in Table 13.1 it is seen that price deviation, price variance, and amplitude are generally larger under the LPCR than without for all levels of experience, but that duration and turnover are about the same with and without LPCR across all experience treatment. We conjecture that a LPCR accentuates the severity of bubbles because traders perceive that their downside risk is limited by the 32 or 48 cent bounds on price declines in each period. Consequently, the boom carries to greater heights, and collapses at about the same time as natural markets.

Figure 13.3a–c charts the mean price and volume results for experiments 304–306, respectively. Experiment 304 with inexperienced subjects yields a substantial bubble that bursts in period 13, then falls the limit without trade in periods 14 and 15. Nine of these 12 subjects returned in experiment 305 (Figure 13.3b). Again we observe a large, though somewhat smaller bubble that crashes in period 6, then declines at the limit in periods 7–14 with zero volume.[2] Only in the final period does trade resume at prices near dividend value. These nine subjects returned for the third experiment shown in Figure 13.3c. Now trading follows closely the declining path of dividend value. The convergence pattern across these three experiments is similar to that for similar sequences with increasing experience without a limit price change rule. Hence, in spite of the procyclic effect of limit price change rules, experience eventually dominates, and we observe a rational expectations pattern of price decline.

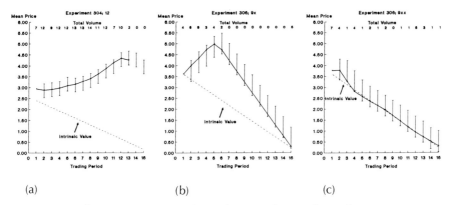

(a)   (b)   (c)

Figure 13.3 Mean price, volume, and price change limits.

Effect of Using Corporate Executives, or Stock Market Dealers, as Subjects

A common criticism of laboratory experiments is that the subjects — usually college students — are not as sophisticated as "real world business men and women," and are likely to yield different behavior. Experimentalists for over a quarter of a century have responded to this critique by reporting studies replicating their experiments with subjects from business and other groups. One of the earliest such studies was that of Siegel and Harnett (1964) replicating their bilateral bargaining experiments using General Electric sales personnel experienced in economic bargaining. Siegel and Harnett (1964, p. 342) report that the "contracts negotiated by college students and the sales personnel were notably similar, and in general corresponded closely to those predicted (by bargaining theory)." In SSW (pp. 1130–1131) one experiment using small business men and women from the Tucson community is reported. This experiment produced one of the largest deviations from intrinsic value observed among the original SSW experiments.

Experiment 280; 15

The subjects in this experiment were from a variety of different industries. They come to the University of Arizona campus to participate once each week in the Arizona Executive Program, a year-long sequence of lectures offered to corporate executives. The experimental design was the same as that used above for experienced subjects except that the reward levels were increased by over 60%; each subject was endowed with one additional (owned) share, and an additional $3.60 in cash. Subjects were also endowed with a capacity to borrow up to three additional shares for short sales, and to borrow up to $10.80 (3 × $3.60) cash for margin purchases.

The mean price, volume and net short sales, by trading period, is shown in Figure 13.4. The sharp drop in mean price in period 7 was due to a buy/sell mode error in which a subject mistakenly sold one share for $0.75. Trading tended to occur in a small range around $6.50 per share until the final period when the market collapsed on a volume of 14 shares of which 4 were short sales at prices above the penalty for failing to cover.

Experiment 293; 6, 3i

The subjects in this experiment were six over-the-counter traders familiar with computerized stock quotation systems. The design parameters and reward levels were the same as in the previous experiment except that short sales and margin purchases were not allowed. In addition three experimenters served as informed insiders, i.e., they were versed in the content of SSW. They also were given no short selling capacity. Figure 13.5 shows a modest bubble pattern in prices with the

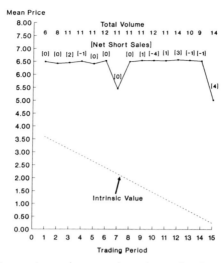

Figure 13.4 Mean price, volume, and net short sales: Experiment 280; 15.

insiders net sellers of shares in most of the first 14 periods. These sales account for a substantial portion of total volume. Although the mean price in period 15 was well above dividend value, the closing contract was at dividend value.

We conclude that the general pattern of trading for first-time participants in these laboratory stock market environments is not altered when the subjects are corporate personnel or when they are stock market dealers.

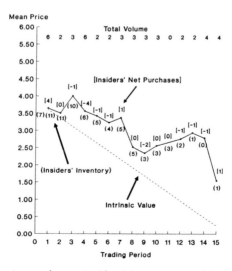

Figure 13.5 Mean price, volume, insiders' inventory, and insiders' net purchases: Experiment 293; 6, 3i.

Table 13.5 *t* Values for Pairwise Comparisons of Regression Coefficients

Pairwise comparison	Normalized absolute price deviation from RE[a]	Price variance[a]	Amplitude[a]	Duration[a]	Turnover[b]
Baseline vs. Treatment					
Inexperienced					
Short selling	3.077(9978)	1.951(9699)	1.277(8944)	-0.463(3323)	2.321(0270)
Margin buying	2.693(9944)	6.751(9999)	4.698(9999)	-0.821(2089)	0.572(5713)
Short sales and					
margin buys	2.963(9971)	-0.420(3388)	-0.709(2418)	1.045(8480)	-0.589(5602)
Equal endowments	3.917(9998)	1.983(9718)	2.186(9818)	-0.132(4778)	1.907(0658)
Exchange Fee	-0.673(2529)	-0.741(2322)	-1.344(0944)	-0.101(4600)	0.840(4072)
Price Limit	1.431(9188)	-1.156(2564)	3.359(9990)	0.152(5597)	0.240(8121)
Insiders	-1.141(1314)	-0.504(3090)	-1.199(1178)	1.045(8480)	-1.785(0840)
Insider short selling	-0.737(2334)	-0.875(1941)	-1.183(1230)	1.045(8480)	-0.540(5930)
Once–experienced					
Short selling	0.455(6740)	0.800(7852)	0.017(5062)	0.071(5282)	0.881(3880)
Margin buying	-0.040(4841)	4.390(9999)	-0.674(7472)	-1.243(1116)	-0.489(6279)
Short sales and					
margin buys	1.764(9562)	-0.800(2150)	-0.215(4156)	1.808(9598)	2.072(0467)
Exchange fee	-0.455(3260)	-0.766(2247)	-0.340(3679)	0.160(5630)	-1.158(2557)
Price limit	-0.209(4178)	-0.609(7266)	2.262(9846)	-0.071(4718)	-0.698(4903)
Insiders	-0.529(3002)	0.446(6702)	-0.720(2384)	1.469(9241)	-0.489(6279)
Insider short selling	-0.500(3100)	-0.000(5014)	-1.154(1286)	-0.715(2400)	1.218(2324)
Twice–experienced					
Short selling	0.305(6190)	0.731(7650)	0.653(7406)	0.286(6116)	0.742(4635)
Price limit	0.033(5129)	0.657(7421)	1.210(8824)	-0.587(2806)	0.126(9006)
Experienced Level					
Inexperienced vs. once–experienced					
Baseline	-1.300(1016)	0.218(5858)	-1.472(0756)	-2.696(0056)	-1.329(1935)
Short selling	-3.494(0008)	-0.635(2652)	-2.579(0079)	-2.159(0135)	-2.398(0227)
Margin buying	-2.635(0065)	-1.320(0982)	-3.619(0005)	-1.661(0534)	-1.443(1591)
Short sales and					
margin buys	-1.362(0915)	-0.240(4060)	-0.335(3700)	-0.554(2919)	1.510(1412)
Exchange fee	-0.773(2226)	-0.100(5398)	-0.226(4113)	-1.716(0481)	-2.707(0109)
Price limit	-2.155(0195)	1.596(9396)	-1.506(0711)	-1.958(0296)	-1.698(0995)
Insiders	-0.191(4296)	0.838(7959)	-0.384(3519)	-0.831(2063)	0.306(7619)
Insider short selling	-0.441(3310)	0.869(8044)	-0.639(2639)	-2.877(0036)	0.656(5167)
Inexperienced vs. twice–experienced					
Baseline	-2.050(0244)	-0.356(3620)	-2.999(0026)	-3.639(0005)	-2.394(0209)
Short selling	-4.097(0002)	-0.998(1630)	-3.251(0014)	-2.990(0027)	-3.339(0022)
Price limit	-2.664(0060)	1.277(8944)	-3.715(0004)	-3.524(0006)	-1.914(0648)

[a] See text for definition. For comparisons of baselines and treatments, the null hypothesis is H_0: baseline $\leq$ treatment. For comparisons of experience level, the null hypothesis is H_0: inexperienced $\leq$ once–experienced, or H_0: inexperienced $\leq$ twice–experienced, as appropriate. *p* values are in parentheses.

[b] See text for definition. For comparisons of baselines and treatments, the null hypothesis is H_0: baseline = treatment. For comparisons of experience level, the null hypothesis is H_0: inexperienced = once–experienced, or H_0: inexperienced = twice–experienced, as appropriate. *p* values are in parentheses.

Regression Analysis of Treatments

We computed OLS estimates of the linear regression of each of the dependent variables — absolute price deviation, price variance, amplitude, duration, and turnover — on the various treatment variables studied in this paper. By defining a dummy (0, 1)variable for each treatment we can assess the marginal impact of each treatment on each of the three measures of a bubble. These dummy variables accounted for 42–61% of the variation in the dependent variables across the 51 experiments used in the regressions.

In Table 13.5 we report pairwise tests of the baseline and treatment coefficients estimated in the regressions.[3] We report one-tailed t values for price deviation, price variance, duration, and amplitude where the prior prediction (research hypothesis) informs us that treatment coefficients listed in the rows will be smaller than the baseline coefficients listed in the columns, and two-tailed t values for turnover. A few statistically significant comparisons emerge — virtually all of them associated with experience. Experience is clearly the most important factor in dampening the intensity and duration of bubbles. None of the treatments arguably thought to introduce a rational reduction in bubbles is statistically effective in accomplishing this prediction.

Conclusions

The behavioral features of laboratory stock markets reported in SSW is extended and corroborated by the greatly increased sample size studied in this paper. Bubbles are dampened by once-experienced subjects and largely disappear for twice experienced subjects. If subjects can sell short, buy on margin, or both, bubbles can be more severe for inexperienced subjects. This suggests that the common social policy of imposing margin requirements may be effective in moderating stock market bubbles. But the common cry for limit price change rules as a bubble retardant following the October 1987 world stock market crash gets no support from our experiments. In fact, for inexperienced subjects, limit price change rules somewhat exacerbate bubbles. We think this may be due to the perceived reduction in down-side risk because of the limit price change rule. Using regression analysis, we find no significant affect on bubbles introduced by any of our treatments, with the exception of experience. Finally, the results of experiments using corporate middle level executives or over-the-counter securities traders do not alter the basic bubble propensity of experimental markets. These bubbles are robust with respect to all of the above treatments; only experience is ultimately reliable in eliminating bubbles. This reinforces the basic findings in SSW: common information is not sufficient to yield common expectations, but through experience subjects come to have common expectations.

Notes

We are grateful to the National Science Foundation for research support to Vernon L. Smith (PI, University of Arizona) and to Arlington W. Williams (PI, Indiana University).

    1. Excluded from Table 13.1 are a number of experiments reported in SSW using special treatments and manipulations designed to explore factors affecting asset trading behavior.

    2. When there was no trade the LPCR was applied as follows: If there was only an offer outstanding at the end of the period, the closing "price" was taken to be the minimum price under the LPCR; if there was a standing bid-offer spread at the close of the period, the midpoint of this spread was taken to be the closing "price." Only one of the periods with zero volume in experiments 305 and 306 fell into the latter category.

    3. We do not make the Bonferroni adjustments for multiple t test comparisons because the resulting adjustments still yield significant t values in those cases that show significance (Miller, 1981).

Bibliography

Miller, Rupert G., Jr., 1981, *Simultaneous Statistical Inference*, 2nd ed., Springer-Verlag, New York.

Muth, John F., 1961, "Rational Expectations and the Theory of Price Movements," *Econometrica*, 29, 315–355.

Siegel, Sidney, and D. L. Harnett, 1964, "Bargaining Behavior: A Comparison Between Mature Industrial Personnel and College Students," *Operations Research*, 12, 334–343.

Smith, Vernon L., Gerry L. Suckanek, and Arlington W. Williams, 1988, "Bubbles, Crashes, and Endogenous Expectations in Experimental Spot Asset Markets," *Econometrica*, 56, 1119–1151.

Tirole, Jean, 1982, "On the Possibility of Speculation Under Rational Expectations," *Econometrica*, 50, 1163–1181.

14

Intraday Nonlinear Behavior of Stock Prices

MELVIN J. HINICH and DOUGLAS M. PATTERSON

The discovery that rates of return to shares of common stock exhibit significant non-linear behavior was first reported in Hinich and Patterson (1985). Subsequently, Ashley and Patterson (1986), Scheinkman and LaBaron (1989), and Brockett, Hinich, and Patterson (1988) also reported finding nonlinear behavior in stock market rates of return. Note that rates of return are analyzed rather than share prices because price series are highly nonstationary in the mean. Hsieh (1989) finds evidence of nonlinear behavior in daily spot foreign exchange rates. Hinich and Patterson (1985, 1989, 1990) and Brockett, Hinich, and Patterson (1988) applied the Hinich (1982) bispectrum based linearity test to daily rates of return of individual common stocks, whereas Ashley and Patterson (1986) used a bootstrap linearity test applied to daily rates of return of individual stocks and two market indices

The finding that stock returns are generated by a nonlinear process is particularly surprising because an extensive empirical literature indicates that these same returns correspond rather nicely to a white noise model. This white noise evidence has led most financial economists (e.g., see Fama, 1965, 1970) to conclude that the stock market can not be forecast to any economically significant extent. However, nonlinearity may imply serial dependence in stock returns, which in turn raises the possibility of finding an economically profitable forecasting rule. On the other hand, many nonlinear processes are also a martingale, and therefore point forecasts of deviations from expected returns cannot be made using historic returns.

The rates of return used in the studies cited above suffer from a problem of aliasing. That is to say, the returns were not properly sampled. The term "aliasing" refers to a phenomenon whereby the high frequency structure of the source time series is reflected back into the lower frequencies of the sampled series with the result that the statistics of the sampled series are no longer representative of the underlying source series. Aliasing is a potential problem whenever the analyst works with sampled data. This is true regardless of whether the data are explicitly sampled by the user, or has somehow been sampled by the provider or collector of the data used in time series analysis. The obvious virtue of sampling data is that the sampled

Table 14.1 Summary of Linearity Test for Treatment of Missing Day for McDonalds Corp. Daily Returns

	1980–1981			1982–1983			1984–1985			1980–1985		
	No treatment	Linear trend	Random walk	No treatment	Linear trend	Random walk	No treatment	Linear trend	Random walk	No treatment	Linear trend	Random walk
SD	.027	.0105	.0105	.0132	.011	.011	.009	.008	.008	.012	.010	.010
Linear[a] Test statistic	1.45	1.59	1.58	1.93	2.94	2.91	-.386	-1.05	-1.08	4.11	7.08	6.94

[a] Distributed as $N(0, 1)$ under the null hypothesis of a linear generating mechanism.

Table 14.2   Linearity Test Results for Daily Returns over 2-Year Periods[a]

Firm	1980–1981	1981–1983	1984–1985
Aluminum Co. Amer.		X	
American Express Co.			X
Bethlehem Stl. Corp.	X	X	X
Chevron Corp.	X	X	
Coca Cola Co.			X
Eastman Kodak Co.		X	X
General Mtrs. Corp.	X		
Goodyear Tire & Rubber		X	X
International Bus. Mach.		X	X
International Paper Co.	X	X	
McDonalds Corp.		X	
Merck & Co.		X	X
Minnesota Mng. & Mfg.	X	X	
Procter & Gamble Co.			X
United Technologies Corp.	X		X

[a] An "X" indicates that the linearity test statistic is significant at the 5% level.

Linearity Test Applied to Individual Days of the Week

One of the more interesting anomalies concerning the behavior of stock market prices is the so-called "weekend effect." Suppose for the moment we define Monday's return as the percentage price change between the Friday close and the Monday close. French (1980) reports that for the period 1953–1977 the mean Monday return for the S&P 500 index was significantly negative, whereas the mean returns for the other 4 days of the week were positive. Rogalski (1984) found that from 1974 to 1984 prices for the DJIA actually tend to rise during Monday trading, but fall between Friday's close and Monday's open. Smirlock and Stark (1986) report that "over the 1963–1983 period the weekend effect has shifted from characterizing active trading on Monday to characterizing the non-trading weekend," that is, the weekend effect during the later part of their sample period was caused by price declines from Friday close to Monday open. In the event, there appears to be something different about weekends in comparison to other periods when the market is closed.

We investigated linearity as a function of day of the week by using 15-minute sampled returns. For example, to study Mondays we estimated the bispectrum for the 24 15-minute returns on a particular Monday. The estimated bispectral estimates for all Monday's over a subperiod were then averaged together and the linearity test performed on the normalized average.

Tables 14.3, 14.4, and 14.5 display the results as a function of the subperiods for each of the stocks. Note from the tables that the linearity test was also applied to the 10:45–3:30 returns for each day; more about that shortly. Considering the returns over the entire day, the tables show that linearity is rejected at the 5% level a total of 34 times out of a possible 45 times for Monday, i.e., 15 stocks times 3

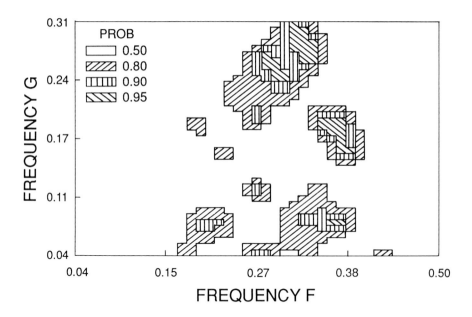

(a)

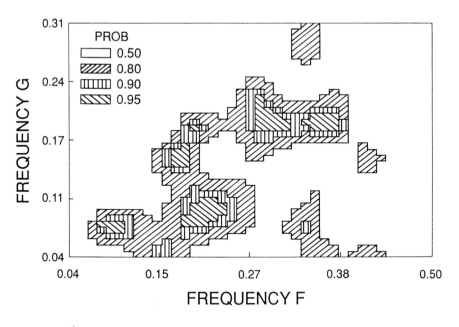

(b)

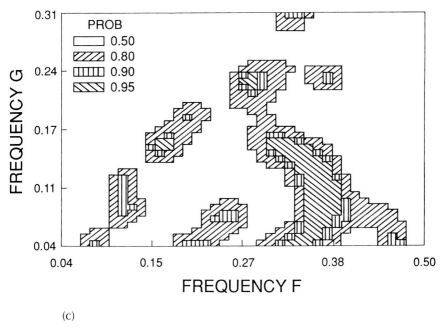

(C)

Figure 14.1 Probability that estimated bispectrum is not zero. (A) IBM Corp. 1980–1981. (B) IBM Corp. 1982–1983. (C) IBM Corp. 1984–1985.

subperiods. The rejection frequencies are not much different for other days of the week: 38 times for Tuesday, 39 times for Wednesday, 33 times for Thursday, and 37 times for Friday. In other words, the data does not seem to point to any particular day or days as being responsible for the observed nonlinear behavior of stock returns.

It has been reported in the literature that stock prices behave differently during the first and last half-hours of trading than during the rest of the day. Wood, McInish, and Ord (1985) found that returns to an equally weighted NYSE market index constructed from trade-by-trade prices are significantly higher during the first and last half-hours of a trading day. Their analysis was not done for separate days of the week. Harris (1986) analyzed transactions data over a 14-month period in order to study the weekend effect. One hypothesis he tested was that the weekend effect is caused by an upward bias in the Friday closing price. Although he found little support for this explanation of the weekend effect, Harris did find that the mean final transaction return for each weekday was significantly higher than the mean return of the previous nine trades. This difference is most dramatic when the closing trade occurs during the last 5 minutes of the trading day. In addition, Harris found that the final trade each day occurred on average 26 to 28 minutes before the close of trading. These results suggest that it might be fruitful to repeat the linearity test on returns that exclude the first and last half-hours of trading.

Table 14.3 Summary of Linearity Test for Day of Week, 1980–1981[a]

Firm	Monday		Tuesday		Wednesday		Thursday		Friday	
	10:00–4:00	10:45–3:30	10:00–4:00	10:45–3:30	10:00–4:00	10:45–3:30	10:00–4:00	10:45–3:30	10:00–4:00	10:45–3:30
Aluminum Co. Amer.	X		X		X		X		X	X
American Express Co.	X		X		X	X	X		X	X
Bethlehem Stl. Corp.	X		X	X	X	X	X		X	
Chevron Corp.	X	X	X	X	X	X	X		X	X
Coca Cola Co.			X	X	X	X	X			X
Eastman Kodak Co.	X		X	X	X	X	X	X	X	X
General Mtrs. Corp.		X	X	X	X	X	X			
Goodyear Tire & Rubber	X	X	X		X	X	X			X
International Bus. Mach.	X	X	X		X	X	X	X	X	X
International Paper Co.	X	X	X		X	X	X	X	X	X
McDonalds Corp.	X	X	X		X		X		X	X
Merck & Co.	X	X			X	X	X	X	X	X
Minnesota Mng. & Mfg.			X	X	X		X		X	
Procter & Gamble Co.	X	X	X		X		X	X	X	X
United Technologies Corp.	X		X	X	X	X	X	X	X	X

[a] An "X" indicates that the linearity test statistic is significant at the 5% level.

Table 14.4 Summary of Linearity Test for Day of Week, 1982–1983[a]

Firm	Monday 10:00–4:00	Monday 10:45–3:30	Tuesday 10:00–4:00	Tuesday 10:45–3:30	Wednesday 10:00–4:00	Wednesday 10:45–3:30	Thursday 10:00–4:00	Thursday 10:45–3:30	Friday 10:00–4:00	Friday 10:45–3:30
Aluminum Co. Amer.		X		X	X	X	X	X	X	X
American Express Co.	X	X		X	X		X	X	X	X
Bethlehem Stl. Corp.		X	X		X	X		X	X	X
Chevron Corp.	X	X	X	X	X		X	X	X	X
Coca Cola Co.	X	X	X	X	X		X		X	X
Eastman Kodak Co.	X	X	X	X	X	X	X		X	X
General Mtrs. Corp.	X	X	X	X	X	X	X		X	X
Goodyear Tire & Rubber			X	X	X	X	X		X	
International Bus. Mach.	X	X	X	X	X		X	X	X	X
International Paper Co.			X		X		X		X	X
McDonalds Corp.	X	X	X	X	X	X	X	X	X	X
Merck & Co.		X	X	X	X		X		X	X
Minnesota Mng. & Mfg.	X	X	X	X	X		X	X	X	X
Procter & Gamble Co.	X	X	X		X	X	X		X	X
United Technologies Corp.	X	X	X	X	X	X	X	X	X	X

[a] An "X" indicates that the linearity test statistic is significant at the 5% level.

Table 14.5 Summary of Linearity Test for Day of Week, 1984–1985[a]

Firm	Monday 10:00–4:00	Monday 10:45–3:30	Tuesday 10:00–4:00	Tuesday 10:45–3:30	Wednesday 10:00–4:00	Wednesday 10:45–3:30	Thursday 10:00–4:00	Thursday 10:45–3:30	Friday 10:00–4:00	Friday 10:45–3:30
Aluminum Co. Amer.	X	X					X	X	X	
American Express Co.	X			X	X	X		X	X	
Bethlehem Stl. Corp.	X		X			X			X	
Chevron Corp.	X		X	X	X	X	X	X	X	X
Coca Cola Co.	X	X	X		X	X		X	X	X
Eastman Kodak Co.	X	X	X		X	X	X	X		
General Mtrs. Corp.	X		X		X	X			X	
Goodyear Tire & Rubber	X	X	X	X		X			X	X
International Bus. Mach.	X	X				X		X		X
International Paper Co.	X		X	X	X	X	X		X	X
McDonalds Corp.	X		X		X			X	X	X
Merck & Co.	X		X		X	X	X	X		
Minnesota Mng. & Mfg.	X	X	X	X	X	X	X	X	X	X
Procter & Gamble Co.			X		X	X	X		X	
United Technologies Corp.	X	X	X	X				X		

[a] An ''X'' indicates that the linearity test statistic is significant at the 5% level.

Tables 14.3, 14.4, and 14.5 also include the significance results for each day of the week when the 10:15, 10:30, 3:45, and 4:00 P.M. Fifteen-minute sampled returns are excluded. In perusing the tables note that the rejection frequency for linearity drops rather sharply. This means that the first, and last, half-hours of the trading day may be responsible for the rejection of linearity over the entire day. For Monday, the number of rejections during the 10:45–3:30 period conditional on rejection for the entire day is 23 times, versus 34 times for the entire day. For Tuesday, the number of conditional rejections drops to 21 from 38, and for Wednesday, Thursday, and Friday the number of conditional rejections are 29, 18, and 28, respectively.

One intriguing aspect of this result is that it reinforces the conclusion of Wood et al. (1985) and Harris (1986): there is something unusual and anomalous about the formation of stock prices at the beginning and end of the day. Furthermore, the anomaly goes beyond just an upward shift in the mean of the return distribution: non-linear dynamic behavior appears to be strongest (most frequently observed) during the first half-hour of trading and/or the last half-hour of the trading day. The cause of this anomaly remains mysterious: does it flow from certain peculiarities (frictions) in the institutional arrangements for stock trading, or how agents formulate expectations or agents' preference functions? Better models of intertemporal decision making surely will lead to a deeper understanding of the market dynamics at the open and close of trading.

Bibliography

Ashley, R., and D. Patterson, 1986, "A Nonparametric, Distribution-Free Test for Serial Independence in Stock Returns," *Journal of Financial and Quantitative Analysis*, 21(2), 221–227.

Ashley, R. A., D. M. Patterson, and M. J. Hinich, 1986, "A Diagnostic Test for Nonlinear Serial Dependence in Time Series Fitting Errors," *Journal of Time Series Analysis*, 7(3), 165–178.

Brockett, P. L., M. J. Hinich, and D. M. Patterson, 1988, "Bispectral Based Tests for the Detection of Gaussianity and Linearity in Time Series," *Journal of the American Statistical Association*, 83(403), "Applications," 657–664.

Fama, E., 1965, "The Behavior of Stock Market Prices," *Journal of Business*, 38, 34–105.

Fama, E., 1970, "Efficient Capital Markets: A Review of Theory and Empirical Work," *Journal of Finance*, 25, 383–417.

French, K., 1980, "Stock Returns and the Weekend Effect," *Journal of Financial Economics*, 8, 55–69.

Harris, L., 1986, "A Transaction Data Study of Weekly and Intradaily Patterns in Stock Returns," *Journal of Financial Economics*, 16(1), 99–117.

Hinich, M. J., 1982, "Testing for Gaussianity and Linearity of a Stationary Time Series," *Journal of Time Series Analysis*, 3, 169–176.

Hinich, M., and D. Patterson, 1985, "Evidence of Nonlinearity in Daily Stock Returns, *Journal of Business and Economic Statistics*, 3(1), 69–77.

Hinich, M., and D. Patterson, 1989, "Evidence of Nonlinearity in the Trade-by-Trade Stock Market Return Generating Process," in W. Barnett, J. Geweke, and K. Shell, eds., Economic Complexity: *Chaos, Sunspots, Bubbles, and Nonlinearity*, Cambridge University Press, Cambridge, MA, pp. 383–409.

Hinich, M., and D. Patterson, 1990, "Relating Sample Bicovariances of a Process to the Parameters of a Quadratic Nonlinear Model," Technical Report, Applied Research Laboratories, University of Texas at Austin.

Hinich, M. J., and M. A. Wolinsky, 1988, "A Test for Aliasing Using Bispectral Analysis," *Journal of the American Statistical Association*, 83(402), "Theory and Methods," 499–502.

Hsieh, D. A., 1989, "Testing for Nonlinear Dependence in Daily Foreign Exchange Rate Changes," *Journal of Business*, 62(3), 339–368.

Rogalski, R., 1984, "New Findings Regarding Day-of-the-Week Returns over Trading and Non-Trading Periods: A Note," *Journal of Finance*, 34(5), 1603–1614.

Scheinkman, J., and B. La Baron, 1989, "Nonlinear Dynamics and Stock Returns," *Journal of Business*, 62(3), 311–337.

Smirlock, M., and L. Stark, 1986, "Day-of-the-Week and Intraday Effects in Stock Returns," *Journal of Financial Economics*, 17, 197–210.

Wood, R. A., T. H. McInish, and J. K. Ord, 1985, "An Investigation of Transactions Data for NYSE Stocks," *Journal of Finance*, 40, 723–741.

V

PROBLEMS OF ESTIMATION AND INFERENCE

This part contains four chapters concerning statistical methodology appropriate for nonlinear models. The first two discuss the problem of inferring the type of mechanism that could have generated a given series of data. Chen reviews in Chapter 15 a number of techniques that derive directly from the theory of deterministic nonlinear systems and outlines some of the pitfalls in their use. He reevaluates his early investigation of chaos in monetary aggregates and then shows that a single differential-difference equation can generate series that possess many of the same attributes as the real data.

Barnett and Hinich follow in Chapter 16 with a reevaluation of Barnett and Chen's earlier work using a more conventional technique of statistical inference, the Hinich bispectrum approach. It has an advantage over the alternative Brock, Dechert, Scheinkman test in that it provides a direct test for nonlinearity (but not for chaos itself). They find "deep nonlinearity" in the Divisia monetary aggregates.

The final two chapters deal with statistical estimation of structural equations. Geweke explores in Chapter 17 the problem of estimating the tent map parameter when data are observed with Gausian error. He finds that the likelihood function is extraordinary complex, possessing a multitude of local maxima. This requires new methods for calculating estimators and forecasts.

In Chapter 18 Kalaba and Tesfatsion introduce a multiple criteria method for estimating nonlinear dynamic models that enables a researcher to take account of the fact that he usually does not have correct model specification but only an approximate one at best. Their test introduces separate "discrepancy terms" or model misspecification error variables and uses both rather than just one as in conventional theory.

15

Searching for Economic Chaos:
A Challenge to Econometric
Practice and Nonlinear Tests

PING CHEN

Chaos research has attracted wide interest in the scientific community. Convincing empirical evidence for it has been found in fluid dynamics (Brandstater and Swinney, 1987), chemistry (Argoul et al., 1987), and biology (Guevara, Glass, and Shrier, 1981). Relatively less convincing reports come from epidemiology, population dynamics, meteorology, and astronomy (Pool, 1989). Evidence for it in economic data has been published in my own work with Barnett (Chen, 1987b, 1988a,b; Barnett and Chen, 1987, 1988) and in others including Brock and Sayers (1988) and Scheinkman and LeBaron (1989). This work is still controversial.

Empirical studies of economic chaos began in mid–1980 (Chen, 1984, 1987b; Sayers, 1985; Brock, 1986; Barnett and Chen, 1987, 1988). Nonlinearity (Ashly, Patterson, and Hinich, 1986; Brock and Sayers, 1988; Scheinkman and LeBaron, 1989), nonnormality (Ashly, Pattern, and Hinich, 1986), and nonindependence (Brock, Dechart, and Scheinkman, 1987; Hsieh 1989) in economic time series is widely discovered. Negative or "mixed" findings are also reported (Sayers, 1985,1989; Brock and Sayers, 1988; Frank and Stengos, 1988; Frank, Gencay, and Stengos, 1988). Little evidence of chaos is found in monetary indexes (Chen, 1987b, 1988a,b), daily stock returns (Chen, 1984; Scheinkman and LeBaron, 1989), and laboratory simulations (Sterman, Mosekilde, and Larsen, 1989). There is a fierce debate about the empirical findings of economic chaos (Chen, 1988b; Brock and Sayers, 1988; Ramsey, Sayers, and Rothman, 1990).

In this chapter I will first introduce some of the techniques for distinguishing between randomly generated data and data generated by deterministic processes. I then analyze pitfalls in statistical tests designed to detect chaos. My work on monetary aggregates serves as an example to discuss the problem of inference with economic time series and to illustrate the usefulness of the continuous time model. This model is just sufficient to generate behavior that closely resembles the data.

Distinguishing between Deterministic and Stochastic Processes

There are at least four possible candidates for describing fluctuating time series: linear stochastic processes, discrete deterministic chaos, continuous deterministic chaos, and nonlinear deterministic chaos plus noise. Testing and modeling the last one are only in its infancy, because a high level of noise will easily destroy the subtle signal of deterministic chaos. I discuss the first three candidates here and give numerical examples of white noise and deterministic chaos as the background for further discussions. They include the linear autoregressive AR(2) model, the discrete time logistic model, which is widely used in population studies and economics, and the continuous-time spiral chaos or Rossler model (1976).

Sample time sequences of these models are shown in Figure 15.1. They all exhibit irregular economic fluctuations very much like economic data when appropriate scales are used. However, a closer examination reveals differences among them.

How can we distinguish between such different theoretical specifications? Can we tell if a given economic time series is generated by one of them? These are the basic questions we shall discuss. Four main tools are available, the "phase portrait," the autocorrelation function, the Lyapunov exponent, and the fractal dimension. I shall describe them briefly in turn.

Phase Space and Phase Portrait

From a given time series $X(t)$, an m-dimensional vector $V(m, T)$ in phase space can be constructed by the m-history with time delay $T : V(m, T) = \{X(t), X(t + T), \ldots, X[t + (m - 1)T]\}$, where m is the embedding dimension of phase space (Takens, 1981). This is a powerful tool in developing numerical algorithms of nonlinear dynamics, since it is much easier to observe only one variable than to analyze a complex multidimensional system.

The phase portrait in two-dimensional phase space $X(t + T)$ versus $X(t)$ gives a clear picture of the underlying dynamics of a time series. Figure 15.2 displays the phase portrait of the three models using the sample data of Figure 15.1. The nearly uniform cloud of points in Figure 15.2a closely resembles the phase portrait of random noise (with infinite degree of freedom). The curved image in Figure 15.2b is characteristic of the one-dimensional unimodal discrete chaos. The spiral pattern in Figure 15.2c is typical of a strange attractor whose dimensionality is not an integer. Its wandering orbit differs from periodic cycles.

Long-Term Autocorrelations

The autocorrelation function is another useful concept in analyzing time series. The autocorrelation function $AC(I)$ is defined by

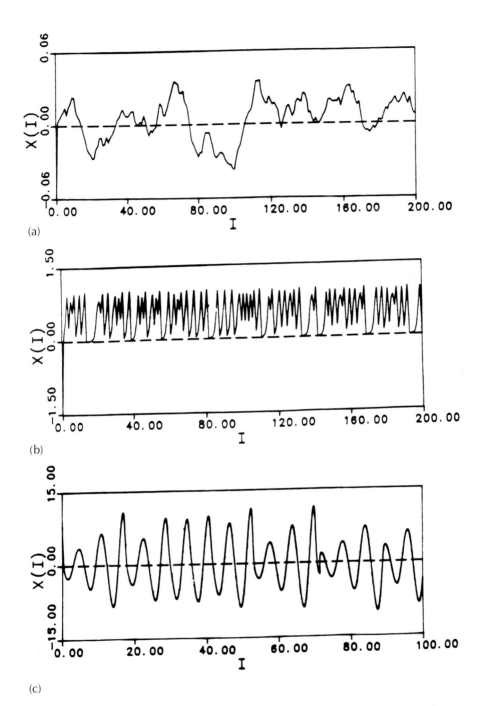

Figure 15.1 Comparison of the time series of model solutions. Their time units are arbitrary. (a) AR(2) linear stochastic model. (b) Discrete logistic chaos generated by mapping $X(t+1) = 4X(t)[1 - X(t)]$. (c) Rossler model of spiral chaos with time interval $dt = 0.05$.

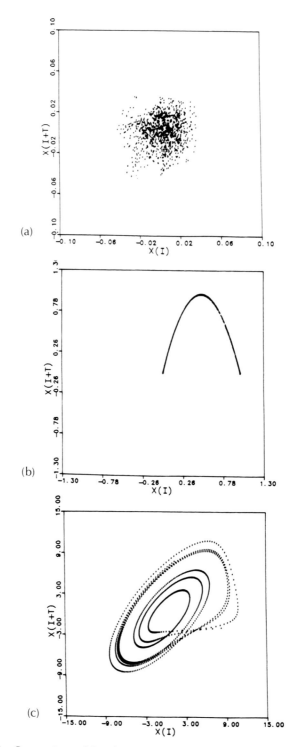

Figure 15.2 Comparison of the phase portraits of model solutions. $N = 1000$. (a) AR(2) model with $T = 20$. (b) Logistic chaos with $T = 1$. (c) Rossler model with $T = 1$ and $dt = 0.05$.

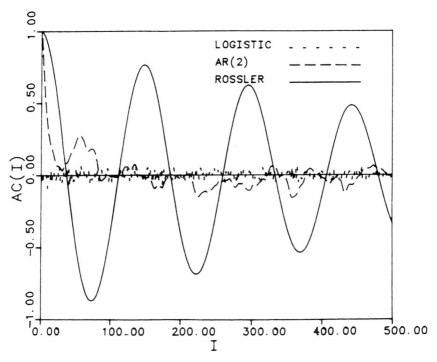

Figure 15.3 Comparison of the autocorrelations of the three model solutions with 1000 data points. The time units are the same as in Figure 15.1. T_d, the decorrelation time, can be determined by the first zero point of autocorrelation function.

$$AC(I) = AC(t' - t) = cov[X(t'), X(t)]/E[(X(t) - M)^2] \qquad (15.1)$$

where M is the mean of $X(t)$ and cov $[X(t'), X(t)]$ is the covariance between $X(t')$ and $X(t)$. The autocorrelation function of stochastic processes, such as an AR(2) process, decays quickly to irregular oscillations (Figure 15.3a). The autocorrelations of discrete time chaos, such as the logistic model, look like that of random noises (Figure 15.3b). In contrast, the autocorrelation function of continuous-time chaos, such as that of the Rossler attractor, shows wave-like oscillations with smooth decay (Figure 15.3c).

The Numerical Maximum Lyapunov Exponent

Chaotic motion is sensitive to initial conditions. This sensitivity is measured by the Lyapunov exponents. Consider a very small ball with radius $\varepsilon_i(0)$ at time $t = 0$ in the phase space. The length of the ith principal axis of the ellipsoid evolved from the ball at time t is $\varepsilon_i(t)$. The spectrum of Lyapunov exponents λ_i from an initial point can be obtained theoretically by (Farmer, 1982).

$$\lambda_i = \lim_{t \to \infty} \lim_{\varepsilon(0) \to 0} \{\ln[\varepsilon_i(t)/\varepsilon_i(0)]/t\} \qquad (15.2)$$

The maximum Lyapunov exponent λ (the largest among λ_i) can be calculated numerically by the Wolf algorithm (Wolf et al., 1985). Its limiting procedure is approximated by an averaging process over the evolution time EVOLV. This algorithm is applicable when the noise level is small. The maximum Lyapunov exponent λ is negative for stable systems with fixed points, zero for periodic or quasiperiodic motion, and positive for chaos. The largest Lyapunov exponent plays an important role in characterizing deterministic dynamics in theoretical studies. It has rather limited use in empirical tests, since random noise may also generate a positive exponent numerically. However, the maximum Lyapunov exponent may reveal some clue of chaos, if the order of $\lambda - 1$ is about T_d the decorrelation time (Nicolis and Nicolis, 1986). If one has any doubt about the possibility of random noise, we recommended to check the phase portrait and compare the reverse of Lyapunov exponent with the decorrelation time. These techniques can tell whether business cycles are likely generated by unit-root random process or chaos (Nelson and Plosser, 1982; Frank and Stengos, 1988; Sayers, 1989).

The Correlation and Fractal Dimensions

The most useful characteristic of chaos is its fractal dimension (Grassberger and Procaccia, 1984), which provides a lower bound to the degrees of freedom for the dynamic system. The popular Grassberger–Procaccia (GP hereafter) algorithm estimates the fractal dimension by means of the correlation dimension D (Grassberger and Procaccia, 1983). The correlation integral $C_m(R)$ is the number of pairs of points in m-dimensional phase space, whose distance between each other is less than R. For random or chaotic motion, the correlation integral $C_m(R)$ may distribute uniformly in some region of the phase space, and it has a scaling relation of R^D. Therefore, we have

$$\ln_2 C_m(R) = D \ln_2 R + \text{constant} \tag{15.3}$$

For white noise, D is an integer equal to the embedding dimension m. For deterministic chaos, D is less than or equal to the fractal dimension.

Pitfalls in Statistical Testing for Chaos

There are two major pitfalls in testing empirical data for chaos that need to be recognized. These involve (1) the common problems caused by insufficient information in empirical tests; and (2) the specific limitations of statistical inference for distinguishing chaotic from stochastic processes.

The Discrepancy between Mathematical Theory and Numerical Experiment

In any scientific discipline, mathematical theory approximates only some aspects of empirical phenomena. Certainly, more difficulties attend empirical work than theoretical study, since the real world is much more complex than simplified models. This is especially true for studies of nonlinear dynamics. I now want to outline some of these difficulties in detecting chaos from empirical data.

Sparse Data

Typical experiments in physics, chemistry, and biology often collect tens of thousands to almost a million data points and sampling time usually cover more than a hundred cycles. However, most economic indicators have only several hundred data points covering only a few cycles. This deficiency prevents many of the powerful tools in nonlinear dynamics, such as the Poincare return map, spectral analysis, mutual information, saddle-orbit analysis, and others based on statistical theory, from detecting intrinsic irregularity even when it is there.

Some algorithms give useful hints even for a small data set, but their power is much reduced. Worse, they may generate numerical artifacts. For example, the autocorrelations of continuous-time chaos models in numerical models show exponential decay when the time span is very large (Grossmann and Sonneborn-Schmick, 1982). However, the autocorrelations of continuous-time chaos look like those of periodic movements when only a few cycles of data are available (Figure 15.3c). Small data sets will introduce spurious low frequency in the power spectrum when there are only about hundreds of data points available (Nelson and Kang, 1981).

The problem of sparse data is especially acute in dimension calculations because their data requirements are severe. The minimum number of data points N_D required in dimension estimation has an exponential relation with the underlying dimension D, i.e., $N_D = h^D$, where h varies with different attractors (Mayer-Kress, 1986). For example, in the case of the Mackey–Glass model (Mackey and Glass, 1977), the required data for $D = 2$ is $N_D > 500$ points; and that for $D = 3$ is $N_D > 10,000$ points (Kostelich and Swinney, 1989). We also investigate the effect of the sample rate in dimension calculation. Generally speaking, 10–100 points per cycle are needed for the Mackey–Glass model. The relative error of the numerical correlation dimension is about 1% for 100 cycles, 3% for 30 cycles, 8% for 10 cycles, and 18% for only 5 cycles.

It is also found that a discrete map needs even more data points than a continuous flow. For instance, the reasonable number of data points is 5000 for Henon attractor (Henon, 1976) with $D = 1.26$ (Ramsey and Yuan, 1989). As a rule of thumb, the observed dimensionality in empirical data cannot be higher than 5 and embedding dimension in calculation should not be larger than 10, when data size is less than 10,000.

Noise

The second major problem is that the subtle information of deterministic chaos can be contaminated by numerical or measurement noise. The question is: To what degree can noise be tolerated in empirical tests? There are several numerical tests in terms of uniform noise. For example, it is found that the phase portrait of the noisy Henon map can be recognized and the correlation dimension can be estimated when random jitter is chosen from $[-0.05, 0.05]$, the up-bond of noise/signal ratio is 0.1% for the correlation dimension of Mackey–Glass model (Ben-Mizrachi, Procaccia, and Grassberger, 1983). In estimating the largest Lyapunov exponent, the allowance is 5% (Wolf et al., 1985).

Continuous and Discrete Time and the Time Unit

For qualitative models in economic theory, the choice between difference and differential equations is a matter of a mathematical convenience or aesthetic taste. For empirical models, however, the choice of time scale can crucially affect estimation and verification. Preferably, it should be determined by the dynamic nature of the process under investigation. For example, in population dynamics, the period of reproduction of nonoverlapping generation insects can be used as the natural unit to construct a difference equation. More general systems that exhibit continuous motion with a natural or intrinsic period should be sampled at intervals that correspond with the intrinsic frequency. The resulting discrete time series can then be described by a difference equation. However, when the natural period of a process is not known, the choice of time unit is an open question. We cannot arbitrarily choose the time unit without theoretical analysis and empirical evidence. This would appear to be the viewpoint we should take in economics as noted by Koopmans. He suggested replacing the discrete-time stochastic model with a continuous-time stochastic model when the serial correlation is much longer than the time unit (Koopmans, 1950).

Figure 15.5 shows that the pattern of the phase portrait is sensitive to the time lag T for discrete mapping, but not sensitive for continuous-time ones. The latter changes its shape only with varying T (Figure 15.4). In either case, the time unit plays a critical role in data analysis.

To illustrate the problem, consider a discrete-time Henon model economy and assume the intrinsic unit is a month. Now look at the phase portrait for "quarterly" or "annual" samples. The phase portraits in Figure 15.5 show that the pattern of quarterly data is more complex than that of monthly data. It also illustrates that the image of the annual data appears like random noise except its square boundary. Fitting the Henon model to quarterly and annual data leads to complete failure. This example illustrates why, if the underlying economic dynamics are truly discrete and its intrinsic time unit is the order of day, or week, or month, the quarterly or monthly economic indicators are not capable of revealing the discrete nature of dynamic process.

Numerical experiments show that the autoregressive and moving average model

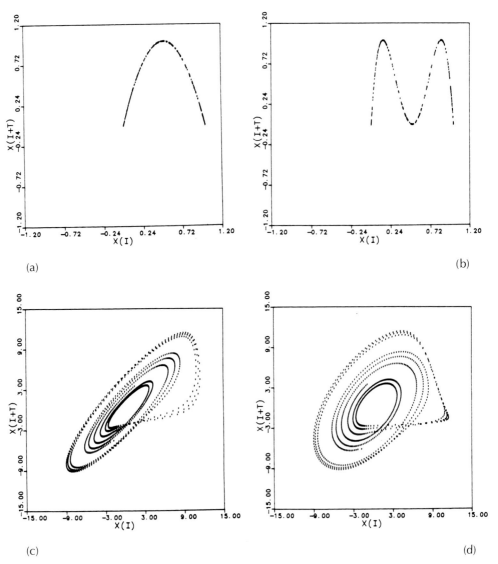

Figure 15.4 The two-dimensional phase portrait $X(I)$ vs $X(I + T)$ of deterministic chaos with varying time lag T. (a) Logistic model with $T = 1$, time interval $\Delta t = 1$, data size $N = 300$. (b) Logistic model with $T = 2$, $\Delta t = 1$, $N = 300$. (c) Rossler model with $T = 0.5$, time interval $\Delta t = 0.05$, and $N = 1000$. (d) Rossler model with $T = 1$, $\Delta t = 0.05$, $N = 1000$.

(ARMA) can well represent data generated by discrete time chaos, such as the Henon and logistic models when the time intervals are the intrinsic ones but not when they are based on a sample at time intervals different than this. For continuous time models, like those of Lorenz (1963) or Mackey–Glass (Mackey and Glass, 1977), the ARMA model can fit the generated data only when the sampling time

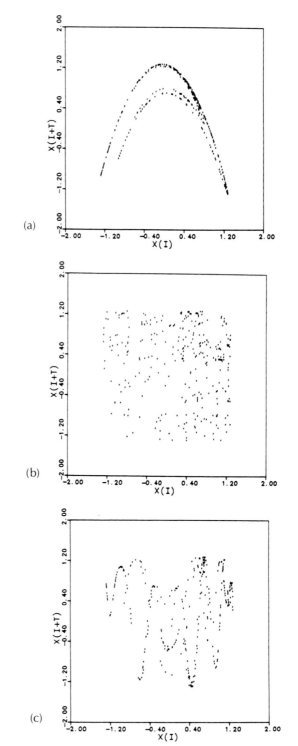

Figure 15.5 The phase portrait of the Henon economy observed from varying time interval Δt, $T = 1$, $N = 300$. (a) Original monthly data with $\Delta t = 1$. (b) Quarterly data with $\Delta t = 4$. (c) Annual data with $\Delta t = 12$.

interval is roughly of the same order as the average orbital time. In either case, success or failure in fitting ARMA models cannot indicate whether the data are generated by noise or chaos.

Spectral analysis and autocovariance function cannot distinguish between discrete-time chaos and random noise (Dale, 1984; Brock, 1986). However, these methods can identify continuous-time chaos (Crutchfield et al., 1980; Grossman and Sonneborn-Schmick, 1982; Nicolis and Nicolis, 1986). Few economic researchers are aware of these differences.

Limitations of Statistical Inference

Statistical inference has been developed to test stochastic process with identical independent distribution (i.i.d.). To what degree statistical inference is capable of dealing with chaotic process is still an open question. Stochastic and chaotic process are polar models based on conflicting assumptions. Most empirical cases lie in the gray zone between chaos and noise. Econometricians will soon be aware of the gap between the static nature of statistical inference and the dynamic complexity of chaotic behavior.

Inseparability of Nonlinear Systems

Currently, econometric reasoning is based on linear stochastic models. Interacting components can be separated and analytical solutions can be obtained in linear systems, because the superposition principle of linear systems mathematically justifies the theoretical framework of homogeneous and additive economies. However, the superposition principle is not valid for nonlinear systems, since the whole is more than the sum of the parts for nonlinear dynamics. Nonlinear dynamic equations rarely have closed forms of analytical solution. This situation casts serious doubt on regression exercises for nonlinear dynamic problems. Nonlinearity imposes a great challenge to time-series analysis in economic studies. The inseparability of nonlinear components may frustrate econometricians when they are developing statistical tools for testing economic chaos. For example, Brock argues that chaotic time series can be detected by using a linear filter such as first differencing, or taking residual of a fitted ARMA model. He believes that the dimensionality of the original and the filtered time series should be the same (Brock, 1986). However, it is difficult to judge the result of the differencing operation because it is sensitive to the time interval of differencing. The concept of fractal dimensionality comes from self-similarity of fractal structures (Hentschel and Procaccia, 1983). Brock did not discuss the issue of self-similarity when he tried to prove the residual test theorem.

The complexity of the problem can be seen from a special case of first differencing. Assume $\{X(t)\}$ denotes the continuous time series generated from a strange attractor, say, the Rossler attractor. The fractal dimension of Rossler attractor D is larger than two but less than three. A one-dimensional chaotic discrete-time series $\{u_n\}$ can be obtained from the Poincare section of $\{X(t)\}$ in a two-dimensional

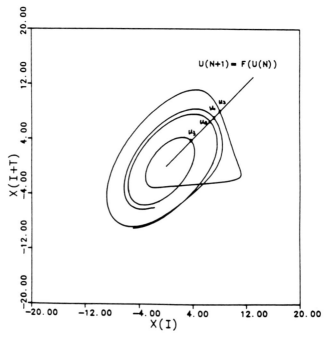

Figure 15.6 The relationship between continuous and discrete chaos. The discrete-time chaos $\{u_n\}$ is obtained from the one-dimensional Poincare section of continuous-time chaos $\{X(I)\}$ in a two-dimensional phase space. Here, $X(I)$ is generated from the Rossler model with $T = 1, \Delta t = 0.05, N = 500$. The time unit of one-dimensional discrete map $u_{n+1} = F(u_n)$ is the average orbital time $T_n = 1/f_n$ around the unstable equilibrium point of continuous-time chaos $\{X(I)\}$. The natural frequency f_n can be determined from the highest peak in the power spectrum.

phase space. Its time interval is equal to the averaging orbital (natural) time T_N of the attractor (see Figure 15.6). Therefore, the fractal dimension D' of $\{u_n\}$ must be less than 1.

For the differenced time series $\{\Delta u_n\}$, the outcome is uncertain if the time interval for differencing is arbitrarily chosen. In practice, the differencing procedure in econometric modeling is a "whitening" process that cuts off the autocorrelation and increases the variance in observed time series. So far as we know, there is no theoretical argument and numerical evidence to show the invariance of dimensionality under a difference transformation.

Changing Strangeness under the Residual Test

It has been noted that correlation dimension is not invariant to a smooth coordinate transformation (Ott, Withers, and Yorke, 1984). The residual of a moving average process introduces random noise into the original data. This procedure may erase the fractal structure (Garcia-Pelayo and Schieve, 1991). For the autoregressive process, the situation becomes more subtle. The metric fractal dimension under a smooth linear deterministic transformation is invariant, but most probability dimensions are not.

To check the validity of the residual test, we tested the Henon attractor with 5000 data points, which is good enough to uncover its dimensionality (Ramsey and Yuan, 1989). We fit the ARMA(6,3) model and AR(6) model, respectively, to the Henon time series. The correlation dimension of ARMA(6,3) residuals is equal to the embedding dimension, which is the characteristic of random noise. The correlation dimension of AR(6) residuals cannot be determined because no parallel line can be identified from the GP plot. Probably, the AR(n) transformation changes the probability density in phase space, and the definition of correlation dimension is related to the square of probability density (Hentschel and Procaccia, 1983). A residual test of the logistic time series has a similar result. For a continuous time model, such as the Lorenz attractor, fitting it to the low-order ARMA model is increasingly difficult, when autocorrelation is long and the time interval is short compared with its natural orbital time. No clear-cut conclusion can be reached from the residual tests in our numerical experiment.

A technical remark should be made here. It is known that only idealized models of pure random noise and well-behaved attractors have well-defined correlation dimension. This means that a time series may not have a well-defined correlation dimension. When no plateau region or no saturated dimension can be identified from the Grassberger–Procaccia plots, the correlation dimension is not tractable. The face value of the numerical mean in dimension calculations should not be readily accepted until its Grassberger–Procaccia plot has been carefully examined.

The Pitfall of Linear Stochastic Filter in Detecting Deterministic Chaos

It is well known that any Gaussian or i.i.d. time series can be represented by an infinite autoregressive process or moving average process (Granger and Newbold, 1986). Some features observed in empirical tests, such as the long autocorrelations in a deterministic time series, can be simulated by a finite-order stochastic process, either in linear or nonlinear form. But a stochastic model cannot simulate a self-similar structure such as that of the Cantor set. Characterizing a strange attractor requires a spectrum with infinite dimensionality (Farmer, Ott, and Yorke, 1983).

The above discussion may help to solve the dispute raised by Ramsey, Sayers, and Rothman (1990). Conflicting results from nonlinear diagnostics and the residual test are reported in testing the monetary indexes (Chen, 1987b, 1988b; Barnett and Chen 1988; Ramsey, Sayers, and Rothman, 1990). Ramsey and co-workers duplicated our results from log-linear detrended data. However, there is no sign of nonlinear structure in the residuals resulted from a double-sided moving average filter. The reason for the absence of such a sign is that the symmetric, low-reject filter used by Ramsey and his colleagues did not wipe out high-frequency noise, but improperly removed the low-frequency deterministic components. As we indicated before, a continuous-time chaos can be considered as an imperfect periodic motion with low frequency and irregular amplitude (Chen, 1988b). In Ramsey's test, the filtered time series did not even become stationary, which was required by attractor modeling. The low-reject filter made the variance of the filtered monetary index increase over time. The seemingly contradictory reports resulting from the residual tests are actually an aid in understanding the essential difference between linear stochastic deduction and nonlinear deterministic logic.

The Roots of Nonstationality and Nonnormality

Nonstationality and nonnormality are widely observed in economic time series because economies are open systems. It is a formidable task for econometricians to deal with these problems within the conventional framework of i.i.d. process. Deterministic approach and stochastic approach in theoretical economics represent conflicting ideas of endogenous and exogenous mechanisms of business fluctuations. However, the deterministic description and probabilistic description of dynamic process in theoretical physics are simply complementary tools in the unified dynamical framework. For example, chemical reactions can be described by (deterministic) differential equations or a master equation. The probability distribution function in master equation can be obtained by solving a (deterministic) partial differential equation. In the case of the Fokker–Planck equation, the peak of the distribution function or the mean value evolves along the path that can be represented by the trajectory of the corresponding deterministic equation. Therefore, these two approaches are equivalent when the distribution function is unimodal (Nicolis and Prigogine, 1977, 1989; Reichl, 1980). However, during bifurcation at the critical point of some control parameter, fluctuations will be so large that the mean value no longer represents the most-likely situation because the distribution function may become multihumped (Baras et al., 1983; Chen, 1987a). Actually, many statistical practitioners have already observed nonnormal, long-tail, and multimodal distribution in empirical studies.

The relationship between deterministic approach and probabilistic approach in nonlinear dynamic systems is illustrated in Figure 15.7.

Roughly speaking, between two bifurcation points, the dynamic process follows a deterministic path, which can be described by averaging when the process has a unimodal distribution. Statistic inference or i.i.d. process can be approximately applied only in this situation. The bifurcation model is quite useful in understanding noncontinuity, nonstationality, and nonnormality in real economies when econometricians are confounded by the multiple phase character of economic evolution (Day and Walter 1989). Changing economies can be one of the major obstacles in detecting economic chaos.

Some Conclusion about Numerical Algorithms

Practically, we have only some clue of low-dimensional attractors with finite data sets. There is no way to identify deterministic chaos with certainty. At present, with data only in the hundreds, the discovery of economic strange attractors whose dimensionality is higher than 3 is unlikely.

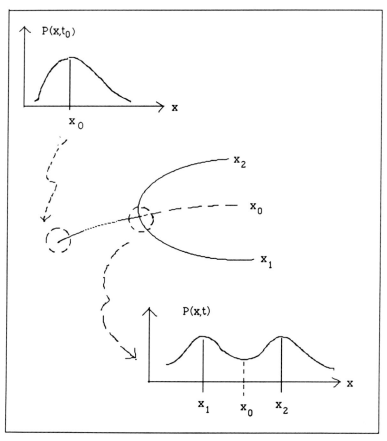

Figure 15.7 The relationship between the probability distribution function of a stochastic equation and the corresponding solution of the deterministic equation.

We can only speculate why we were unable to identify correlation dimensions for other types of economic time series, such as GNP, IPP, and the Dow–Jones index, in our numerical tests. Either their dimensions are too high, or their noise levels are too large, or they do not in fact reflect intrinsic characteristics of complex behavior, or changing economies caused by series of bifurcations. Current observational scope and analytical technique are not capable of solving these problems.

Testing Economic Chaos in Monetary Aggregates

With the pitfalls well in mind, I shall briefly reconsider my work on monetary aggregates to illustrate techniques for detecting chaos. The Federal Reserve's monetary indexes include M1, M2, M3, and L. These are simple-sum aggregate indexes (denoted by SS hereafter). There are also parallel Divisia theoretical indexes such as

Divisia demand indexes (denoted by DD hereafter) and Divisia supply indexes (denoted by DS hereafter).

We tested 12 types of monetary index time series covering the period from 1969 to 1984. Five of them suggested strangeness: Federal Reserve's simple-sum SSM2, Divisia demand DDM2, DDM3, DDL and Divisia supply DSM2 monetary aggregates (Chen, 1987b, 1988a,b). The behaviors of Divisia aggregates are very similar. We discuss only SSM2 and DDM2 here for brevity. Previously, the weekly data were used in our test. Now, the tests of the original monthly data are added here. Our data source is Fayyard. Monthly and weekly indexes are distinguished by the letter m and w, respectively. All the data are log-linear detrended, since no strange attractors have been identified from the first differencing data.

Data Processing and Path Smoothing

Ramsey and co-authors noted that the weekly monetary data used in our previous test were largely generated from monthly raw data by spline interpolation and model reconstruction (Ramsey, Sayers, and Rothman, 1990). The question is whether the interpolation procedure may introduce additional correlation or alter the original dimensionality. For this reason, we reexamined the original monthly monetary data. The numerical results of correlation dimension n, decorrelation time T_d, and the largest Lyapunov exponent λ of the monthly data are essentially in the same order as weekly data. It is not surprising that interpolation does not change the primary characteristics of deterministic movements in our case. The interpolation procedure is equivalent to a smoothing technique for noise reduction.

In fact, interpolation is widely used in the scientific community when raw data are incomplete (Charney, Halem, and Jastrow, 1969; Tribbia and Anthes, 1987). Interpolation and smoothing were also used in testing chaos from climate, ecological, and epidemic time series (Grassberger, 1986; Schaffer, 1984; Schaffer and Kot, 1985).

Detrending Methods and Attractor Models

Testing economic aggregate time series for chaos or randomness is a formidable task. The intrusion of growth trends raises a critical problem of how to characterize a growing economy by means of mathematical attractors. Various methods of detrending have been used in econometrics. We are interested in their theoretical implication: the choice of reference system in observing economic behavior. We attempted to explore this problem through numerical experiments on empirical data.

For example, the percentage rate of change and its equivalent form, the logarithmic first differences, are widely used in fitting stochastic econometric models (Osborne, 1959; Friedman, 1969). It can be defined as follows:

$$Z(t) = \ln S(t+1) - \ln S(t) = \ln \{S(t+1)/S(t)\} \qquad (15.4)$$

where $S(t)$ is the original time series, and $Z(t)$ is the logarithmatic first difference.

An alternative method called log-linear detrending has been used in chaos models (Dana and Malgrange, 1984; Brock, 1986; Barnett and Chen, 1988). We have

$$X(t) = \ln S(t) - (k_0 + k_1 t) \tag{15.5}$$

or

$$S(t) = S_0 \ \exp(k_1 t) \ \exp[X(t) \tag{15.6}$$

where $S(t)$ is the original time series, and $X(t)$ is the resulting log-linear detrended time series, k_0 is the intersection, k_1 the constant growth rate, and $S_0 = \exp(k_0)$.

Our numerical experiments indicate that the percentage rates of change are whitening processes based on short time scaling. Log-linear detrending, on the other hand, retains the long-term correlations in economic fluctuations, since its time scale represents the whole period of the available time series. Findings of evidence of deterministic chaos mainly from log-linear detrended economic aggregates lead to this conclusion.

Figure 15.8a shows the time sequences of the log-linear detrended (denoted by LD) monetary aggregates SSM2. Its almost symmetric pattern of nearly equal length of expansion and contraction is a typical feature of growth cycles in economic systems. The usual business cycles are not symmetrical. Their longer expansions and shorter contractions can be obtained in such a way, when a trend with constant growth rate is adding to symmetric growth cycles. The logarithmic first-difference time series (denoted by FD) SSM2 is given in Figure 15.8b as a comparison. The latter is asymmetric and more erratic.

Empirical Evidence of Deterministic and Stochastic Processes

Based on the phase portrait and autocorrelation analysis, we can qualitatively distinguish a stochastic process from a deterministic one. Figure 15.9a presents the phase portrait of detrended monetary aggregates LD SSM2. It rotates clockwise like the spiral chaos in Figure 15.2c. The complex pattern is a potential indication of nonlinear deterministic movements and eliminates the possibilities of white noise or simple periodic motions. To compare with a series that appears like white noise, the phase portrait of IBM daily stock returns is shown in Figure 15.9b. The autocorrelations of the detrended time series are shown in Figure 15.10. Readers may compare these with the autocorrelations in Figure 15.3c.

If we approximate the fundamental period T_1 by four times the decorrelation time T_d, as in the case of periodic motion, then, T_1 is about 4.7 years for LD SSM2. This result is very close to the common experience of business cycles. We will return to this point later.

The Numerical Maximum Lyapunov Exponent and Autocorrelations

Let us now consider the tests using the Lyapunov experiments and autocorrelations. In theory, the choice of evolution time EVOLV, embedding dimension m and time

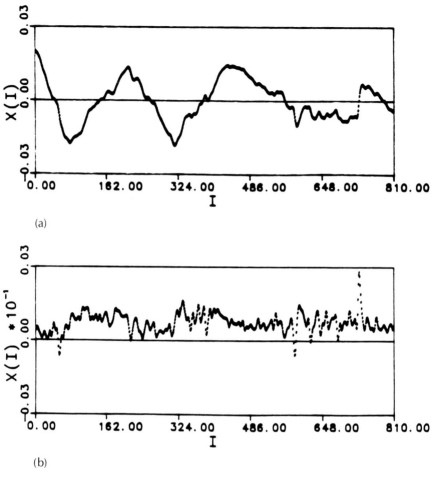

Figure 15.8 Comparison of the detrended weekly time series SSM2w. (a) Symmetric LD SSM2w: the log-linear detrended SSM2w with a natural growth rate of 4% per year. (b) Asymmetric FD SSM2w: the logarithmic first differences of SSM2.

delay T, has no relevance to the maximum Lyapunov exponent. In practice, the value of the Lyapunov exponent does relate to the numerical parameters. The range of evolution time EVOLV must be chosen by numerical experiments. The positive maximum Lyapunov exponents of the investigated monetary aggregates are stable over some region in evolution time. The numerical Lyapunov exponent is less sensitive to the choice of embedding dimension m. In our tests, we fixed m at 5 and time delay T at 5 weeks based on the numerical experiments. For example, the stable region of EVOLV is 45–105 weeks for SSM2 and 45–150 weeks for DDM2. Their average maximum Lyapunov exponents over this region are 0.0135 and 0.0184 (bit per week), respectively.

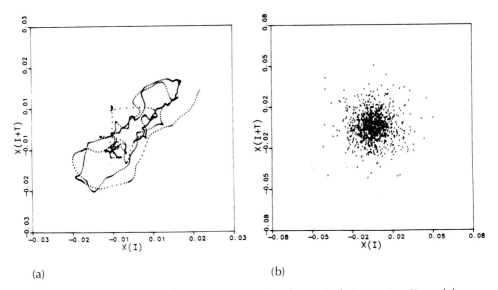

(a)   (b)

Figure 15.9 Comparison of the phase portraits of empirical time series. Time delay $T = 20$. (a) LD SSM2w weekly time series. $N = 807$ points. (b) IBM daily common stock returns. $N = 1000$ points, beginning on July 2, 1962.

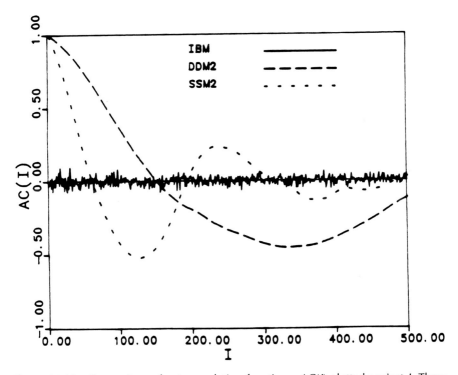

Figure 15.10 Comparison of autocorrelation functions; $AC(I)$ plotted against I. There are three time series: LD SSM2w and LD DDM2w weekly data, and IBM daily stock returns, each in the same time units as in Figure 15.9. $N = 807$.

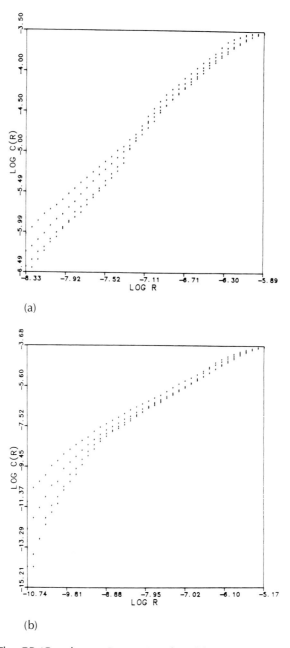

(a)

(b)

Figure 15.11 The GP (Grassberger–Procaccia) plot of $\ln_2 C_m(R)$ versus $\ln_2 R$ for log-linear detrended monthly monetary indexes beginning from January 1969. The embedding dimension, $m = 1, \ldots, 5$, is taken as a parameter. The plots rotate downward and to the right as m increases. The time lag $T = 10(m)$. (a) SSM2m, $N = 195$ observations. (b) DDM2m, $N = 195$ observations.

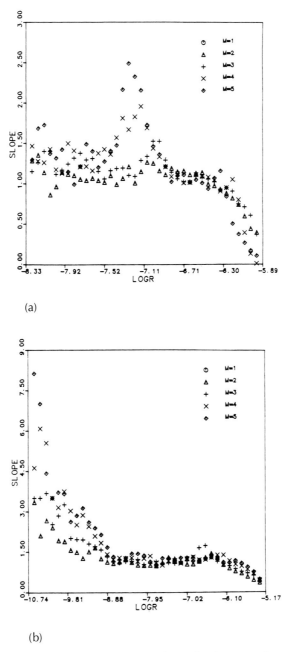

(a)

(b)

Figure 15.12 The GP Plot of SLOPE$_m$ versus $\ln_2 R$ for the same detrended monetary indexes. The correlation dimension n is estimated from the saturated slope in plateau regime, which corresponds to the linear regime of lines in Figure 15.11. (a) SSM2m, $N = 195$ observations. (b) DDM2m, $N = 195$ observations.

The characteristic decorrelation time T_d of the LD SSM2 is 61 weeks. The reciprocal of the maximum Lyapunov exponent $\lambda^{-1}(= 74.1)$ for LD SSM2 is roughly of the same order of magnitude as the decorrelation time T_d. This relation does not hold for pure white noise.

The Correlation Dimension

The correlation dimension ν can be estimated by the Grassberger–Procaccia algorithm. Plots of $\ln C_m(R)$ versus $\ln R$ and slope versus $\log R$ for LD SSM2 and LD DDM2 are shown in Figure 15.11 and Figure 15.12. The existence of linear regions of intermediate R, which reflect the fractal structure of the attractors, is shown in Figures 15.11a and 15.12a. The correlation dimension can be determined from the up-bond slope of the plateau region in Figures 15.11b and 15.12b. The level of uniform noise in the data can be estimated from the left end of the plateau when R is small.

We calculated the correlation dimension with the time lag T varying from 4 to 38 (the decorrelation time of DDM2m). The pattern is not sensitive to changing T. The first zero-autocorrelation time is not the best choice for T in our cases, because a large T may cause folding in the phase space.

We found that the correlation dimensions of the investigated five monetary aggregates were between 1.3 and 1.5. They include four Divisia monetary indexes and one official simple-sum monetary index. For other monetary aggregates, no correlation dimension could be determined.

A Continuous Time Model of Growth Cycles with Delayed Feedback and Bounded Expectations

Given the evidence just presented, and given our comments on the desirability of a continuous-time model, let us consider a continuous-time representation of economic data with low-dimensional chaos.

The observed low correlation dimension and long decorrelation–time set constraint on the modeling of growth cycles. For a typical discrete model, T_d is approximately the same order of the time unit. The decorrelation time T_d for monetary attractors is more than 60 weeks. A continuous time model would seem to be appropriate to describe monetary growth cycles. The minimum number of degrees of freedom required for chaotic behavior in autonomous differential equations is 3. The low dimensionality of monetary attractors leads to the assumption that the monetary deviations are separable from other macroeconomic movements. The background of growth cycles can be approximately represented by a constant exponential growth trend, or the so-called natural growth rate.

After comparing the correlation dimension and the phase portraits of the data and alternative models, a differential-delay equation suggests itself as a good candidate. For simplicity, we consider only one variable here.

Deviations from Trend and Time Delay in Feedback

The apparent monetary strange attractors are mainly found in log-linear detrended data. This is an important finding to study control behavior in monetary policy. I assume that the general trends of economic development are perceived by people in economic activities as a common psychological reference or as the anchor in observing and reacting (Tversky and Kahneman, 1974). Administrative activities are basically reactions to deviations from the trend. Accordingly I choose the deviation from the "natural growth rate" as the main variable in the dynamic model of monetary growth in the following equation:

$$dX(t)/dt = aX(t) + F[X(t - \tau)] \tag{15.7}$$

$$F(X) = XG(X) \tag{15.8}$$

where X is the deviation from the trend, τ is the time delay, a is the expansion speed, F is the feedback function, and G is the control function. There are two competing mechanisms in the growth system. The first is the immediate response to market demand. It is described by the first term on the right of equation (15.1). The second term represents the endogenous system control described by the feedback function F. This consists of feedback signal $X(t - \tau)$ and control function G. The time delay τ exists in the feedback loop because of information and regulation lags.

There are several considerations in specifying F and G. We argue that the monetary policy follows a simple rule based on the bounded expectations of monetary movements. We assume the feedback function $F(X)$ has two extrema at $\pm X_m$ for the control-target floor and ceiling as argued by Solomon (1981). To describe the overshooting in economic management and the symmetry in growth cycles, $G(X)$ should be nonlinear and symmetric, $G(-X) = G(X)$. A simple exponential function describes the assumed nonlinear control function with flexible floor and ceiling. Its control behavior is similar to that driving in a freeway with lower and upper speed limits.

$$G(X) = -b \, \exp(-X^2/\sigma^2) \tag{15.9}$$

where b is the control parameter, the minus sign of b is associated with negative feedback, σ is the scaling parameter, and the extremas of $F(X)$ are located at $X_m = \pm\sigma/\sqrt{2}$. Substituting equation (15.9) into equations (15.7) and (15.8) gives the following differential-delay equation:

$$dX(t)/dt = aX(t) - bX(t - \tau) \, \exp[-X(t - \tau)^2/\sigma^2] \tag{15.10}$$

We may change the scale by $X = X'\sigma$ and $t = t'\tau$, then drop the prime for convenience:

$$dX(t)/dt = a\tau X(t) - b\tau X(t - 1) \exp[-X(t - 1)^2] \tag{15.11}$$

What Can We Learn from the Model

No empirical phenomenon can be understood without theoretical reasoning. Only some empirical tests offer supportive arguments for theoretical judgment. The choice of chaotic model over stochastic model largely depends on whether we can obtain more information based on the same set of empirical data. Our answer is yes. The mechanism of intrinsic instability and the pattern of irregularity illustrated in non-linear chaotic models are entirely foreign to linear stochastic models.

Phase Transition and Pattern Stability

Figures 15.13a–b displays qualitatively the phase diagram of equation (15.11) in the parameter space. The broad diversity of dynamic behavior includes steady-state ST, limit cycle or periodic motion C1, and the explosive solution EP. The complex regime CP includes multiperiodic (C1, C2, C3) and chaotic regime CH. When parameter values change within each region, the dynamic behavior is pattern-stable, because the dynamic mode occupies a finite area in the parameter space. The phase transition occurs when parameters cross the boundary between different phases. It is observable when the wave pattern changes.

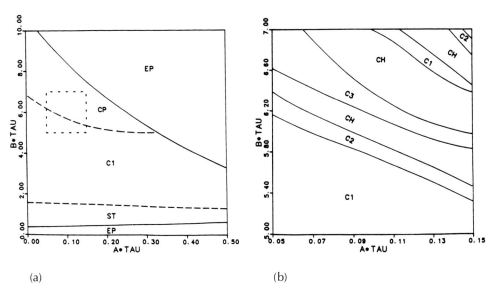

(a)　　　　　　　　　　　　　　　　　　(b)

Figure 15.13　The phase diagram of numerical solutions of equation (15.11) in parameter space $a\tau$ and $b\tau$. The dashed area in (a) is enlarged in (b). Here, EP, ST, and CP represent explosive regime, steady state (after damped oscillation), and complex regime, respectively. CH is chaotic regime. C1, C2, and C3 are periodic patterns, whose longer wave consists of one, two, or three shorter waves in turn.

Long Wave and Short Cycles

In addition to seasonal changes, several types of business cycles have been identified by economists: the Kitchin cycles (3–5 years), the Juglar cycles (7–11 years), the Kuznets cycles (15–25 years), and Kondratieff cycles (45–60 years) (Van Duijn, 1983). Schumpeter suggested that these cycles were linked. Each longer wave may consist of two or three shorter cycles. This picture can be described by the periodic phase C2 or C3 in the CP regime of our model. The irregularity in long waves can also be explained by the chaotic regime CH. Our model gives a variety of possibilities of periodicity, multiperiodicity and irregularity in economic history, although our data show the chaotic pattern only in monetary movements. It is widely assumed that the long waves are caused by long lags, a belief coming from the linear paradigm (Rostow, 1980). This condition is not necessary in our model, because the dynamic behavior of equation (15.13) depends both on $a\tau$ and $b\tau$. A strong overshooting plus a short time delay has the same effect as a weak control plus a long time delay, a point also made by Sterman (1985). This model is so simple and general, it could have applications beyond the monetary system in the market economy we discussed here. For example, the growth cycles and long waves caused by overshooting and time delay may also happen in centrally planned economies.

Simulating Empirical Cycles and Forecasting Basic Trends

In comparing model-generated patterns with empirical data, we may confine our experiments to certain regions of the parameter space. For example, we can estimate the average period T from 4 times the decorrelation time T_d. The time delay τ in monetary control due to regulation lag and information lag is between 20 and 56 weeks (Gordon, 1978). If we estimate the time delay τ to be 39 weeks, we can simulate LD SSM2 time series by the solution by setting $\tau = 39, a = 0.00256, b = 0.154$, and $\sigma = 0.0125$. The model results match well the average amplitude A_m, decorrelation time T_d, positive maximum Lyapunov exponent λ, and correlation dimension D of the empirical time series.

We tested the theoretical models with power spectra and autocorrelation analysis. The approximated period T of the chaotic solution can be estimated from T_d measured by 3–5 cycles. It is close to the fundamental period $T_1(=f_1^{-1})$. The fundamental frequency can be determined by power spectra. The error can be less than 3% when observation period covers 100 cycles. For LD SSM2 time series, the difference of T_d measured between 10 and 15 years is less than 5%. We can obtain valuable information about the fundamental period T_1 without knowing the exact parameters of the deterministic model.

The small data sets cause the estimation of the correlation dimension to be biased downward (Ramsey and Yuan, 1989). In our theoretical simulation of monetary cycles, the numerical result of the correlation dimension is 1.7 calculated with 1000 data points and 2.08 with 16,384 points for the same model. The error is 18% in dimension estimation of the growth-cycle model. The results of monthly monetary

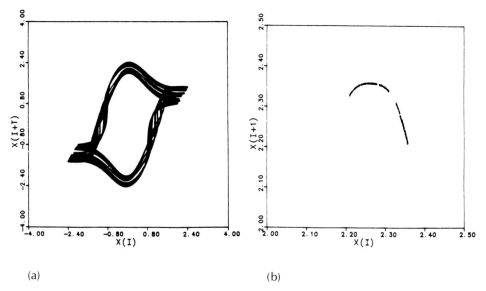

(a)   (b)

Figure 15.14   The two-dimensional phase portrait and the maximum map of theoretical monetary strange attractor (Chen, 1987b). The scale is arbitrary. (a) The two-
dimensional phase portrait of theoretical monetary strange attractor, which rotates
clockwise, $N = 25,000, T = 1, \Delta t = 0.01$. (b) The maximum map obtained from the
one-dimensional Poincare section in two-dimensional phase space. The time unit is the
averaging orbital time T_n.

data are still within the margin of numerical reliability because of their low dimensionality (Chen, 1988b). Certainly, the numerical estimation of the correlation dimension for monetary indexes is only suggestive since the amount of data is small.
Further empirical observations are needed to provide better evidence of monetary
chaos.

The phase portrait and maximum map of a theoretical model of monetary chaos
are demonstrated in Figure 15.14. The theoretical monetary strange attractor rotates
clockwise (Figure 15.14a), which mimics the movement of the monetary growth cycle in Figure 15.9a. The maximum map shows the qualitative picture of discrete-time
chaos typically created by the Poincare section (Figure 15.14b). A brief summery of
both empirical and simulating results is given in Table 15.1. The time unit of weekly
data is converted to monthly for comparison. Here, the time scales are 1 year = 12
months = 52 weeks, and 1 month = 4.3 weeks. SSM2t is the simulating time series
generated by the theoretical monetary growth model and its correlation dimension n
is calculated with 1000 and 16,384 data points, respectively (Chen, 1988b).

Implications for Forecasting and Control Policy

The predictive power of a chaotic economic time path is limited by the magnitude of
the maximum Lyapunov exponent. Nevertheless, we may potentially recover more
information from chaotic motion than from randomly generated movements. We
know that a long-term prediction of the chaotic orbit is impossible from the view

Table 15.1 Empirical and Theoretical Evidence of Monetary Chaos

Name	N (obs)	$\lambda(/m)$	$\lambda^{-1}(m)$	$T_d(m)$	ν
SSM2m	195	0.0242/m	41.3m	14m	1.3
DDM2m	195	0.0489/m	20.4m	38m	1.3
DDM3m	195	0.0218/m	45.9m	37m	1.3
DDLm	192	0.0397/m	25.2m	35m	1.3
SSM2w	807	0.0581/m	17.2m	14.2m	1.5
DDM2w	807	0.0791/m	12.6m	34.9m	1.4
DDM3w	807	0.0774/m	12.9m	34.2m	1.5
DDLw	798	0.0525/m	19.1m	32.3m	1.5
DSM2w	798	0.0585/m	17.1m	32.6m	1.3
SSM2t	1000w	0.0688/m	14.5m	14.2m	1.7
	(16384)				(2.08)

of nonlinear dynamics. A medium-term prediction of approximate period T can still be made, if we identify strange attractors from the time series.

Let us discuss the meaning of the control parameters in equation (15.13). When $b = 0$, the monetary deviation from the natural rate will grow at a speed e^{at}. We define a characteristic doubling time t_a, which measures the time needed to double the autonomous monetary expansion $X(t)$ without control. Similarly, we can define a characteristic half time t_b, which measures the time needed to reduce the money supply to half its level, when $a = 0$ and $X(t - \tau)$ reaches the control target $X_m = \sigma/\sqrt{2} = 1.4\%$ per year. The same is true for the contraction movements, since the feedback function $G(X)$ is symmetric. Here t_a is 5.2 year and t_b is 7.4 week for SSM2 in our simulation. We see that even modest time delay and overshooting may generate cycles and chaos.

For policy considerations, the phase diagram of the model suggests that the steady state in money supply can be achieved by carefully adjusting the control parameter b or the time delay τ (see Figure 15.13). For example, we can fix a $(= 0.1)$ and $\tau(= 39$ weeks) and set b in stable regime ($0.41 < b < 1.51$ or 29.5 weeks $< t_b < 108.7$ weeks); we may also fix $a(= 0.1)$ and $b(= 6.0)$ but choose τ in ST regime (14.4 minutes $< \tau < 1.3$ day). Obviously, reducing overshooting is much easier than cutting time delay in monetary control. These figures give a qualitative picture of monetary target policy (Chen, 1988b).

Linear Approximations of a Nonlinear Model

Let us study the relationship between the nonlinear dynamic model (15.10) and its linear approximation under some simplifying conditions.

A different equation can be obtained as an approximation of a nonlinear difference-differential equation (15.10) when the time unit is chosen to be the time delay $\tau(\tau = 1)$ and $X(t)$ is much less than the control target σ, and b is less than σ^2, we have

$$dX(t)/dt = X(n + 1) - X(n) = aX(n) - bX(n - 1) \ \exp(-X(n - 1)^2/\sigma^2) \quad (15.12)$$

$$= aX(n) - bX(n - 1) - bX(n - 1)3/s2 \quad (15.13)$$

or

$$X(n + 1) = c_1X(n) + c_2X(n - 1) + \omega X(n - 1)^3 \quad (15.14)$$

where $c_1 = (1 + a), c_2 = -b, \omega = b/\sigma^2$. Equation (15.14) looks like an AR(2) process when the nonlinear term $\omega X(n - 1)^3$ is ignored and replaced by some noisy residual term. Although AR(2) approximation may be very useful and convenient in econometric analysis, its drawbacks and limitations are also significant. First, the sampling time unit should be the time delay that is between 20 and 56 weeks, equivalent to quarterly or annual data (Gordon, 1978). Second, the AR(2) model is misleading in its stochastic nature, because the residual is generated by the nonlinear term with long-term correlations, not random noise without correlations.

We may also have a differential version of equation (15.13) when the time delay is ignored,

$$dX(t)/dt = -aX(t)g\{\exp[-X(t)^2/\sigma^2] - 1\} \quad (15.15)$$

where $g = b/a \gg 1$, so the equation has a fixed point solution. Friedman believes that the natural rate in economies can be achieved in so-called long-run equilibrium (Friedman, 1969). In our case, constant growth rate can be realized when the time delay in control process is zero. Obviously, this is an idealistic case but unrealistic situation. The concept of long-run equilibrium in static analysis can be considered as the fixed point solution in nonlinear dynamic systems. Although steady state is hard to achieve due to time delay and overreaction in human behavior, equilibrium or steady state can still serve a reference regime for control target.

This example demonstrates the close connection between nonlinear economic dynamics and linear dynamics. Static equilibrium analysis could be integrated in the generalized framework of disequilibrium dynamics.

Brief Summary and Future Directions

So far we have little evidence of economic chaos from empirical data. However, theoretical powers of modeling complex behavior and mathematical generality of nonlinearity strongly support the development of chaotic economic dynamics. The prerequisite for this advancement is its tremendous demand of empirical information and computational power to handle nonlinear problems.

The question is how to extend our scope of economic analysis and advance our study of economic chaos. Four directions should be explored in the near future.

- Rethinking the operational framework of chaos theory for empirical studies.

The standard definition of deterministic chaos is based on the positive Lyapunov exponent. Fractal dimension is also important in characterizing the strange attractor (Hao, 1990). These criteria are useful in studies of theoretical models and computer experiments, but very restricted in empirical analysis. We should develop operational guidelines for choosing chaotic or stochastic approaches in empirical analysis.

Prigogine pointed out that deterministic chaos is only a partial feature of complex systems. Long-range correlation is the fundamental character of complex dynamics (Nicolis and Prigogine, 1989). This definition of chaotic process may help econometricians in understanding chaos and noise, since econometric analysis is based on stochastic process with short correlations.

In my experience in analyzing large numbers of economic time series, taintless cases of economic chaos are rare, but long-term correlations appearing in empirical data are abundant. The real problem is always more complicated than theoretical models. It is true both for natural sciences as well as social sciences. For example, discovering the beautiful structure of hydrogen spectra is a rare case even in physics. However, the discontinuity of frequency distribution widely observed in optical spectra strongly support the quantum theory.

No empirical observation can be done without theoretical reasoning, whether it works in an explicit or implicit way. The difference lies deeply in theoretic foundation. Some econometricians use a whitening technique such as multiple differencing to eliminate correlations and justify stochastic models. We try long-term detrending methods to extract correlation signals and recover deterministic mechanisms.

- Reexamining the theoretical foundation of econometrics.

Economists often compare economy with weather (Goodwin, 1990). Although the irregularities of their behavior are very similar, their theoretical perspectives are just the opposite. The failure of econometric forecasting based on a stochastic approach (Dominguez, Fair, and Shapiro, 1988; Wallis, 1989) and the success of weather forecasting based on a deterministic approach (Tribbia and Anthes, 1987) dramatize the difference in their methodological foundation.

- Expanding the empirical base of economic studies.

Genuine economic dynamics cannot be discovered by curve fitting in terms of statistical techniques. The current controversy of chaos versus noise cannot be completely settled by numerical tests based on limited contaminated data.

Consider the oldest problem of planet motion in astronomy. The irregular time paths of planet motion are easily seen in short-time observations. Linear stochastic models may fit the data and give a good explanation of the short history. However, cumulative observations reveal regularity in recurrent patterns. Although arithmetic rules in calendar calculation can be established from empirical data, theoretical understanding went a long way from Copernicus's idea of heliocentric reference system, to Kepler's law of planet motion, and Newton's law of classical mechanics.

The improvement in weather forecasting has been achieved by expanding the data base through global weather-station networks and satellite-surveillance techniques. Increasing computer power also facilitates increasing precision of nonlinear models and weather forecasting. However, current resource constraints in empirical economic research result in an economic profession basically confined in thought experiments and linear models because of the lack of empirical data and computing power in the information age. Long-term investment in "economic weather-station network" and research efforts in complex economic dynamics is essential for advancing empirical economic science.

Exploring economic chaos opens new ways to understand human behavior and social evolution. The interdisciplinary character in developing evolutionary dynamics and nonlinear economics has not only changed the way we think, but also the institution in which we organize economic research.

Appendix A. A Direct Test for Determinism in Monetary Time Series

A new algorithm of direct testing determinism has been developed by Daniel Kaplan and Leon Glass (1992a,b) at McGill University. It turns out to be a useful tool to distinguish between determinism and randomness. Their idea is simple.

At each state a deterministic dynamic flow has only one direction, while a stochastic system has more than one possible value. By calculating local coarse-grained flow averages and statistics Λ, one may have a better chance of dealing with noisy and short time series than calculating Lyapunov exponents and correlation dimensions.

We sent two time series of 807 points in length, DLSM2 and PCSM2, to Kaplan. PCSM2 is a simulated time series generated by equation (15.11). DLSM2 is the log-linear detrended SSM2 weekly time series in Figure 15.9a. Kaplan finds clear conclusions for both time series. We now provide further evidence of deterministic monetary chaos, courtesy of Kaplan (private communication, April 9, 1992).

PCSM2 easily passes the test of determinism as shown in Figure 15.15a: the lambda-bar is close to 1 for the deterministic signal, and the contrasting Gaussian random process with the same autocorrelation function Ψ is much less and near zero, as is expected from the theory.

DLSM2 in Figure 15.15b shows that the signal is more deterministic than a Gaussian random noise. Its low resolution is due to short time series and high level of noise. It would be helpful for economic studies to have a longer time series of empirical data in the future.

Figure 15.15   Kaplan-Glass plots for testing determinism. Λ vs. τ for tested time series and a Gaussian random process (GRP) with identical autocorrelation $\Psi(\tau)$ are marked by open symbols and filled symbols, respectively. For a deterministic system, Λ is close to 1. For a stochastic system, Λ is much less than 1 and near 0. (a) PCSM2, $N = 807$. Embedding dimension $m = 3$, and resolution = $1/512$. (b) DLSM2, $N = 807$. Embedding dimension $m = 3$, and resolution = $1/8$.

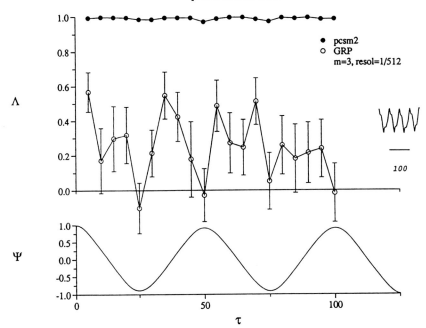

pcsm2 from P. Chen

(a)

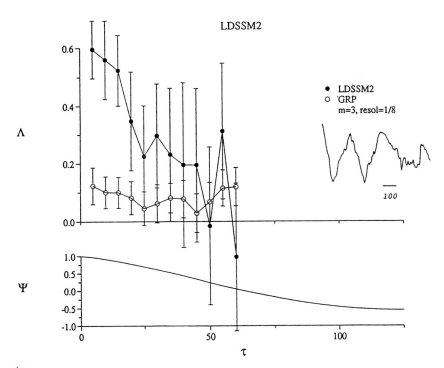

LDSSM2

(b)

Appendix B. Testing Correlation Resonances in Searching for Chaos

In Chapter 1, Professor Prigogine pointed out that complex spectral theory plays a critical role in dealing with unstable dynamic systems. Of special importance is the concept of correlation resonances (Ruelle, 1986) which are the peaks of correlation spectra of time series data. We call this approach "the complex spectral analysis of correlations (CSAC)."

A complex Fourier spectrum is a natural generalization of conventional Fourier spectrum when unstable states are present. The complex spectral representation in physics originated from the problem of decaying states and resonances in quantum mechanics (Gel'fand and Vilenkin, 1964). The CSAC shifts interest from the original time series to the correlation functions. Resonances in Henon map were studied by Isola (1988). The complex spectral theory for nonintegrable large Poincare system developed by Petrosky and Prigogine (1991) has been applied to studies of highly chaotic maps by Hasegawa and Saphir (1992). These developments form the foundation for empirical applications of CSAC approach.

Zhang, Wen, and Chen (1992) have improved the CSAC numerical technique for empirical testing with limited data points. The procedure is to first calculate autocorrelations of the time series data, then calculate the power spectra and locate complex singularities of correlations by means of the Pade rational function approximation, and, finally, estimate resonance frequencies and their exponential decay rates.

We tested several log-linear detrended data, including S&P 500, Federal Reserve M2, crude oil prices, and real GNP data. Our initial results, which are reported in Table B.1, provide strong evidence of economic chaos in monetary data, and weak evidence in stock market and oil price data. Weaker evidence is provided in the case of GNP.

The CSAC approach is just one possible test that should be added to the package of numerical tests briefly outlined in this chapter. Each test may reveal one or two aspects of nonlinearity and long-range correlation. The tests are complementary and should all be used in a weighted judgment.

The empirical findings shed important light on endogenous economic dynamics. First, the generalized concept of unstable periodic modes breaks the intellectual barrier between chaos and noise— the two idealized models of complex reality. Now we may define the peaks (resonances in correlation power spectra) with exponential decays as one of many operational indicators of typical chaos.

Second, the existence of correlation resonances in economies builds a link between nonequilibrium evolutionary processes and static equilibrium representations. The correlation resonances reveal the coexistence of various characteristic fluctuations. The lifetime of metastable modes provides a quantitative measure of the transition from disequilibrium to equilibrium.

Table 15.2 Testing Economic Chaos Based on Various Methods

Name	LFDS&P	S&P	M2	GNP	Brent	WTI
N-points	1499	1500	807	164	580	580
Period	1952–81	1952–81	1969–84	1946–88	1983–85	1983–85
Time unit (Δ)	5 days	5days	week	quarter	day	day
$T_d(\Delta)$	2	136	61	22	44	44
$\lambda(\Delta^{-1})$	0.014	0.0145	0.013	0.032	0.020	0.018
$\lambda^{-1}(\Delta)$	71.4	69	74.1	31	50	56
D	no	2.0	1.5	2.5(?)	1.5	2.2
P-Portrait	random	spiral	spiral	spiral	spiral	spiral
KG Test	no	no	yes	?	no	no
T_1	no	43.8 ys[?]	4.39ys	33.4ys	140.9 ds	110.5 ds
τ_1		43.9 ys[?]	2.44 ys	*	55.7 ds	74.4 ds
T_2	no	3.33 ys	1.98 ys	12.5 ys	24.2 ds	21.3 ds
τ_2		13.0 ys	0.91 ys	?	47.7 ds	*
T_3	no	1.09 ys		5.6 ys	18.5 ds	
τ_3		*		?	20.6 ds	
chaos evidence	no	weak	strong	weaker	weak	weak

[a] Where λ is Lyapunov exponent, T_d is decorrelation time measured from the first zero of autocorrelations, D is correlation dimension, P-portrait represents phase portrait, and KG stands for Kaplan-Glass direct test. T ($=2\pi/\omega$) is the period of correlation resonance, $\tau(=1/\alpha)$ is the lifetime of unstable mode $e^{-\alpha t}e^{i\omega t}$.
Note: The question mark (?) casts doubt on the numerical reliability when data are short. The asterisk (*) indicates that the extremely slow decay actually means persistent oscillation within the numerical precision.

The results of the observed resonance frequencies are consistent with the common experience of business cycles (Gordon, 1986). The different rates of exponential decay provide good indicators of adjustment speed for persistent medium business cycles and faster dissipative innovation shocks.

Note

The author is grateful to Professor I. Prigogine for his continuous support, Professor W. A. Barnett for providing monthly monetary data, and Professor R. Day for his careful reading of my manuscript and for his valuable suggestions. He also thanks T. Stangos and C. Sayers for bringing the problems of the unit-root hypotheses, and the data processing effect to the attention of the author. The stimulating comments from W. A. Brock, E. Mosekilde, R. M. Goodwin, C. W. J. Granger, J. B. Ramsey, J. Conlisk, and anonymous referees are greatly appreciated. I have incorporated, with permission of the publishers (MIT Press), a considerable amount of material from Chen (1988b).

Bibliography

Argoul, F., A. Arneodo, P. Richetti, and J. C. Roux, 1987, "Chemical Chaos: From Hints to Confirmation," *Accounts of Chemical Research*, 20, 436–442.

Ashly, R., D. Patterson, and M. Hinich, 1986, "A Diagnostic Test for Nonlinear Serial Dependence in Time Series Fitting Errors," *Journal of Time Series Analysis*, 7, 165–178.

Baras, F., G. Nicolis, M. Malek Mansour, and J. W. Turner, 1983, "Stochastic Theory of Adiabatic Explosion," *Journal of Statistical Physics*, 32, 1–23.

Barnett, W.A., and P. Chen, 1987, "Economic Theory as a Generator of Measurable Attractors," in I. Prigogine and M. Sanglier, eds., *Laws of Nature and Human Conduct*, Task Force of Research Information and Study on Science, Brussels.

Barnett, W.A., and P. Chen, 1988, "The Aggregation-Theoretic Monetary Aggregates Are Chaotic and Have Strange Attractors: An Econometric Application of Mathematical Chaos," in W. A. Barnett, E. R. Berndt, and H. White, eds., *Dynamic Econometric Modelling*, Cambridge University Press, Cambridge, pp. 199–245.

Ben-Mizrachi, A., I. Procaccia, and P. Grassberger, 1983, "Characterization of Experimental (Noisy) Strange Attractors," *Physical Review A*, 29, 975–977.

Blatt, J.M., 1978, "On the Econometric Approach to Business-Cycle Analysis," *Oxford Economic Papers*, 30, 292–300.

Bohm, A., 1986, *Quantum Mechanics, Foundations and Applications*, 2nd edition, Springer-Verlag, Berlin.

Brandstater, A. and H. L. Swinney, 1987, "Strange Attractors in Weakly Turbulent Couette-Taylor Flow," *Physical Review A*, 35, 2207–2220.

Brock, W. A., 1986, "Distinguishing Random and Deterministic Systems: Abridged Version," *Journal of Economic Theory*, 40, 168–195.

Brock, W. A., W. D. Dechart, and J. Scheinkman, 1987, "A Test for Independence Based on the Correlation Dimension," SSRI Working Paper #8702, University of Wisconsin-Madison.

Brock, W. A., and C. Sayers, 1988, "Is the Business Cycles Characterized by Deterministic Chaos?" *Journal of Monetary Economics*, 22, 71–80.

Charney, J., M. Halem, and R. Jastrow, 1969, "Use of Incomplete Historical Data to Infer the Present State of the Atmosphere," *Journal of the Atmospheric Sciences*, 26, 1160–1163.

Chen, P., 1984, "A Possible Case of Economic Attractor," Research Note, Prigogine Center for Studies in Statistical Mechanics, University of Texas at Austin.

Chen, P., 1987a, "Origin of the Division of Labour and a Stochastic Mechanism of Differentiation," *European Journal of Operational Research*, 30, 246–250.

Chen, P., May 1987b, "Nonlinear Dynamics and Business Cycles," Ph.D. Dissertation, University of Texas at Austin, Austin.

Chen, P., 1988a, "Multiperiodicity and Irregularity in Growth Cycles: A Continuous Model of Monetary Attractors," *Mathematical and Computer Modelling*, 10(9), 647–660.

Chen, P., 1988b, "Empirical and Theoretical Evidence of Economic Chaos," *System Dynamics Review*, 4(1–2), 81–108.

Chen, P., 1989, "The Bridge Between the Two Cultures: Some Fundamental Issues in Advancing Empirical Economic Science," IC² Institute Working Paper #89–12–01, University of Texas at Austin, Austin, December.

Crutchfield, J., J. Farmer, N. Packard, N. Shaw, G. Jones, and R. J. Donnely, 1980, "Power Spectral Analysis of a Dynamical System," *Physics Letters*, (26A) (1), 1–4.

Dana, R.A., and P. Malgrange, 1984, "The Dynamics of a Discrete Version of a Growth Cycle Model," in J. P. Ancot, ed., *Analyzing the Structure of Econometric Models*, Martinus Nijhoff, The Hague, 115–142.

Day, R.H., and J.L. Walter, 1989, "Economic Growth in the Very Long Run: on the Multiple-Phase Interaction of Population, Technology, and Social Infrastructure," in W. A. Barnett, J. Geweke, and K. Shell, eds., *Economic Complexity: Chaos, Sunspots, Bubbles, and Nonlinearity*, Cambridge University Press, Cambridge, pp. 253–289.

Dominguez, K.M., R.C. Fair, and M.D. Shapiro, 1988, "Forecasting the Depression: Harvard versus Yale," *American Economic Review*, 78(4), 595–612.

Farmer, J.D., 1982, "Chaotic Attractors of an Infinite Dimensional Systems," *Physica D*, 4, 366–380.

Farmer, J.D., E. Ott, and J.A. York, 1983, "The Dimension of Chaotic Attractors," *Physica D*, 7, 153–180.

Frank, M., and T. Stengos, 1988, "Some Evidence Concerning Macroeconomic Chaos," *Journal of Monetary Economics*, 22, 423–438.

Frank, M., R. Gencay, and T. Stengos, 1988, "International Chaos," *European Economic Review*, 32, 1569–1584.

Friedman, M., 1969, *The Optimum Quantity of Money and Other Essays*, Chapter 11, Aldine, Chicago.

Garcia-Pelayo, R., and W. C. Schieve, 1991, "Noisy Fractals," submitted to *Journal of Mathematical Physics*.

Gel'fand I.M., and N.Na. Vilenkin, 1964,,, *Generalized Functions*, Academic Press, New York.

Gordon, R.J., 1978, *Macroeconomics*, Little, Brown, Boston, pp. 468–471.

Goodwin, R.M., 1990, *Chaotic Economic Dynamics*, Oxford University Press, Oxford.

Granger, C.W.J., and P. Newbold, 1986, *Forecasting Economic Time Series*, 2nd ed., Academic Press, New York.

Grassberger, G., 1986, "Do Climatic Attractors Exist?" *Nature* (London), 323, 609–612.

Grassberger, P., and I. Procaccia, 1983, "Measuring the Strangeness of Strange Attractors," *Physica D*, 9, 189–192.

Grassberger, P., and I. Procaccia, 1984, "Dimensions and Entropies of Strange Attractors From a Fluctuating Dynamic Approach," *Physica D*, 13, 34–54.

Grossmann, S., and B. Sonneborn-Schmick, 1982, "Correlation Decay in the Lorenz Model as a Statistical Physics Problem," *Physical Review A*, 25, 2371–2384.

Guevara, M.R., L. Glass, and A. Shrier, 1981, "Phase Locking, Period-Doubling Bifurcations and Irregular Dynamics in Periodically Stimulated Cardiac Cells," *Science*, 214, 1350–1353.

Hao, B.-L., *Chaos I, Chaos II*, 1984, 1990, World Scientific, Singapore.

Hasegawa, H.H., and W.C. Saphir, 1992, "Decaying Eigenstates for Simple Chaotic Systems," *Physics Letters A*, 161, 471–476.

Henon, M., 1976, "A Two Dimensional Mapping with A Strange Attractor," *Communications of Mathematical Physics*, 50, 69–77.

Hentschel, H. G. E., and I. Procaccia, 1983, "The Infinite Number of Generalized Dimensions of Fractals and Strange Attractors," *Physica D*, 8, 435–444.

Hsieh, D., 1989, "Testing for Nonlinear Dependence in Foreign Exchange Rates," *Journal of Business*, 62, 339–368.

Isola, S., 1988, "Resonances in Chaotic Dynamics," *Communications in Mathematical Physics*, 116, 343–352.

Kaplan, D.T., and L. Glass, 1992, "Direct Test for Determinism in a Time Series," *Physical Review Letters*, 68 (4), 427–430.

Koopmans, T.C., 1950, Models Involving a Continuous Time Variable, in *Statistical Inference in Dynamic Economic Models*, John Wiley & Sons, New York, p. 384.

Kostelich, E., and H. Swinney, 1989, "Practical Considerations in Estimating Dimension from Time Series Data," *Physics Scripta*, 40, 436–441.

Kostelich, E., and J. A. York, 1988, "Noise Reduction in Dynamic Systems," *Physical Review A*, 38, 1649–1652.

Lorenz, E.N., 1963, "Deterministic Nonperiodic Flow," *Journal of Atmospheric Science*, 20, 130–141.

Mackey, M.C., and L. Glass, 1977, "Oscillation and Chaos in Physiological Control Systems," *Science*, 197, 287–289.

Mayer-Kress, G., 1986, *Dimensions and Entropies in Chaotic Systems*, Springer-Verlag, Berlin.

Nelson, C.R., and H. Kang, 1981, "Spurious Periodicity in Inappropriately Detrended Time Series," *Econometrica*, 49, 741–751.

Nelson, C.R., and C.I. Plosser, 1982, "Trends and Random Walks in Macroeconomic Time Series, Some Evidence and Implications," *Journal of Monetary Economics*, 10, 139–162.

Nicolis, C. and G. Nicolis, 1986, "Reconstruction of the dynamics of the climatic system from time series-data," *Proceedings of the National Academy of Sciences*, USA, 83, 536–540.

Nicolis, G., and I. Prigogine, 1977, *Self-Organization in Non-equilibrium Systems*, Wiley, New York.

Nicolis, G., and I. Prigogine, 1989, *Exploring Complexity*, Freeman, New York.

Osborne, M.F.M., 1959, "Brownian Motion in the Stock Market," *Operation Research*, 7, 145–173.

Ott, E., W.D. Withers, and J.A. York, 1984, "Is the Dimension of Chaotic Attractors Invariant under Coordinate Changes?" *Journal of Statistical Physics*, 36, 687–697.

Pool, R., 1989, "Is It Chaos, Or Is It Just Noise?" *Science*, Vols. 243, 25–28, 310–343, 604–607, 893–896, 1290–1293; Vols. 245, 26–28.

Ramsey, J.B., C.L. Sayers, and P. Rothman, 1990, "The Statistical Properties of Dimension Calculations Using Small Data Sets: Some Economic Applications," *International Economic Review*, 31, 991–1020.

Ramsey, J.B., and H.J. Yuan, 1989, "Bias and Error Bars in Dimension Calculation and Their Evaluation in Some Simple Models," *Physics Letters A*, 134, 287–297.

Reichl, L.E., 1980, *A Modern Course in Statistical Mechanics*, University of Texas Press, Austin.

Rossler, O.E., 1976, "An Equation for Continuous Chaos," *Physics Letters A*, 57, No. 5, 397–398.

Rostow, W.W., 1980, *Why the Poor Get Richer and the Richer Slow Down*, University of Texas Press, Austin.

Ruelle, D., 1986, "Resonances of Chaotic Dynamical Systems," *Physical Review Letters*, 56, 405–407.

Sayers, C.L., 1985, "Work Stoppages: Exploring the Nonlinear Dynamics," Working Paper, University of Wisconsin-Madison.

Sayers, C.L., 1989, "Chaos and the Business Cycle," Working Paper, University of Houston.

Schaffer, W.M., 1984, "Stretching and Folding in Lynx for Returns: Evidence for a Strange Attractor in Nature," *American Naturalist*, 124, 798–820.

Schaffer, W.M., and M. Kot, 1985, "Nearly One-Dimensional Dynamics in an Epidemic," *Journal of Theoretical Biology*, 112, 403–427.

Scheinkman, J., and B. LeBaron, 1989, "Nonlinear Dynamics and Stock Returns," *Journal of Business*, 62, 311–337.

Solomon, A.M., 1981, "Financial Innovation and Monetary Policy," in Sixty-Seventh Annual Report, Federal Reserve Bank of New York.

Sterman, J.D., 1985, "A Behavioral Model of the Economic Long Wave," *Journal of Economic Behavior and Organization*, 6, 17–53.

Sterman, J.D., E. Mosekilde, and E. Larsen, 1989, "Experimental Evidence of Deterministic Chaos in Human Decision Making Behavior," *Journal of Economic Organization and Behavior*, 12, 1–28.

Takens, F., 1981, "Detecting Strange Attractors," in *Dynamical Systems and Turbulence*, Lecture Notes in Mathematics, No. 898, D. A. Rand and L. S. Young, eds., Springer-Verlag, Berlin, pp. 366–381.

Tribbia, J.J., and R.A. Anthes, 1987, "Scientific Basis of Modern Weather Prediction," *Science*, 237, 493–499.

Tversky, A., and D. Kahneman, 1974, "Judgement under Uncertainty: Heuristics and Biases," *Science*, 185, 1124–1131.

Van Duijn, J.J., 1983, *The Long Wave in Economic Life*, Allen and Unwin, London.

Wallis, K.F., 1989, "Macroeconomic Forecasting: A Survey," *Economic Journal*, 99, 28–61.

Wolf, A., J. Swift, H. Swinney, and J. Vastano, 1985, "Determining Lyapunov Exponents from a Time Series,"*Physica D*, 16, 285–317.

Zhang, Z.L., K.H. Wen, and P. Chen, 1992, "Complex Spectral Analysis of Economic Dynamics and Correlation Resonances in Market Bheavior," IC^2 Institute Working Paper, 90–09–02, University of Texas at Austin.

16

Has Chaos Been Discovered with Economic Data?

WILLIAM A. BARNETT and MELVIN J. HINICH

The claim of successful detection of chaos by Barnett and Chen (1986, 1988a,b) and Chen (1987) has generated considerable controversy, as in Ramsey, Sayers, and Rothman (1988). We believe that the controversy cannot be resolved by using the usual algorithms, and therefore introduce an alternative method owing to Hinich (1982), which, however, can only confirm the finding of nonlinear dynamics. Nonlinear dynamics is necessary but not sufficient for chaos. Further research is needed before we can confirm or reject the discovery of chaos.[1]

The reason for the apparent success of Barnett and Chen's research is the unusually high quality of the data. Instead of using data produced from governmental accounting identities, they used Barnett's (1980, 1987) Divisia monetary aggregates, which are produced from the Törnqvist discrete time approximation to the continuous time Divisia line integral. The latter is within Diewert's "superlative" class, defined to consist of index numbers producing a second-order approximation to the exact theoretical aggregate of economic aggregation theory. In contrast, the highest quality data typically available from governmental sources are based on Laspeyres or Paasche indexes, which produce only first-order approximations. The Federal Reserve System's simple sum monetary aggregates are not even first-order approximations to the economic variable, and hence have first-order remainder terms. In brief, the noise in the Divisia monetary aggregates is very low, relative to that of most economic data.

In the current chapter we use these and an even newer set of monetary aggregates: the exact theoretical rational expectations monetary aggregates (hereafter called the Theoretical aggregates) described in Barnett, Hinich, and Yue (1989). We also use simple sum and Divisia data, as in the earlier studies, but we use monthly data of higher quality than the weekly data used in the earlier research.

The Maintained Hypothesis

The tests used in Barnett and Chen are those commonly used in the experimental physics literature. With noise free data, the connection between those tests and chaos is well understood (see, e.g., Brock and Dechert (1988) for proofs of the relevant theorems). But the appropriate way to use those tests with noisy data is not entirely clear, because the sampling distributions of the test statistics are not known. This ambiguity is at the center of the controversies that have arisen in economics regarding testing for chaos. As we shall see, the issue in fact is at least partially philosophical, as well as being statistical.

In classical statistical methodology, a deterministic model is maintained, and estimation methods then are used to select the parameters in a manner that permits the model to explain as much of the variability in the data as possible. The remaining residuals are then imputed to the stochastic disturbances presumed to be produced from an assumed statistical error distribution. Model evaluation then commonly is concentrated on error structure tests designed to determine whether the residuals could have been random drawings from the assumed distribution of the stochastic disturbances under both maintained and null hypotheses. Tests of the null are based on comparison of the residuals under the null and maintained hypotheses. In Barnett and Chen's tests, chaos was the deterministic null hypothesis, which was permitted to explain as much of the variability in the data as possible under the null. The residuals were assumed to be random.

However, an alternative view seems to have been adopted by some researchers working on tests for chaos. It reverses the conventional methodology by imputing chaos only to the residuals remaining after as much of the data's variability as possible has been explained by conventional stochastic processes. According to this view, once all possible means of detrending and prewhitening have been exhausted, the remaining residuals can be tested for chaos. So, e.g., if much of the variability in the data could have been explained equally as well by chaos or by an $AR(n)$ process for some n, then the $AR(n)$ becomes the accepted null rather than chaos. This basic view underlies the tests run in Ramsey, Sayers, and Rothman (1988).

It is well known that solution paths produced from chaotic systems look very much like stochastic processes. This fact produces a virtually insolvable problem: should we view chaos as a potential explanation for stochastic appearing data, or should we view stochastic processes as a potential explanation for chaotic appearing data? With the former view, the approach taken by Barnett and Chen seems appropriate. They preprocessed the data only through detrending, and then applied conventional tests for chaos. But with the latter view, the approach taken by those, such as Ramsey, Sayers, and Rothman, who preprocess the data more extensively, seems appropriate.

We feel that the former approach more closely corresponds with conventional statistical methodology. It seems to us that the alternative approach is open ended and could rule out any possible findings of chaos. If an $AR(1)$ process cannot explain the data, then there is an $AR(2)$. But what about an $AR(459)$, etc? What about high order nonlinear detrending? If carried to its logical extreme, that approach seems to leave no room for chaos.

Even if a clear basis for choice existed between the two approaches, there remains a serious obstacle to useful application of the chaos testing algorithms. In particular, those algorithms, once they have detected chaos, are not yet capable of using that information to uncover much else about the underlying dynamic system, other than its dimension. Moreover, the available methods for measuring dimension of chaotic systems, such as the Grassberger–Procaccia algorithm, are severely biased downward, especially with small samples. This defect in those methods was an additional reason for using a conventional statistical test.[2]

There are two important conventional stochastic process tests currently in use for testing for nonlinearity: the BDS [Brock, Dechert, and Scheinkman (1986)] test and the Hinich bispectrum test. The BDS test provides an important advance in testing for stochastic dependence, but it does not provide a direct test either for nonlinearity or for chaos, because the sampling distribution of the test statistic is not known, either in finite samples or asymptotically, under the hypotheses of nonlinearity, linearity, chaos, or the lack of chaos. The asymptotic distribution is known only under the null of independence.[3]

The Hinich bispectrum approach provides direct tests for nonlinearity and Gaussianity. It produces a test statistic having known asymptotic sampling distribution under the null of Gaussianity.

The Hinich Bispectral Approach

Definitions and Background

If $\{x(t)\}$ is a zero mean third order stationary time series, then the mean $\mu_x = E[x(t)] = 0$, the covariance $c_{xx}(m) = E[x(t)]$, and the general third-order moments $c_{xxx}(s, r) = E[x(t + r)x(t + s)x(t)]$ are independent of t. If $c_{xx}(m) = 0$ for all nonzero m, the series is white noise. Priestley (1981) and Hinich and Patterson stress that although a series may be white noise, $x(n)$ and $x(m)$ may be stochastically dependent unless $\{x(t)\}$ is multivariate Gaussian. Only under multivariate Gaussianity are lack of correlation (whiteness) and stochastic independence the same. If the distribution of $\{x(n_1), \ldots, x(n_N)\}$ is multivariate normal for all $n_1, \ldots, n_N$, then the series is defined to be Gaussian, where N is the sample size.[4] Hinich and Patterson (p. 70) fault Box and Jenkins (1970, p. 8 vs. p. 46) and Jenkins and Watts (1968, p. 149 vs. p. 157) for blurring the definitions of whiteness and independence.

We define a pure white noise series as one in which $x(n_1), \ldots, x(n_N)$ are independent random variables for all values of $n_1, \ldots, n_N$. All pure white noise series are white. All white noise series are not pure white noise, unless, in addition, they are Gaussian.

In addition to stationarity, whiteness, and pure whiteness, another often assumed property of a time series is linearity. Many researchers implicitly assume the errors of their models are Gaussian, and test for pure white noise by using the covariance function $c_{xx}(m)$, but ignore the information regarding possible nonlinear relationships which are found in the third order moments $c_{xxx}(s,r)$.

The above discussion suggests the need to test for both nonlinearity and Gaussianity, in addition to testing in the usual manners for whiteness.

The Test Method

Hinich argues that the bispectrum in the frequency domain is easier to interpret than the multiplicity of third order moments $\{c_{xxx}(r,s) : s \leq r, r = 0, 1, 2, \ldots\}$ in the time domain. For frequencies f_1 and f_2 in the principal domain

$$\Omega = \{(f_1, f_2) : 0 < f_1 < .5, \quad f_2 < f_1, \quad 2f_1 + f_2 < 1\},$$

the bispectrum, $B_{xxx}(f_1, f_2)$, is defined by

$$B_{xxx}(f_1, f_2) = \sum_{r=-\infty}^{\infty} \sum_{s=-\infty}^{\infty} c_{xxx}(r, s) \exp[-2\pi(f_1 r + f_2 s)]. \tag{16.1}$$

The bispectrum is the double Fourier transformation of the third-order moments function.[5]

The skewness function $\Gamma(f_1, f_2)$ is defined in terms of the bispectrum as follows:

$$\Gamma^2(f_1, f_2) = |B_{xxx}(f_1, f_2)|^2 / S_{xx}(f_1) S_{xx}(f_2) S_{xx}(f_1 + f_2), \tag{16.2}$$

where $S_{xx}(f)$ is the (ordinary power) spectrum of $x(t)$ at frequency f. Since the bispectrum is complex valued, the absolute value (vertical) lines in equation (5.2) designate modulus. Brillinger (1965) proves that the skewness function $\Gamma(f_1, f_2)$ is constant over all frequencies $(f_1, f_2) \in \Omega$, if $\{x(t)\}$ is linear; while $\Gamma(f_1, f_2)$ is zero over all frequencies, if $\{x(t)\}$ is Gaussian. Linearity and Gaussianity can be tested using a sample estimator of the skewness function $\Gamma(f_1, f_2)$. We now outline the procedure we use to obtain the bispectrum.

Computation of the Test Statistics

Let $f_k = k/N$ for each integer k. For the example $\{x(0), x(1), \ldots, x(N-1)\}$, define $F_{xxx}(f_j, f_k)$ to be an estimate of the bispectrum of $\{x(t)\}$ at the frequency pair (f_j, f_k) such that

$$F_{xxx}(f_j, f_k) = X(f_j) X(f_k) X^*(f_j + f_k)/N, \tag{16.3}$$

where

$$X(f_j) = \sum_{t=0}^{N-1} x(t) \exp(-2\pi f_j t).$$

The asterisk in equation (16.3) designates complex conjugate.

The function $F_{xxx}(f_j, f_k)$ must be smoothed as follows to form a consistent estimator. Let $< B_{xxx}(f_m, f_n) >$ denote a smoothed estimate of $B_{xxx}(f_m, f_n)$, which is obtained by averaging over values of $F_{xxx}(f_j, f_k)$ at adjacent frequency pairs such that

$$< B_{xxx}(f_m, f_n) >= M^{-2} \sum_{j=(m-1)M}^{mM-1} \sum_{k=(m-1)M}^{nM-1} F_{xxx} F_{xxx}(f_j, f_k). \qquad (16.4)$$

This estimator, $< B_{xxx}(f_m, f_n) >$, is the average of the $F_{xxx}(f_j, f_k)$ over a square on M^2 points. It is a consistent and asymptotically complex normal estimator of the bispectrum $B_{xxx}(f_1, f_2)$, if the sequence (f_m, f_n) converges to (f_1, f_2) (see Hinich, 1982).

As discussed earlier, the estimated skewness function, $\Gamma(f_m, f_n)$, will not be significantly different from a constant at any frequency pair in Ω under the null hypothesis of linearity. If the null hypothesis is Gaussianity as well as linearity, then that constant is zero. The skewness function can be used to motivate construction of the normalized test statistic, $2|\delta(f_m, f_n)|^2$, where

$$\delta(f_m, f_n) =< B_{xxx}(f_m, f_n) > / [(N/M^2) < S_{xx}(f_m) > \ < S_{xx}(f_n) >$$

$$< S_{xx}(f_m + f_n) > |^{1/2}. \ (16.5)$$

In this formula, $< S_{xx}(\cdot) >$ is defined to be a consistent and asymptotically normal estimator of the power spectrum $S_{xx}(\cdot)$, and f_m is defined by $f_m = (2m - 1)M/2N$ for each integer m. Hinich has shown that $2[\delta(f_m, f_n)]^2$ is approximately distributed as an independent noncentral chi-squared variate with two degrees of freedom at frequency pair (f_m, f_n).

The larger M, the less the finite sample variance and the larger the sample bias. Because of this trade-off, there is no one unique M that is appropriate to use for performing nonlinearity and Gaussianity tests based on the estimated statistics given by (16.5). When M is large, the bandwidth is large, the variance is reduced, and the resolution of the tests is small, since there are too few terms for the linearity test. If M is small, there is a large number of terms to sort for the linearity tests, the variance may be too large, and the chi-square approximation used for the linearity test may not be good. Hinich has suggested that M should be selected to be approximately the square root of the number of observations, N.

Let P denote the number of frequency pairs in the principal domain, Ω, and let

$$D = \{(m, n) : (f_m, f_n) \in \Omega\},$$

so that P is the cardinal number of the set D. Hinich has shown that the P values of $1|\delta(f_m, f_n)|^2$ for $(m, n) \in D$ are approximately distributed as independent, noncentral chi-square variates with noncentality parameter $\lambda(f_m, f_n)$, where

$$\lambda(f_m, f_n) = (2M^2/N)|B_{xxx}(f_m, f_n)|^2/S_{xx}(f_m)S_{xx}(f_n)S_{xx}(f_m + f_n)$$
$$= (2M^2/N)\Gamma^2(f_m, f_n). \tag{16.6}$$

Define the test statistic

$$\text{CHISUM} = 2\sum\sum_{(m,n)\in D}|\delta(f_m, f_n)|^2. \tag{16.7}$$

The distribution of CHISUM is approximately a noncentral chi-square with $2P$ degrees of freedom with a noncentrality parameter that is the sum of the $\lambda(f_m, f_n)$ over all $(m, n) \in D$.

Under the null hypothesis that $\{x(t)\}$ is Gaussian and thus the skewness function, $\Gamma(f_m, f_n)$, is identically zero over all $(m, n) \in D$, CHISUM is approximately a central chi-square $2P$ variate. Equation (5.7) gives us an asymptotic chi-square test of the Gaussianity hypothesis. If the time series is linear but not necessarily Gaussian, then the skewness function is constant, which implies from (16.6) that the noncentrality parameters are constant. The Hinich linearity test uses the empirical distribution function of $\{2|\delta(f_m, f_n)|\}$ in the principal domain to test the null hypothesis that the $\lambda(f_m, f_n)$s are all the same. A robust single test statistic for this dispersion is the 80th quantile of these statistics.

For details of the test, see Hinich (1982), Hinich and Patterson (1985, 1989), and Ashley, Patterson, and Hinich (1986). In particular, the final transformed test statistics are distributed as standard normal random variates under the respective null hypotheses. When the null is Gaussianity, the resulting test statistic is denoted by H. When the null is linearity, the test statistic is denoted by Z. In both cases the distribution of the standard normal is used to produce a one-sided test in which the null is rejected if the test statistic is large.

Ashley, Patterson, and Hinich (1986, p. 174) presented an equivalence theorem that proves that the Hinich bispectral linearity test statistic is invariant to linear filtering of the data. This important result proves that *the linearity test can be applied either to the raw series or to the residuals of a linear model fitted to the data.* Hence, there is no need to choose between possible linear methods of detrending or prefiltering the data. An additional important implication of the theorem is that if $x(t)$ is found to be nonlinear, then the residuals of a linear model of the form $y(t) = f[x(t)]$ will also be nonlinear, since the nonlinearity in $x(t)$ will pass through any linear filter, f. The above paper further reported tables on the power of the Hinich linearity test for detecting violations of the linearity and Gaussianity hypotheses for a number of sample sizes and M values. The table indicates substantial power for both tests, even when N is as small as 256, if the value of M used is between 12 and 17. For this sample size, the power of the test falls off, as M increases above 17.

The Data

Because of the sample size problems that exist in using the testing algorithms produced within the literature on chaos, Barnett and Chen used weekly data. However, some degree of interpolation exists in virtually all governmental sources of weekly data, since not all component variables used in computing the aggregates are available weekly. On the other hand, monthly monetary data are of very high quality and make use of no interpolated component variables in the generation of the data. In this chapter we use the monthly data. The resulting low sample size is tolerable (although not desirable) with the Hinich test.

In addition, we eliminate the need for the implicit assumption of risk neutrality by using the new exact theoretical rational expectations aggregates available from Barnett, Hinich, and Yue (1989). We call those new aggregates the theoretical aggregates. Those aggregates were derived and estimated in a manner motivated by the earlier work of Poterba and Rotemberg (1987).

As a further check, we preprocess the data by logarithmic first differencing to acquire growth rates. Barnett and Chen preprocessed the data by fitting a linear regression on time and then using the residuals as the detrended data.[6] It should be observed that the results that we report in this paper would be invariant to further linear filtering of the data, as through the use of $AR(1)$ residuals, because the Hinich test is invariant to linear filters (see Ashley, Patterson, and Hinich, 1986, p. 174). Hence, the approach discussed in this chapter is more robust than the tests used in Barnett and Chen.

Results

The detailed results of the bispectral tests are available in Barnett and Chen (1988a).

The results are limited to the first two ($M1$ and $M2$) levels of monetary aggregation. The reason is that production of the estimated theoretical aggregate is extremely expensive, when the number of components over which aggregation occurs becomes large. In particular, the estimation procedure is generalized method of moments estimation applied to a deeply nonlinear economic structure. In Tables 16.1 and 16.2 we provide the values of the Hinich test statistics.

At both levels of aggregation, the Hinich Gaussianity test statistic, H, exceeded 6.0 for the Divisia, simple sum, and theoretic aggregate, as well as for the pairwise differences between the estimated theoretic and the Divisia or simple sum aggregate. Those pairwise differences can be viewed as estimates of the approximation error in

Table 16.1 Test Statistics: Bispectrum Tests with $M1$ Data[a]

Process	Gaussianity H	Linearity Z	Whiteness	% of Bifreqs with Gaussianity $P < .05$
Divisia	6.98	21.66	.58	28.57
Simple sum	14.39	2.29	1.86	33.33
Theoretic	14.19	2.29	1.74	33.33
$D - T$	7.34	1.322	.95	23.81
$SS - T$	9.12	2.291	1.97	33.33
Gaussian noise				5.00

[a] All data are in growth rate form. The "residual" series are $D - T$ = Divisia growth rate minus estimated theoretic growth rate, and $SS - T$ = simple sum growth minus estimated theoretical growth rate.

the statistical index numbers relative to the estimated theoretic aggregate. The test statistic H is distributed as a standard normal under the null of Gaussianity, and the test is a one-sided test, which rejects for large values of H. Relative to usual test levels, rejection of Gaussianity would occur for values of H exceeding 2.0 or 3.0. Based upon the H values, the data clearly are non-Gaussian.

From Tables 16.1 and 16.2 we can accept whiteness for all of the aggregates at each of the two levels of aggregation. But the nonlinearity results in that paper are very striking, especially at the $M1$ level of aggregation. Using Hinich's nonlinearity test statistic Z, we find that Divisia $M1$ is extremely deeply nonlinear. The test statistic was 21.66, which is so far above 2.0 or 3.0 as to provide dramatically convincing evidence of nonlinearity. Like H, the statistic Z is normally distributed under the null, and the test is one sided, rejecting the null for large values of Z. But the Z, the null hypothesis is linearity. Linearity is overwhelmingly rejected for Divisia $M1$ monthly data.[7]

Table 16.2 Test Statistics: Bispectrum Tests with $M2$ Data[a]

Process	Gaussianity H	Linearity Z	Whiteness	% of Bifreqs with Gaussianity $P < .05$
Divisia	7.52	1.542	1.54	0.00
Simple sum	6.09	1.573	1.18	6.25
Theoretic	9.96	.761	1.60	12.50
$D - T$	21.49	1.426	1.50	12.50
$SS - T$	8.03	1.595	2.59	18.75
Gaussian noise				5.00

[a] All data are in growth rate form. The "residual" series are $D - T$ = Divisia growth rate minus estimated theoretic growth rate, and $SS - T$ = simple sum growth minus estimated theoretical growth rate.

Conclusions

Although the statistical properties of the currently available tests for chaos are not well understood, a test for nonlinearity does exist, which has known level and power, and which is produced from a test statistic having known asymptotic sampling distribution under the null of linearity. The test is the Hinich test, which we apply successfully in this paper to produce very strong rejection of linearity with the Divisia $M1$ data. That data are very deeply nonlinear.

Notes

1. By conventional statistical standards there presently exists no means for accepting chaos with a finite sample at known test level. Neither Type 1 nor Type 2 error is known for any available test for chaos. At best, one can only report whether or not the data pass all the currently available tests for chaos. It is perhaps worth mentioning that all of the results in Barnett and Chen, including the Liapunov exponent computation and the Grassberger–Procaccia dimension calculation, were replicated successfully by Ramsey, Sayers, and Rothman (1988, Section III, p. 16), who view those successful replications to be a "testimony to the care taken by all of the above mentioned researchers." For a more recent and more extensive investigation of the Barnett and Chen results, see DeCoster and Mitchell, who use shuffle and residual tests as well as the conventional correlation dimension tests for chaos. DeCoster and Mitchell (1991, p. 12) conclude that their "results reinforce the Barnett and Chen finding of nonlinearity in Divisia M2, Divisia M3, and simple sum M2."

2. Nevertheless, it should be acknowledged that conventional econometric methods for estimating dimension at present seem to be no more reliable than the Grassberger–Procaccia algorithm, as has been shown by Barnett and Choi (1989) through Monte Carlo comparisons. Hence, we test for nonlinearity without estimating dimension.

3. Hence, the hypotheses of nonlinearity and chaos are nested within the alternative hypothesis, which included both nonwhite linear and nonwhite linear processes. In conventional statistical methodology, one tests an hypothesis by equating it with the null or with the total alternative hypothesis — not by using the power of the test to try to discriminate between subsets of the alternative hypothesis. Under the latter nonstandard approach, virtually every known hypothesis would be a "test for nonlinearity or chaos," since every statistical test contains nonlinearity and chaos as subsets somewhere within either the null or the alternative hypothesis. Despite our reservations about the use of the BDS test in testing for whiteness (the true null), there have been a number of recent attempts to apply the BDS test to nonlinearity testing. For one such interesting example, see Scheinkman and LeBaron (1989).

4. In accordance with time series conventions, we equate Gaussianity of the time series with multivariate Gaussianity.

5. The bispectrum is the third-order polyspectrum, while the ordinary power spectrum is the second-order polyspectrum. Strictly speaking, the polyspectrum of order k is the Fourier transform of the cumulant function (not the moment function) of order k. Cumulants are defined to be the coefficients of the terms in the power series expansion of the *logarithm* of the characteristic function of a distribution, while the moments are the coefficients of the terms in the power series expansion of the *level* of the characteristic function of the distribution.

Unlike the moments, the cumulants have the merit of being simiinvariants. However, for a stationary time series with zero mean, the second- and third-order cumulant functions are identical to the second- and third-order moment functions. Only at the fourth and higher orders do the cumulant functions differ from the moment functions. But since we here use only the second and third orders under the assumption of stationarity and zero mean, we need draw no distinction between moments and cumulants.

6. They checked for robustness to the detrending method by alternatively using logarithmic cubic detrending.

7. No other result regarding nonlinearity was as dramatic as that acquired with Divisia M1. With the other aggregates, either linearity was accepted or only marginally rejected with values of Z slightly in excess of 2.0. Also, by investigating the degree of nonlinear structure in the pairwise differences relative to the estimated theoretic aggregate, we found that the dynamic structure of the Divisia aggregates at both levels of aggregation more closely captures that of the theoretical aggregate than does the simple sum aggregate.

Bibliography

Ashley, Richard, Douglas M. Patterson, and Melvin Hinich, 1986, "A Diagnostic Test for Nonlinear Serial Dependence in Time Series Fitting Erros," *Journal of Time Series Analysis*, 7(3), 165–178.

Barnett, William A., 1980, "Economic Monetary Aggregates: An Application of Index Number and Aggregation Theory," *Journal of Econometrics*, 14, 11–48.

Barnett, William A., 1987, "The Microeconomic Theory of Monetary Aggregation," in William Barnett and Kenneth Singleton, eds., *New Approaches to Monetary Economics*, Proceedings of the Second International Symposium in Economic Theory and Econometrics, Cambridge University Press, Cambridge, pp. 115–168.

Barnett, William A., and Ping Chen, 1986, "Economic Theory as a Generator of Measurable Attractors," *Modes en Development*, 14, 453; reprinted in I. Prigogine and M. Sanglier, eds., *Laws of Nature and Human Conduct: Specificities and Unifying Themes*, G.O.R.D.E.S., Brussels, pp. 209–224.

Barnett, William A., and Ping Chen, 1988a, "The Aggregation-Theoretic Monetary Aggregates are Chaotic and Have Strange Attractors: An Econometric Application of Mathematical Chaos," in W. Barnett, E. Berndt, and H. White, eds., *Dynamic Econometric Modeling*, Proceedings of the Third International Symposium in Economic Theory and Econometrics, Cambridge University Press, Cambridge, pp. 199–246.

Barnett, William A., and Ping Chen, 1988b, "Deterministic Chaos and Fractal Attractors as Tools for Nonparametric Dynamical Econometric Inference," *Mathematical Computer Modeling*, 10, 275–296.

Barnett, William A., and Seugmook S. Choi, 1989, "A Comparison Between the Conventional Econometric Approach to Structural Inference and the Nonparametric Chaotic Attractor Approach," in W. Barnett, J. Geweke, and K. Shell, eds., *Economic Complexity: Chaos, Sunspots, Bubbles, and Nonlinearity*, Proceedings of the Fourth International Symposium in Economic Theory and Econometrics, Cambridge University Press, Cambridge, pp. 141–212.

Barnett, William A., M. Hinich, and W.E. Weber, 1986, "The Regulatory Wedge Between the Demand-Side and Supply-Side Aggregation-Theoretic Monetary Aggregates," *Journal of Econometrics*, 33, 165–185.

Barnett, William A., M. Hinich, and Piyu Yue, 1989, "The Exact Theoretical Rational Expectations Monetary Aggregates," University of Texas, Austin, TX.

Box, G.E.P., and G.M. Jenkins, 1970, *Time Series Analysis — Forecasting and Control*, Holden-Day, San Francisco, CA.

Brillinger, David R., 1965, "An Introduction to Polyspectrum," *Annals of Mathematical Statistics*, 36, 1351–1374.

Brock, William A., and W.D. Dechert, 1988, "Theorems on Distinguishing Deterministic from Random Systems," in W. Barnett, E. Berndt, and H. White, eds., *Dynamic Econometric Modeling*, Proceedings of the Third International Symposium in Economic Theory and Econometrics, Cambridge University Press, Cambridge, pp. 247–268.

Brock, William A., W.D. Dechert, and J. Scheinkman, 1986, "A Test for Independence Based on the Correlation Dimension," University of Wisconsin-Madison and University of Chicago.

Brockett, P.L., Melvin Hinich, and G.R. Wilson, 1987, "Nonlinear and Non-Gaussian Ocean Noise," *Journal of Acoustic Society of America*, 82(4), 1386–1394.

Brockett, P.L., Melvin Hinich, and Douglas Patterson, 1988, "Bispectral-Based Test for the Detection of Gaussianity and Linearity in Time Series," *Journal of the American Statistical Association*, 83(403), 657–664.

Chen, Ping, 1987, "Nonlinear Dynamics and Business Cycles," Ph.D. Dissertation, Department of Physics, University of Texas, Austin, TX.

DeCoster, Gregory P., and Douglas W. Mitchell, 1991, "Nonlinear Monetary Dynamics," *Journal of Business and Economic Statistics*, 9(October), 455–462.

Diewert, W. Erwin, 1976, "Exact and Superlative Index Numbers," *Journal of Econometrics*, 4, 115–145.

Hinich, Melvin J., 1982, "Testing for Gaussianity and Linearity of a Stationary Time Series," *Journal of Time Series Analysis*, 3(3), 169–176.

Hinich, Melvin J., and Douglas Patterson, 1985, "Identification of the Coefficients in a Nonlinear Time Series of the Quadratic Type," *Journal of Econometrics*, 30, 269–288; reprinted in W. Barnett and R. Gallant, eds., 1989, *New Approaches to Modelling, Specification Selection, and Econometric Inference*, Proceedings of the First International Symposium in Economic Theory and Econometrics, Cambridge University Press, Cambridge.

Hinich, Melvin J., and Douglas Patterson, 1989, "Evidence of Nonlinearity in the Trade-by-Trade Stock Market Return Generating Process," in W. Barnett, J. Geweke, and K. Shell, eds., *Economic Complexity: Chaos, Sunspots, Bubbles, and Nonlinearity*, Proceedings of the Fourth International Symposium in Economic Theory and Econometrics, Cambridge University Press, Cambridge, pp. 383–409.

Hulten, C.R., 1973, "Divisia Index Numbers," *Econometrica*, 63, 1017–1026.

Jenkins, G., and D. Watts, 1968, *Spectral Analysis and Its Applications*, Holden-Day, San Francisco, CA.

Minsky, Hyman, 1975, *John Maynard Keynes*, Columbia University Press, New York.

Poterba, James M., and Julio J. Rotemberg, 1987, "Money in the Utility Function: An Empirical Implementation," in W. Barnett and K. Singleton, eds., *New Approaches to Monetary Economics*, Proceedings of the Second International Symposium in Economic Theory and Econometrics, Cambridge University Press, Cambridge, 219–240.

Priestley, M., 1981, *Spectral Analysis and Time Series*, Vol. 2, Academic Press, New York.

Ramsey, James B., Chera L. Sayers, and Philip Rothman, 1988, "The Statistical Properties of Dimension Calculations Using Small Data Sets: Some Economic Applications," Department of Economics, New York University, New York, NY, August 16.

Scheinkman, José, and Blake LeBaron, 1989, "Nonlinear Dynamics and GNP Data," in W. Barnett, J. Geweke, and K. Shell, eds., *Economic Complexity: Chaos, Sunspots, Bub-*

bles, and Nonlinearity, Proceedings of the Fourth International Symposium in Economic Theory and Econometrics, Cambridge University Press, Cambridge, pp. 213–227.

Semmler, Willi, 1985, "Financial Crisis as Bifurcation in a Limit Cycle Model: A Nonlinear Approach to Minsky Crisis," Department of Economics, New School for Social Research, New York, NY.

Woodford, Michael, 1989, "Imperfect Intermediation and Complex Dynamics," in W. Barnett, J. Geweke, and K. Shell, eds., *Economic Complexity: Chaos, Sunspots, Bubbles, and Nonlinearity*, Proceedings of the Fourth International Symposium in Economic Theory and Econometrics, Cambridge University Press, Cambridge, pp. 309–338.

17

Inference and Forecasting for Deterministic Nonlinear Times Series Observed with Measurement Error

JOHN GEWEKE

Forecasting, one of the central problems of science, demands approaches appropriate to the complexity of the application and our understanding of it. When motion is complicated, involving many independent irreducible degrees of freedom, or when first principles are not understood, then the time series may appropriately be regarded as the realization of a random process. The modern theory of forecasting and signal extraction (e.g., Whittle, 1983) may be applied in these situations, ranging from the sunspot cycle (Yule, 1927) to the business cycle (Doan, Litterman, and Sims, 1984).

Even in simple systems arising from well understood first principles, apparent randomness can arise from deterministic but nonlinear behavior: an example well known to statisticians is the "random number" generator. Surveys of such systems are provided by Ott (1981), Ford (1983), Crutchfield et al. (1986), and Gleick (1987). If the appropriate initial conditions were measured without error then these systems could be predicted perfectly, in the same way that knowledge of the construction of a random number generator and the initial seed implies knowledge of the nth number generated. As a practical matter perfect knowledge of initial conditions is unobtainable for a variety of reasons, including inherent limitations on instrumentation or the need to measure a continuum in three dimensions.

The realization that deterministic nonlinear systems can generate the sort of apparent randomness seen in turbulence (Ruelle, 1976) or convection (Libchaber, 1982) has motivated considerable progress in the *detection* of the existence of such a system underlying an observed time series (Takens, 1980; Grassberger and Procaccia, 1983). These detection methods allow one to confirm that a time series can be produced by a system in which the dimensionality of the state vector is small. However, they provide no direct guidance in the actual process of forecasting. There

seems to have been little attention to actual forecasting procedures for deterministic nonlinear time series. There are (at least) two distinct ways to proceed. One is
to embed the time series in a state space and model the relationship nonparametri-
cally; Farmer and Sidorowich (1987) constitute the only exploration of this approach
that has come to the author's attention. A second is to proceed from first principles,
with a well-specified deterministic model and a stochastic structure for measurement
error. This second approach is taken in the work reported here. We think it is new,
and it leads to statistical problems very different from those associated with random
processes.

The focus of this chapter is on a particular, very simple deterministic nonlinear time series model. The findings are specific to this model, but it is apparent
that many of them will extend to more complicated deterministic nonlinear models applied in the physical sciences. We introduce the model in the next section,
and describe some of its properties. Most of these will be unsurprising, if not already known, to those familiar with the recent nonlinear time series literature. In the
third section a conventional stochastic structure for measurement error is added. The
likelihood function turns out to have multitudinous local maxima, and a global maximum that isolates plausible parameters in a very small region. As a consequence
standard methods for maximization of a function — or even response surface exploration — utterly fail, and new methods are required. One solution is presented in
the fourth section that goes on to fully develop procedures for Bayesian inference.
These methods are then applied to the problem of extracting the signal of the deterministic process itself from the noisy observations, and to forecasting the signal. The
concluding section suggests further exploration of the models and extensions of the
methods taken up in this paper.

A Simple One-Dimensional Noninvertible Map

The nonlinear time series model we consider is

$$x_t = a(1 - 2|x_{t-1} - 0.5|); \quad 0.5 < a < 1; \quad 0 < x_0 < 1; \quad t = 1, 2, 3, \ldots .(17.1)$$

Because of the model's geometric portrayal (Figure 17.1) it is often called the tent
map. Since this model is deterministic we may write

$$x_t = f_t(x_0; a).$$

Explicit expressions for f_t rapidly become cumbersome as t increases, because of the
nonlinearity. There are several characteristics of this model that are important for the
interpretation of the results that follow.

A critical property is that subsequent x_t are quite sensitive to small changes
in the initial condition x_0. For our model, we note $\partial x_1/\partial x_0 = 2a$ or $-2a$ as $x_0 <$
0.5 or $x_0 > 0.5$, and by recursion $\partial x_t/\partial x_0 = \pm(2a)^t$. Given a small discrete change

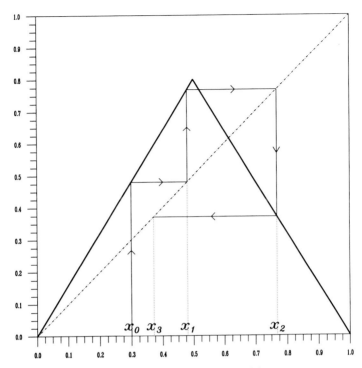

Figure 17.1   Geometric interpretation of the tent map.

$\Delta x_0, \Delta x_t \approx \pm(2a)^t \Delta x_0$, but this approximation will be valid only if $(2a)^t \Delta x_0 \ll 1$, i.e., $t < \log_{2a}(1/\Delta x_0)$. The effects of some small changes in x_0 are shown in Figure 17.2. The perturbation 8.272×10^{-m} in x_0 is chosen because our approximation implies a perturbation of 10^{5-m} when $t = 20$. We also expect the perturbed path to begin to bear little apparent relation to to original before $t = 29$ for the perturbation 8.272×10^{-7}, before $t = 34$ for the perturbation 8.272×10^{-8}, before $t = 39$ for the perturbation 8.272×10^{-9}, and before $t = 44$ for the perturbation 8.272×10^{-10}. These characteristics can be discerned in Figure 17.2, but they are much clearer in Figure 17.3, which provides $\log_{10}|x_t^* - -x_t|$ for the original series $\{x_t\}$ and the sequence $\{x_t^*\}$ arising from the perturbation of the initial condition.

This sensitivity to initial conditions is characteristic of models exhibiting chaos (Crutchfield et al., 1986). Chaos cannot be demonstrated analytically for the sequence $\{x_t\}$ generated by (17.1), but from experiments it is clear that any periodicities must be quite long and it can be shown that beyond some point the values of the sequence will be restricted to the interval $[2a(1-a), a]$ (Ott, 1981). The relative frequency of these values for the case $a = 0.8$ is provided in Figure 17.4. This diagram was produced from the sequence of length 10^9 with initial condition $x_0 = 0.45$, sorted into 400 cells.[1] The "wobbles" between vertical breaks are statistically insignificant, suggesting that as simulated series length approaches infinity these segments would become flat. The arithmetic mean for the 10^9 values is 0.5864 and the standard deviation is 0.1303.

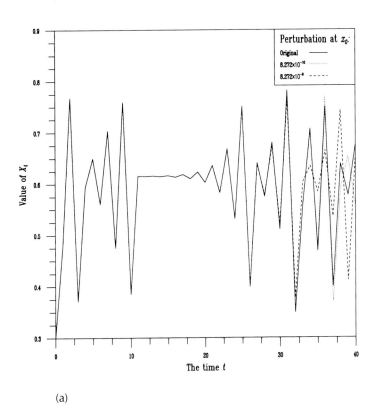

(a)

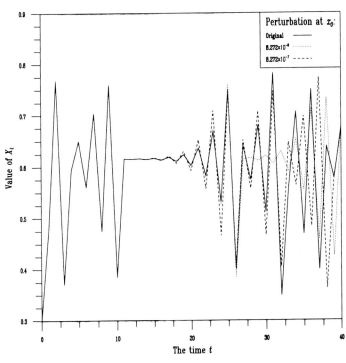

(b)

Figure 17.2 (a,b) Paths from tent map.

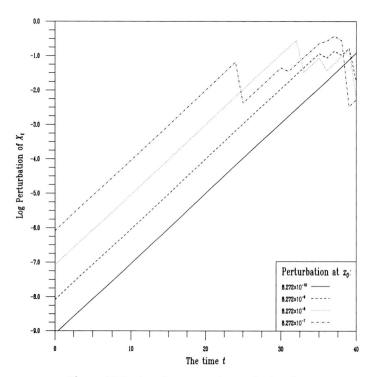

Figure 17.3 Log departure of perturbed path.

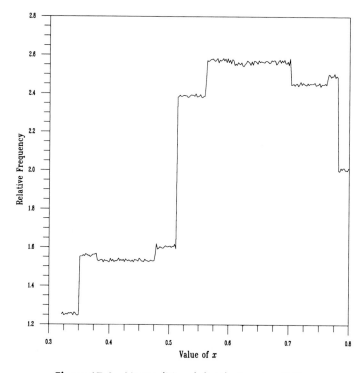

Figure 17.4 Unconditional distribution ($a = 0.8$).

The last important characteristic of the tent map is its irreversibility. Given x_0 and a, values $x_1, x_2, \ldots$ are implicit. But a given value $x_t = x_t^0$ could have arisen either from $x_{t-1} = 0.5 + 0.5(a - x_t^0)$ or $x_{t-1} = 0.5 - -0.5(ax_t^0)$, and in general there are 2^m possibilities for x_{t-m}.

The Likelihood Function

We now turn toward the central task, inference and forecasting when x_t cannot be measured with complete accuracy, addressing the cases in which a is known and a is unknown, respectively, as we proceed. A simple appealing stochastic structure for measurement error is

$$y_t \sim IIDN(x_t, \sigma^2) \quad (t = 1, \ldots, N) \tag{17.2}$$

where $\{y_t\}$ is the sequence of measurements and $\{x_t\}$ is known to evolve according to (17.1). The log-likelihood function (LLF) in a, x_0, and σ is

$$LLF(a, x_0, \sigma | y_1, \ldots, y_N) = -N \log(\sigma) - (1/2\sigma^2) \sum_{t=1}^{N} [y_t - f_t(x_0; a)]^2.$$

Since this expression as a function of σ is conventional, and since the parameter σ generally will be of less interest than a and x_0, we work with the concentrated log likelihood function,

$$LLF^*(a, x_0 | y_1, \ldots, y_N) = -(N/2) \log \left\{ \sum_{t=1}^{N} [y_t - f_t(x_0; a)]^2 / N \right\} - (N/2)$$

in this section.

Figure 17.5 portrays some aspects of this function for 20 data points generated from $a = 0.8, x_0 = 0.3, \sigma = 0.01$; the measurement errors were generated from the IMSL (Edition 10) function DRNNOF with a seed of 12,345. Figure 17.5a–f shows cross sections of LLF* as a function of a with the argument x_0 fixed at 0.3. Figure 17.5a provides a global portrayal of LLF*, Figure 17.5b exhibits LLF* in a neighborhood of $a = 0.8$, and the following panels provide successive magnifications by a factor of 10 of the neighborhood of $a = 0.8$. Figure 17.5 g–l goes through the same process for x_0 in a neighborhood of 0.3 with a fixed at 0.8. (In all figures, asterisks denote arguments of LLF*, to distinguish them from true values of the parameters.) These figures exhibit several notable aspects of the concentrated log-likelihood function, which are characteristic of the model (17.1, 17.2).

First, LLF* exhibits multitudinous local extrema. This is the reason that its characteristic behavior cannot be portrayed in a single figure of reasonable size. There are on the order of 10^4 local maxima between $a = 0.5$ and $a = 1.0$ in Figure 17.5a, but most of these are not detected by the plotting program, which worked with only 1000 points over this range. A second striking characteristic of the log-likelihood as a function of either a or x_0 is the height of the global maximum relative

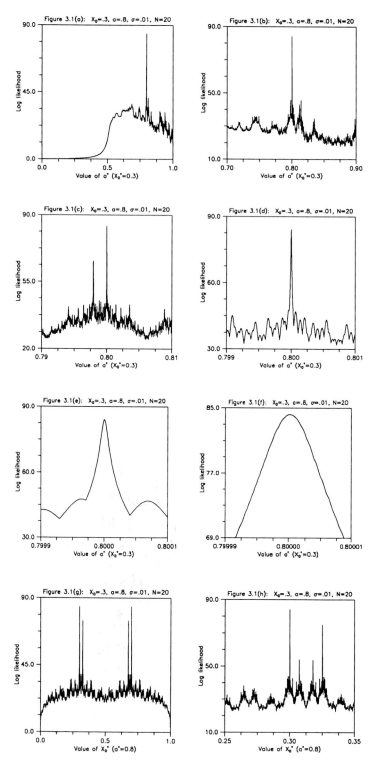

Figure 17.5 Log-likelihood I.

to the other maxima; the second largest maximum is 10 below the largest one (Figure 17.5c).

These aspects of the likelihood function are directly attributable to the fact that very small perturbations in x_0 will lead to changes in x_t that are substantial in a sample of size 20, as was seen in Figures 17.2 and 17.3. As x_0 is varied for a given value of a, the implied sequence $\{x_t\}$ changes very fast, and consequently there are rapid fluctuations in LLF*. If a is fixed at its true value, then only values of x_0 very close to the true one produce a sequence $\{x_t\}$ that matches $\{y_t\}$ within a tolerance of about .01 over the range $t = 1, \ldots, 20$. Consequently, the global maximum is relatively quite high. The similar local and global behavior in LLF* viewed as a function of a with x_0 fixed at its true value is attributable to the local near-symmetry of (17.1) in x_{t-1} and a, implying (as may be verified numerically) that subsequent x_t are very sensitive to small changes in a. The implications for inference are also clear: conventional optimization methods cannot possibly find the global maximum, of which there are on the order of 10^8 in this example if a is unknown. It is reasonable to surmise that stochastic formalizations of measurement error in other nonlinear deterministic models displaying sensitivity to initial conditions will produce likelihood functions whose local extrema are multitudinous and whose global maximum cannot be isolated by conventional methods.

Figure 17.5a shows that multitudinous local extrema are confined to the interval $(0.5, 1)$. This is attributable to the fact that if $a < 0.5$ then the sequence generated by (17.1) is not sensitive to initial conditions, but converges to 0 or 1, and therefore the implied $\{x_t\}$ does not resemble measured $\{y_t\}$ at all. In Figure 17.5g it is seen that LLF* as a function of x_0 is symmetric about $x_0 = 0.5$; this arises from the same characteristic that leads to the irreversibility of $\{x_t\}$, the fact that x_0 and $1 - x_0$ imply the same value of x_1. Two more curious patterns are evident. First, the log-likelihood function exhibits many local, nearly mirror images as inspection of Figure 17.5c–d and h shows. Second, LLF* as a function of x_0 in a neighborhood of $x_0 = 0.3$, and LLF* as a function of a in a neighborhood of $a = 0.8$, display very similar behavior, LLF*$(0.8 + 1.74z, 0.3) \approx$ LLF*$(0.8, 0.3 + z), |z| < 10^{-3}$. We presently have no explanation for either phenomenon.

Varying the parameters a and σ, and the number of observations N, provides a fuller understanding of the characteristics of the likelihood function. The effects of these variations are indicated in Figures 17.6 through 17.11, whose organization is indicated in Table 17.1. We survey the effects first quantitatively, and then proceed with a more analytical approach.

Table 17.1　Organization of Figures 17.5 – 17.11

Aspect of likelihood function	Figure
Base case: $N = 20$, $\sigma = 0.01$, $a = 0.8$, $x_0 = 0.3$	7.5
Variation in N: $N = 10$, $N = 30$	17.6, 17.7
Variation in σ: $\sigma = 0.1$, $\sigma = 0.001$	17.8, 17.9
Variation in a: $a = 0.6$, $a = 0.95$	17.10, 17.11

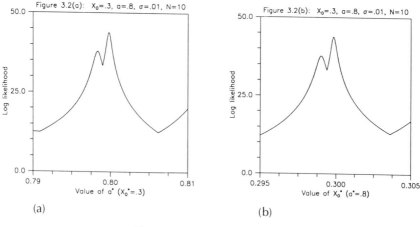

Figure 17.6   Log-likelihood II.

Changes in the number of observations modify the roughness of the likelihood function dramatically: compare Figures 17.6a, for $N = 10$, and 17.7a, for $N = 30$. These show the log-likelihood function over the range $0.79 \leq a \leq 0.81$, with x_0 fixed at 0.3, and with data generated from the model (17.1, 17.2) with $a = 0.8, x_0 = 0.3, \sigma = 0.01$. Similar behavior is shown in comparing Figures 17.6b and 17.7b for the range $0.295 \leq x_0 \leq 0.305$, with a fixed at 0.8. As N increases the number of local maxima in any given interval increases quite rapidly. This is fundamentally a consequence of the exponential departure of a perturbed path from the original as t increases, in the model (17.1). It is evident that the increase in numbers of local maxima is geometric in N, and continues without bound. Thus, while the likelihood function is locally (only) smooth for fixed N, in the limit it is arbitrarily rough in the sense that any

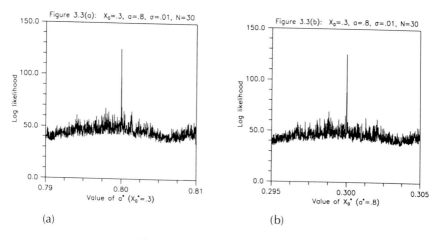

Figure 17.7   Log-likelihood III.

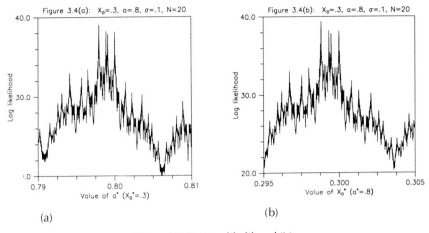

Figure 17.8 Log-likelihood IV.

fixed Lipschitz condition is almost surely violated. The limiting likelihood function therefore shares some of the characteristics of other transformations of deterministic nonlinear models, such as phase diagrams and the Mandelbrot set.

As the standard deviation of the measurement error decreases peak-to-trough ratios increase and the global maximum is increasingly well defined, but the intervals between local maxima are not much affected. For general behavior, compare Figure 17.8a, for $\sigma = 0.1$, and 17.9a, for $\sigma = 0.001$; similarly 17.8b and 17.9b. Note the vertical scale in these figures, which shows the effect of σ on the global maximum. It appears that as $\sigma \to 0$ the global maximum of the log likelihood function attains increasingly higher values, while the likelihood function elsewhere is unaffected.

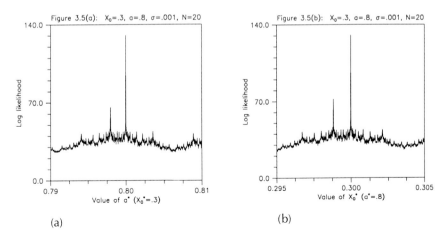

Figure 17.9 Log-likelihood V.

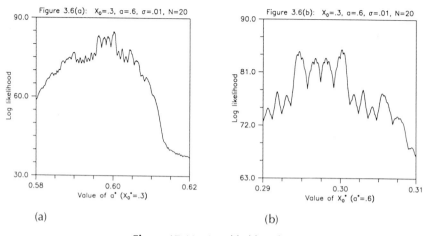

Figure 17.10　Log-likelihood VI.

Figure 17.10 provides perspectives on LLF* for $a = 0.6$, which implies a substantially weaker effect of initial perturbations on subsequent x_t than when $a = 0.8$, and Figure 17.11 provides these same perspectives for $a = 0.95$, in which case the effect is much stronger. As revealed in Figure 17.5a, the concentration of local extrema increases with a as an argument of the likelihood function. Figures 17.10 and 17.11 show that it is not much affected by the true value of a. Global behavior of LLF* as a function of x_0 is so different in Figures 17.10b and 17.11b because the argument, a, at which LLF* is evaluated is much higher in Figure 17.11 than in Figure 17.10. This behavior is just what our analysis of small perturbations in (17.1), and the near-symmetry of x_{t-1} and a in that expression, would suggest: when $a = 0.6$, a

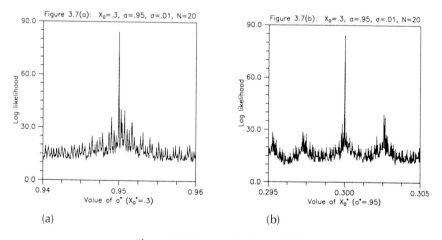

Figure 17.11　Log-likelihood VII.

perturbation Δ in x_0 produces a change in x_t on the order of $\Delta(1.2)^t$, whereas when $a = 0.95$ the effect is on the order of $\Delta(1.9)^t$. Since changes in x_0 or a have a relatively weak effect when $a = 0.6$, the global maximum is not well isolated (contrast Figures 17.10 and 17.11). For comparably reliable inference about a, substantially larger sample sizes are required as $a \to 0.5$.

These predominating characteristics of the likelihood function are consistent with a first-order analysis of the map (17.1). Consider first the frequency of local maxima. The basin of attraction of x_t is $[a, 2a(1 - a)]$ (Ott, 1981), an interval of length $a(2a - 1)$. Following the argument of the previous section, an initial perturbation d would move x_N this length if $d(2a)^N = a(2a - 1)$, suggesting that peak-to-peak distances in LLF* evaluated as a function of x_0 for fixed a would be on the order of $d = a(2a - 1)(2a)^{-N}$. The implications of this analysis for the situations of Figures 17.5–17.11 are indicated in Table 17.2, along with the peak-to-peak distances typically observed in those figures. The anticipated and observed distances agree well. As anticipated, peak-to-peak distance is not a function of the degree of measurement error σ.

The value of the global maximum and the value of the likelihood function elsewhere are easy to anticipate. At the global maximum the differences between the unobserved x_t and $f_t(x_0; a)$ will be negligibly small relative to σ, so that LLF* will take a value near $p = -N \log(\sigma) - N/2$. Elsewhere, the residual $y_t - f_t(x_0; a)$ will consist of three essentially unrelated components, $y_t - x_t, x_t$, and $f_t(x_0; a)$. This suggests that the sum of squared residuals will be about $N(\sigma^2 + 2M)$, where $M = 0.5864$ is the sample second central moment from the series of length 10^9 used to generate the frequency distribution in Figure 17.4. Hence the "base value" of LLF* away from the global maximum should be about $b = -(N/2)\log(2M + \sigma^2) - (N/2)$. The implications of this analysis for the peaks and bases in Figures 17.5 though 17.11, along with those typically observed, are anticipated in Table 17.3. That the observed global maximum always falls short of the anticipated one by 5 may be attributed to the fact that the same, short sequence of measurement errors was used in each case. Anticipated and observed base values agree well, and as implied neither peak nor base values are a function of the value of a.

Table 17.2 Peak–to–Peak Intervals\ $[d = a(2a - 1)(2a)^{-N}]$

Figure	a	Ng	σ	d	Typical observed intervals
1	0.8	20	0.01	3.97×10^{-5}	$3 \times 10^{-5} - 4 \times 10^{-5}$
2	0.8	10	0.01	4.37×10^{-3}	$1 \times 10^{-3} - 7 \times 10^{-3}$
3	0.8	30	0.01	3.61×10^{-7}	$3 \times 10^{-7} - 4 \times 10^{-7}$
4	0.8	20	0.1	3.97×10^{-5}	$3 \times 10^{-5} - 4 \times 10^{-5}$
5	0.8	20	0.001	3.97×10^{-5}	$2 \times 10^{-5} - 4 \times 10^{-5}$
6	0.6	20	0.01	3.13×10^{-3}	$2 \times 10^{-4} - 1 \times 10^{-3}$
7	0.95	20	0.01	2.275×10^{-6}	$5 \times 10^{-7} - 4 \times 10^{-6}$

Table 17.3 Peak and Base Values
$[p = -N \log(\sigma) - N/2, b = -(N/2) \log(2M + \sigma^2) - (N/2)]$

Figure	a	N	σ	p	b	Observed peak	Observed base
1	0.8	20	0.01	82.1	27.8	77.8	25 - -42
2	0.8	10	0.01	41.1	13.9	37.8	9 - -18
3	0.8	30	0.01	123.	41.8	118.2	32 - -57
4	0.8	20	0.1	36.1	24.2	32.4	18 - -31
5	0.8	20	0.001	128.2	27.9	123.5	23 - -40
6	0.6	20	0.01	82.1	27.8	77.5	34 - -37
7	0.95	2	0.01	82.1	27.8	77.0	9 - -28

Inference

The intractable shape of the likelihood function makes inference about the parameters a and x_0 of (17.1) challenging. Classical inference appears to be precluded altogether, and any approach to Bayesian inference must be numerical rather than analytical.

Given the symmetry of the model in x_0 and $1 - x_0$ and assuming very little about the magnitude of measurement error, let the parameter space for (a, x_0, σ) be $(0.5, 1) \times (0, 0.5) \times (0, \infty)$. On this space we consider the family of improper prior densities $\pi(a, x_0, \sigma) \propto \sigma^{-q}$. This family is chosen for illustrative purposes only. In what follows the only step that would be rendered more difficult by assuming different prior distributions, including those that are perhaps quite informative, is the marginalization in σ. So long as the posterior distribution of σ conditional on x_0 and a is tractable — which surely will be the case given the form of LLF(a, x_0, σ) — the marginalization step could be avoided and s could be integrated by standard numerical procedures conditional on a and x_0.

The posterior density for a, x_0, and σ is

$$p(a, x_0, \sigma) \propto \sigma^{-(n+q)}[- \exp \text{SSR}(x_0; a)/2\sigma^2],$$

where SSR$(a, x_0) \equiv \sum_{t=1}^{N}[y_t - f_t(x_0; a)]^2$. Interest in σ is presumably secondary to interest in a and x_0 in particular; it will turn out to be the case that the predictive density for $\{x_t\}$ can be constructed directly from the marginal posterior density for x_0 and a. Standard techniques (Zellner, 1971, pp. 66–67) yield the conditional posterior distribution

$$\text{SSR}(x_0, a)/\sigma^2]|(a, x_0) \sim \chi^2(n + q + 1)$$

and the marginal posterior density

$$p(a, x_0 | y_1, \ldots, y_N) \propto SSR(x_0; a)/2]^{-(n+q-1)/2}.$$

In what follows we take $q = 1$.

Examination of the likelihood function has established the futility of gradient methods for determination of the posterior mode, and a direct grid search is impractical for more than a dozen observations or so. Indeed, the central problem is not determination of the posterior mode, since multiple unconnected regions in the parameter space of (a, x_0) may contribute substantially to the posterior density. The method described here is based on the fact that when N is quite small, grid methods are practical for finding those regions of the parameter space in which $p(a, x_0)$ is relatively large. Beginning with a small subsample at the start of the series, regions of importance may be identified tentatively through grid search, and as sample points are added subsets of these regions may be eliminated, again through grid search. From the grids remaining when the entire sample has been incorporated, a uniform random sample in (a, x_0) may be employed to construct the marginal posterior density $p(a, x_0)$. We now detail the method, which consists of a search procedure followed by an accelerated Monte Carlo integration procedure.

We begin with an initial approximation p^* to $\sup_{a, x_0} p(a, x_0)$ and the implied $SSR^* = 2(p^*)^{-2/N}$. The inference procedure itself will reveal a poor guess, and suggest improvements in the approximation; the procedure then can be repeated with a more informed approximation. The objective of the search procedure is to find a subset of the parameter space (a, x_0) that contains all points whose posterior odds relative to the posterior model exceeds a small probability p_{min}. The results reported in the next section employed $p_{min} = 10^{-6}$, and $N = 20$.

The parameter space (a, x_0) is divided into a 100×100 grid, that is, 10,000 blocks each of dimension 0.005×0.005. $SSR(a, x_0)$ is computed for the point in the center of each block, using just the first seven observations. The rationale for this procedure is that local minima in $SSR(a, x_0)$ should have separations of more than 0.01 for all values of a over the range $(0.5, 0.98)$; for $a = 0.8$, used to generate the data, separations should be about 0.018. Consequently substantial dips in $SSR(a, x_0)$ are not likely to be missed altogether. If $SSR(a, x_0)$ exceeds SSR^* by a factor of more than $2 \times 2(p_{min})^{-2/N}$, then the block is dropped from further consideration, and the next block in the 100×100 grid over the parameter space is examined in the same way. The factor of 2 is a conservative choice, allowing for the fact that there will be some variation in $SSR(a, x_0)$ between evaluated points in the middle of each block. Substantial gains in efficiency are achieved by stopping the computation of $SSR(a, x_0) = \sum_{t=1}^{N} [y_t - f_t(x_0, a)]^2$ as soon as the partial sum exceeds $4(p_{min})^{-2/N} SSR^*$.

If $SSR(a, x_0)$ is less than this value, the block is further divided into a 100×100 grid, that is, 10,000 blocks each of dimension $(5 \times 10^{-5}) \times (5 \times 10^{-5})$. The same procedure is repeated, but using 16 observations rather than 7. As soon as any partial sum exceeds $4(p_{min})^{-2/N} SSR^*$ the next of the 10,000 blocks is considered. If the sum using all 16 observations does not exceed this value, then the block is divided into a 10×10 grid, defining 100 blocks each of dimension $(5 \times 10^{-6}) \times (5 \times 10^{-6})$. $SSR(a, x_0)$ is evaluated at the center of each block, and if this sum is less than $2(p_{min})^{-2/N} SSR^*$, then the value of (a, x_0) for the center of the block is recorded in a file for subsequent use in the integration procedure. For the artificial data described in the base example of the previous section, 110,237 points are so recorded.

If the parameter a is known, search takes place in only one dimension, using the obvious modification. For the base example, 770 points are so recorded. Experimentation with grid sizes and criteria for retaining points showed that the choices described here are conservative, that is, the results reported in the next section remain essentially unchanged for finer grids and/or larger elimination criteria for $SSR(a, x_0)$ and considerably coarser grids or smaller elimination criteria are required before results are affected.

The Monte Carlo integration procedure generates a random sample of pairs (a, x_0), or of x_0 values in the case that a is known. We detail this procedure for the former case, modification for the latter being obvious. The procedure is basically Monte Carlo integration with importance sampling (Geweke, 1989), with grid acceleration (Geweke, 1988), and mixed weighting and rejection (Barnett, Geweke, and Yue, 1991).

There are n iterations. For computation of posterior means and standard deviations in the next section $n = 100$, and for computation of posterior densities including interquartile ranges, $n = 8$. At the start of each iteration independent drawings a^+ and x_0^+ from a uniform distribution on $[-2.5 \times 10^{-6}, 2.5 \times 10^{-6}]$ were made. Each point (a, x_0) saved in the search procedure is then read from the file, and the posterior density $p(a + a^+, x_0 + x_0^+)$ is evaluated. This value is compared with $p^* = \sup_{a, x_0} p(a, x_0)$ as determined from the search procedure. If $p(a + a^+, x_0 + x_0^+) > p^*$ (which occurs, but rarely) the point $(a + a^+, x_0 + x_0^+)$ is retained in the random sample with a weight of $p(a + a^+, x_0 + x_0^+)/p^*$. If not, then the point is retained with probability $p(a + a^+, x_0 + x_0^+)/p^*$ and if retained assigned a weight of 1. From this sample, moments and posterior distributions of functions of interest of the parameters a and x_0 may be approximated numerically as detailed in Geweke (1989).

To provide an interpretation of this procedure, observe that in each iteration a $10^5 \times 10^5$ grid is laid out randomly; the randomness guarantees that numerical approximation of moments, quantiles, etc., will be unbiased. By examining each of these grid points we would be employing a uniform importance sampling density. The preliminary search procedure is simply a way of efficiently eliminating the vast majority of the grid points that contribute essentially nothing to the posterior density. Straightforward Monte Carlo integration with importance sampling would retain each point with the appropriate weight, but $110,237n$ points — to say nothing of $10^{10}n$ points — is not a practical number. Given considerations of computation time and disk space, it is much more efficient to employ rejection methods.

Signal Extraction and Forecasting

Given a sample $y_1, \ldots, y_N$, a random sample from the posterior distribution of a and x_0 has been formed. A random sample from the posterior distribution of the functions of interest $(x_t, t = 1, 2, \ldots, N, \ldots, N + F)$ can be generated directly by applying (17.1) recursively to each point (x_0, a) drawn from the posterior density. We undertake this procedure for three examples, as detailed in Table 17.4.

Posterior means and standard deviations for three examples are presented in Tables 17.5 – 17.7, along with standard errors for the numerical approximation of the posterior means computed as described in Geweke (1989). When both parameters are unknown (Table 17.5) the posterior standard deviations of the extracted signals $x_1, \ldots, x_{18}$ are of similar orders of magnitude. Beginning with the extracted signal x_{19} and continuing through the forecasted signal x_{24} each successive standard deviation is almost 1.6 times the previous one. This progression is not surprising based on the features of the model previously discussed. Beginning with x_{25} standard deviations level out, and begin to scatter around the standard deviation of the very long sequence used to generate Figure 17.4. Thus, uncertainty about all but the last signals is dominated by uncertainty about a; for the last signals and early forecasts uncertainty about x_0 dominates; and for subsequent forecasts essentially nothing is known.

Tables 17.6 ($\sigma = 0.01$) and 17.7 ($\sigma = 0.0001$), reporting on cases in which a is known, reinforce this interpretation. The progression of posterior standard deviations is evident beginning with x_9 in Table 17.6, and with x_1 beginning in Table 17.7. For the example of Table 17.6, the larger posterior standard deviations for early x_t were traced to areas of low, but consequential, probability far from most of the main cluster relative to the size of that cluster. These points have the property that early values of $x_t = f_t(x_0; a)$ differ from those implied by the main cluster, but later values do not. This anomaly bears further investigation: it seems to arise from particular configurations of a and x_0 for which the local exponential approximation previously

Table 17.4   Organization of Examples
for Signal Extraction and Forecasting

	Example I	Example II	Example III
True a	0.8	0.8	0.8
True x_0	0.3	0.3	0.3
σ	0.01	0.01	0.0001
a known?	No	Yes	Yes
N	20	20	20
F	20	20	20
Grid points retained	110,237	770	26
Computing time (hours)	16.8	6.0	1.2

Table 17.5 Signal Extraction and Forecasting for $x(t)$, Example I: $\sigma = 0.01$, a Unknown, x_0 Unknown

Value of t	Posterior mean	Posterior standard deviation	Standard error of numerical approximation
1	7.210871E-01	4.149480E-03	8.086198E-06
2	4.474603E-01	1.963849E-03	3.838822E-06
3	7.179398E-01	4.373274E-03	8.515225E-06
4	4.525064E-01	2.269751E-03	4.424589E-06
5	7.260315E-01	3.970307E-03	7.743924E-06
6	4.395297E-01	1.765732E-03	3.462129E-06
7	7.052183E-01	4.578960E-03	8.900244E-06
8	4.729155E-01	2.411910E-03	4.674097E-06
9	7.587710E-01	4.153222E-03	8.087757E-06
10	3.869944E-01	2.603342E-03	5.076555E-06
11	6.209084E-01	2.341127E-03	4.558836E-06
12	6.082325E-01	2.643153E-03	5.154028E-06
13	6.285668E-01	2.409935E-03	4.677937E-06
14	5.959437E-01	2.541936E-03	4.937619E-06
15	6.482878E-01	3.082058E-03	5.931777E-06
16	5.642919E-01	2.215899E-03	4.105847E-06
17	6.990939E-01	5.958216E-03	1.140012E-05
18	4.827314E-01	5.660715E-03	1.049516E-05
19	7.743579E-01	7.445239E-03	1.374184E-05
20	3.620051E-01	1.101962E-02	2.031395E-05
21	5.808406E-01	1.822795E-02	3.406235E-05
22	6.724843E-01	2.828576E-02	5.232901E-05
23	5.255228E-01	4.582142E-02	8.525172E-05
24	7.351706E-01	5.069637E-02	1.009489E-04
25	4.248397E-01	8.115530E-02	1.625267E-04
26	6.471278E-01	8.622475E-02	1.421200E-04
27	5.646081E-01	1.358519E-01	2.192160E-04
28	5.972651E-01	1.273296E-01	1.866557E-04
29	5.841683E-01	1.361304E-01	2.090255E-04
30	5.821093E-01	1.324008E-01	2.075637E-04

developed does not apply, and it implies that the extreme tails of the posteriors can be thick relative to the normal and hence measures of dispersion like standard deviation must be cautiously interpreted. When measurement error is much reduced ($\sigma = .0001$, in Table 17.7) the mass of the posterior is much more concentrated as noted. No outlying values of (a, x_0) were included in the 240,522 points sampled, and the posterior standard deviation displays a steady progression by a factor of 1.6^2 up through the forecast of x_{34}, after which the long-sequence standard deviation is evident.

In all three cases, observe that the posterior standard deviation of x_{20}, the signal underlying the *final* observation y_{20}, is close to the standard deviation of the measurement error. Significantly, exact knowledge of the form of the underlying process and even of the parameters of that process does not contribute to knowledge of the final signal x_{20}, which is critical for forecasting. We believe this important phenomenon may be attributed to the sensitivity to initial conditions and irreversible

Table 17.6 Signal Extraction and Forecasting for $x(t)$, Example II: $\sigma = 0.01$, a Unknown, x_0 Unknown

Value of t	Posterior mean	Posterior standard deviation	Standard error of numerical approximation
1	4.801065E-01	2.052144E-03	4.103249E-06
2	7.680015E-01	3.574055E-05	7.010556E-08
3	3.711976E-01	5.718487E-05	1.121699E-07
4	5.939162E-01	9.149580E-05	1.794719E-07
5	6.497341E-01	1.463933E-04	2.871552E-07
6	5.604254E-01	2.342293E-04	4.594485E-07
7	7.033194E-01	3.747668E-04	7.351177E-07
8	4.746890E-01	5.996269E-04	1.176188E-06
9	7.594911E-01	5.956520E-05	9.139085E-08
10	3.848142E-01	9.530434E-05	1.462257E-07
11	6.157027E-01	1.524869E-04	2.339610E-07
12	6.148756E-01	2.439791E-04	3.743377E-07
13	6.161990E-01	3.903666E-04	5.989404E-07
14	6.140816E-01	6.245865E-04	9.583047E-07
15	6.174694E-01	9.993384E-04	1.533288E-06
16	6.120490E-01	1.598941E-03	2.453260E-06
17	6.207217E-01	2.558306E-03	3.925216E-06
18	6.068453E-01	4.093290E-03	6.280346E-05
19	6.290475E-01	6.549264E-03	1.004855E-05
20	5.935240E-01	1.047882E-02	1.607768E-05
21	6.503616E-01	1.676612E-02	2.572430E-05
22	5.594215E-01	2.682579E-02	4.115887E-05
23	7.043532E-01	4.163004E-02	6.278796E-04
24	4.730327E-01	6.659755E-02	1.004240E-04
25	7.076301E-01	6.843770E-02	9.256496E-05
26	4.675302E-01	1.087032E-01	1.460004E-04
27	6.455127E-01	9.530263E-02	1.145200E-04
28	5.562548E-01	1.343316E-01	1.229224E-04
29	6.020522E-01	1.229358E-01	1.166020E-04
30	5.822067E-01	1.338557E-01	1.222421E-04

character of $\{x_t\}$. Because of sensitivity to initial conditions the "window" of measurement error defines increasingly tighter regions for plausible signals the farther back in time one moves, if one is certain about a. Because the process is irreversible, alternative values of x_N have essentially no implications for the sequence $\{x_t\}$, and consequently the values of $y_t, t < N$, are of no incremental help in inferring x_N given y_N.

This interpretation is reinforced by examination of interquartile ranges for the signals and forecasts. The base 10 logarithms of these ranges are plotted in Figure 17.12. When a is known, the exponential nature of the effects of small perturbations and the implied fraction of 1.6 completely dominates the behavior of the interquartile range: observe the similar properties of Figures 17.3 and 17.12. When a is unknown, the interquartile range for any x_t has a lower limit set by this uncertainty. Larger sample sizes, presumably, would diminish this lower limit.

Table 17.7 Signal Extraction and Forecasting for $x(t)$, Example III: $\sigma = 0.0001$, a Unknown, x_0 Unknown

Value of t	Posterior mean	Posterior standard deviation	Standard error of numerical approximation
1	4.800000E-01	1.406266E-08	0.000000E+00
2	7.680000E-01	0.000000E+00	0.000000E+00
3	3.712000E-01	3.429493E-08	2.102730E-11
4	5.939200E-01	3.951267E-08	1.410554E-10
5	6.497281E-01	8.932932E-08	0.000000E+00
6	5.604351E-01	1.441837E-07	2.169993E-10
7	7.033039E-01	2.312682E-07	3.390550E-10
8	4.747138E-01	3.718206E-07	5.823461E-10
9	7.595421E-01	5.936318E-07	9.143854E-10
10	3.847327E-01	9.505460E-07	1.471235E-09
11	6.155723E-01	1.521005E-06	2.346924E-09
12	6.150843E-01	2.433587E-06	3.763769E-09
13	6.158651E-01	3.894132E-06	6.022514E-09
14	6.146158E-01	6.230646E-06	9.636355E-09
15	6.166147E-01	9.968910E-06	1.541769E-08
16	6.134165E-01	1.595039E-05	2.466889E-08
17	6.185337E-01	2.552059E-05	3.947052E-08
18	6.103461E-01	4.083296E-05	6.315288E-08
19	6.234462E-01	6.533274E-05	1.010444E-07
20	6.024861E-01	1.045324E-04	1.616710E-07
21	6.360222E-01	1.672518E-04	2.586737E-07
22	5.823644E-01	2.676029E-04	4.138780E-07
23	6.682169E-01	4.281647E-04	6.622048E-07
24	5.308530E-01	6.850635E-04	1.059528E-06
25	7.506352E-01	1.096102E-03	1.695244E-06
26	3.989837E-01	1.753763E-03	2.712391E-06
27	6.383739E-01	2.806020E-03	4.339825E-06
28	5.786018E-01	4.489632E-03	6.943720E-06
29	6.742371E-01	7.183411E-03	1.110995E-05
30	5.212207E-01	1.149346E-02	1.777592E-05
31	7.654792E-01	1.730029E-02	2.579754E-05
32	3.752334E-01	2.768046E-02	4.127607E-05
33	6.003669E-01	4.425934E-02	6.595925E-05
34	6.394130E-01	7.081494E-02	1.055348E-04
35	5.736728E-01	1.066298E-01	1.517915E-04
36	6.305209E-01	1.194934E-01	1.474119E-04
37	5.509466E-01	1.346745E-01	1.140762E-04
38	6.057873E-01	1.239247E-01	1.220641E-04
39	5.762090E-01	1.337206-01	1.277304E-04
40	5.905075E-01	1.294479E-01	3.502568E-04

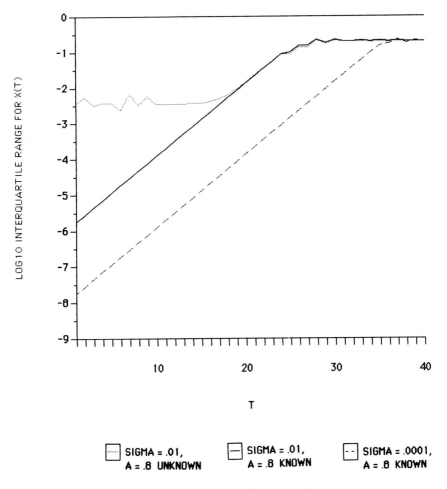

Figure 17.12   Comparison of interquartile ranges.

Unanswered Questions

This work has shown that a specific deterministic nonlinear process, observed with measurement error, leads to a statistical model with bizarre properties. It has introduced procedures for inference that work well in this particular case, when sample size is modest. Exact posterior distributions for past, present, and future values of the process itself have been obtained and interpreted.

The process studied was chosen for its simplicity rather than for any physical application. However, it is widely conjectured that deterministic nonlinear processes with only a few more degrees of freedom account for many phenomena. We may therefore speculate that in situations where forecasts of these processes are used analytically, statistical problems very much like the ones studied in this article will be found, and unconventional methods will be required for their solution. Undoubtedly, substantial improvements can be made on the first solutions introduced here. The immediate research agenda includes several questions raised in this research.

First, the behavior of the likelihood function reported here should be similar in other noninvertible maps. For example, analogous peak-to-peak distance rules like $d = a(2a - 1)(2a)^{-N}$ should be verified. Generalizations of this kind of behavior in terms of properties of the maps, like the effects of small perturbations, should be verified.

Second, attention must be given to the development of efficient search algorithms for processes with more than one degree of freedom, or even for processes with just one degree of freedom if the sample size is much larger than the samples employed here. This is a challenging task, but it need not be overwhelming for two reasons. One is that the number of degrees of freedom known or conjectured in most physical applications is quite modest. The other has to do with another item on the research agenda, the effects of sample size.

Third, the issue of just what determines forecast quality deserves specific attention. In our example sample size was of no consequence when a was known and of little consequence when a was unknown. On the other hand, measurement error is critical; it appears in particular that the accuracy of the last observation in the sample is almost entirely responsible for the quality of forecasts. Predictive densities for other sample sizes and for other noninvertible maps need to be computed to verify this pattern and learn more about the ingredients of a good forecast. Findings in even simplified and abstract settings may have implications for measurement and the design of experiments.

Fourth, much of what was observed in the example studied may be specific to *non*invertible processes. A parallel study should be conducted with one or more simple invertible processes.

Notes

The views expressed herein are those of the authors and not necessarily those of the Federal Reserve Bank of Minnesota or the Federal Reserve System.

This work was supported by NSF Grants SES–8605867 and SES–8908365. The chapter has benefited from comments by Bill Barnett, Hans-Walter Lorenz, and participants in the International Symposium on Evolutionary Dynamics and Nonlinear Economics (Austin, April 1989) and the Workshop on Econometric Estimation and Inference for Nonlinear, Dynamic Macroeconomic Models (University of Southern California, April 1989). Guofu Zhou and Zhenyu Wang provided research assistance. Responsibility for any errors rests with the author.

1. The simulation was conducted in double precision (64-bit) floating point arithmetic on a Sun IPC 4/40 and required about 14 hours. Because of the finite precision of these computations and the sensitivity of the model to changes in initial conditions, the fact that the generated numbers are not quite the true ones is important. Based on experiments with 32-bit,

64-bit, and 128-bit computations, it is clear that the approximation error in 64-bit arithmetic becomes important at about $t = 80$. Whether or not the relative frequencies in Figure 17.4 are affected by this approximation is not clear and is currently under investigation. Other computational work in this chapter uses series of length at most 40, and so inaccuracies in floating-point arithmetic are not a factor except possibly in Figure 17.4.

2. Posterior standard deviations for x_1 through x_4 and standard errors of numerical approximation for x_1 through x_7 are all but meaningless due to rounding error: they are formed as the difference of two numbers whose order of magnitude is 10^0, and 64-bit arithmetic produces mantissas with about 15 significant figures. The square roots of such differences are reported as standard deviations and standard errors in Table 17.7.

Bibliography

Barnett, William A., J. Geweke, and P. Yue, 19891, "Semiparametric Bayesian Estimation of the Asymptotically Ideal Model: the AIM Demand System," in W.A. Barnett, J. Powell and G.E. Tauchen, eds., *Nonparametric and Semiparametric Methods in Econometrics and Statistics*, Cambridge University Press, Cambridge, pp. 127–174.

Crutchfield, J. P., J. D. Farmer, N. H. Packard, and R. S. Shaw, 1986, "Chaos," *Scientific American*, 255, 46–57.

Doan, T., R. Litterman, and C. A. Sims, 1984, "Forecasting and Conditional Projection Using Realistic Prior Distributions," *Econometric Reviews*, 3(1), 1–100.

Farmer, J .D., and J. J. Sidorowich, 1987, "Predicting Chaotic Time Series," mimeo, Los Alamos National Laboratory, *Physical Review Letters*, 59, 845–848.

Ford, J., 1983, "How Random is a Coin Toss?," *Physics Today*, 1, 40–47.

Geweke, John, 1988, "Acceleration Methods for Monte Carlo Integration in Bayesian Inference," *Proceedings of the 20th Symposium on the Interface: Computing Science and Statistics*, 587–590.

Geweke, John, 1989, "Bayesian Inference in Econometric Models Using Monte Carlo Integration," *Econometrica*, 57, 1317–1340.

Gleick, J., 1987, *Chaos: Making a New Science*, Viking, New York.

Grassberger, P., and I. Procaccia, 1983, "Estimation of the Kolmogorov Entropy from a Chaotic Signal," *Physical Review A*, 28, 2591–2593.

Libchaber, A., 1982, "Experimental Study of Hydrodynamic Instabilities. Rayleigh-Bernard Experiment: Helium in a Small Box," in T. Riste, ed., *Nonlinear Phenomena at Phase Transitions and Instabilities*, Plenum, New York.

Ott, E., 1981, "Strange Attractors and Chaotic Motions of Dynamical Systems," *Reviews of Modern Physics*, 53. 655–671.

Ruelle, D., 1976, *The Lorenz Attractor and the Problem of Turbulence*, Springer-Verlag, Berlin.

Takens, F., 1980, "Detecting Strange Attractors in Turbulence," in D. Rand and L. Young, eds., *Dynamical Systems and Turbulence*, Springer-Verlag, Berlin.

Whittle, P., 1983, *Prediction and Regulation by Linear Least-Square Methods*, University of Minnesota Press, Minneapolis.

Yule, G. U., 1927, "On a Method of Investigating Periodicities in Disturbed Series, with Special Reference to Wolfer's Sunspot Numbers," *Philosophical Transactions*, A226, 267–275.

Zellner, Arnold, 1971, *An Introduction to Bayesian Inference in Econometrics*, Wiley, New York.

18

A Multicriteria Approach
to Dynamic Estimation

ROBERT KALABA and LEIGH TESFATSION

The theoretical relations postulated for socioeconomic processes typically fall into four conceptually distinct categories. *Cross-sectional* relations restricting the behavior of theoretical variables at a point in time might be given, such as demand and supply relations for goods, services, and financial assets. *Measurement* relations connecting empirical observations to theoretical constructs might be specified. *Dynamic* relations governing theoretical variables at successive points in time would also presumably be postulated; for example, relations describing how physical and human capital stocks change over time. Finally, *probability* relations might be assumed for some of the theoretical variables.

Inevitably, an observed socioeconomic process will behave in a manner that is incompatible to some degree with each of these postulated theoretical relations. Associated with any set of estimates for the theoretical variables, therefore, will be a set of model discrepancy terms reflecting the various ways in which the theoretical relations are incompatible with the process observations. These discrepancy terms are derived terms incorporating everything unknown about the cross-sectional, measurement, dynamic, and probabilistic aspects of the process.

Considered in this way, the estimation of socioeconomic models would seem, intrinsically, to be a *multicriteria* optimization problem. Any such estimation typically entails various conceptually distinct types of discrepancy terms, and a statistician undertaking the estimation would presumably want *each* type of discrepancy to be small.

Nevertheless, multicriteria optimization techniques have played only a minor role in econometrics to date, and it is interesting to consider why this is so. The explanation is that the standard statistical inference techniques used in econometrics routinely require the statistician to couch his inference problem in an all-encompassing stochastic framework. That is, the actual data generating process is assumed to be describable by means of some well-defined probability distribution either objectively, i.e., apart from any observer, or subjectively, as a coherent reflection of the statistician's current beliefs. See, for example, the standard econometric text by Judge et al. (1985).

In particular, within this all-encompassing stochastic framework, discrepancy terms (model specification errors) are interpreted as random quantitities governed by joint probability distributions known up to a parametrization. Consequently, the determination of the separate and joint behavior of the theoretical variables in relation to process observations reduces to the determination of some appropriately derived likelihood function or posterior probability distribution. The problem of reconciling imperfect theory with observations is thus transformed into the problem of determining the most probable parameter values for a stochastic model whose structure is assumed to be correctly and completely specified.

What are the strengths and weaknesses of this standard statistical inference approach? On the plus side, it provides the statistician with a powerful and elegant way in which to scale and weigh disparate sources of information. All discussion of theoretical variables is conducted in terms of assumed joint probability relations, so that a common level of abstraction is achieved. This permits the construction of a single *real-valued* measure of incompatibility between theory and observations, e.g., a likelihood function. Incommensurability problems simply do not arise. To use an analogy from decision theory, it is as if the preferences of one or more decision makers with potentially conflicting objectives were always assumed to be representable in aggregate form by a single real-valued utility function.

On the minus side, the statistician is forced to undertake his or her inferential study under the generally false presumption of correct model specification. This standard "null hypothesis" is to be employed even when the statistician is fully aware that he or she has resorted to conventional or otherwise arbitrary probability assessments for model discrepancy terms.

Residuals (estimates for the model discrepancy terms) can of course subsequently be subjected to various diagnostic procedures to check for model misspecification. Specifically, one can check whether the probabilistic properties postulated for these residuals are in reasonable agreement with their empirically determined statistical properties. Specification testing against alternative models can also also be undertaken using some form of likelihood or posterior odds ratio test. Yet the fact remains that all incompatibilities between theory and observations, whatever their actual source, are *forced* to reveal themselves as inconsistencies between postulated and empirical *probability* relations; the cross-sectional, measurement, and dynamic relations are either pushed into the background or lost sight of entirely through various analytical manipulations. Untangling the true source of any diagnosed specification problem can thus be difficult.

In Kalaba and Tesfatsion (1989, 1990a,b), the problem of estimation is reexamined from a multicriteria perspective. In particular, a framework for estimation is developed that encompasses a broad range of views concerning the appropriate interpretation and treatment of model discrepancy terms. On the one hand, conceptually distinct discrepancy terms can be considered without forced amalgamation, as illustrated by the "flexible least squares" (FLS) approach. The basic FLS objective is to determine the extent to which conceptually distinct types of discrepancy terms can simultaneously be made as small as possible, in the sense of vector minimization. Alternatively, if available, joint probability assessments can be used to achieve a complete amalgamation of the discrepancy terms into a single real-valued measure of theory and data incompatibility.

The next section illustrates the FLS approach for a time-varying linear estimation problem in which a data analyst is unable or unwilling to provide probability assessments for model discrepancy terms. The FLS approach to this estimation problem is then contrasted with the standard statistical inference approach in which probability assessments for discrepancy terms are assumed to be available. A multicriteria framework for more generally specified estimation problems is then outlined and concluding remarks are given.

Multicriteria Estimation: An Illustrative Example

Suppose scalar observations $y_1, y_2, \ldots, y_T$ have been obtained on a process at successive discrete time points $1, 2, \ldots, T$. The basic estimation objective is to understand the way in which the process has evolved over the course of the observation period.

The state of the process at each time t, $t = 1, \ldots, T$, is described by an $N \times 1$ column vector x_t of unknown state variables.[1] An approximately linear relation is postulated between the observation y_t and the state vector x_t at each time t:

Measurement Relations [Approximately Linear Measurement]:

$$y_t - h'_t x_t \approx 0 , \quad t = 1, \ldots, T , \tag{18.1}$$

where h'_t is a $1 \times N$ row vector of known exogenous variables.

The dynamic motion of the state vectors x_t is not well understood a priori. It is anticipated that some systematic time variation in these state vectors might have occurred over the observation period. However, it is also anticipated that any such evolution will have been gradual, so that successive state vectors do not differ too much from one observation time to the next. These prior anticipations are modeled by a smoothness constraint on the evolution of the state vector:

Dynamic Relations [Gradual State Evolution]:

$$x_{t+1} - x_t \approx \mathbf{0} , \quad t = 1, \ldots, T - 1 . \tag{18.2}$$

In accordance with the basic estimation objective, suppose an attempt is now made to determine all possible estimates $\hat{\mathbf{X}}_T = (\hat{x}_1, \ldots, \hat{x}_T)$ for the state sequence $\mathbf{X}_T = (x_1, \ldots, x_T)$, which are in some sense minimally incompatible with the given theoretical relations (18.1) and (18.2), conditional on the given observation sequence $\mathbf{Y}_T = (y_1, \ldots, y_T)$. The multicriteria nature of this estimation problem is seen as follows. Two conceptually distinct types of model specification error can be associated with each possible state sequence estimate $\hat{\mathbf{X}}_T$. First, the choice of $\hat{\mathbf{X}}_T$ could result in measurement specification errors consisting of nonzero discrepancy terms $y_t - h'_t\hat{x}_t$ in (18.1). Second, the choice of $\hat{\mathbf{X}}_T$ could result in dynamic specification errors consisting of nonzero discrepancy terms $\hat{x}_{t+1} - \hat{x}_t$ in (18.2). To conclude that the theoretical relations (18.1) and (18.2) are in reasonable agreement with the observations, *each* type of discrepancy would have to be small.

Suppose a measurement cost $c_M(\hat{\mathbf{X}}_T, \mathbf{Y}_T, T)$ and a dynamic cost $c_D(\hat{\mathbf{X}}_T, \mathbf{Y}_T, T)$ are separately assessed for the two disparate types of model specification errors entailed by the choice of a state sequence estimate $\hat{\mathbf{X}}_T$. On the basis of both tractability and general intuitive appeal, these costs are taken to be sums of squared discrepancy terms. More precisely, for any given state sequence estimate $\hat{\mathbf{X}}_T$, the measurement cost associated with $\hat{\mathbf{X}}_T$ is taken to be

$$c_M(\hat{\mathbf{X}}_T, \mathbf{Y}_T, T) = \sum_{t=1}^{T}[y_t - h'_t\hat{x}_t]^2 , \tag{18.3}$$

and the dynamic cost associated with $\hat{\mathbf{X}}_T$ is taken to be

$$c_D(\hat{\mathbf{X}}_T, \mathbf{Y}_T, T) = \sum_{t=1}^{T-1}[\hat{x}_{t+1} - \hat{x}_t]'D[\hat{x}_{t+1} - \hat{x}_t] , \tag{18.4}$$

where D is a suitably selected positive definite scaling matrix.[2]

If the prior beliefs (18.1) and (18.2) concerning the measurement and dynamic relations hold true with absolute equality, then selecting the actual state sequence $\mathbf{X}_T$ as the state sequence estimate would result in zero values for both c_M and c_D. In all other cases, each potential state sequence estimate $\hat{\mathbf{X}}_T$ will entail positive measurement and/or dynamic costs. Nevertheless, not all of these state sequence estimates are equally interesting. Specifically, a state sequence estimate $\hat{\mathbf{X}}_T$ that is cost subordinated by another estimate $\mathbf{X}_T^*$, in the sense that $\mathbf{X}_T^*$ yields a lower value for one type of cost without increasing the value of the other, should presumably be excluded from consideration.

Attention is therefore focused on the set of state sequence estimates that are not cost subordinated by any other state sequence estimate. Such estimates are referred to as *flexible least squares* (FLS) estimates. Each FLS estimate shows how the state vector could have evolved over time in a manner minimally incompatible with the prior measurement and dynamic relations (18.1) and (18.2). Without additional modeling criteria, restricting attention to any proper subset of the FLS estimates is a purely arbitrary decision. Consequently, the FLS approach envisions the generation and consideration of all of the FLS estimates in order to determine the similarities and divergencies displayed by these potential state sequences. The similarities might be used to construct more structured hypotheses regarding the evolution of the state vector. The divergencies reflect the uncertainty inherent in the problem formulation regarding the nature of this evolution.

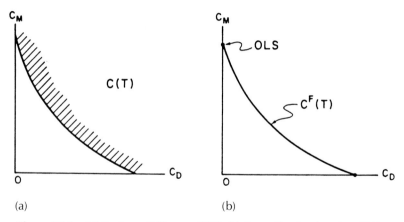

Figure 18.1   (a) Cost possiblity set, $C(T)$; (b) Cost-effective frontier, $C^F(T)$.

Define the *cost possibility* set to be the collection

$$C(T) = \{c_D(\hat{\mathbf{X}}_T, \mathbf{Y}_T, T), c_M(\hat{\mathbf{X}}_T, \mathbf{Y}_T, T) \mid \hat{\mathbf{X}}_T \in E^{TN}\} \tag{18.5}$$

of all possible configurations of dynamic and measurement costs attainable at time T, conditional on the given observation sequence $\mathbf{Y}_T$. The *cost-efficient frontier* $C^F(T)$ is then defined to be the collection of all cost vectors $c = (c_D, c_M)$ in $C(T)$, which are not subordinated by any other cost vector c^* in $C(T)$ in the sense that $c^* \leq c$. Formally, letting vmin denote vector-minimization,

$$C^F(T) = \text{vmin} \, C(T). \tag{18.6}$$

By construction, then, the cost-efficient frontier is the collection of all cost vectors associated with the FLS state sequence estimates.

If the $N \times T$ matrix $[h_1, \ldots, h_T]$ has full rank N, the cost-efficient frontier $C^F(T)$ is a strictly convex curve in the $c_D - c_M$ plane giving the locus of vector-minimal costs attainable at time T, conditional on the given observations. In particular, $C^F(T)$ reveals the measurement cost c_M that must be paid in order to achieve the OLS solution entailing zero dynamic cost (time-constant state vector estimates) (see Figure 18.1).

Once the FLS estimates and the cost-efficient frontier are determined, three different levels of analysis can be used to investigate the degree to which the theoretical relations (18.1) and (18.2) are incompatible with the observations $y_1, \ldots, y_T$. First, the frontier can be examined to determine the efficient attainable trade-offs between the measurement and dynamic costs c_M and c_D. Second, for a rough grid of points spanning the frontier, one can generate the FLS estimates whose cost vectors correspond to these points. Recalling that each FLS estimate is an estimate for the evolution of the actual state vector, descriptive summary statistics (e.g., average value and standard deviation) can be constructed for each of these FLS estimates.

These summary statistics provide rough indicators of the extent to which the FLS estimates deviate from the OLS solution associated with the extreme point of the frontier where dynamic cost is zero. Finally, the time paths traced out by the FLS estimates can be directly examined for evidence of systematic movements in individual state variables—e.g., unanticipated jumps at dispersed points in time. These movements might be difficult to discern from summary statistical characterizations of the time paths.

In Kalaba and Tesfatsion (1989), this three-stage FLS analysis is applied to a time-varying linear regression problem, a special case of (18.1) and (18.2) in which the time t state vector x_t denotes the vector of time t regression coefficients, and the time t exogenous vector h_t denotes the vector of time t regressor variables. The basic estimation objective is to determine whether the regression coefficients have exhibited any systematic time variation over the course of the observation period.

A FORTRAN program for generating the FLS estimates is provided in an appendix Kalaba and Tesfatsion (1989), together with an explanation of the program logic. Various simulation experiments demonstrating the ability of the FLS estimates to track linear, quadratic, sinusoidal, and regime shift motions in the true regression coefficients, despite noisy observations, are reported and graphically depicted. In Tesfatsion and Veitch (1990), a variation of this program is used to undertake an empirical investigation of the well-known Goldfeld (1976) log-linear regression model for U.S. money demand over the volatile period 1959:Q2–1985:Q3. Interesting insights are obtained concerning shifts in the money demand regression coefficients at economically reasonable points in time. In Dorfman and Foster (1991), the FLS approach is used to develop a new measure of productivity change by allowing the coefficients characterizing the production process to evolve slowly over time in an ex ante unknown manner. The new measure compared favorably with more traditional measures when tested for U.S. agricultural data.

A more general FLS procedure for the sequential estimation of approximately linear measurement and dynamic relations—referred to as GFLS—is developed in Kalaba and Tesfatsion (1990a). A FORTRAN implementation is provided, and conceptual and computational distinctions between GFLS and Kalman filtering are clarified. A detailed discussion of the FLS approach or more general nonlinear systems can be found in Kalaba and Tesfatsion (1990b). This latter work is briefly reviewed below.

In summary, the basic FLS objective is to characterize the state sequence estimates that achieve vector-minimal incompatibility between process observations and imperfectly specified theoretical relations, whatever form these theoretical relations might take. Although probability relations can be incorporated along with other types of theoretical relations, they do not play a distinguished role. Indeed, as illustrated above, they may be absent altogether. In contrast, standard statistical estimation techniques (e.g., maximum a posteriori estimation and maximum likelihood estimation) are point estimation techniques that attempt to determine the most probable state sequence estimate for a stochastic model whose structure is assumed to be correctly and completely specified. The crucial distinction between the two approaches lies in the use of probability theory to transform potentially disparate model discrepancy terms into apparently commensurable quantities.

The next section illustrates this distinction by reformulating the state estimation problem (18.1) and (18.2) in accordance with standard practice.

Standard Treatment of the Problem

Suppose scalar observations $y_1, \ldots, y_T$ obtained on a process are postulated to be approximately linearly related to a sequence of state vectors $x_1, \ldots, x_T$. The prior measurement relations take the following form:

Measurement Relations [Approximately Linear Measurement]:

$$y_t = h_t' x_t + v_t, \quad t = 1, \ldots, T, \tag{18.7}$$

where x_t denotes an $N \times 1$ column vector of unknown state variables, h_t' denotes a $1 \times N$ row vector of known exogenous variables, and v_t denotes a scalar measurement discrepancy term.

If no restrictions are placed on the discrepancy term v_t, then equation (18.7) is simply a defining relation for v_t. That is, v_t is a slack variable, and equation (18.7) is true by definition whether or not an approximately linear relation exists between y_t and x_t in actuality. The slack variable v_t depends on everything affecting y_t that is not captured by the term $h_t' x_t$—that is, everything unknown, or not presumed to be known, about how y_t might depend on higher order terms in x_t, on missing variables, and so forth. To give content to the prior of "approximately linear measurement," the discrepancy term v_t must further be restricted to be small in some sense.

Suppose in addition to (18.7) that the state vector x_t is assumed to evolve gradually over time. The prior dynamic relations take the following form:

Dynamic Relations [Gradual State Evolution]:

$$x_{t+1} = x_t + w_t, \quad t = 1, \ldots, T - 1, \tag{18.8}$$

where the $N \times 1$ vector w_t denotes a dynamic discrepancy term. As before, if no restrictions are placed on the discrepancy term w_t, then equation (18.8) simply defines w_t to be a slack variable incorporating everything unknown, or not presumed to be known, about how the differenced state vector $[x_{t+1} - x_t]$ depends on higher order terms in x_t, on missing variables, and so forth. Consequently, as it stands, equation (18.8) is true regardless of the actual relation between x_{t+1} and x_t. To give content to the prior of "gradual state evolution," the discrepancy term w_t must further be restricted to be small in some sense.

If no additional theoretical relations are introduced, the estimation problem described above is simply an alternative representation for the multicriteria estimation problem outlined in the previous section. Each possible estimate for the state sequence $(x_1, \ldots, x_T)$ entails two conceptually distinct apple-and-orange types of discrepancy terms—measurement and dynamic—and a data analyst undertaking this estimation would presumably want *each* type of discrepancy to be small.

However, standard statistical estimation techniques invariably do introduce a third type of theoretical relation at this point in the description of a state estimation problem: namely, probability relations governing both the individual and the joint behavior of the measurement and dynamic discrepancy terms and the initial state vector. Consider, for example, the following commonly assumed relations:

Probability Relations:

$$(v_t) \text{ and } (w_t) \; = \; \text{mutually and serially independent processes} \qquad (18.9)$$

$$(PDF \text{ for } v_t) \; = \; P(v_t), \quad t = 1, \ldots, T; \qquad (18.10)$$

$$(PDF \text{ for } w_t) \; = \; P(w_t), \; t = 1, \ldots, T-1; \qquad (18.11)$$

$$x_1 \text{ distributed independently of } v_t \text{ and } w_t \text{ for each } t; \qquad (18.12)$$

$$(PDF \text{ for } x_1) \; = \; P(x_1). \qquad (18.13)$$

The relations (18.9)–(18.13) imply that the discrepancy terms v_t and w_t appearing in (18.7) and (18.8) are random quantities with known probability density functions (PDFs) governing both their individual and their joint behavior. Since (18.7) and (18.8) are still interpreted as equations in the usual exact mathematical sense, v_t and w_t now appear in these equations as commensurable "disturbance terms" impinging on correctly specified theoretical relations. The previous interpretation for v_t and w_t as conceptually distinct apple-and-orange discrepancy terms incorporating everything unknown about the measurement and dynamic aspects of the process is thus dramatically altered.

Once the commensurability of the discrepancy terms w_t and v_t is assumed, a single real-valued measure of theory and data incompatibility can be constructed. Specifically, combining the measurement relations (18.7) with the probability relations (18.9)–(18.13) permits the derivation of a probability density function $P(\mathbf{Y}_T \mid \mathbf{X}_T)$ for the observation sequence $\mathbf{Y}_T = (y_1, \ldots, y_T)$ conditional on the state sequence $\mathbf{X}_T = (x_1, \ldots, x_T)$. Combining the dynamic relations (18.8) with the probability relations (18.9)–(18.13) permits the derivation of a "prior" probability density function $P(\mathbf{X}_T)$ for $\mathbf{X}_T$. The joint probability density function for $\mathbf{X}_T$ and $\mathbf{Y}_T$ then takes the form

$$P(\mathbf{X}_T, \mathbf{Y}_T) \; = \; P(\mathbf{Y}_T \mid \mathbf{X}_T) \cdot P(\mathbf{X}_T). \qquad (18.14)$$

The joint probability density function (18.14) elegantly combines the two distinct sources of theory and data incompatibility—measurement and dynamic—into a single *real-valued* measure of incompatibility for any considered state sequence $\mathbf{X}_T$.

An objective commonly assumed for estimation problems described by relations of the form (18.7)–(18.13) is maximum a posteriori (MAP) estimation, i.e., the determination of the state sequence $\mathbf{X}_T$, which maximizes the posterior probability density function $P(\mathbf{X}_T \mid \mathbf{Y}_T)$. Since the observation sequence $\mathbf{Y}_T$ is assumed to be given, this objective is equivalent to determining the state sequence $\mathbf{X}_T$, which maximizes the product of $P(\mathbf{X}_T \mid \mathbf{Y}_T)$ and $P(\mathbf{Y}_T)$. By the agreed on rules of probability theory,

$$P(\mathbf{X}_T \mid \mathbf{Y}_T) \cdot P(\mathbf{Y}_T) = P(\mathbf{Y}_T \mid \mathbf{X}_T) \cdot P(\mathbf{X}_T), \qquad (18.15)$$

where, as earlier explained, the right-hand expression can be evaluated using the relations (18.7)–(18.13). Determining the state sequence with greatest posterior probability is thus equivalent to determining the state sequence which minimizes the real-valued incompatibility cost function

$$c(\mathbf{X}_T, \mathbf{Y}_T, T) = -\log[P(\mathbf{Y}_T \mid \mathbf{X}_T) \cdot P(\mathbf{X}_T)]. \qquad (18.16)$$

In summary, what ultimately has been accomplished by the augmentation of the measurement and dynamic relations (18.7) and (18.8) with the probability relations (18.9) through (18.13)? *The multicriteria problem of achieving vector-minimal incompatibility between imperfectly specified theoretical relations and process observations has been transformed into the single-criterion problem of determining the most probable state sequence for a stochastic model whose structure is assumed to be correctly and completely specified.*

One basic objection to this standard estimation approach is that it entails a disturbance-term interpretation for model discrepancy terms that is inappropriate and overly restrictive, particularly with regard to the dynamic discrepancy terms w_t. Another important objection is that the required specification of joint probability relations for conceptually distinct types of discrepancy terms can be difficult to implement in a way that other researchers find compelling. A third objection is that the amalgamation of conceptually distinct discrepancy terms into a single real-valued incompatibility measure such as (18.16) makes it difficult to detect and correctly sort out which aspects of the model, if any, are seriously misspecified.

In what sense is the disturbance-term interpretation particularly inappropriate and overly restrictive for the dynamic discrepancy terms w_t? Modeling these discrepancy terms as random vectors assumes the existence of a potentially jagged discontinuity between successive state vectors, the opposite of the "gradual evolution" prior belief which (18.8) was originally intended to capture. A counter to this criticism might be that the variances of the discrepancy term components are anticipated to be small. However, a significant change occurs in the interpretation of the dynamic relations (18.8) when this probabilistic conception of "smallness" is applied to the discrepancy terms w_t.

Consider the nature of the discrepancy terms $w_t = [x_{t+1} - x_t]$ when the state vector x_t is systematically evolving over time. Suppose, for example, that each component of x_t exhibits a smooth but irregular cyclical motion. This time variation satisfies the prior assumption of gradual state evolution. However, the prior assumption that the discrepancy terms w_t are generated in accordance with a stationary probability distribution is simply wrong and misleading, no matter what one assumes about the size of the variances for the components of w_t. Relaxing stationarity is certainly a necessary first step toward realism; but consider how much more structured and complicated the relations (18.9)–(18.13) would have to become to capture adequately the general idea of a "smooth but irregular cyclical motion" through the use of formal probabilistic assumptions. And, once modified to reflect this possibility, would relations (18.9)–(18.13) still be able to capture adequately the idea of other forms of gradual state evolution, e.g., a gradual shift from one level to nother?

"Small discrepancy terms" and "small discrepancy variances" are not conceptually equivalent concepts. For approximate reasoning purposes, probability can be an overly restrictive concept. See, for example, the thoughtful discussion of this point in Ruspini (1991).

The second objection raised above concerns public incredulity. The probability relations (18.9)-(18.13) imply that the mutual behavior of the measurement and dynamic discrepancy terms w_t and v_t is governed by the joint probability distribution $P(w_t, v_t) \equiv P(w_t) \cdot P(v_t)$. Consequently, w_t and v_t are now assumed to be cardinally comparable. For many processes—in particular, for socioeconomic processes—it is hard to maintain such an assumption in a publicly credible way. For example, the observations $y_1, \ldots, y_T$ might be the outcome of a nonreplicable experiment, implying that probability assessments for the discrepancy terms w_t and v_t cannot be put to an objective test. Alternatively, as previously stressed, the theoretical relations (18.7) and (18.8) might represent tentatively held conjectures concerning a poorly understood process, or a linearized set of relations obtained for an analytically intractable nonlinear process. In this case it is questionable whether the discrepancy terms are governed by any meaningful probability relationships. A data analyst may then have to resort to specifications determined largely by convention if forced to provide a probabilistic characterization for the discrepancy terms.

The third objection raised above concerns the confounding of conceptually distinct specification errors. There is of course no way to determine from the single real-valued measure (18.16) that a serious specification error has occurred, e.g., in the dynamic relations (18.8) rather than the measurement relations (18.7). In fact, (18.16) is constructed under the premise that no specification error has occurred, and there is no way to use it per se to check for any kind of modeling difficulty. Rather, subsequent diagnostic tests must be conducted to check whether specific theoretical assumptions are at variance with empirically determined properties.

A further difficulty here, as detailed in Kalaba and Tesfatsion (1990b, Section 5.1), is that standard diagnostic procedures force all incompatibilities between theory and observations to reveal themselves as incompatibilities between theoretically anticipated probability relations and empirically determined statistical properties. For example, suppose the dynamic relations (18.8) are fundamentally misspecified because the true dynamic dependence of x_{t+1} on x_t is highly nonlinear. Using standard diagnostic tests on the dynamic residual terms $\hat{w}_t \equiv [\hat{x}_{t+1} - \hat{x}_t]$, the data analyst would presumably perceive that the empirically determined properties of these residuals are at variance with the probability relations assumed for w_t in (18.9) and (18.11). The tendency of the data analyst would then be to modify the probability assumptions for w_t in a purely statistical way—e.g., to replace serial independence with first-order serial correlation, or to assume that w_t has a time-varying covariance matrix—rather than to think more carefully about the actual physical or socioeconomic relationships connecting x_{t+1} to x_t.

These three objections—inappropriateness and overrestrictiveness, public incredulity, and the confounding of conceptually distinct errors—would be of purely academic interest if treating discrepancy terms as commensurable random disturbance terms constituted the only way to turn the estimation crank. However, as suggested previously, an alternative multicriteria treatment of discrepancy terms can feasibly and fruitfully be undertaken.

Generalizations

The multicriteria approach has been generalized in Kalaba and Tesfatsion (1990) to a much broader class of estimation problems. The present section briefly reviews this work.

Consider a situation in which a sequence of observations $\mathbf{Y}_T = (y_1, \ldots, y_T)$ has been obtained on a process at successive discrete time points $1, \ldots, T$. The basic objective is to learn about the sequence of states $\mathbf{X}_T = (x_1, \ldots, x_T)$ through which the process has passed.

Suppose the degree to which each possible state sequence estimate $\hat{\mathbf{X}}_T$ is incompatible with the given observation sequence $\mathbf{Y}_T$ is measured by a K-dimensional vector $c(\hat{\mathbf{X}}_T, \mathbf{Y}_T, T)$ of incompatibility costs. These costs may represent penalties imposed for failure to satisfy criteria *conjectured* to be true (theoretical relations), and also penalties imposed for failure to satisfy criteria *preferred* to be true (objectives). Let $C(T)$ denote the set of all incompatibility cost vectors $c = c(\hat{\mathbf{X}}_T, \mathbf{Y}_T, T)$ corresponding to possible state sequence estimates $\hat{\mathbf{X}}_T$. The *cost-efficient frontier*, denoted by $C^F(T)$, is then defined to be the collection of cost vectors c in $C(T)$, which are not subordinated by any other cost vector c^* in $C(T)$ in the sense that $c^* \le c$.

By construction, the state sequence estimates $\hat{\mathbf{X}}_T$ whose cost vectors attain the cost-efficient frontier are characterized by a basic efficiency property: For the given observations, no other possible state sequence estimate yields lower incompatibility cost with respect to each of the K modeling criteria included in the incompatibility cost vector. Each of these state sequence estimates thus represents one possible way the actual process could have evolved over time in a manner minimally incompatible with the prior theoretical relations and objectives.

The basic multicriteria estimation problem can be summarized as follows:

The Basic Multicriteria Estimation Problem: *Given a process length T,* an observation sequence $\mathbf{Y}_T$, and a vector-valued incompatibility cost function $c(\cdot, \mathbf{Y}_T, T)$, determine all possible state sequence estimates $\hat{\mathbf{X}}_T$ that vector-minimize the incompatibility cost $c(\hat{\mathbf{X}}_T, \mathbf{Y}_T, T)$. That is, determine all possible state sequence estimates $\hat{\mathbf{X}}_T$ whose cost vectors $c(\hat{\mathbf{X}}_T, \mathbf{Y}_T, T)$ attain the cost-efficient frontier $C^F(T)$.

A vector-valued recurrence relation is established for the cost-efficient frontiers in Kalaba and Tesfatsion (1990b). This recurrence relation is readily recognizable as a multicriteria extension of the usual scalar dynamic programming equations.

To give a rough idea of this result, consider the estimation problem at any intermediate time t. Suppose a K-dimensional vector $c(\hat{\mathbf{X}}_t, \mathbf{Y}_t, t)$ of incompatibility costs can be associated with each t-length state sequence estimate $\hat{\mathbf{X}}_t = (\hat{x}_1, \ldots, \hat{x}_t)$, conditional on the sequence of observations $\mathbf{Y}_t = (y_1, \ldots, y_t)$. Let $C(\hat{x}_t, t)$ denote the set of all cost vectors $c(\hat{\mathbf{X}}_t, \mathbf{Y}_t, t)$ attainable at time t, conditional on the time–t state estimate being $\hat{x}_t$; and let $C^F(\hat{x}_t, t)$ denote the cost-efficient frontier for $C(\hat{x}_t, t)$.

Given certain regularity conditions, it is shown that state-conditional frontiers at time t are mapped into state-conditional frontiers at time $t + 1$ in accordance with a vector-valued recurrence relation having the form

$$C^F(\hat{x}_{t+1}, t + 1) = \text{vmin}\left(\bigcup_{\hat{x}_t}[C^F(\hat{x}_t, t) + \Delta c(\hat{x}_t, \hat{x}_{t+1}, y_{t+1}, t + 1)]\right), \quad (18.17)$$

where vmin denotes vector-minimization and $\Delta c(\cdot)$ denotes a vector of incremental costs associated with the state transition $(\hat{x}_t, \hat{x}_{t+1})$. Moreover, the cost-efficient frontier at the final time T satisfies

$$C^F(T) = \text{vmin}\left[\bigcup_{\hat{x}_T} C^F(\hat{x}_T, T)\right]. \quad (18.18)$$

Various well-known state estimation algorithms are derived in Kalaba and Tesfatsion (1990b) as single-criterion special cases of the multicriteria recurrence relations (18.17) and (18.18): for example, the Kalman filter (Kalman, 1960) for sequentially generating maximum a posteriori (MAP) probability estimates. In addition, an algorithm for sequentially generating the FLS estimates for the problem discussed above is derived as a bicriteria special case of (18.17) and (18.18).

Concluding Remarks

To date, statistical inferential techniques have primarily been designed for situations where theoretical specifications are essentially correct and model discrepancy terms are reasonably modeled as random quantities with known probability distributions. Nevertheless, for numerous important socioeconomic processes, the underlying relations are not yet well understood. Model misspecification is thus an endemic problem, and procedures are needed for coping with this reality.

As this chapter demonstrates, interesting challenges arise for statistical inference when model discrepancy terms are explicitly treated as disparate and incommensurable model specification errors. In particular, multicriteria methods take on a new and critical importance, providing a powerful new tool for nonlinear estimation.

Notes

This work was partially supported by NIH Grant DK 33729. Preliminary versions of this chapter were presented at the International Symposium on Evolutionary Dynamics, the IC^2 Institute, Austin, Texas, April 16–19, 1989; at the Olin School of Business, Washington University, St. Louis, Missouri, November 8, 1989; at the Econometric Society Meeting, Atlanta, Georgia, December 28, 1989; and at the Fifth Annual Tax Research Symposium, sponsored by Deloitte and Touche and the Center for Accounting Research, Redondo Beach, California, January 19, 1990. The authors are grateful to symposium and seminar participants for helpful comments.

1. In the present estimation context, the state vector x_t represents a vector of unknown process attributes at time t, which the data analyst is attempting to estimate. For example, for a time-varying linear regression problem, x_t would typically be the vector of time t regression coefficients, possibly augmented to include other unknown structural parameters. For an economic growth problem, x_t might include the time t aggregate stocks of human capital, physical capital, and financial assets, together with various unknown structural parameters.

2. The scaling matrix D can be specified so that the "FLS" estimates obtained below for the state vectors x_t are essentially invariant to the choice of units for the components of the exogenous vectors h_t. See Tesfatsion and Veitch (1990, footnote 3).

Bibliography

Dorfman, J.H., and K.A. Foster, 1991, "Estimating Productivity Changes with Flexible Coefficients," *Western Journal of Agricultural Economics*, 16, 280–290.

Goldfeld, S., 1976, "The Case of the Missing Money," *Brookings Papers on Economic Activity* 3, 683–730.

Judge, G.G., W.E. Griffiths, R.C. Hill, and T.C. Lee, 1985, *The Theory and Practice of Econometrics*, Wiley, New York.

Kalaba, R. and L. Tesfatsion, 1989, "Time-Varying Linear Regression Via Flexible Least Squares," *Computers and Mathematics with Applications*, 17, 1215–1245.

Kalaba, R., and L. Tesfatsion, 1990a, "Flexible Least Squares for Approximately Linear Systems," *IEEE Transactions on Systems, Man, and Cybernetics*, 20, 978–989.

Kalaba, R., and L. Tesfatsion, 1990b, "An organizing principle for dynamic estimation," *Journal of Optimization Theory and Applications*, 64, 445–470.

Kalman, R.E., 1960, "A New Approach to Linear Filtering and Prediction Problems," Transactions of the ASME: *Journal of Basic Engineering*, 82, 35–45.

Ruspini, E.H., 1991, "Approximate Reasoning: Past, Present, and Future," *Information Sciences*, 57–58, 297–317.

Tesfatsion, L., and J. Veitch, 1990, "U.S. Money Demand Instability: A Flexible Least Squares Approach," *Journal of Economic Dynamics and Control*, 14, 151–173.

VI

HONORARY LECTURE

Richard Goodwin is one of the first to develop nonlinear models of the business cycle and probably the first to notice that intrinsic fluctuations can be nonperiodic. His early papers are classics. At an age when most professionals have long since retired, he launched an energetic program of research in which he reconsidered the business cycle using concepts of nonlinear dynamics that had been developed after his own seminal contributions. Part of this recent work was summarized in Chapter 4. His earlier essays on nonlinear dynamics are collected in his *Essays in Economic Dynamics* (1989).

Richard was asked to give a special lecture at the conference banquet. This Part VII contains the transcript of his remarks, which delightfully encapsulates a lifetime of work that intersects with some of the most important figures in twentieth-Century economics.

19

My Erratic Progress
Toward Economic Dynamics:
Remarks Made at Banquet,
Tuesday, April 18, 1989

RICHARD M. GOODWIN

Being a student in the middle of the Great Depression, I naturally became interested in trying to understand why and how such catastrophic events came about. So, I turned to economics. At that exciting time in the 1930s, precise, quantitative dynamics was first really formulated. The subject began in a rather primitive form. I propose to talk about its subsequent unfolding.

I was introduced to the subject by a very remarkable teacher, Jacob Marschak. He organized a seminar for the entire year at Oxford, announcing at the beginning: "I will allow no one to talk in this seminar about anything if he cannot provide proper numbers, or at least how one might find them." That was a remarkable statement and potent: economists talk and talk, and half of the time there are no numbers corresponding to the concepts. In the midst of a collapse of the world's economies, our subject was business cycles. It was organized around a survey article in one of the earliest issues of *Econometrica* by Tinbergen; he discussed the nature of the problem and what had been done up to that time.

One of the topics treated was a paper given at one of the early meetings of the Econometric Society by the Polish economist Kalecki. I think of it as the first really quantitative, rigorous formulation of an economic cycle — no abstract theorem but about the economic storm we were in the midst of in the 1930s. It was really an original piece of work; the subject has never been the same since, though the elaboration has been slow. However, poor Kalecki had the misfortune to give his paper at a meeting with Frisch present. Frisch was a very intelligent man but also blunt and a harsh critic. He tended to say quite simply what he thought, regardless of the consequences. In effect he said, "Kalecki, you're talking nonsense." What he said touches on a central problem in all linear cycle theory (and it all was linear then). Kalecki's model ended up as a second-order difference equation; he knew that for a linear equation the first-order term determined the stability; if positive, damped

cycle and if negative, explosive. Hence, neither could be used to explain the continued existence of cycles in capitalism. The parameter of the first difference consisted
of the sum of two parameters, of which he had a good estimate for one and not the
other, so he happily chose the sum to be zero, thus avoiding extinction and explosion
in his model.

Frisch simply destroyed the theory as an explanation of the cycle; one can
never in applied work set a parameter at precisely one value: this became later
what is known as structural stability. It was not called that then, but the concept
was familiar to applied mathematicians and engineers. Mathematicians can specify
an exact value, but not applied scientists. Kalecki made several attempts to put the
matter right but, though his theory remained important, his solutions were doubtful.
I was impressed by the problem, and it occupied me for 15 years in an effort to
reformulate the analysis so as to achieve structural stability.

About a decade later a Hungarian economist, Kaldor, admired Kalecki's work
and realized that he had the right basic ideas, actually prior to Keynes. Kaldor
combined the ideas of Keynes and Kalecki, and by careful logic solved the problem
in spite of the fact that he had no mathematical training. His was a somewhat over-
specified geometrical analysis, which gave qualitatively a plausible solution. I do
not think it was too good an answer, but it gave a nonlinear solution. It involved
what would later be called a catastrophe, an endogenous bifurcation which produced
a limit cycle. That was the solution which Kalecki never found. Unfortunately, I did
not benefit from Kaldor's discovery, since it was published during the war, while I
was teaching Physics.

Before the war I had been taught by Roy Harrod, who was very intelligent but
also vain and obstinate. While I was his student he published a small book on the
trade cycle, which I read with interest. He had participated in the writing of Keynes'
General Theory and he realized that Keynes had made a mistake in giving a purely
statical formulation. He dynamized the theory, adding the accelerator, but, giving it
another name, left the impression that it was his own idea, in spite of the fact that it
had been much discussed in America. Harrod showed that the multiplier–accelerator
model is dynamically unstable, so the economy grows until it hits full employment
and collapses. Harrod, like Kaldor, could successfully carry out some economic
arguments in spite of having no mathematics. He simply said the economy reaches a
boundary and bounces back; what he meant was there was a single nonlinearity. I did
not understand it as a nonlinearity, nor, I think, did anyone else. I read Tinbergen's
review of the book and was stunned to read his statement that this implied a first
order linear equation and, hence, it could not give a cycle. *False*. It took me a
long time to understand that, and Tinbergen should have known better. Particular
nonlinear first order equations can perfectly well give one a cycle. Tinbergen was
thinking of linear equations, as was I and everyone else.

This leads back to an earlier event, which is also of interest. Early in the 1930s
Alvin Hansen, a middle western economist, gave a paper in which he developed a
seemingly plausible argument that the accelerator would generate a cycle. When you

invest, you grow; when you grow, you invest more; when you have invested enough, you do not invest and you decline. That made sense, but Frisch again said, in effect, you do not know what you are talking about; this gives exponential growth, never a cycle. Alas, poor Hansen, like Kalecki, was destroyed. Hansen had to accept the rebuff, but privately never gave up the idea, and when the General Theory appeared, he thought — that's it! He, like Kaldor, had no mathematics, so he asked the brightest young man of that generation, Paul Samuelson, to formulate it, and the result is the justly famous Hansen–Samuelson theory. Again, it was a linear theory but basic to all subsequent work on cycles. I should add that Samuelson has recently written a generous and interesting account of his collaboration with Hansen and how they worked together, and how it went on being a relationship even later. The moral of the stories is that what Tinbergen said of Harrod, and Frisch said of Kalecki, was that they were all really speaking of steady-state growth theory that, as you all well know, became the dominant paradigm postwar.

I was left by all this still bothered about Harrod's problem. I tried to convince Schumpeter of its usefulness. As a result, he agreed to attend the first lectures I ever gave; they were on linear cycles, allowing me the unique status of being both pupil and teacher of Schumpeter. In my spare time I continued to think about all this. Frisch, in correctly criticizing Kalecki, nonetheless gave the wrong answer: in the Cassel Festschrift he said the model must be stable but be kept alive by exogenous shocks, which had the added advantage of producing irregularities. There is nothing wrong in this; indeed, it became standard econometric methodology. But it is not the whole story: what we know now is that with nonlinear theory there can be endogenous irregularity, so there is not one but two possible explanations of irregular motion.

Frisch, Tinbergen, and Schumpeter had a discussion at an American Economic Association meeting and decided that they must form an econometric society — on the basic and splendid trinity of principles of good theory, good statistics, and good mathematics. In one of the early issues of *Econometrica* the French mathematician, Le Corbeiller, produced a brief note in which he told economists that they needed nonlinear dynamics to explain the existence of cycles. Frisch, who was editor of the journal, *must* have read it. What was he thinking about when he told Kalecki he had to have exogenous shocks to explain the cycle? The *nonlinearities* can maintain the cycle, which is what Le Corbeiller was trying to convince economists of; he referred to the fundamental work of van der Pol, which had been of great help to electronic analysis and promised to be so for economists. I cannot imagine why Frisch ignored this advice, and now one can never find out!

One day in the physics lab, I was walking down a corridor and I saw a name on the door, "Le Corbeiller." Happily, I remembered that was the name of the man who wrote that article. I had noticed the article but did not understand its significance because, like everyone else, I too, was thinking in linear terms. I knocked on the door and asked if he was the man who wrote that article: he said, "Yes, come in." He was a kindly, generous man and he helped to educate me in nonlinear dynamics.

I would never have arrived without his help. Later, still bothering about Harrod's full employment boundary, I came to him and said an upper and a lower boundary are sufficient for a limit cycle but a single boundary is necessary and sufficient. He expressed grave doubts, telling me that all limit cycle theories employ something like a cubic, but after some discussion he decided to go away and think about it over the weekend; after which he agreed with me.

As a student at Harvard I took the elementary course in mathematics, which was taught by a famous mathematician, Marston Morse. His teaching was not on my level and destroyed me in one go, just like that. So I gave up mathematics; I have no feeling for formal mathematics. Happily, Le Corbeiller helped me to understand what I needed to know to solve my problem. Proceeding by trial and error, I developed a first-order nonlinear difference model that would give a limit cycle. In fact, it exemplifies one of René Thom's elementary catastrophes. Then I elaborated it into a second-order system that can yield a limit cycle in the manner of Poincaré. That resolves the problem of explaining the continued existence of cycles, so that I felt satisfied that I had arrived at what I was looking for. It did not satisfy many others and received almost no attention until now, when apparently it does arouse interest.

There remained only one thing that bothered me; the solution was around a constant level; it should involve growth, and it took me another 10 or 15 years to arrive at that. Looking back, it seems strange that it takes me so long to find solutions to problems — *simple* problems. I finally realized that I could formulate a Volterra prey–predator system in ratios; then it becomes independent of scale, but if the variables are properly chosen, they imply growth. Then I thought I've arrived — that's what I've spent my life looking for; I've found it. At first, few others were interested, but I felt satisfied.

This happy state of mind persisted until Dick Day came to Siena in March of 1985 to see a mathematician, Giulio Pianigiani, and agreed to give us a seminar on chaos. I had read a bit about chaos, but I thought that it was for pure mathematicians, not for us economists. Listening to him worked on me a bit like a religious conversion. For the past 4 years I have done little else but work on economic forms of chaos, and it is all due to him. It is no doubt true that we have not undeniably established that it is empirically significant for economics. Dr. Chen and others will have to accomplish that. For myself, I have no doubts; some large part of the irregularities evident in economic behavior are to be explained by this fascinating new analytic tool.

I feel I must apologize for a rather subjective account. I was asked to talk about the history of doctrine; instead of an objective survey, I have chosen to talk about the development of economic dynamics that I have witnessed.

VII

ROUND TABLE DISCUSSION

The conference ended with a Round Table discussion. Some participants amplified views made during their formal presentations. Others raised controversial points and criticisms. Two major themes stand out from the discussion. First, the new work continues and extends a strong flow of previous scientific work. Second, it does involve new theoretical and methodological developments. Some think that these break with tradition or even constitute an intellectual revolution. Others see them rather as a widening and deepening of the discipline. Most would agree that new insights are forthcoming and that much work remains to be done. The following section presents a severely edited version of the transcript. Hopefully, it retains something of the spirit of the occasion.

20

Round Table Discussion

ROUND TABLE DISCUSSANTS: Peter Allen, Brian Arthur, William Brock, Ping Chen, John Conlisk, Richard Day (Chair), Giovanni Dosi, Sidney Winter.

FLOOR DISCUSSANTS: Richard Goodwin, Jacques Lesourne, Richard Lipsey, Michael Mackey, Richard Nelson, Ilya Prigogine, Peter Schwefel, John Sterman.

DAY: For this Round Table discussion we have a totally unstructured situation. We're going to watch it self-organize into something interesting, probably according to the laws of statistical mechanics, but hopefully without leading to total chaos. Let us proceed in order down the table, beginning with Peter Allen.

ALLEN: It's been an exciting and interesting conference. What is intriguing is that people are thinking about similar problems, but because they come from different directions and have different training, they bring different points of view. Still, there is a commonality sufficiently great that we can actually understand each other enough so that real cross fertilization can occur.

I won't summarize my talk — but that doesn't mean I'll give it in full, either! I would like to underline the need to broaden outlooks. I think that this new scientific paradigm of complex nonlinear systems is a great unifier of areas of knowledge that have separated out over time through "positive feedback traps." What we're beginning to see, I hope, is a new holistic approach.

I gave a talk recently about this model that I'd cooked up about how a population can learn. The audience was absolutely bored to tears. I was told afterward that, "Well, not to worry because they were single organism zoologists." And I thought how utterly *staggering* that this kind of partition can exist in people's minds; that they may love a particular organism, like a snail, but they can't see that this snail is part of a system and that its whole existence is conditional on the rest of the system.

I would end by commenting on optimization. We talk about climbing *hills*, but a hill exists only if you know what the vertical axis is, but that vertical axis depends on who you are and what your history is; and therefore there is really no hill. There is simply a system interaction.

ARTHUR: I'm struck that so many people turned up for an evolutionary economics meeting. I take it that means something new is happening in economics. I've been trying to figure out what it is. As I see it, adaptive economics is the next necessary step that economics must take. Let me explain why.

309

Neoclassical economics, as far as I can see, has three major deficiencies. One is that it does not tell us what happens *out of equilibrium*. It's very good at saying what happens exactly at equilibrium, but trading out of equilibrium in most economic models is not well defined.

Second, neoclassical economics does not say what we ought to do when there are *multiple equilibria*. Even with benign assumptions, general equilibrium theory usually finds multiple equilibria. And game theory finds that most noncooperative multiperson games have many more than one equilibrium. How, then, is an equilibrium outcome *selected*? One possibility is to throw in more assumptions to narrow the set of candidate equilibria until only one is left. But that's an artificial way to handle multiplicity.

The third deficiency, and possibly the most serious one, is that once we introduce expectations in sequential-decision neoclassical problems, we ask that economic agents perform *extraordinary feats of calculation*. One could caricature this sort of economics by picturing two rational expectations economists sitting down to play a chess game. They just stare at the board; no moves are made; and finally after 95 minutes, one of them gets up and says, "You win. There is no way I could beat you given the last two moves you would have made." If we dismiss perfect rationality as absurd and turn to bounded rationality instead, this also has its problems. People are not infinitely smart, but then where in our models do we set the dial of nonsmartness?

These three problems then are where neoclassical economics is currently stuck: what happens out of equilibrium; what happens when there's more than one equilibrium; and what happens if people are boundedly rational and not infinitely smart.

It turns out that these three problems are taken care of to quite a degree if we assume that people start off making arbitrarily good or bad decisions, which they can improve. People learn. If we define the learning algorithm they use, we automatically define out-of-equilibrium behavior. If there are multiple equilibria, "learning" may home in one of the equilibria, thus "selecting" it. (Of course, if randomness is present, the algorithm might "learn its way" to a different equilibrium in different reruns of the dynamics.) So the equilibrium-selection problem is taken care of. The bounded rationality problem is also taken care of. We may calibrate agents' learning in our models against *actual* human learning adapts decisions toward better and more plausible actions. Of particular interest is whether the solutions that emerge in this case coincide with the textbook, perfect-rationality solutions.

BROCK: I'm going to deal with a technical problem: how can one adduce evidence of low-dimensional, deterministic chaos that's persuasive to time series econometricians? As I see it, there's a lot of difference between nonlinearity and low-dimensional, deterministic chaos. The latter is generated by a map whose largest Lyapounov exponent is positive and is completely deterministic. The class of nonlinear processes is much broader. There are tests that are designed to detect various kinds of nonlinearities. People have done tests on economic time-series and have found evidence of it, for example, in pig iron production. Many econometricians can therefore accept the presence of nonlinearity. But is this rather special type of nonlinearity present, namely, deterministic chaos?

To tell you about this I'll refer to an experiment. A house from Wall Street wanted to find out whether our team could detect anything or not. They sent us five series and said, "Identify these series, if you can." We got a thousand observations from each series. We took the autocorrelation function of all of the series. For two of them, the autocorrelation function was white noise. Then we squared those two series and took the autocorrelation function of the squares. It's well known in finance that the autocorrelation function of stock returns is approximately white noise, but the autocorrelation function of the squares of stock returns has a fairly large positive first-order lag, and then the lags drop, but they stay positive and they stay outside the Bartlett bounds for quite a few lags. The bottom line is that volatility is forecastable but not returns themselves. The squares of our two test series also looked like white noise. We're beginning to get suspicious that maybe we've got two random series.

We then ran the series through our own test for chaos, which has high power against deterministic chaos as well as other forms of nonlinearity in fairly small samples. Again, the two series showed what looked like IID. Finally, we plotted the unconditional histograms of those two series. One of them appeared to be from a IID uniform distribution, and the other one looked like IID from a Gaussian distribution. We sent a message back to Wall Street by E-Mail that those two are random number generators and we got back the answer, "Yes."

We took the autocorrelation function of the remaining series. Two of them looked like white noise. We took the squares and the autocorrelation functions were positive. They had a downward slope, so we thought, "Hey, there's a pretty good chance they're financial series." We prewhitened them with so called autoregressive conditional heteroscedastic models that are used a lot in finance, and ran the standardized residuals through the autocorrelation function. It looked like white noise. We guessed that they were financial series, and they said, "Yeah, they are, but what are they?" Well we couldn't tell.

So now we've got one series left. Its autocorrelation function did not die out as lag length increased, so we ran it through our chaos test and that barked: gave a loud signal that it might be deterministic chaos, but it also might be a fractionally differenced process. We weren't really able to get rid of that alternative, so we tried forecasting it with nearest neighbors using the powerful Frank and Stengos algorithm. If you take a Mackey–Glass chaos, for example, of dimension 7, there'll be some persistence in that. Act like you're a Box–Jenkins guy and prewhiten the series and look at the residuals. They will look like random noise in any linear test, but if it's really Mackey–Glass, you can forecast it somewhat with nearest neighbors. Now, you're going to get a fairly small r^2, but one way to check to see if r^2 is significant is: You take the series that you're forecasting and you shuffle it. So you've created an IID series with all the same moments. This is called "bootstrapping." Then conduct, say, 5000 replications of the nearest-neighbor forecasting experiment.

You get 5000 values of $\hat{r}^2$, multiply each by the sample length, which is 1000 in our case, and you get a histogram of these statistics. If your actual data value lies in the 5% rejection region, then you say you've got something. We did that and couldn't discard the possibility that it was fractionally differenced because we didn't have the software up at that time. It turned out that there were some number theorists at Wall Street that had generated, by a complicated number theoretic algorithm, a series that had a long-term dependence in it but is perfectly deterministic. But we hadn't caught that.

The bottom line is that when you're trying to convince people that you've found low-dimensional deterministic chaos in economic data, you have got to discard all of these alternative processes that Chris Sims, that Clive Granger, that any time-series econometrician is going to throw at you.

DAY: Consider the complex economic system with thousands, nay, millions of feedback loops. Contrast this against the idea that it's worth testing for low-order chaos, which means roughly that you believe you could potentially describe a real data series with a very small number of equations of relatively simple nonlinear structure. Is it likely that the appearance of randomness is due to the fact that real data are generated by high-order nonlinear processes? We should be very lucky to find economic processes that can be modeled by low-order models. The point is that we use low-order nonlinear models to gain theoretical insight using analytical methods. We should expect usually to need fairly high-order models for empirical work. As a lower bound on the number of state variables for business cycle models, I would give roughly a dozen and these should enter with a number of lags.

In addition to chaos another important aspect of nonlinear models is that in a finite length of time they usually exhibit only a part of their repertoires of behavior. It could take quite a long time to get into a regime where qualitative change occurs, and some of the most significant structural properties of the system may not show up in the data that are available.

CONLISK: I came here expecting to enjoy shots against conventional economics. And I did. However, about halfway through the first day, the shots seemed to be getting a bit too numerous and the aim a little too wild. A list of the seven most frequent targets might be mathematical equilibrium, economic equilibrium, optimizing models of behavior, linearity, exogenous stochastic shocks, exogenous nonstochastic shocks, and rational expectations. My comment is that these are not the seven deadly sins. In fact, they are perfectly reasonable modeling ingredients. Economists may overuse them, and may inappropriately reject other ingredients, but that is not the fault of the ingredients. All seven ingredients will arise quite naturally in some learning models. The job is not to banish the ingredients of conventional economics, but rather to subsume them within a broader framework.

CHEN: I would like to share some interesting remarks by a leading economist related to Conlisk's question. Leontief once pointed out:

Not having been subjected from the outset to the harsh discipline of systematic fact-finding, traditionally imposed on and accepted by their colleagues in the natural and historical sciences, economists developed a nearly irresistible predilection for deductive reasoning. . . . Year after year economic theorists continue to produce scores of mathematical models and to explore in great details their formal properties; and the econometricians fit algebraic functions of all possible shapes to essentially the same sets of data without being able to advance, in any perceptible way, a systematic understanding of the structure and the operation of real economic systems.   Wassily Leontief, 1982, "Academic Economics," *Science*, 217, 104–107.

As a physicist, I share the belief that economic science should be an empirical science. The targets just mentioned by John Conlisk are not our enemies, but hypotheses that should be subject to empirical tests and theoretical examinations.

Let us examine the debate among economists on equilibrium versus disequilibrium economics. First, I would like to quote Kaldor:

The powerful attraction of the habits of thought engendered by "general equilibrium economics" has become a major obstacle to the development of economics as a science — meaning by the term "science" a body of theorems based on assumptions that are empirically derived (from observations) and which embody hypotheses that are capable of verification both in regard to the assumptions and the predictions.   Nicholas Kaldor, 1972, "The Irrelevance of Equilibrium Economics," *Economic Journal*, 82, 1237–1238.

Weintraub, an equilibrium economist, amplified this view:

The "equilibrium" story is one in which empirical work, ideas of facts and falsification, played no role at all. There are thus some lessons and implications for both the history and philosophy of economics.   E. Roy Weintraub, 1983, "On the Existence of a Competitive Equilibrium: 1930–1954," *Journal of Economic Literature*, 21, 1–39.

Current debate on equilibrium versus disequilibrium economics reminds me of a story in the history of physics. After the Michelson–Morley experiment rejected the validity of the Galilean relativity principle for light, Lorenz proposed a contraction hypothesis to save classical mechanics. Einstein's relativity theory simply combined a new relativity principle of the constancy of the light velocity with the Lorentz transformation. We can see how the two approaches were clashed at the beginning, but were unified at the fruitful end.

On the controversy of chaos vs. noise in business cycle theory, I have some suggestions for Brock's test. Brock used a line to connect the subsequent points in the phase portrait. This causes big trouble to tell whether it's chaotic. If you just put points there, it's quite easy to identify whether it is chaos or noise. The only requirement is that the time interval of the observed time series should not be very large. It is hard to judge for annual aggregate data, but monthly or weekly data may reveal essential information about the deterministic component in economic movements.

One obstacle in advancing empirical economic science is analogous to short-term profit seeking in business. It is the struggle for quick publication. The competition in the States is so high that most people rush for the short-term goal without undertaking long-term investment. In business, perhaps, that is why Americans gradually lose to the Japanese. In the winter of 1987, when the *New York Times* published my response to the article on stock market chaos by James Gleick, I immediately received many phone calls from bankers and brokers. They hoped we can provide some easy tools to predict the stock market movement and make day-to-day decisions to make a fortune! After I told them that there would be a long way to go in developing empirical economic science, their enthusiasm quickly disappeared.

Actually, there is no short-cut for economic studies. We physicists have spent years — maybe 10 years, or even 100 years — to find out the particular mechanism to understand a specific phenomenon. After that, we could make useful predictions. I think we should keep public expectations low for a while. At the same time we need to encourage public support.

DOSI: I'm going to follow up on the comparison of an evolutionary approach vis-à-vis the standard theory. We see in the practice of the discipline two quite different strategies: "incrementalist" and "radical" models. The incrementalist view involves marginal changes in the assumptions and initial restrictions: add an epsilon of "irrationality" to behaviors (as, for example, in Akerlof and Yellen), marginally change informational availability, or even simply change the form of the postulated utility functions and see what happens. Usually, the theoretical outcomes radically change. This raises the question: could you make incremental relaxations on that research program and still say something useful about the particular empirical object that you are trying to understand?

To answer this we need to ask what the economic discipline is about. Is it in an exercise of empirical interpretation, or is it a deductive exercise simply about notional and logically coherent worlds? I share the "naiveté" of Ping Chen and believe that economics is about an economic object, that it's about explaining something that empirically happened.

My impression is that you can indeed use semineoclassical models, say, with equilibrium assumptions but relaxing other highly demanding auxiliary assumptions, e.g., on information availability, market completeness, and the like. Important results can and have come from this approach. In my view, however, these results, e.g., on the multiplicity of equilibria, the importance of history, and the importance of various kinds of extraeconomic institutions, are essentially negative: while they don't help directly the interpretation of particular empirical "stylized facts," they provide a fortiori theoretical results on the importance of the above phenomena. But, then, if one theoretically obtains, e.g., multiple equilibria, what is the process leading to their selection, if any? How do agents actually behave in a highly nonlinear environment?

In particular, let me briefly address two issues central to both neoclassical and "evolutionary" theories. One is the problem of choice, behavior, and institutions. In my view, even at a theoretical level, there is often *no* optimal behavior. The agents develop robust problem-solving routines that apply to entire classes of problems that emerge in a world that continues to change and "expand." One way to put it is that the more complex the environment, the less you can expect maximization.

Hence, institutions emerge, meaning also repeated behavior: routines (and metarules to change them) to cope with a complex world ridden with unexpected circumstances. This, in my view, is the general story. People are socialized in institutions, they develop community structures in institutions, and under certain circumstances they develop particular classes of institutions called markets. Individuals also evolve norms and beliefs, context dependent notions of "interest" and "rationality," but in this evolutionary/institutionalist story even the pursuit of self-seeking goals is *learned*, but on the ground of the community structure that they already have. Here, the challenge for evolutionary theories is to show that norms (and innovative changes in the norms themselves) are *emergent properties* of far-from-equilibrium interactions. (In this respect, works such as those by Axelrod and John Miller are initial explorations of a fruitful research perspective.)

The second issue concerns the notion of equilibrium and relates the concept of *opportunity* with the existence/inexistence of a *hill-climbing process*. If you focus on the properties of equilibria, you also implicitly or explicitly assume that the opportunities offered by an environment are limited and that ultimately it is some sort of "scarcity constraint" that defines its asymptotic properties. Here I see also a potentially misleading application of genetic algorithm methods. Assume a stationary world, start with very "bounded-rational" agents, allow them to learn, and sooner or later they will converge to a traditional equilibrium.

The crucial point, however, is, in my view, nonstationarity and the endogeneity of opportunities that the system explores. As Prigogine and Allen have told us in this conference, dissipative systems, even in natural sciences, hardly show such hill-climbing properties. This is more so in social systems, which are, loosely speaking, "hyperdissipative:" agents explore only a minute subset of the whole opportunity space and are often constrained not by the "objective world" but by their own competences. Free lunches are always potentially there.

For modeling strategies, one should look for two kinds of robust empirical generalizations, namely (1) *micro*generalizations on behaviors, building on the type of evidence that John Sterman and Vernon Smith have discussed in this conference, and (2) more aggregate evidence on variables such as prices, productivity, investment, innovation diffusion, and income growth. The big theoretical challenge ahead is how meaningfully to link the two. My guess is that you will end up with history-dependent stories with hills that disappear in the process of climbing them, other hills that endogenously emerge, and a lot of diversity, exploration, mistakes, and selection.

I will conclude with an even more philosophical remark. If there is a robust, evolutionary strength of the market, it's not that of optimally allocating resources. Actually, the market allocates resources with a lot of waste. What markets do is they allow decentralized processes of exploration of things that do not yet exist, and that, of course, a planner could not forecast. But markets themselves are *in-*

stitutions, made up, among other things, of (1) mechanisms of interaction among agents, (2) norms of behavior, and (3) specific contributions of competences and (non-Bayesian) "models-of-the-world." Indeed, contemporary political experience and urgent normative challenges force the whole profession ("evolutionary" or not) to think about prescriptions well beyond standard exercises on the Pareto properties of different equilibria.

WINTER: I've taught a one-semester economics course at the Yale School of Management for several years now. For many students it's an introductory course; for some it's also a terminal course in economics. The idea is to try to tell them in the space of one semester something that's helpful for future managers. I have a very simple design principle that I use in trying to decide what kind of things to include and how to treat them. The design principle is "nothing but the truth."

To suggest how I approach the problem of "the truth," I tell them about the law of one price and, as Vernon Smith would probably say, that even in markets that are not face to face it has a lot of force. For example, in posted price markets the opportunity for customers to switch among sellers in order to find price advantages is a discipline that tends to enforce this law. I explain that, but get some skepticism.

Well, one time I spent a Saturday afternoon going up and down a three-mile stretch of New Haven road, looking at gasoline prices and got 64 observations. After a little controlling for cash versus credit and regular versus unleaded, etc., I computed the price dispersion. The standard deviation was about 7 cents/gallon. Given that the price was about $1.00/gallon, that's about 7%. So, I take that back to my course and I say, "See, it works. The law of one price holds." And they say, "What?! You just said that there was standard deviation of 7 cents/gallon." And I say, "Yes, but it wasn't 70 cents/gallon."

Nobody in his right mind believes the law of one price for an unrigged market has to be right to the last decimal place. Nonetheless, there's a quantitative question: how accurate is the law of one price as a description of gasoline prices on that road? Next, I said, "Okay, 7 cents/gallon is the standard deviation; that's how accurate the law of one price is for this particular problem, and so that gives you some kind of feel for what the reality's like." Is such a number of surprising or unsurprising? That's one of the problems.

Turning to the modeling of novelty or emergent structures or creativity, there's always a sense in which the novelty isn't true novelty because you put it into the logical structure. Nonetheless, I think that examples we've seen here illustrate that we may be getting close to being able to show the appearance of new structures and new levels of rationality in economic actors. The question that I want to raise about this is (it's analogous to the question about the law of one price), how are you going to calibrate the results of that effort? How are you going to describe whether you've done a good job of giving a model of the emergence of novelty or improvement in performance, or learning?

What I want to warn against is bias based on our particular historical and social and personal positions. If we get a model of an artificial actor of some sort that turns out to be a lot smarter than we are, should we reject it because it conflicts with bounded rationality; saying, "Okay, we've got too much computation power, we have to turn it back?" Or, suppose you get one that's a lot dumber than we are and say, "Heck, human beings are a lot smarter than that," so that's not a good model either?

You have to recognize that in the real world there are big performance improvements, at least over extended periods of time. For example, semiconductors achieved large orders of magnitude improvement over several years. Contrastingly, John Sterman's example shows that at least without much practice, some smart people can do some pretty dumb things on some pretty simple problems. Evidently, there's a big span to human levels of performance in terms of practice, in terms of resources available to support research. Given such a big span, we don't want to reject models because they don't look just like what we would be able to do at the time. We want to compare them with a realistically broad span of levels of human performance.

LIPSEY: To make a revolution, you must kill some people and destroy some human capital, usually, however, much more than is absolutely necessary. I suspect this revolution in economics will be no exception. I want, however, to put in a little plea for the orthodox, and their ideas, that we do not try to use the intellectual guillotine any more than absolutely necessary.

Making innovation and technical change endogenous, and developing the requisite dynamics, will be revolutionary enough. But we should not throw out the baby of great neoclassical insights. If we do make that mistake, those who are in the business of applying economics to current, everyday issues will part company with the revolutionaries. The applied economists will use what works, no matter how imperfect it is. And they will go on doing so until it is replaced with something that deals with dynamic, long term behavior better, while incorporating what economists now understand about the working of those individual markets that are not unreasonably handled using static equilibrium models.

CHEN: A scientific revolution is both different from and similar to a political revolution. For example, relativity only extended our understanding — it didn't *kill* Newtonian mechanics, but it generalized it. Sometimes, however, the dominating paradigm kills innovative ideas.

We hope this conference will help improve the dialog among scholars with diversified backgrounds. If we want to progress in economics, we should — to paraphrase Newton — stand on the shoulders of the giants!

NELSON: Let me continue that and suggest some things that one might try to remember as this revolution goes forward. We want a deeper structural understanding of those situations in which positive feedback generates instabilities, generates self-reinforcement and self-organization, but we should also keep in mind the large class of circumstances in which negative feedback or the absence of feedback gives to classical economics some substantial purchase on what we could expect to happen.

While we're doing this, we should try to keep in mind that while history matters in some cases history is stronger, and in other cases it's weaker, that real dynamic processes run at different rates in real time. In specifying systems it is therefore important to identify the characteristic rates in real time relative to the other dynamic processes, so that we don't imagine a world is dimensionless in the time scale.

I think it's terribly important to remember that human beings have cognitive beliefs and/or theories about processes that coevolve with behavioral states, information systems, or culture, and that some of those systems coevolve very slowly so that they become anchors for many of the shorter processes. But it would be wrong to imagine that they are totally exogenous. Instead, endogeny and exogeny are aspects of the time scale that we're considering. Finally, I would say that history itself is not just a string of events, because human systems don't observe all of the events; they are selected. Consequently, one of the things that happens in the evolution of cognitive states is a continual attempt to recover better observations on past events, and so our history in the sense of the sequence of reigning models or theories is subject to discontinuous updating and nonlinear switching from one theory or another about the world. That can become a disturbing force, a disturbing aspect that impinges on other systems. It's only when we can move to that level that we will begin to get close to dealing with the histories of human organization and human society. That should be our mission.

STERMAN: I'm excited about many of the developments here. We've seen models which generate complex nonlinear dynamics, which learn, and which evolve — all phenomena of great importance for economics. What concerns me is the validity of the decision processes posited for the actors in these models. Compared to empirical studies of decision making reported here and elsewhere, the simulated actors are often much smarter than we humans are and sometimes much too limited. While models in which the rationality of the actors differ from that of real people may be quite useful at the beginning of a new field, we must not be content with such models but strive to capture the cognitive, informational, institutional, and historical limitations that bound human rationality. Yet we will never be able to discriminate among competing models of decision making by considering the outputs of the systems alone — the *results* of decision making. We must enlarge the definition of "data" to include field study of decision-making *process*. Observation of the processes by decisions are actually made — in the lab and in the field — will both suggest and constrain the heuristics that may be usefully included in our models. Research coupling such psychological, organizational, and institutional studies with modern nonlinear systems theory offers the best hope for a behaviorally sound disequilibrium foundation for the study of economic and social dynamics.

MACKEY: I'd like to make three comments that reflect my experience in a totally different area from this.

Ten years ago in mathematical biology quite a few people got very excited by "catastrophe theory," and were making wild and fantastic claims: it was going to help us understand propagation of nervous impulse, it was going to help us understand cell division, the onset of cancer, prison riots, etc., etc. All of these claims turned out to be a gross exaggerations.

There is a similar danger for chaos theory. The point is, in my mind, not whether there's chaos. It's not a question of chaos versus no chaos. The question is, Where is the phenomenon that you're looking at coming from? What's giving rise to it?

The second point is that the purpose of any revolution in science is to try to upgrade your discipline, to try to give it new insights, new ways of looking at things. How do you impress people? In biology we have taken systems or subsystems in which we've got good data and where we feel we have a good idea about the way they work. We were able to construct physiologically realistic models of those, and show that the consequence of those models was precisely what we were seeing in the laboratory or clinically. That's the important thing for people to do in mathematical economics.

The third point, and this is not a criticism, it is simply an observation. There is currently great excitement within the scientific world about "neural networks." There was a meeting in Boston last August on neural networks attended by 10,000 people! Many neurophysiologists started to get very excited about neural networks, many subscribing to the *Journal of Neural Networks*. They are now starting to realize that what we called neural networks have absolutely nothing to do with the way the nervous system functions! It's a name that got tacked onto an area that considers how you can construct artificial systems that learn to do things. Are we seeing the same kind of thing here? So the question that I have — I don't expect an answer, but it's something that is important to think about is — are you really talking about an artificial system that you can't validate?

SCHWEFEL: One possible criterion of whether nonlinear economics might be a success may be the answer to the question, "What does it mean for economic policy?" If one has macroeconomic time series that are irregular and generated by very simple deterministic chaotic systems, what does it mean for economic policy? Does it mean that economic policy can't do anything because we don't know the initial conditions? Or would that mean we should set up some rules and framework for economic policy within which the economies operate?

ARTHUR: I'd like to respond to a couple of comments. I'm old enough to remember catastrophe theory. Point well taken. I think we should watch out for fads; techniques shouldn't be *too* far in advance of actual economic problems.

But I want to come back to what Dick Lipsey said. And that is, is there a revolution going on, and are babies getting thrown out with the bath water? What I would like ideally is to teach my students to look at an economic problem, the one that they're looking at, and say, "Okay, what axioms are at work here? Are there diminishing returns at work here? Is this perfectly continuous? Are we assuming it's reasonable that people are making maximizing choices, etc? People ought to be trained to know the domain they're working in. If you're working on a simple problem with diminishing returns, you can expect an equilibrium and there's no sweat. If you're working with increasing returns, and it's a game, you might expect multiple Nash. Then you have to start to worry about the selection problem. In graduate economic theory courses we teach students the equivalent of one tool. We teach them to use a hammer and then we complain that they treat everything else as if it were a nail. We should teach them that not everything is a nail; that in some cases you need a screwdriver, or a Phillips screwdriver, or something else. So the important thing in economics is not that you can apply this or that fad; the important thing, I believe, is to recognize the problem for what it is. It contains a learning component, or it contains an adaptive component, or it contains increasing returns, or there's a possibility of chaos; recognize it for what it is and bring to bear the appropriate analysis. So, I see something like what we're talking about here not at all as a revolution, I just see it as a widening.

LESOURNE: I would like to come back to the question raised by Sidney Winter about the appropriate level of bounded rationality. You may have processes in which, whether the behavior of individuals is sophisticated or very primitive, has no impact at all on the development of the process. In other processes the evolution is very sensitive to the type of sophistication of the routine. And in still other processes, if you have only a minority with a sort of sophisticated behavior, even though it is a minority, it has an impact on the whole evolution of the process.

WINTER: On this issue of the quantitative magnitudes, one big difference between economic evolution and biological evolution is the drastically different time scales that are interesting. Take two behaviors in an economic context that have a difference of growth of 2% a year. That is an enormously fast selection by biological standards. To drive the inferior type out of the population does not take millions of years at 2% a year. But for lots of economic purposes, that means that the proportion of the types in the population 5 years from now is not really all that much different from what it is right now. So, even though there may be these performance differentials out there, if you want to base arguments on one type driving out, you have to ask, "Well, how fast does that spread?" or "How fast does that grow relative to the other type of behavior?"

ALLEN: The ideas that we're discussing can change the nature of the scientific method considerably. The view that a model that can be totally falsified or validated has to be changed. Instead, I think, we need to find models which are *useful*. We must restrict our ambitions a little.

The process of modeling nonlinear systems is a learning experience. When you put together the micromechanisms that seem to be present in a system, then you can get out of it macroscopic behavior which you may have observed, or you may *not yet have observed*. One simple case is a fishing model that had two regimes of operation that were very different, which I hadn't thought of before running the model. I ran the fishing model of a thousand years, and I didn't see anything extraordinary. I ran it again with identical conditions but the noise sequence was slightly different and it fell into a second basin of attraction after 40 years and then sat there for a very long time. What does that mean? It means that I could have run "life," if you like, for a thousand years and not have seen that second regime. Whether or not incredibly sophisticated techniques could have in some way inferred the properties of the second regime from the trajectory of the first one, it is much easier to just put the mechanisms together and run the model and find there are two regimes. So, in fact, you could *discover* something that you didn't know, essentially. I'm sure there's a lot of other things lurking in that system that I still don't know. I do know what I put in the model; but then there's the real world "out there." So I keep on, in a sense, *with humility* submitting my model to the empirical test. If I do, then I will probably keep on learning things.

Now I would like to invent a word which I call *robustish*. Because of irreversibility in open systems, learning isn't going to stop, and heuristics maybe get to a sort of *robustish* state through successive accidents and catastrophes. We should use our models to avoid doing completely stupid things. Whether we can do optimal things, I say, is a completely different question.

A final remark on fads. There's a school of English philosophers known as the Monty Python Flying Circus. There is one particular telling passage in its classic work, which is called *The Life of Brian*, where the new messiah (who is Brian) is being acclaimed by the crowd who say, "Speak to us! Speak to us! Speak to us!" And he says, "Okay. Look, why should I speak to you? You're all individuals." And they say, "Yes! We're all individuals. We're all individuals. But speak to us!" And he says, "You're all individuals, think for yourselves! Think for yourselves!" And they say, "Yes! We're all individuals. Think for ourselves! Think for ourselves!" And a voice says, "But what shall we think?" And the crowd takes up the cry, "What shall we think?" The point of this simply is that people always want a new recipe, and one has to be very careful, for there is no new recipe which will solve all your problems. I think that the message of the new recipe is that you never solve all your problems because as soon as you do something, you will discover that there are aspects that you haven't thought of that emerge.

Summing up, then: Life in the universe is actually just positive and negative feedback loops and noise.

DAY: Since you brought us back to irreversibility, Peter, this might be a good point to call on Professor Prigogine.

PRIGOGINE: Many years ago I read a book by Levi-Strauss who made the distinction between mechanical societies and thermodynamic societies. He, by the way, preferred mechanical societies in which nothing is supposed to happen — let's say New Guinean type societies, small societies that are involved in small wars between themselves, but essentially trying to keep a steady state — over thermodynamic societies that are running down, according to Levi-Strauss, he believed in the "malediction" of time. I am simplifying a little. I believe that rationality would be quite differently understood in these societies. I suppose that in a mechanical society, as he imagined, you have this warfare going on, killing one or two of your neighbors from time to time was considered to be very rational, but killing too many would be irrational. The concept of rationality is obviously historically bounded, that is what I want to mention first. When we speak of bounded rationality, we must keep in mind the historical context.

Second, we have been speaking about a revolution of some kind. Certainly, in mathematics and physics there has been a revolution. The revolution is coming from two directions: one is of the classification of dynamic systems, which marks the end of the universality of dynamics; and second, there is, if I may say so, the discovery of role novelties. Of course, you can discuss the question: what is a novelty? You can push it further and further and further. But anyway, there are discontinuities and the appearance of new structures — you can see them in the laboratory; you can see them everywhere. The question whether this change will have some consequences for economics or not — that is something that you have to decide, after all, not me. But certainly there is a different scientific atmosphere that appears today.

One of the lessons is that even relatively simple systems have different modes of functioning. In other words, you take the same molecules with the same type of interactions, and put them into different environments and you have approach to equilibrium, limit cycles, chaos, bursting . . . all kinds of things. With the *same* molecules. Only the environment or the macroscopic constraints are different. That, perhaps, marks the difference between simple and complex systems. In this sense a harmonic oscillator has only one type of function, but a population of molecules — with very *simple* interactions — has already many types of functions. This is a quite remarkable feature because it shows that if this is so for very rudimentary objects, obviously it will be even *more* so for the more complicated objects such as living beings.

We are living in a period of the decline of rationality in the traditional sense. It is very remarkable that classical science started with the most empirialistic claims. Essentially, the claim was a transparent, complete understanding of the physical world, on all levels. Newtonian laws, written in general form by Lagrange and Laplace, were an attempt to describe the universal behavior of the universe in the sense that it was only a question of scaling it up with the right interactions. This is the type of thinking that has been decaying since the beginning of this century. It is decaying because universal constants appear, it is decaying because of the classification of dynamic systems, it is decaying because we make a distinction between "close to equilibrium" and "far from equilibrium," and so on. It is going in the direction of classification, of finding mechanisms, of splitting things into groups where novelties can appear, where things have to be categorized according to the circumstances. So, we are losing the possibility of simple, universal laws.

From this point of view we are just at the beginning, and I think that in some way or another, this type of understanding will spill over to economics, like it's spilling over already to biology, to artificial intelligence, and to other fields. The discussions that we have here are taking place at a well-defined moment in the history of science, and that they are only one aspect of discussions that — using other terminologies — are also taking place at other meetings.

DAY: Thank you very much, Professor Prigogine. Well, the afternoon is drawing to a close. It's time to end this Round Table discussion, which has been extremely interesting. I thank all of the panelists and the audience. At this point, at Professor Prigogine's request, I shall make some closing remarks.

Many people are recognizing an adaptive, evolutionary, nonlinear economics as a new field of play, a new set of intriguing ideas to explore — and not only that — there are other people to talk to about them. That's fine, but I see little to be gained from attacking previous developments in economics, any more than there would be from attacking mainstream physics. One recalls Walras' excitement — you can feel it on every page as he transformed economic insights into mathematical notation. He attempted already to model the adaptive nature of the price system. And Marshall, also one of the founders of neoclassical economics, is a source of inspiration for adaptive, evolutionary economics. Schumpeter, who should probably be credited with being the real father of evolutionary economics, was an admirer of Walras and Pareto and based his own theory solidly on the neoclassical core. Most of us who have been working on ideas of adaptation and evolution in economics have been inspired by his ideas. We would like to build on the foundations of our science as he did, even if it means taking some "revolutionary" departures.

In this connection I remember one of Charlie Chaplin's funniest scenes, perhaps the funniest scene in all cinema. Charlie is walking along when a lumber truck drives by with a load of long beams. Stapled on the end of one beam is a red flag. The truck lurches over a bump and the red flag falls. Charlie notices this, waddles over to the red flag, raises it and begins waving wildly after the truck as it lumbers on down the street. As he goes running after the truck, waving the red flag, a huge army of burly workers comes marching around the corner, five thousand strong, carrying on a workers' demonstration. And here's Charlie, waving the red flag at the very front of the procession. Naturally, the police, who were just around the next corner, nabbed him as a revolutionary. Maybe some here who have been working in this area for some time feel a little like that!

Actually, as the field matures, scholars will be doing exactly what's been going on in neoclassical economics for the past 50 years. We'll be trying to give greater precision to ideas that are growing up in this field; we'll be trying to formulate them in more general and more effective ways; we'll be trying to give empirical body to the ideas that are emerging; and we'll be exploring the policy relevance to an ever-broadening range of problems.

As these developments are pursued, certain distractions should be avoided. One is discrete versus continuous time. This is partially a matter of convenience, it's partially a matter of the particular phenomenon we're considering. Neural nets and more general switching phenomenon are frequently studied with discrete state spaces and iterated maps. Continuous time, while possibly at the foundation of what's going on, would simply clutter the analysis, and so we wouldn't want to use it. In other cases, we should be using continuous time.

Macro versus micro is another foolish thing to argue about. We *have* to have macroeconomics because we have to have some simple ways of organizing our knowledge and making decisions. I should hope that adaptive, evolutionary, non-linear economics can help identify the way we ought to specify macro models.

As models are refined, generalized, and developed further, the really important ingredients of this general approach should be kept in the forefront.

First is the explicitly dynamic explanation of economic phenomena. Second is the representation of adaptive behavior. Third is the concern with out-of-equilibrium or disequilibrium aspects of economic processes. And fourth is the recognition that complex dynamic behavior can be explainable in part by endogenous variables and forces, and not only by exogenous shocks.

As far as chaos is concerned, I would judge it to be a side show: but sideshows *are* important parts of the circus. Chaos illustrates something fundamental about the concerns that we have here. Chaos is *not* a theory any more than "catastrophe theory" is a theory. Nonlinear dynamics is the fundamental method. Chaos is just one of the properties of dynamic systems that we now know is worth looking for. It illustrates very well how certain qualitative properties of the real world that may have seemed inexplicable before *can* in fact be explained in terms of intrinsic hypotheses of structure.

Editors' Note

The preceding discussion is a substantially abbreviated version of the original tape recording. Each discussant has had final approval of the edited version of his own remarks.

Author Index

Alchian, Armen A., 19, 20, 132, 147
Allen, Peter M., 91, 101, 102, 103, 104, 107
Anderson, Philip, 20
Andersson, A. E., 93
Anthes, R. A., 232, 245
Argoul, F., 217
Arrow, Kenneth J., 20
Arthur, W. B., 59, 97, 102
Ashley, R., 201, 205, 259, 260

Bak, P., 59, 75
Bakken, B., 61
Baldwin, W. L., 92
Bandura, A., 96, 132
Baras, F., 230
Barnett, H. G., 93, 217
Barnett, W. A., 202, 229, 233, 254, 260,
    262n2, 280
Batten, David, 20, 22
Belair, J., 60
Benhabib, Jess, 170
Ben-Mizrachi, A., 224
Bennetin, G., 77
Bieshaar, H., 58
Blanchard, O. J., 127
Bohr, T., 59
Box, G. E. P., 256
Boyd, Robert, 132, 138, 142, 145, 148
Bradford, James, 172
Brandstater, A., 217
Brillinger, David R., 257
Brock, W. A., 217, 227, 233, 255, 256
Brockett, P. L., 201
Bronfenbrenner, M., 64
Buchanan, J. M., 97
Burns, Arthur, 59

Casti, J., 20, 22
Cavalli-Sforza, L. L., 133
Charney, J., 232
Chen, P., 233, 217, 229, 230, 232, 242, 243,
    248, 249, 254, 260

Choi, Seugmook S., 262n2
Cigno, Alessandro, 20
Clark, Colin, 16
Cohen, Kolman J., 19
Colding-Jorgensen, M., 59, 75
Conlisk, John, 114, 118, 131, 132
Cournot, A. A., 19
Crutchfield, J. P., 227, 266, 268
Cumming, A., 77
Cyert, Richard, 19

Dale, 227
Dana, Rose-Anne, 170, 233
Darwin, Charles, 18
David, P., 97
Day, Richard H., 20, 22, 28, 30, 32, 39, 91,
    93, 98, 169, 170, 175, 230
Dechert, W. D., 217, 255, 256
DeCoster, Gregory P., 262n1
Denekere, Raymond, 170
Doan, T., 266
Dominguez, K. M., 245
Dorfman, J. H., 293
Dosi, Giovanni, 20, 93, 96
Dunford, C., 133, 145
Durham, W. H., 145

Edgerton, R. B., 132
Eigen, M., 93
Eliasson, Gunnar, 20
Engle, R. F., 127

Fair, R. C., 245
Fama, Eugene, 201
Farmer, J. D., 221, 229, 267
Feigenbaum, M., 77
Feldman, M. W., 133
Ford, J., 266
Forrester, J. W., 23, 43, 60, 63, 64
Foster, K. A., 293
Frank, M., 217, 222
Freeman, Christopher, 20, 93

French, Kenneth, 207
Friedman, M., 19, 232, 244
Fritzsch, Harold, 18
Fuller, J. L., 132

Garcia-Pelayo, R., 228
Gel'fand, I. M., 248
Gencay, R., 217
Geweke, John, 280, 281
Gilad, B., 95
Glass, L., 60, 75, 217, 223, 225, 246
Glazier, J., 60
Gleick, J., 266
Goldfeld, S., 293
Goldstein, J., 63
Goodwin, R. M., 245, 301
Gordon, R. J., 241, 244
Gordon, Robert A., 58
Graham, A., 59
Grandmont, Jean-Michel, 170
Granger, C. W. J., 127, 229
Grassberger, P., 222, 224, 232, 266
Griliches, Z., 96
Grossmann, S., 223, 227
Groves, Theodore, 20, 22
Gu, Mu, 181n1
Guevara, M. R., 217

Hagen, E. E., 95
Halem, M., 232
Hansen, Alvin, 16
Hao, B.-L., 245
Harnett, D. L., 196
Harris, L., 209, 213
Harrod, Roy, 16
Hasegawa, H. H., 12, 248
Hayek, F. A., 97, 98n1, 132, 147
Henon, M., 223
Hentschel, H. G. E., 227, 229
Herman, Robert, 88
Hinich, Melvin J., 201, 202, 205, 254, 256,
     258, 259, 260
Hirshleifer, Jack, 131, 148
Holland, J., 104
Holst, J., 63
Hoyt, H., 58
Hsieh, D. A., 201, 217
Huang, Weihong, 169, 175

Isola, S., 248

Iwai, Katsuhito, 20

Jastrow, R., 232
Jenkins, G. M., 256
Jensen, M. H., 59, 75, 77
Johansson, B., 20, 22
Jovanovic, B., 114
Judge, G. G., 289

Kahneman, D., 239
Kalaba, R., 289, 293, 297, 298, 299
Kaldor, Nicholas, 313
Kalman, R. E., 299
Kang, H., 223
Kaplan, David, 246
Katz, S., 147
Kaufman, Stuart A., 21
Keynes, John Maynard, 45
Kleinknecht, A., 58
Knight, Frank, 19
Kondratiev, N. D., 58
Koopmans, T. C., 224
Kostelich, E., 223
Kot, M., 232
Kuznets, Simon, 14, 15–16, 58

LaBaron, B., 201
Laffond, G., 151
Larsen, E., 217
Lasota, Andrzej, 26, 170, 175, 179
Laws of Nature and Human Conduct, 3
LeBaron, Blake, 262n3
Leibniz, G. W., 4, 18
Leontief, Wassily, 313
LeRoy, Stephen F., 169
Lesourne, Jacques, 151
Lesser, M., 107
Libchaber, A., 266
Lighthill, J., 4
Lin, Tsong Yau, 30, 32, 39
Linsay, P. S., 77
Litterman, R., 266
Long, C. D., Jr., 58, 64
Lorenz, E. N., 14, 225
Lucas, Robert E., 19, 21, 30
Lumsden, C., 133, 145

MacDonald, G. M., 114
McGlade, J. M., 101, 103, 104
McInish, T. H., 209, 213

Mackey, Michael C., 170, 175, 223, 225
Malgrange, P., 233
Malthus, Thomas, 15
Mandelbrot, B. B., 75
March, James G., 19, 94
Mark, Hans, 16
Marshall, Alfred, 15, 19, 20
Marx, Karl, 15, 45
Matthews, R. C. O., 98n3
May, Robert, 23
Mayer-Kress, G., 223
Mill, J. S., 15
Miller, J. H., 104
Miller, Rupert G., Jr., 200
Minsky, Hyman, 59
Mitchell, Douglas W., 262n1
Mitchell, Wesley C., 16, 58, 59
Modigliani, Franco, 19
Montrucchio, Luigi, 170
Moore, G. H., 58
Mosekilde, E., 60, 63, 64, 217
Muth, John F., 183

Nelson, Charles R., 127, 222, 223
Nelson, Richard R., 20, 91, 97, 114, 118,
    132, 143, 147
Newbold, P., 229
Nicolis, C., 222, 227
Nicolis, G., 102, 222, 227, 230, 245

Ord, J. K., 209, 213
Osborne, M. F. M., 232
Ott, E., 228, 229, 266, 268, 277

Papandreau, A. G., 20
Patterson, Douglas M., 201, 202, 205, 256,
    259, 260
Pelikan, Steve, 170
Petrosky, T., 6, 248
Pianigiani, Giulio, 26, 28, 170, 175
Pines, David, 20
Plosser, C. I., 127, 222
Poincaré, Henri, 6–9, 11–12, 48
Polanyi, M., 93
Pool, R., 217
Popper, Karl, 91
Poterba, James M., 260
Priestly, M., 256
Prigogine, Ilya, 3, 6, 93, 102, 230, 245, 248
Procaccia, I., 222, 224, 227, 229, 266

Pulliam, R., 133, 145

Quah, D., 127

Ramsey, J. B., 217, 229, 232, 241, 254, 255,
    262n1, 223
Randers, J., 61
Rasmussen, S., 63, 64
Reichl, L. E., 230
Reinganum, J. F., 92
Ricardo, David, 15
Richardson, G., 60
Richerson, Peter J., 132, 138, 142, 145, 148
Riggleman, J. R., 58
Riley, J., 131
Robertson, D. H., 16
Rogalski, R., 207
Rogers, A., 133
Rogers, E. M., 96
Rosenberg, N., 95
Rosenthal, T., 132
Rossler, O. E., 218
Rostow, Elspeth D., 14
Rostow, W. W., 58, 61, 241
Rotemberg, Julio J., 260
Rothman, P., 217, 229, 232, 254, 255, 262n1
Ruelle, D., 248, 266
Ruspini, E. H., 297

Sahal, D., 93
Samuelson, Paul, 16
Sanglier, M., 102, 103
Saphir, W., 12, 248
Sayers, C. L., 217, 222, 229, 232, 254, 255,
    262n1
Scarr, S., 132
Schaffer, W. M., 232
Schein, E. H., 132
Scheinkman, J., 201, 256, 262n3
Schieve, W. C., 228
Schrödinger, Erwin, 18
Schumpeter, J., 14, 15–16, 20, 45–47, 58,
    92, 95, 97
Scitovsky, Tibor, 94
Scott, J. T., 92
Segerstrom, P. S., 114
Semmler, W., 59
Senge, P., 59, 66
Shackle, G. L. S., 98n2
Shafer, Wayne, 170

Shapiro, M. D., 245
Shrier, A., 60, 217
Sidorowich, J. J., 267
Siegel, Sidney, 196
Silverberg, Gerald, 20
Simon, Herbert, 3, 4, 19, 20, 94
Sims, C. A., 266
Smale, Stephen, 23
Smirlock, M., 207
Smith, Adam, 15
Smith, S. S., 132
Smith, Vernon L., 183, 184. 196
Soete, Luc, 20
Solomon, A. M., 239
Sonneborn-Schmick, B., 223, 227
Stark, L., 207
Steiner, G. A., 95
Stengers, I., 3, 4, 102
Stengos, T., 217, 222
Sterman, J. D., 58, 59, 60, 63, 64, 65f, 66, 68, 217, 241
Stokey, Nancy L., 30
Stoll, Hans R., 172
Sturis, J., 60
Suchanek, Gerry L., 183, 184, 196
Swinney, H. L., 217, 223
Szebehely, Victor G., 5, 6

Takens, F., 218, 266
Tesfatsion, L., 289, 293, 297, 298, 299, 300n2
Thompson, R. W., 132
Tirole, Jean, 183
Togeby, M., 60, 75
Tribbia, J. J., 232, 245
Tse, Raymond, 30, 39
Tversky, A., 239

Vanberg, V. J., 97
Van Duijn, J. J., 58, 63, 241
Van Maanen, J., 132

Van Valen, L., 106
Vasko, T., 63
Veitch, J., 293, 300n2
Vilenkin, N. Na., 248
von Boehm, J., 75
von Neumann, John, 26

Wallace, Alfred Russel, 18
Walliss, K. F., 245
Walras, Leon, 19
Walter, J. L., 28, 230
Watts, D., 256
Weidlich, W., 93
Weinberg, R. A., 132
Weintraub, E. Roy, 313
Weisskopf, W. A., 4
Wen, K. H., 248
Whittle, P., 266
Williams, Arlington W., 183, 184, 196
Wilson, E. O., 133, 145
Winter, Sidney G., 20, 91, 97, 98n3, 114, 118, 132, 143, 147
Withers, W. D., 228
Witt, U., 92, 96, 97
Wolf, A., 77, 222, 224
Wolinski, M. A., 202
Wood, R. A., 209, 213

Yorke, James A., 26, 175, 179, 228, 229
Yuan, H. J., 223, 229, 241
Yue, Piyu, 254, 260, 280
Yule, G. U., 266

Zabel, Edward, 172
Zarnowitz, Victor, 58, 59, 60, 81n1
Zeeman, E. C., 170
Zellner, Arnold, 278
Zhang, Z. L., 248
Zimmerman, B., 132
Zou, Gang, 34

Subject Index

Adaptation. *See also* Imitator firms; Innovation; Innovator firms
  in endogenous labor union formation, 154–56
  in evolutionary drive, 104–12
  in evolutionary economics, 19–21
  in neoclassical growth model, 31–37
Aliasing phenomenon, 201–04
Angle-action systems, 7
Arnol'd tongues, 75–77
Attractors. *See also* Lorenz attractor; Rossler attractor; Strange attractors
  Lorenz, 229
  low-dimensional, 230
  mathematical, 232
  modeling of, 230, 232–38
  Rossler Band as, 48, 53–54
Autocorrelation function, 218, 221, 228–29, 233–38. *See also* Correlation dimension

Baker transformation, 6, 7f, 12
Beliefs
  acquisition by imitation, 132–33
  in heterogeneous environment, 138–41
  model of distribution and modification, 133–34
  shaped by selection, 132
Bellman's principle of optimality, 29–30
Bernouilli shift, 6
Bispectrum test
  for chaos, 256–62
  in daily stock market returns, 202
Bootstrapping, 311
Bounded rationality. *See also* Unbounded rationality
  in analyzing growth, 130
  concept of, 3, 5
  in cyclical output growth, 113–14
  interaction with random innovation, 129
  of investment decision, 61, 68
  in long wave model, 64
  in neoclassical growth model, 30

relation to dynamical systems, 12–13
  in Schumpeter's work, 19
Business cycles. *See also* Juglar cycle; Kitchin cycle; Kondratiev wave or cycle; Kuznets cycle; Real business cycle
  durability of short, 58–59
  with entrainment of long wave, 68–75
  linking of different, 241
  nonlinearity in modulating amplitude, 63–64
Business cycle theory, 43

Cantor set, 229
Car-following equation, 84–85
Chaos. *See also* Correlation dimensions
  detecting economic, 230–38
  detection by maximum Lyapounov exponent, 221–22, 233–38, 242–43
  in dynamic economic process, 23
  in economic data, 254
  fractal dimension of, 222
  frustration, 77
  implications for economics, 49
  imputation in data residuals, 255
  research in economic, 244–45
  testing in monetary aggregates for, 231–38
  topological, 26, 27
Chaos, deterministic
  defined, 245
  identification of, 230
  presence of, 76–77
  time scale, 224–27
Chaotic process
  compared with statistical inference, 227
  examples of, 5
Cobweb theory of competitive markets, 22
Collisions, 9–10
Complex economic dynamics, 24, 28–30
Complex spectral theory, 6, 248. *See also* Bispectrum test
Construction cycle. *See* Kuznets cycle

Correlation coefficient, 85
Correlation dimensions. *See also* Fractal
  dimension
  estimates of, 238
  in estimating fractal dimension, 222
  identification of, 231
  in residual test, 228–29
Correlation resonances concept, 248–49
Correlations
  in classical dynamics, 10–11
  as distinct from forces, 9
  pre- and postcollision, 9–10
Creativity, 95, 103
Cycles. *See* Business cycle; Kondratiev wave
  or cycle; Kuznets cycle
Cyclical output growth model, 113–16

Data. *See also* Time series
  generated randomly or by deterministic
    process, 217–18
  problems of sparse, 223
  in statistical testing for chaos, 222–31
  time scale in chaos analysis, 22–27
Data sources
  for detection of chaos in economics,
    254–55
  in testing for chaos, 254, 260
  for test of nonlinearity and Gaussinity,
    260
Decision making
  in adaptive neoclassical model, 37–38
  distribution of beliefs in, 133–37
  in endogenous labor union formation,
    153–54
  optimal, 97
  tradition in, 131
Determinism, 246–47. *See also* Randomness
Deterministic process, 230, 233–38
Detrending, 232–33, 245
Devil's staircase, 74–75, 77, 78f
Discrepancy terms
  in multicriteria dynamic estimation,
    289–90
  residuals as estimates for, 289
  in stochastic analysis, 289
Disequilibrium system model, 64–68
Disequilibrium theory, 22, 24
Disorder, 11. *See also* Order
Distortion, 201–02
Dynamical systems. *See also* Bernouilli

shift; Estimation, dynamic;
  Evolutionary theory; Large Poincare
  systems (LPS); Maps, tent or quadratic;
  Multiple phase systems
  ergodic, 26–27
  linear and nonlinear, 25, 28, 102
  nonintegrable, 8
Dynamical systems, unstable, 4–6, 9. *See
  also* Kolmogorov systems; Large
  Poincare systems (LPS)
  correlation resonances concept in, 248
  irreversibility of, 12
  in nature, 12
  as property in socioeconomic systems, 12
Dynamics, classical, 3–4
  direct and inverse motion in, 9, 11
  limitation of, 11
Dynamics, economic, 21–24. *See also*
  Estimation, dynamic; Nonlinear
  dynamics

Economic systems
  neoclassical, 310
  nonlinear, 16–17, 60, 62–64
Entrainment process
  with change in amplitude, 75–77
  in disequilibrium system model, 64–75
  in economic fluctuations, 59–60
  nonlinear, 62–75, 80–81
Equilibrium
  intertemporal, 19, 22–24, 29–30
  statistical, 27
Equilibrium dynamics, 21–22
Ergodic theory. *See also* Maps, tent or
  quadratic
  derivations from, 28
  dynamic systems in, 26–27
  in economics, 170
Errors
  in evolution, 105–12
  during learning, 138
Estimation, dynamic
  flexible least squares approach to, 290–94
  multicriteria, 289–94, 298–99
  standard statisitical approach to, 293,
    294–98
Evolution
  defined, 91
  information for, 139–41
  in multicriteria estimation, 290–94

Evolution *(continued)*
    selection by, 103–12
    self-transformation in, 91
    of structure, 102–03
    using nonlinear dynamics, 34–38
Evolutionary drive concept, 104
Evolutionary theory. *See also* Innovation
    criteria for, 91–92
    dynamic approach to, 21–22
    pre- and postrevelation analysis, 92
    task of, 98
Expectations. *See also* Rational expectations
    assumption
    adaptive, 30–31
    bounded, 238–44
    in human systems, 101
    self-fulfilling, 59

Feedbacks
    delayed, 238–44
    in disequilibrium system model, 64–68
    loops in economic theory, 59–60
    positive and negative economic, 109, 111
Fiscal policy, compensatory, 52–56
Flexible least squares (FLS) estimation,
    289–94
Forces, 9. *See also* Sinusoidal forcing
Forecasting
    for deterministic nonlinear time series,
    266–67, 281–84
    econometric, 245
    using deterministic process, 241–43
    weather, 245–46
Fractal dimensions. *See also* Correlation
    dimensions
    concept of, 227–28
    of devil's staircase, 75
    estimate of, 222
Fractal structures, 227, 228–29
Frequency in phase, 28
Frobenius-Perron operator, 179

Gaussianity test, 256–62
General flexible least square (GFLS)
    approach, 293
Grassberger-Procaccia (GP) algorithm, 222,
    238, 256

Hamiltonian equations, 6–8
Hénon attractor, 229

Hénon model, 224
Hinich bispectrum test, 202, 256–62

Ignorance, 103–04, 112
Imaginative thinking model, 93–94
Imitation. *See also* Beliefs; Traditions
    to acquire subjective probabilities, 132
    based on information, 139–40
    biased, 141–42, 144, 147
    positive feedback mechanisms as process
    of, 109
    as precondition for optimization, 133
    when imitator firms dominate, 114
Imitator firms
    behavior of, 119–20
    decision making of, 114
    defined, 113
Inference. *See also* Likelihood and
    log-likelihood functions
    in multicriteria estimation, 289–94,
    298–99
    in nonlinear time series, 278–80
    standard statistical approach to, 288–89
    in standard stochastic estimation, 294–98
    static nature of statistical, 227–31
Information
    in classical dynamics, 11
    in evolutionary theory, 103–04
    genetic, 93
    in imaginative thinking, 93
    in large Poincare systems, 11
    in learning process, 101
    loss on time scale of, 1, 6
    in novelty, 94–96
    quality of, 131, 137
    in recombination, 93
    in socioeconomic systems, 12
Innovation
    analysis in economic theory, 20
    costs to innovator firm of, 114, 118, 121
    defined, 92
    endogenous, 51–52
    occurrence and dissemination of, 94–98,
    111
    random, 129–30
    relation to novelty, 92
    in Schumpeter's analysis, 46–47
Innovativeness, 95–96
Innovator firms
    in cyclical output growth model, 116–19

Innovator firms *(continued)*
  decision making of, 114, 121
  defined, 113
  imitators copy, 114
Instability. *See also* Dynamical systems,
    unstable; Irreversibility; Probability
  in dynamical systems, 12
  in stock market, 169
Integrable systems, 8
Interpolation, 232
Intertemporal analysis. *See* Time
Intertemporal equilibrium
  model of, 29, 32
Invention, 92
Irreversibility
  of nonlinear deterministic time series,
    273, 282–83
  in self-organization model, 162–66
  of tent map, 271
  when time symmetry is broken, 12

Juglar cycle, 46, 241

KAM (Kolmogorov-Arnold-Moser) theory, 8
K-flows. *See* Kolmogorov systems
Kitchin cycle, 46, 241
Knowledge base (in innovation), 93, 95
Kolmogorov systems, 5–6
Kondratiev wave or cycle, 46, 58–59, 241
  in MKS model of economic growth,
    50–51, 54–55
  model of, 64–68
  nonlinear entrainment in, 62–64
  with perturbation, 68
Kuznets cycle, 241
  with entrainment of long wave, 68–75
  in Kondratiev and business cycles, 64
  in MKS model of economic growth,
    58–59

Labor market
  endogenous labor union formation in,
    151–57
  skill creation by, 157–62
Large Poincare systems (LPS), 5, 6–9
  complex spectral theory applied to, 248
  dynamics of, 9, 11–12
  irreversibility in, 12
Lasota-Yorke Theorem, 175

Learning process. *See also* Ignorance;
    Information
  for attitudes toward tradition, 144–46
  determinants of individual, 137–38
  effect on beliefs, 133–34
  role of information in, 103–04, 112
Least-action principle, 4
Likelihood and log-likelihood functions,
    271–79, 286
Limit price change rule, 192t, 194–95, 199
Linear analysis, 22, 59
Linearity test
  in detection of chaos, 257–62
  for sampled stock market return series,
    205, 207, 209–13
  in weekends and missing days, 204–06
Linear models. *See also* Nonlinear models
Lipschitz condition, 275
Long wave. *See* Kondratiev wave or cycle
Lorenz attractor, 229
Lotka-Volterra predator prey model, 48
LPS. *See* Large Poincare systems (LPS)
Lyapounov exponents
  calculation and values of, 77–79
  in deterministic chaos, 245
  maximum, 221–22, 233–38, 242–43
  measure temporal horizon, 5–6, 233–38,
    242–43
  value of, 234

Mandelbrot set, 275
Maps, tent or quadratic, 170, 174–76, 179,
    267–71
Marx-Keynes-Schumpeter (MKS) system,
    45–46
Maximum a posteriori (MAP) probability
    estimation, 295–96, 299
Mechanics, classical, 3, 6–7. *See also*
    Hamiltonian equations
Migration theory, 162–63
Mode locking. *See also* Arnol'd tongues
  effect on cycles of, 68–75
  in natural sciences, 59–60
  at rational winding numbers, 70, 74,
    80–81
  sources of economic, 60
Monte Carlo integration procedure, 279–80
Multiple phase systems, 27–28, 31–32. *See
    also* Phase structures; Phase zones

Natural resource management, 103–04
N-body system, 9
Neoclassical economics, 29–30, 310
Nonanticipatability condition, 92–93
Nonintegrability, 8
Nonlinear dynamics
    development of ideas in, 16–17
    in economics, 22–24
    tools in, 223
Nonlinearities
    analysis in business cycle theory, 43
    bispectrum test for, 256–62
    as constraints, 67
    in disequilibrium system model, 64–75
    in economics and economic fluctuations,
        16–17, 59–60, 102
    Hinich bispectrum test for, 256–62
    in modulation of business cycle, 63–64
    in sampled stock prices, 205, 208–09f
    stochastic process tests for, 256
    in stock market prices, 202
    in time series data, 60–61, 63, 202
Nonlinear models. See also Linear analysis
    linear approximations of, 243–44
    mode locking in, 59–60
Novelty
    concept of, 91–92
    generation of, 93
    information in, 96

Order. See also Disorder
    creation of, 11
    deceptive, 27, 32
Oscillatory process. See also Business
        cycles
    in economic systems, 58–64
    in entrainment, 80
    in long wave model, 67

Perturbation. See also Entrainment; Mode
        locking
Perturbations
    implied, 268–71
    nonaverage, 101–02
    in nonlinear deterministic time series,
        267–69, 273, 276–77, 286
    sensitivity to, 25–26, 38
    using sinusoidal forcing, 68–75
Phase diagrams, 275
Phase portrait

of detrended monetary aggregates, 233,
        235f
    of noisy Hénon map, 224
    in nonlinear dynamics, 218, 220
    sensitivity of, 224
Phase space. See also Lyapounov exponents;
        Multiple phase systems
    in nonlinear dynamics, 218, 221
    projection of steady-state behavior, 69–70,
        74
    resonance distribution in, 8
    system distribution in, 6
Phase structures, 28
Phase zones, 28
Poincare theorem of large systems. See
        Large Poincare systems (LPS)
Positive feedback systems, 107–09
Postrevelation analysis, 92
Prerevelation analysis, 92–93
Price bubbles
    with equal endowments, 189
    with fee for exchange, 190
    with informed traders, 190–94
    with margin buying, 188–89
    with short selling, 186–88
Price distribution model, 170–75
Prices. See also Limit price change rule
    adjustment mechanism in stock price
        distribution model, 173–75, 176–77,
        179–81
    density function of, 175–76
    movement in stock market, 169–70
Probability, 12
    distribution in stochastic extimation, 289
    with lost information, 6
    in phase switching, 28
    prior probability distribution (L), 137–38

Quantum theory, 4

Randomness
    in deterministic, nonlinear behavior, 266
    distinct from determinism, 246–47
    in time series, 232–33
    in turbulence, 266
Rational behavior. See Rationality
Rational expectations
    limit price change rule under, 194–95
    moetary aggregates, 254
    price bubble predictions using, 190

Rational expectations assumption, 30
Rationality
  concept of, 3–4
  dependence on prior beliefs, 146
  distinction between bounded and
    objective, 12
Real business cycle, 22–23, 30, 32, 36
Recombination, 93–94
Relativity, 4
Residuals (in stochastic analysis), 289
Resonances
  concept of correlation, 248–49
  in disequilibrium system model, 75
  in unstable dynamical systems, 8–9
Rossler attractor, 227
Rossler Band
  as chaotic attractor, 48
  as dynamic control parameter, 53–54

Selection. *See also* Sociobiological theory
  beliefs shaped by, 132
  of culturally transmitted behaviors,
    142–48
  evolutionary, 101–12
Self-organization. *See also* Labor market
  aggregate demand as agent of, 46
  in spatial evolution, 102–03
  in studies of the economy, 45
Self-similarity
  by Cantor set, 29
  of fractal structures, 227
Self-transformation, 91
Sensitivity
  of chaotic motion, 221
  criteria for, 25–26
  of Lyapounov exponent, 234
  of nonlinear time series, 268, 282–83
  of phase portrait to time, 224
Sensitivity coefficient, 84, 85, 86
Signal extraction, 281–84
Sinusoidal forcing, 68–75
Sociobiological theory, 148
Stochastic process
  discrepancy terms in, 289
  empirical evidence of, 233–38
  statistical inference tests, 227
  tests for nonlinearity, 256
Strange attractors
  economic, 230
  monetary, 239

sprectrum for, 229
Superposition principle
  of linear systems, 227
  for nonlinear systems, 68, 227

Theoretical aggregates, 254
Time. *See also* Baker transformation;
    Irreversibility; Lyapounov exponent;
    Trajectories
  in behavior of stock prices, 202–13
  breaking of symmetry in, 12
  intertemporal aspects of, 19, 22–24,
    29–38
  in Kolmogorov systems, 5–6
  in long wave model, 68–77
  model of growth cycles with continuous,
    238–44
  in vehicular traffic case, 84–87
Time lags, 85, 86
Time scale
  in chaotic process, 227
  loss of information on, 1, 6
  in mode locking, 77–80
  in stochastic analysis, 24, 224–27
Time series
  aliasing in sampled, 201–02, 203–04
  analyzing, 217–22
  definition of pure white noise, 256–57
  detection of randomness in, 266–67
  economic nonlinearities in, 60–61, 63
  i.i.d. (identical independent distribution),
    227, 229, 230
  nonlinear deterministic model of, 267–71
  nonstationality and nonnormality in, 230
  testing for chaos or randomness in,
    232–33
  time sequences of models of, 218, 219f
Traditions. *See also* Beliefs; Imitation
  determinants of importance of, 137
  in economic decision making, 131–32
  in hetergeneous environment, 138–41
  reliance on, 143–48
  theory of, 133
Trajectories
  bounded chaotic, 24
  chaotic, 26
  concept of, 4–6
  in frustration chaos, 77
  in intertemporal equilibrium, 29–30
  Lyapounov exponents measure, 77

Trajectories *(continued)*
  periodic and nonperiodic, 26–27
Trajectories concept. *See also* Dynamical
  systems; Kolmogorov systems;
  Lyapounov exponent
Trapping set
  in dynamic cyclical output growth model,
    125–26
  in stock price distribution, 175, 176, 180
Turbulence, 266

Unbounded rationality, 14
Uncertainty
  in classical dynamics, 4

in experimental stock markets, 183–200
intertemporal equilibrium under, 19
in nonlinear time series, 281, 283
rational choice theory under, 131–32
Universality (in mode-locking behavior), 75

Viability creating mechanisms, 38–39

Walrasian tâtonnement, 22
Winding numbers
  defined, 70
  in devil's staircase, 77
  in long wave model, 74
Wolf algorithm, 222